Catherine de' Medici and the French Reformation

Edith Sichel

Alpha Editions

This edition published in 2020

ISBN: 9789354185175 (Hardback)
ISBN: 9789354187148 (Paperback)

Design and Setting By
Alpha Editions
www.alphaedis.com
email - alphaedis@gmail.com

As per information held with us this book is in Public Domain.
This book is a reproduction of an important historical work. Alpha Editions
uses the best technology to reproduce historical work in the same manner
it was first published to preserve its original nature. Any marks or number
seen are left intentionally to preserve its true form.

PREFACE

THE greater functions of history, the discovery of new documents, the revelation of new facts, demand great scholars. To the achievement of such ends a study like the present one—a study of persons, not an ordered narration of events—makes no kind of pretension. But history has its bye-paths and its lesser purposes, and one of the chief tasks of the minor historian is to read the books that no one has leisure for. It is customary to question the use of writing fresh works when so many have already been written. But we too frequently forget how many of these books are no books.

There are unknown contemporary records, buried either in remote publications or between the dusty covers of inconceivably tedious tomes, which have to be gone through for the sake of the solitary paragraph, perhaps the solitary sentence, that may serve the occasion in view. And there are always the volumes, old and modern, which are compiled, not written, out of which a book might be evoked. To gather together some such old fragments, to prevent waste of truth, to rescue the few vivid facts and impressions embedded in ruinous remains—still more, if possible, to throw some light upon the characters of an age, and thus, indirectly, upon its events—these seem aims not altogether incompatible with usefulness, or with the modest means at an ordinary chronicler's disposal. And if the following pages, which disclaim any larger ambition, should succeed in lending vitality to a single personage, a single occurrence of the past, they will not have been written in vain.

My thanks are due to Messrs. Longman and to the editor of the *Edinburgh Review* for permitting me to reproduce parts of an article on "The Women of the Renaissance," published in that periodical last April.

EDITH SICHEL.

CONTENTS

BOOK I

CHAPTER I
CATHERINE DE' MEDICI 3

CHAPTER II
THE YOUTH OF CATHERINE DE' MEDICI 29

CHAPTER III
DIANE DE POITIERS 43

CHAPTER IV
THE COURT OF HENRI II 71

BOOK II

CHAPTER V
THE REIGN OF FRANÇOIS II 101

CHAPTER VI
THE PRINCESSE DE CONDÉ 119

CHAPTER VII
JEANNE DE NAVARRE 137

CHAPTER VIII
THE COUNCIL OF POISSY 159

CHAPTER IX
THE HUGUENOTS 189

CONTENTS

CHAPTER X
Catherine and the Prince de Condé 205

CHAPTER XI
Why the Reformation Failed in France 231

CHAPTER XII
Ronsard and the Pléiade 241

CHAPTER XIII
Ronsard and the Elizabethans 265

CHAPTER XIV
Catherine and the Arts 291

CHAPTER XV
Bernard Palissy 305

LIST OF ILLUSTRATIONS.

Catherine de' Medici. By *Pourbus* (Uffizi Gallery,
    Florence) . . . . *Frontispiece*
Catherine De' Medici. By *Clouet* (Musée de Versailles) *to face page* 32
Henri de Valois (Henri II.) in his Youth. By *François*
    Clouet (Château de Chantilly) . . . ,, ,, 38
Diane de Poitiers. Portrait in enamel, by *Léonard*
    Limousin (Collection Soltikoff) . . . ,, ,, 48
Marguerite de Valois, Reine de Navarre (La Reine
    Margot) Vers. 1555. Portrait anonyme. Bibliothèque Nationale . . . . . ,, ,, 76
The Three Colignys: The Cardinal de Châtillon;
    The Admiral; The Maréchal d'Andelot.
    Drawing of the French School, in the Bibliothèque
    Nationale . . . . ,, ,, 88
Marguerite de Valois, Duchesse de Savoie. By
    François Clouet (Bibliothèque Nationale) . ,, ,, 94
Antoine de Bourbon, Roi de Navarre. By *François*
    Clouet (Château de Chantilly) . . . ,, ,, 102
Renée de France, Duchess of Ferrara. By *Jean*
    Clouet (Château de Chantilly) . . . ,, ,, 138
Jeanne d'Albret, Reine de Navarre. By *François*
    Clouet (Bibliothèque Nationale) . . . ,, ,, 142
Louis de Bourbon, Prince de Condé, Vers. 1565.
    Portrait anonyme (Bibliothèque Nationale) . ,, ,, 206
Anne de Montmorency. By *Jean Clouet* (Château de
    Chantilly) . . . . ,, ,, 222

SUMMARY OF HISTORICAL EVENTS FROM 1547—1562

HENRI II
1547-59
Married Catherine de' Medici.

CONTEMPORARY SOVEREIGNS

POPES CLEMENT VII, PAUL III, JULIUS III, MARCELLUS II, PAUL IV.

EDWARD VI, MARY and ELIZABETH, of ENGLAND, the EMPEROR CHARLES V, FERDINAND of AUSTRIA, and PHILIP II of SPAIN.

Alliance with the Protestant Princes of Germany against Charles V for political, not religious purposes—Passing of Edict of Chateaubriant, a decree against the Protestants published by Henri II to exonerate himself from the charges of heresy which followed upon his negotiations with Germany 1551

Campaign against Charles V—He besieged Metz, which was occupied by the French under François Duc de Guise, but after two months he was compelled to raise the siege—The French took Metz, Toul, and Verdun . . 1552-3

War raged in the Netherlands—Truce of Vaucelles, between the French and Charles V—He abdicated in 1556 and retired to the Monastery of Yuste, leaving Austria with the imperial title to his brother, Ferdinand, and Spain, the Netherlands and his possessions in Italy to his son, Philip 1553-6

Henri II formed an alliance with Pope Paul IV against Philip, from whose encroachments the Pope saw himself obliged to defend Italy—One French army was sent to Italy under the Duc de Guise ; another was sent to the Netherlands under the Connétable de Montmorency . . . 1556

Guise defeated near Civitella—Great defeat of Montmorency's army at Saint-Quentin—That town was occupied by Coligny, to whose aid Montmorency was hastening when he was met and routed by the enemy under Philibert Emmanuel, Duke of Savoy 1557

Guise hastened back from Italy and retrieved the fortunes of France by the recapture of Calais 1558

SUMMARY OF HISTORICAL EVENTS

Treaty of Câteau-Cambrésis between Henri II and Philip II, by which the French kept Metz, Toul and Verdun—They also kept Calais, pledging themselves to pay England 500,000 crowns if they did not restore the town at the end of eight years—The two sovereigns restored to each other their respective conquests on the frontiers of Italy and the Netherlands, excepting in Piedmont, where Henri II kept several towns until such time as the rights of his grandmother, Louise de Savoie, should have been determined. On the other hand, 189 important French towns and castles in France, Italy and the Netherlands were made over to Philip II—Death of Henri II . . 1559

FRANÇOIS II

1559–60

Married Mary Stuart, Queen of Scotland.

CONTEMPORARY SOVEREIGNS

POPE PIUS IV.
ELIZABETH of ENGLAND, FERDINAND of AUSTRIA, PHILIP II of SPAIN.

Conspiracy of Amboise—a plot of the Huguenots, secretly promoted by Condé, to abolish the tyranny of the Guises. The King and his mother, Catherine de' Medici summoned Antoine de Navarre and the Prince de Condé to Court, promising them safety; but directly they arrived Condé was arrested at the instigation of the Guises and subsequently condemned to death—He was saved by the death of the King 1560

CHARLES IX

1560–74

Married Elizabeth of Austria.

CONTEMPORARY SOVEREIGNS

POPES PIUS IV, PIUS V.
ELIZABETH of ENGLAND, FERDINAND of AUSTRIA, PHILIP II of SPAIN.

Catherine appointed Regent—Antoine de Navarre made Lieutenant-General—Condé released—Passing of the "Ordinance of Orleans" (L'Hôpital's measure) which aimed at reforming the corruptions of the Church and the administration of justice 1560
Passing of the Edict of July which declared the holding of Protestant services to be illicit, but proclaimed a general amnesty as regards religion—The assembling of the Council of Poissy at which Catholics and Protestants met to discuss their chief points of difference and if possible arrive at reconciliation—Failure of this attempt . . 1561

SUMMARY OF HISTORICAL EVENTS

The meeting of the Council of Saint-Germain to debate the religious question and the passing of the Edict of January which allowed Protestant services to be held outside towns though not in them, but forbade Huguenots to molest the exercise of the old religion 1562

Massacre of the Protestants at Vassy and religious disturbances all over the country—Condé took up arms in the Protestant cause and the first religious war broke out—The Catholic party invited the help of Spain, the Protestant party that of England, and foreign troops arrived from both countries—Elizabeth sent soldiers to help in the defence of Rouen which was taken by the Catholics—Death of Antoine de Navarre from a wound received before this city—Battle of Dreux between the Prince de Condé and the Duc de Guise—Condé was taken prisoner. . . 1562

Murder of the Duc de Guise by a Protestant—Negotiations between the Regent and the Prince de Condé—Liberation of Condé and conclusion of the Peace of Amboise which abolished the Protestants' liberty of worship and gave away the Protestant Cause 1562

AUTHORITIES CONSULTED

CONTEMPORARY

Lettres de Catherine de' Medici (5 vols.).
Lettres d'Antoine et de Jeanne d'Albret.
Correspondance de Diane de Poitiers with Introduction—*Guiffry*.
Correspondance de Marie Stuart.
Memoirs de Vielleville.
Memoirs de Gaspard de Tavannes.
Memoirs de Guillaume de Tavannes.
Memoirs de Marguerite de Navarre.
Memoirs du Prince de Condé.
Memoirs du Duc de Guise.
Memoirs de Rochechouart.
Memoirs de Philippi.
Memoirs de Henri II—*Claude d'Aubépine*.
Histoire des Choses Mémorables—*Fleurange*.
Journal de Claude Hâton.
Journal de Pierre L'Estoilles.
Journal de l'an 1562—*Revue Rétrospective*.
Sur le règne de François II—*Régnier de la Planche*.
Discours de Michel Soriano, Vénitien, touchant son Ambassade de France.
Le Livre des Marchands ou du Grand et loyal devoir.
Histoire de l'Église Réformée—*Théodore de Bèze*.
Histoire Universelle—*Agrippine d'Aubigné*.
Histoire de Lyon—*Paradin*.
Mélanges pour l'histoire de François I et Henri II, de Simon Goulart—*Archives Curieuses*.
Lettre de Renée de Ferrara à Jean Calvin—*Archives Curieuses*.
Siège de Metz—*Archives Curieuses*.
Trépas et Obsèques de Henri II—*Archives Curieuses*.
Grand et magnifique Triomphe fait au mariage de François de Valois avec très-excellente Princesse, Madame Marie Stuart, Reine d'Écosse—*Archives Curieuses*.
Lettres envoyées à la Reine Mère—*Archives Curieuses*.
Le Fort inexpugnable de l'honneur féminin—*François Billon*.
Les femmes illustres—*Brantôme*.
Récepte véritable—*Bernard Palissy*.
Discours admirables—*Bernard Palissy*.
Lettres et poésies de Henri II.
Poèmes de Charles IX.
Vie de Ronsard—*Claude Binet*.

AUTHORITIES CONSULTED

Oeuvres Poétiques—*Ronsard*:
L'Art poétique—*Ronsard.*
Préface sur la Musique—*Ronsard.*
Des Vertus—*Ronsard.*
Oeuvres choisies de Ronsard—Edited by *Sainte-Beuve.*
l'Illustration de la Poésie française—*Joachim Du Bellay.*
Lettres au Cardinal Du Bellay, etc.—*Joachim Du Bellay.*
Oeuvres Poétiques—*Joachim Du Bellay.*
Oeuvres Poétiques—*Rémy Belleau.*
French Lyric Poets—Ed. by *Saintsbury.*

BIOGRAPHICAL

Introductions Biographiques aux "Lettres de Catherine de' Medici"—*Le Comte de la Ferrière.*
Catherine de Médicis—*Capefigue.*
Catherine de Médicis—*Henri Bouchot.*
Eléonore de Roye—*Le Comte Delaborde.*
Jeanne d'Albret—*Miss Freer.*
Biographical Preface to the works of Bernard Palissy—*Anatole France.*
Biographical Preface to the works of Joachim Du Bellay—*Becq de Fouquières.*
Biographical Preface to the works of Joachim Du Bellay—*Marty-Laveaux.*
Biographical Preface to the works of Ronsard—*Blanchemain.*
Biographical Preface to the works of Ronsard—*Sainte-Beuve.*
Tableau du seizième siècle—*Sainte-Beuve.*
Vie de Philibert de l'Orme—*Vachon.*
Philibert de l'Orme (Architectural Review, Feb. and March, 1904)—*Reginald Blomfield.*
Germain Pilon et le Tombeau de Birague—*Courajod.*
Notes sur la Chapelle des Orfèvres—*Pichon.*
Biographie Universelle—*Michaud.*
Nouvelle Biographie Générale.
Dictionnaire de Bayle.

LITERARY AND CRITICAL

Causeries du Lundi—*Sainte-Beuve.*
Manuel de l'histoire de la littérature française—*Brunetière.*
Les Moeurs polies de la Cour de Henri II—*Bourciez.*
Les femmes de la Renaissance—*Maulde de la Clavière.*
Les femmes de Brantôme—*Henri Bouchot.*

HISTORICAL

Rélations de la Diplomatie Vénitienne—*Baschet.*
The French Renaissance—*Mrs. Pattison.*
Histoire de France—*Martin*, Vol. ix.
Histoire de France—*Michelet.*
History of the Papacy—*Mandell Creighton.*
Florence—*Herbert Gardner.*
   For contemporary historical authorities see under " Contemporary."

BOOK I

Catherine and Diane

CHAPTER I

Catherine de' Medici

*AUTHORITIES CONSULTED

Lettres de Catherine de' Medici.
Biographical Introductions—*Le Comte de la Ferrière*.
Rélations de la Diplomatic Vênitienne—*Baschet*.
Catherine de Médecis—*Capefigue*.
Catherine de Médecis—*Bouchot*.
Memoirs de Vielleville.
Memoirs de Tavannes.
Memoirs de Guillaume de Tavannes.
Memoirs de Marguerite de Navarre.
Les femmes de Brantôme—*Bouchot*.
Les femmes de la Renaissance—*Maulde de la Clavière*.
Histoire de France—*Michelet*.
Histoire de France—*Martin*.
Dictionnaire de Bayle.

* Mr. Whitehead's scholarly *Gaspard de Coligny* appeared after the completion of this work.

CHAPTER I

Catherine de' Medici

A TIME of decadence is a time of over-attention to detail—a time when the large outline of life is effaced and fine ideals are lost sight of, when great means are used for little ends and small issues are taken for big ones. In such phases of the world's history the whole spiritual currency becomes debased; observance is substituted for religion, common-sense for wisdom, intrigue for statesmanship, while art degenerates into artifice and a noble generosity into an ignoble extravagance. For beauty itself loses rank, and from being the true servant of the princes who once bowed before it becomes the insignificant slave of tyrannical caprice. That a period of abnormal energy of mind tends to produce abnormal enervation in the succeeding age is no new discovery; nor need we go far to find proofs of it in modern history, whether we seek them in the corruption of the Stuart Restoration following upon the great political upheaval, or in the laxity and nullity of the Directoire —the immediate sequel of the French Revolution.

But nowhere is this truth so strongly embodied, so plainly visible, as in the latter half of the sixteenth century—the period born of the Renaissance — in France and in Italy. The impressionable Latin races, highly strung for good and evil, fell the most easily a prey to the emotional excesses and moral disorders belonging to a time of febrile exhaustion, when will was weak, and temperament defenceless,

CATHERINE DE' MEDICI

The richer the summer, the completer and the deadlier its autumnal decay. Miasmic vapours and chill mists close round us, and strange scents of dead leaves oppress us as we follow the last hectic pomp, the pale gold funeral pageant of the dying Renaissance.

In Italy, where the movement first began and soonest reached maturity, it also showed most quickly signs of degeneration, and the earlier half of the sixteenth century had already witnessed its decline. But in France, where it developed later, its splendour was maintained throughout the reign of François I, and, indeed, it may almost be said to have continued through that of his successor. For if we except a growing decadence in art and an absence of romance in life, the general degeneration was hardly felt till the death of Henri II and his wife's accession to the Regency, in 1559.

Every movement has its person, its representative; and since men are entangled in actions and actions disguise motives, it is in women, the clear mirrors of current feelings and tendencies, that integral types of an age will be found. In Italy the prevailing corruption was so subtly interwoven with poetry, its women were surrounded by so rich a glamour, that real outlines are hard to distinguish; but in France, with its brilliant scepticism, its dry, scintillating atmosphere of matter-of-factness, types stand out as crisp and lucid as French aphorisms. In France, therefore, we shall not be slow to find figures that sum up whole periods: women who are, as it were, epigrams, expressive of profound experience.

If Margaret of Angoulême, the sister of King François, queen, poet, philosopher, æsthete, mystic, was the epitome of the Renaissance, no less was Catherine de' Medici, regent, politician, trimmer, patroness, cynic, the epitome of the decadence.

Half French, half Italian, the daughter of a Bourbon princess and of a degenerate Medici prince, the niece also of Leo X, a characteristic Renaissance Pope, Catherine had every aid by nature and by training to become an accomplished cynic. She has hitherto figured as a kind of stage-villain, a mysterious figure surrounded by astrologers and secret drawers of poison-bottles, an effect to which Dumas and occasionally Michelet, in a day when history was still an art and not a science, have contributed not a little. Nowadays science has mercilessly exterminated the race of villains and replaced them by the victims of constitutional infirmities. Perhaps truth lies, as usual, between two extremes. Her poison-cupboard at Blois, which once made history and is now proved to be a fable, is but a symbol of a whole mythology that has gathered round her name. Personages who intensify the tendencies of their time, more memorable than their neighbours, are often made responsible for the crimes of their more anonymous contemporaries and we shall see that most of the sensational accusations against Catherine are based on no solid foundation. We may be sure that people—especially women—must always have seemed possible to themselves, and hence monsters are necessarily unhistorical. Hence, too, whatever work of clearing helps to free the picture and make it tone with its surroundings, whether it be cleared from layers of encrusting black or of whitewash, must be a work in the cause of truth. History is not written in black and white, but in subtle greys and half-tints, and studying some character from the past is often like looking at a figure in a faded fresco on which we cannot get a full light. At first we see its robes as black; then, as we search more closely and grow accustomed to the obscurity, we find that the draperies are not of one colour, but of manifold twilight shades, and it is only for the sake of convenience that we use positive terms at all. Catherine, with Medician craft in her veins, was far too diplomatic to be anything positively. Frankness, even in sin, would have been to her a breach, not of morals, but of manners. She dealt in negative evil—a disease no less actual, and perhaps more poisonous, than the common sort ascribed to her. This sixteenth century princess was very like " der Geist der stets verneint." She was indeed as great, if not as startling a villain as tradition has made her, not, as tradition says, from having bad feelings, but from having no feelings at all. Catherine de' Medici was a mass of indifference. Indifference was the dominant note of her character—was no longer a negative quality, but a positive power—and entire indifference means entire cynicism. The person who becomes a cynic is often no more than a sentimentalist in disguise, but Catherine was a serious cynic, because she was an unconscious one, a person who sees things as they are, never as they may be. She drove common-sense to its absolute conclusion and judged every issue by its standards. Perhaps there is not one of her alleged crimes which condemns her so severely as does the Spanish envoy's description of her a few days after

CATHERINE DE' MEDICI

St. Bartholomew's Eve: "She has grown ten years younger," he wrote, "and always seems to me like one who has come out of a bad illness."

Even her finer characteristics, when examined, seem rather due to the absence than the presence of a quality. It is remarkable that she should have kept her reputation intact, living, as she did, at a time of signal immorality, when illegitimate love affairs were part of the normal life of every lady of position. It would have been impossible for a princess to go unscathed by malicious tongues; the scandals breathed against Catherine, however, such as her rumoured connection with François, Duc de Guise, obtained scant credence even at the time and were manifestly the invention of her enemies. She was indeed the most respectable bad woman on record, but her respectability is due to a want of inclination, of emotion, not to any standard of conduct. That she had no standard is evident from her dealings with other women, as with her "Flying Squadron" of attendants, for whom she deliberately planned *liaisons de convenance* for political purposes. Her severity was reserved, not for the crime, but for the criminal who allowed it to be found out. Before a breach of decorum or any moral clumsiness she was implacable, and the ladies who could not keep their faults to themselves were rigorously expelled from her Court. Her own immunity from blame shows that she was not, at any rate, the slave of low impulses, but it proves no sort of moral scruple. To say that she was free from prejudice is to say little: she was incapable of forming any judgments save those dictated by convenience. This freedom produces the effect, to some extent real, of a large mind. But the largeness that proceeds from fine proportions is one thing, that which comes from emptiness another; and Catherine's mind had the width of an unfurnished room in a marble palace—vast, mysterious, unlived in, and perilously cold.

The tolerance which distinguished her (for all her acts of persecution were matters of political tactics), the Renaissance impartiality which should have served the world in good stead, ever fell short of nobility; for it came from no moral outlook, no intellectual philosophy, but from a lack of conviction; and since life is dignified only by conviction, her life remains undignified. The same may be said in many cases of her extraordinary self-control, even during the most trying period of her married life and of her rivalry with Diane de Poitiers—

the period through which we shall follow her in these pages with admiration but with hatred. For her patience under contumely, her friendship with her husband's mistress, her long waiting for the moment of her power and her prompt use of it when it came, were all helped by her lack of spontaneity as much as by her Medician skill in dissimulation. The brutality of the later Medici lurked in her too. When self-control no longer served a purpose; when the Court retired and she dropped the amazing etiquette to which she clung as a defence against her own violence, she sometimes gave way to accesses of blind rage which were almost insane. Her children, even the bold Princess Margot, learned to dread them and shrank before the loud insulting tones and rough indignities to which their mother subjected them. "*Elle jetait feu,*" wrote this daughter, "*et disait tout ce qu'une colère outrée et démesurée peut jeter dehors.*" But the distant step of a courtier readjusted the balance and brought back her queenly demeanour. It is only when we have glimpses of the savage in her that we can realize the strength of her grip over her own nature; or the effort she made to sustain that impenetrable calm on which she reckoned in herself. It was thus that she appeared to the world: "She from whose soul prudence was never parted, who moderated her actions according to her desire, demonstrating plainly that the discreet person doeth nothing he willeth not to do; she who, in truth, never deigned to amuse herself by showing her pleasure to others," so again wrote Princess Margot, who ought to have been a true reporter, since she had often been the victim of her mother's wrath.

Catherine de' Medici, once removed from the footlights cannot but be a baffling figure; and perhaps the only way to know her better is to get some general outline of her before entering upon the tangled and crooked story of her life. Most great ladies keep their public self apart from their private one. Catherine de' Medici perhaps united the two characters more closely than most people, but how she did so and where her two rôles resembled one another will best be understood by looking at her in both aspects—by passing from Catherine the woman to Catherine the Regent.

Moral indifference, as we saw, had possession of Catherine's nature; but one desire was hers, by no means a moral one, which governed her quite as potently as her apathy and perhaps with more obvious effect. "All her actions," wrote a

CATHERINE DE' MEDICI

Venetian ambassador, describing her to his government, "have ever been ruled and guided by a most powerful desire— the desire to reign": "*un affetto potentissimo . . . un affetto di signoreggiare.*" It is this "affetto" alone which makes Catherine comprehensible in her private, as in her public capacities. Like a strong weed, it usurped the place of every other desire and exhausted the soil around her. It gave her a terrible vitality. It made her policy and guided her religious views. It destroyed all confidence in her neighbourhood, creating enemies and withering friendships for her. Her children, and the Prince de Condé, so willing to be loyal to her, and Coligny, who might have been her support, were all sacrificed to it, and every bad deed she committed may with truth be ascribed to its workings.

It has been already said that crimes not her own were probably ascribed to her. That profound historian, Bishop Creighton, has pointed out how this happened in the case of Alessandro Borgia; and his conclusion that the frequent ascription of such crimes to high personages was a proof, not of their guilt, but of the low morality of their day, applies as much to Catherine as to the Borgias. We must remember that she lived at a moment when the classics and the history of later Rome were diligently searched for models of life, no longer with the scholar's zeal of the young Renaissance, but with the desire of the sated to find a new sensation; that she kept Roman empresses as ideals before her eyes and easily adjusted their standards to those of the cardinals around her. Each age sets up its own virtues to admire, and common-sense and a determined policy, rather than mercy and honour, were the idols that her contemporaries had chosen to imitate. Macchiavelli was no Mephistopheles, but the normal philosopher and voice of his generation, and Cæsar Borgia, strong, prudent and self-contained, was to him the pattern prince. Catherine was not the only Medici who was this great casuist's pupil, and jesuitry applied to things temporal is, after all, not so shocking as jesuitry applied to things spiritual. She certainly did not find much that was better than herself in her immediate surroundings. Diane de Poitiers and the Guises kept a special staff of doctors at Paris to put an unobtrusive end to the owners of benefices; and Margaret of Angoulême, the patroness of Reformers, was forced to celebrate mass in her bedroom so as to avoid the poison which a prelate in high place was anxious to administer to her in the Communion cup. And in addition to such facts, we must also bear in mind the religious conviction of kings that kings could do no evil, that they were part of the eternal order of things—a belief which even at funerals robed all Crown officials in red, the colour of eternity. It is small wonder that the actions of sovereigns waxed insolent and that they credited the Deity with their own indulgence for rank. "I think this very strange," wrote Catherine, when the Pope refused to make a cardinal of the Bastard of Angoulême, Henri II's illegitimate son—"and surely the College should feel it a high honour to count among their ranks the natural son of so great a king. I think that herein the Pope judges very badly, for he should rather buy such a noble chance than refuse the King and myself such a just and reasonable demand." This is the opinion not only of Catherine but of her whole generation, and though in her abnormal nature she *was* worse than her time—and than most times—she can hardly be said to be worse in her actual deeds. Of course, the heinous conception of St. Bartholomew's Eve, perhaps the most heinous ever imagined by a woman, must be excepted. But St. Bartholomew's Eve cannot be taken as a measure of her actions, for it was not a deliberate plan, but a forcing of her hand through her own shortsightedness. She had made the mistake natural to her. She had underrated Coligny and his power, which threatened to vie with her own. His removal became necessary and the Guises were only too willing to be her agents in the matter. It was when they failed to kill him, when the rumour ran that the Protestants vowed an instant and general vengeance for this plot against their chief, that panic seized her. She felt she must effectually forestall them, and the result was the massacre. At this point it would be premature to enter into the strange pact, made seven years before, between her and Alva; nor is it possible to say whether or how she would have fulfilled it, had not fear precipitated her into action. But thus much may here be hazarded—that St. Bartholomew's Eve would not have been the form of the fulfilment, and that therefore this terrible achievement of hers throws no real light upon her nature, excepting as it proves that she felt no bar in herself to such a business. It could hardly, however, have been the result of cold-blooded meditation, for she herself, who desired peace at almost any price, would have been the first to reject it as a blunder.

The two murders for which she can be charged for certain are those of Coligny and Lignerolles. It may be held, indeed, that intentions count as crimes and that a letter like the following ranks as manslaughter: "Try at whatever price to ruin his House" (so she writes to Tavannes about Maligny, the Protestant conspirator); "if it is needful, put your hand upon his collar and—if you can catch him—have him taken . . . secretly to some place so safe and hidden that no one can have news of it, and let me know of this with the utmost diligence." Catherine would have exculpated herself by the saving clause, "If it is needful." At all events, this cannot be reckoned as one of her direct deeds. Let us come to such as are direct.

We know her motive and the means she took for the death of Coligny; the reason for Lignerolles' disappearance was much the same. Once a "Mignon" of Henri, Duke of Anjou's, but fallen into disgrace, "he betrayed himself to King Charles, imprudently prated against the Queen-Mother, and proposed that the King should escape from her tutelage. His Majesty, incapable of so great a design, repeated everything to his mother, who, with the full consent of her children, had him killed . . ." This is the matter-of-fact account of a contemporary diarist—wonderfully devoid of dark lanterns and stage-effects. As for the other enormities of which she was accused, it would be as tedious as it is unnecessary to go through the long list of them, for they are all founded on scandal invented by her foes, chiefly by the Huguenots, and there were no greater scandal-mongers than the Huguenots. She shared the brunt of such evil reports with every monarch and prominent prelate of her day. There was a good instance of this when she and Charles V were both charged with poisoning the young son of François I, who died suddenly at Angers. Yet his death was obviously from pleurisy. He had overheated himself by jousting and had drunk a glass of iced water with speedy ill consequences. Catherine was far away at Fontainebleau. There was not a shadow of evidence against her, except the fact that the murder would make her Dauphine. The impeachment at this date, not many years after her marriage, was simply the result of the popular hatred for her as "the Florentine" and the general suspicion of her as a Medici. It was little better in the case of the Emperor. A Spaniard, under torture, confessed that Charles V had ordered him to poison the prince, but after the moment no one of weight gave credence to this unaccredited outburst from a poor pain-stricken wretch.

CATHERINE DE' MEDICI

These details are worth considering, not in themselves, but because they reveal how full then was men's consciousness of murders and sudden death.

It was unlucky for Catherine that she happened to have a taste for astrology and to have established an Italian astrologer in a tower near her room. Yet nothing was more natural. Like all her contemporaries, she had a profound belief in stars and their influence. Astrologers were consulted in as commonplace a way as doctors about the welfare of actions, expeditions, or even human affections. Such consultations were bound to take place in private, and love-potions and magic medicaments were their normal accessories; but because, like other ladies, Catherine kept a store of phials in her sumptuous drawer at Blois, it does not follow that they need all be labelled "poison."

These mysteries have also surrounded her with an atmosphere of moroseness. Yet this is far from the truth. To be, like her, devoid of the power of charming and yet to bend men and women to her will as she did, she must have possessed some strange fascination. And so it was. Her indifference did not betray itself socially. She was brilliant, acutely alive. She had French wit and Italian *verve* in conversation, and she must have known how to amuse, or she would not, in the early days of her marriage, have been the constant companion of François I. Her wit, salt and shrewd, was of the broad colloquial kind, well suited to cheer a jaded monarch. She understood how to laugh, not often, but aptly. "Then," wrote a Venetian envoy, "she began to laugh a great deal, as she always does when something takes her fancy." . . . "*Elle riait son saoul comme un autre, car elle riait volontiers*," reports Brantôme, "*et aimait à dire le mot et rencontrait fort bien, et connaissait bien où il fallait jeter sa pierre et son mot et où il y avait à redire.*" Her power lay not so much in what she did as in her science of doing. She knew the right moment for laughing, and for weeping. For Catherine was, if we may say so, immensely feminine, and none grasped better than she that a woman's strength is in weakness. Several times ambassadors found her in tears, sometimes, more effectively still, with the tears in her voice.

"One day she said to me" (writes the same envoy), "that if her misfortunes had happened to her, alone, amongst all the queens of France, she would think herself the unhappiest woman in the world, but she was consoled when she remembered that during the minority of kings, the great always plotted to get power . . . . And she added that she had once read at Carcassonne . . . a manuscript chronicle which told how the mother of the King, St. Louis, who was left a widow with a little son of eleven, immediately encountered the opposition of all the great nobles of the kingdom; for they rose in revolt to escape being ruled by a woman, above all, by a foreign woman . . . It pleased God to give the victory to King Louis . . . Her Majesty, when she told me these things, applied them to the affairs of to-day; she saw herself a stranger, without any one near her she could trust, and with a child between eleven and twelve years old . . . Whereupon I said to her: 'Madam, Your Majesty should feel a great consolation in your heart, for since the things of the day seem, as it were, a mirror of the things of the past, you may be well certain that their end also will not be unlike' . . . 'But,' she answered me, 'I should not like any one to know that I had read this chronicle, for they would say that I was acting according to the example of this lady-queen, who was called Blanche, and was the daughter of the King of Castile.'"

The part of the pathetic widow evidently impressed the ambassador and probably helped Catherine to get something she wanted out of Venice. And the intimacy, the *bonhomie* which this remote woman knew how to assume, must have been very endearing. She would invite the envoys to walk with her in the palace gardens, and pacing up and down the rich grass-paths and pleached alleys of the Tuileries, where Palissy's majolica toads and dragons peered out at unexpected corners, she would discuss matters of State with them. "With those in whom she has confidence she gladly becomes expansive," so writes one of these diplomats. "You see with what confidence I talk to you," she said to another; "well, I will say this much—that the Pope is no more than a man who understands nothing about State affairs." This looked like an indiscretion, but she probably meant the envoy to repeat it, and to set his government by the ears with the Pope. This vaunted expansiveness of hers was not always the best sign. Her courtiers were alarmed when she called them *mon ami*, for they knew that it meant she was angry, or that she thought them fools. "I entreat you, Madam," said one thus addressed, "to say *Mon ennemi* at once."

It must be added that her tears and smiles were not exactly hypocritical; they were always near at hand. She was an

CATHERINE DE' MEDICI

Italian, and therefore demonstrative, emotional. Little Mary Stuart, writing to her mother who was harassed by insurgents in Edinburgh, dwells on Catherine's sympathy: "The Queen"—she says—"did you the honour to cry bitterly." It is astonishing to find how caressive, how almost exaggerated in expression she becomes to the few friends she chose from among her relations and dependents. "If you care for my life," she wrote to her sister-in-law, "take care of your own health"; and she begins a letter announcing a change of plan to an official, with a deprecatory, "I'm afraid you will be angry." Sometimes she is almost high-spirited: "You are having such good cheer where you are," she says to a friend, "that you quite forget to send me any news of you. And as I know that your good husband and your good brother and you make up only one person, like the Trinity, I am not going to write three letters." Or again she writes to Montmorency:

"My good gossip—Lansac told me that you asked if the King and I were going to stop more than one night at Chantilly. If you ask me for a day, I will give it you, on condition that I see *you*. As for more, now that you have heard me talk I am sure you will chase me from your house, though such is by no means your custom. Votre bonne cousine, Catherine."

Her amenity was no doubt her best policy and deportment was part of her creed, but there must have been a real social amiability about her and a visitor at her Court is probably truthful when he tells us that she had "a most beautiful manner, and that both in her words and her gestures she made for pleasing everybody." This "need of pleasing" brought her plenty of work. The letters which she wrote, like most princesses of her day, to plead for numberless protégés, or to get them suitable posts, were a work if not of kindness, at least of benevolence. Directly moral sympathy came into play Catherine was at a loss, and her letters of condolence are shocking to our modern notions. "I advise you while you are at home to dress yourself as comfortably as possible . . . and to grieve as little as you can for things that cannot be mended." This is how she wrote to a lady who had just lost a much-loved parent. She had, it must be confessed, the qualities of her failings. Her mental endurance, her unruffled stoicism were admirable. Like many Stoics, she had no faith in doctors for herself and often neglected her health, "for that she was of her nature very slow to complain." Thus writes her son Charles IX, who saw her in every contingency.

CATHERINE DE' MEDICI

"We must all do the same thing," she said of dying, "and it will come when God pleases, but I tell you firmly that nothing will induce me to take waters." And again, after a serious illness from an accident: "You ask for news of my fall, so I will tell you that it was a bad and a heavy one; but, thank God, I was hardly hurt, and I am only marked on my nose, like the sheep of Berri."

Nowhere perhaps do we feel her want of sympathy so much as in her relations to her children. It has been customary to believe that whatever Catherine was, she was an exemplary mother. But this was hardly the case. While she fought fiercely for their interests, she was usually fighting for her Regency and it cost her nothing to marry one daughter to a morose Spanish bigot and another—a reluctant little bride—to the profligate King of Navarre. It is true that during their childhood she was the most devoted parent, lavishing care upon them, giving them lessons, knowing every detail of their lives. But this was when they could not contradict her. Directly they developed wills of their own, it was another story. In the case of the vigorous Princess Margot, it was a story of constant scenes, sometimes of beatings. And yet she, the rebel, was fascinated by her mother, and when Catherine treated her as an equal companion and asked her opinion about affairs she enjoyed transports of pride. Fascination, a word which may imply terror as well as pleasure, best describes the Queen's effect upon her children. François II, of a weak and waxen character, was, as it were, mesmerized by her, and when he came to the throne he practically, if not formally, abdicated the crown in her favour. Charles IX, as weak, but with the intervals of sudden self-assertion common in feeble characters, was always the object of her contempt, her daughter says of her dislike; yet she hid this feeling towards her son beneath the purple and ermine cloak of her outward deference to her King, and the vacillating boy bowed before her and yielded while he rebelled. For her two less prominent children, the Duchesse de Lorraine and the Duc d'Alençon, she does not seem to have had much sentiment of any sort. Decorum drove her to make much of them in public and to treat them with a ceremonious maternal affection; but the affection was like a court-dress of stiff brocade mounted upon a framework of whalebone. Elizabeth, the little Queen of Spain, she did love, with a love which increased considerably after the girl married Philip II, and became an all-important ally. However that may be, she made a confidante of her, and felt her premature death as she felt few other griefs. When Charles IX came to break the tragic news to her, Catherine was stupefied and retired speechless to her apartments. After a few hours only, she entered the Council Chamber: "Gentlemen," she said, "God has taken from me all my hopes in this world. From His hand alone I wait for comfort. I will dry my tears and dedicate myself wholly to the cause of the King, my son, and to the cause of God." Then, not without majesty, she proceeded to business.

Perhaps the most human touch in her affection was given long after, when with a letter of minute injunctions, as important as if they had been for a campaign, she sent two splendid dolls to her little grandchildren in Spain. It is the one piece of gaiety in all the mass of her papers; her only acknowledgement, it would seem, that such a thing as play in life existed. Her real idol, however, the child whom, as Princess Margot tells us, she always adored, was the perverted Henri III, with his beautiful hands and his decadent mind. But when, after his accession, he went against her wishes and endangered her power, she did not scruple to desert him or to join his enemies. Her *affetto di signoreggiare* was more to her than he was. Matters might have been different if her children had loved her; but though they admired her with awe, though she was the excitement of their lives and her praise their chief desire, they lived in too much dread of her to give her a place in their hearts.

One feeling Catherine had, apart from ambition and self-interest, one feeling that slumbered deep, like some subterranean current, in her enigmatic nature, actuating deeds and producing results that the world has ascribed to other causes. This feeling was her love for her husband, a love that was never requited. The fact has been too much overlooked in the general interest that surrounds his attachment to Diane de Poitiers. And Catherine, "slow to complain," kept her secret with dignity. She never reproached him, and she served him faithfully with a wistful and thankless devotion. Perhaps the primitive woman in her came out the most clearly in this—that she kept her love for the one being who spurned her. Henri even roused fear in her, and this caused a certain shyness which made her awkward in his presence and probably prevented her from pleasing the naturally taciturn King. But her sentiment influenced her life in ways that have hardly been recognized. It kept her from rebelling against his wishes, even when for her they meant indignity; and, had it not been for this attachment, she would not have waited for his death to oust Diane de Poitiers. It was not till she was a widow that she told her trouble to the one confidante she had, her daughter, Elizabeth of Spain. This letter is the only bit of self-revelation amidst the multitude of papers that make up Catherine's correspondence, and as such, it is a precious human document, touching enough from such a woman.

"*M'amye*," she wrote, "commend yourself very much to God, for you have seen me of old as contented as you are now, and believing that I should never have any trouble but this one, that I was not loved in the way I wished by the King, your father, who doubtless honoured me beyond my deserts; but I loved him so much that I was always afraid of him, as you know well enough. And now God has taken him away from me ... In so far, *m'amye*, think of me and let me serve as a warning to you not to trust too much in the love of your husband." Those who care to pierce beneath the surface need not wait for her to tell them her secret. Some years earlier she had let her disappointed heart speak between the lines of a note that she sent the Connétable Montmorency, the man whom at that time she most trusted:

"It was not the water that made me ill"—it ran—"so much as not having had any news of the King, for I thought that he and you and all the rest had quite forgotten that I was in existence .. Be sure that there is nothing which gives me such pain as to believe that I am out of his good graces, and out of his remembrance. So, as for me, my good gossip, if you wish me to live, sustain me as often as you can and give me constant news of him: that is the best régime I could possibly have." And again that same year: "I know full well that I must not have the happiness of being near him—which makes me wish that you had my place and I yours so long as the war lasts—and that I could do him as much service as you have done."

Her longings were not satisfied, for she never gained his heart, or even a corner of it. But after her diplomatic successes in his service at Paris, at the time of his defeat at St. Quentin, he paid her greater deference. We can measure the extent of his neglect by the manner of his reward; for from this date onwards, he made it his habit to come to her rooms every evening for an hour, instead of retiring at once to the company of Diane. Before this, except in public, she seems hardly ever to have seen him.

It is impossible not to admire the dignity with which she bore this trial, a dignity born of absolute common-sense. It was a quality which ever distinguished her. Common-sense, indeed, sums up all the best side of her. Her letters to her children are full of it—letters by the side of which those of Lord Chesterfield seem spiritual. They are full of prescriptions, mundane and medical, for though Catherine disbelieved in remedies for herself, like many other people she believed in them for others. At one moment, she commands the poor little Queen of Spain to send away a lady-in-waiting of whom she had grown more fond than a queen should be; at another, she begs the Bishop of Limoges, her ambassador at Madrid, to see that her daughter drinks pigeons' blood and cream for her complexion and takes regular exercise. She warns Philip that the girl has only been used to have meat twice a day and will suffer if she eats more; and she daringly begs him, when Elizabeth is dangerously ill, to try some newly found cure. "In every country," she says, "illnesses are the same, but cures are different." Her notions of hygiene are wonderfully advanced, and in a time which dreaded air and exercise like poison and shrank from innovations, it needed some courage to advocate them. But Catherine was an *esprit positif*. She had the scientific mind, much more than the artistic one, and even had some reputation as a mathematician. Had she lived at a period when science was more developed, she would have delighted in its discoveries. How little there was in her of the real artist, and how much of the luxury-loving patroness will be discussed later on.

Common-sense makes a good administrator but a poor statesman, unless larger qualities accompany it, and Catherine had no larger qualities to bring. Hence, as a woman of affairs she failed. Her *affetto di signoreggiare* would lead one to expect a strong policy from her, and at first sight it is bewildering to find how shifting, how wavering, how wanting in strength was her rule. But reflection soon shows us that a government determined by no central principle, good or bad, must of necessity be weak. Catherine's only pivot was her own personal power: her one aim to keep the Regency at all costs. Hence her tactics changed with the chances of every day and were as variable as a woman's mood. The rule directed by personal likes and dislikes, of which her sex is usually accused, was stability compared to that of Catherine. For she depended on parties—and parties altered every week, or oftener. "*Il faut diviser pour règner*" was one of her favourite maxims, and she sought to strengthen herself by sowing dissension between factions, a negative and hopeless programme which reduced politics to intrigue. At one moment, she was an extreme Catholic with the Guises; at another, she attached herself to the Bourbons and their Huguenot followers, according as she thought that her power depended on the support of either. She made love to Spain while she flirted with Elizabeth, so that she might have an ally in either case, and she destroyed the confidence of both. She pretended to be Alva's admirer when Louis of Nassau was promising her son the Netherlands, and she ended by gaining nothing. Cæsar Borgia, who sought his personal aggrandizement, at least desired a united empire and thus gave solidity and a certain splendour to his schemes. Elizabeth of England may have been whimsical, but she was not so ignoble as her "dearest sister of France," and she had the luck to possess a band of consummate counsellors. "Women rule in an unseemly fashion," comments Catherine's friend, shrewd old Tavannes in his Memoirs; "kingdoms are not like possessions and fortunes to which they can succeed. And few there are whose reigns have prospered like unto that of Elizabeth of England . . . These feminine enterprises are faulty for that they be timorous, vindictive, credulous, irresolute, inconstant, sudden, indiscreet, vainglorious and ambitious—more than in any reign of man." Tavannes had not lived amongst French Court ladies for nothing. And other of his contemporaries tell the same story. "In the administration of the realm," so writes one of them, "one would wish to see more ardour and more promptitude in Her Majesty, above all in her decisions. . . . She seemeth ever to proceed in fear." Her vacillation was indeed surprising, not only in public business, but in the little things of every day. "The truth is," says an envoy, "that her irresolution is extreme, and that from one hour to another one hears her conceiving new plans. She changes her designs at morning—at evening—three times a day. Yesterday morning Her Majesty was at the Palace of Madrid, then she came to dine in Paris. After that she thought of going to the Pont de Charenton, but at the eleventh hour she changed her mind and went to the Bois de Vincennes. . . . And nobody at Court knows what he is expected to do."

CATHERINE DE' MEDICI

She was, in short, a paradox—a compound of indecision and masterfulness. She hated emotion, and much in her that looks like indulgence was merely self-preservation. It was generally for politic ends that she promoted peace and ensued mercy. "When she wishes," says another Venetian diplomat, "she gives an answer which, while it seems quite decided and definite, will none the less turn out to contain no conclusion at all." Other and more recent politicians have tried this method, but it has seldom failed to land a nation in embarrassments.

Catherine would certainly be almost intolerable to read about had she not been unhappy. And this she was, in public as in private life. Her tears were sometimes warranted and the want of some one she could trust, the machinations of those she thought her friends, were a sore trial to her. She was incapable of inspiring devotion and rarely inspired affection. And she was unlike other queens in this, that no tradition of romance has remained to surround her name with glamour. We hear of no lovers, no deeds of daring done for her sake. We may at least pity her for this, that she was a very lonely woman. "I know," writes one who saw her often, "that she hath many times been found in her closet weeping; but of a sudden she hath dried her eyes, dissembled her sorrow, and, to the end that she might deceive those who judged of the true state of affairs by the expression of her countenance, she hath shown herself to the world with a calm and joyous mien." It was only with Alava, the Spanish envoy, that she allowed herself to break down. One day, as she came from the Council Chamber, she took him by the hand. "Why do you smile?" said she. "Will Your Majesty allow me to tell you?" "Speak," she replied sharply. "Well, Your Majesty's eyes are swollen with sleep, one would think you were waking from a dream." "It is but too true," and the tears rose to her eyes, "I have every reason to appear dreamy, for alone and single-handed I bear the burden of affairs. You would be amazed (so she spake) if you understood what has just happened. I no longer know in whom I trust." And yet through weal and woe her spirit wore its regal armour—polished and curiously inlaid, like the Renaissance armour in museums. "She it is," writes Correr, one of the ambassadors from Venice, "who has preserved at Court the only vestige of royal majesty which is still to be found there. That is the reason why I have ever rather pitied than blamed her." Here again we feel how much the Queen-Mother was a woman.

There existed, as it were, four main currents in her life which compelled her course—four shaping influences successively at work—and the names of these four influences are Diane de Poitiers, Philip of Spain, the House of Guise, and the party of the Huguenots. In her attitude to these forces lies the secret of all her actions. The first three are so closely interwoven with her story that they can only be dealt with in their due place. Of her relations to the Huguenots we must take a preliminary view, for without such a view the roughest survey of her would be incomplete.

That Catherine coquetted with the Protestants in England and the Netherlands for political ends, that she dallied with Elizabeth and the House of Orange, is a well-known history. It is more interesting to investigate her own opinions and to discover from contemporaries how much in her earlier and middle life she leaned towards Protestantism. It need hardly be added that the leaning was an intellectual one. Religious beliefs she had none. But she considered that Protestantism was the faith of *ceux de l'entendement*, as her son Henri d'Anjou and his friends expressed themselves when in their first youth they, too, frankly affected the Huguenots. Catherine would always have been on the side of cleverness, and besides this, the Reformers' tenets of freedom of conscience and personal responsibility appealed to her strong sense. So did their attitude towards the Pope, whom Catherine was always rather willing to defy as "no more than a man." When she was still Dauphine, a wave of fashionable Protestantism swept over the Court and it lasted well into Henri II's reign. But it meant little more than that every one, from King to secretary, was in love with Marot's Psalms, and sang them whereever he or she went, whether with hawk on wrist or at the *prie-Dieu*. Each individual at Court had his favourite Psalm —a courtier's paraphrase, as different from the original as his religion was from real piety. "And if there was one person who loved . . . and sang them habitually, it was the late King Henri," wrote a Court secretary, "so that Diane and all his favourites loved them too, or usually pretended so to do. And they said, '*Sire*, may not this one be mine ? ' or ' Do give me that one, please ' . . . And oftentimes he set about singing the aforesaid Psalms with lutes, viols, spinets, flutes, among which rose the voices of his choristers." Catherine found her own private consolation for the King's neglect in singing the one she had made her own: "*Vers l'Eternel, des oppressés le Père*," and she had it constantly on her lips. Private readings of the Bible also came into vogue under the influence of that really serious woman, the mystic, Margaret of Angoulême, and Catherine—unlike her fellows who enjoyed dabbling in a kind of drawing-room heresy—took a real interest in this new study. "At that time," says one who wrote to her in later days, "you recognized Him, you honoured His Holy Bible, which was in your coffers or on your table, in the which you looked and read—and your women and your servants had the happy privilege of reading the Scriptures, and only the nurse, who did not love you any more than she loved God, was furious thereat." With Catherine the taste remained after the fashion died out, and showed itself plainly enough in the first years of the Regency—a taste no doubt sharpened by the fact that Diane was the head of the Catholic faction. It may be objected that the executions that took place after the Huguenot conspiracy of Amboise, that Catherine's treacherous conduct in first inviting the Huguenot, Condé, and then imprisoning him, did not look much like a tendency towards Protestantism. But the cruelties at Amboise were mainly the doing of the Duc de Guise, and whatever voice Catherine had then, as well as her behaviour to Condé, were strictly political matters. At that moment she believed that her Regency depended on the Guises, so she let them work their will and ruin their foes. But directly the support of Condé and his brother of Navarre enabled her to do without them, she gladly threw them over, and it was, as always, with relief that she resumed her dealings with the Protestants. It was when she organized the Conference of Poissy (1561) that she first fully embodied her views: the Council in which Catholics and Protestants, the Cardinal of Guise, and, if possible, Calvin, were to meet together and thrash out their differences in amicable discussion before Queen and Court. Such a conception fitted well with her policy of moderation and peace, her knowledge that the pacification of the Church meant the pacification of the State; but at this time there was more in it than that—there was a sincere desire for conciliation. Catherine's fine moments were not too many, but this was the finest of her life. Her intellect, not her moral insight, made her see that truth was not synonymous with any creed, that each sect fought for its own hand, and that the best chance for true religion was that all should come to some agreement. Her letters of this date are full of it; they, too, rise to a different level from any of the others. And when her preparations were complete and the Protestant ministers arrived, her welcome to them was warmer than mere expediency required. Calvin did not come, but she treated their chief, Théodore de Bèze, with flattering familiarity, summoned him to her private room and made him discuss his tenets with her. She even went so far as to hold "Prêches," as the Huguenots called their form of worship, in her own apartments, with all the Court as congregation. Her son, Henri, frankly avowed his adherence to the Huguenots and, without interference from Catherine, persecuted his little sister, Marguerite for her orthodoxy. There is no stranger page in the annals of this strange family than Marguerite's account of how her brother came to her—a child of eight—and found her reading her Office; how he threw her prayer-book into the fire, telling her that only stupid people were Catholics, that all cultivated folk were Protestants, and that if she continued to read it she should be beaten every day. "All the Court (she says) was infected with heresy," and many lords and ladies urged her to change her opinions as strongly as her brother. No wonder that such doings drew down the angry remonstrance of Philip's envoy, who sent his master detailed accounts of these vagaries. From that year, 1561, until St. Bartholomew's Eve, in 1572, the complaints of Spain against Catherine's heterodoxy never ceased, even when political changes had transformed her attitude into one of severity.

Her Regency was a protracted quarrel with the various ambassadors from Madrid. Those from Venice, too, express themselves boldly on the subject: "It is well-known," writes Suriano, "that several of the women who are most intimate with the Queen are suspected of heresy and of bad conduct; and everybody is aware that the Chancellor in whom she trusts is an enemy of the Roman Church and of the Pope. We saw, too, how tepid were her efforts to protect the Catholic party." One might pick out a score of passages like this one from diaries, letters, despatches, official and unofficial, which show how the land lay. "The Queen favours the Huguenots as usual," Tavannes ironically observes in 1562, and he might have added that, owing to her influence, the Huguenot party was increasing at Court, especially among great ladies. Her choice of the Chancellor, l'Hôpital, one of the only noble figures of this ignoble generation and a man with strong Protestant leanings, was in itself a bold stroke. At first, before it became too perilous, she was frank and even courageous in her espousal of the Protestant cause. The people of Paris, none too fond of their foreign Regent, at one time made a demonstration against her because she tried to stay their cruelties and insisted that the right to punish heretics must be reserved for her magistrates. Decrees of indulgence like this were constantly proclaimed by her. But when the Huguenot revolts broke out in the provinces, when the flame of religious war burst forth, when Condé, tired of her jesuitry, wielded his sword unconditionally against her, her attitude began to alter. The Protestants had become a political danger; Spain suspected her; her Regency was in jeopardy; everything must yield to that. She still, however, when she could, gave way to the mood of leniency and the change in her was not definitive till after the murder of François, Duc de Guise, by the hand of a Protestant in 1562; still more so, after her mysterious journey to the Spanish frontier (on the pretext of seeing her daughter) and her secret conference there with Alva. What really passed between her and that dread man will never be known, since it was not matter for pen and paper. But after their meeting she stepped forth as the declared foe of the ever rebellious Huguenots, and worked in this capacity till the final catastrophe of St. Bartholomew's Eve. Nevertheless, one has only to read her letters to understand that her conduct sprang from no change of opinion. Its cause lay only in her insecurity; in the hostility that threatened her on all sides from the rebels within her realm, and from Philip of Spain, who was watching lynx-eyed for the chance of incriminating her orthodoxy. The feat which she accomplished two days before the massacre, her daughter Marguerite's marriage with Henri de Navarre, the chief of the Huguenot party, proved her dread of Spain; for this match with the King of Navarre was a last diplomatic attempt to rivet to herself an ally against Philip and to make herself sure of the country that lay between the Pyrenees and France. But no less clearly did it show that her old liking for the Protestants was not extinct. The bridegroom was allowed to lead his bride up to the church-door only, and, after the marriage ceremony on the threshold, to withdraw and leave her, so that his ears might be saved from hearing Mass.

Catherine's crest of a rainbow, with her accompanying

CATHERINE DE' MEDICI

motto, *J'apporte la lumière et la sérénité*, seems at first sight something of an irony. But though it never was true of her practice, it was at least true of her aspiration in the earlier years of her Regency. The Catherine of 1560 respected light and cultivated serenity. The Catherine of 1572 had lost her way and her calm had become a mask. And it is these two Catherines that we find in her many portraits. We can trace her development from the day when she was a plump little girl of twelve, with rather heavy cheeks and prominent eyes and thick coils of hair. The bride of fifteen, the young woman of twenty to twenty-five, grows maturer in expression and improves in outline; but the Catherine of thirty to forty is Catherine at her best. "She is a beautiful woman when her face is veiled," says another writer; "I express myself thus because she is tall, her figure is elegant, and her skin delicate; but as for her face, it is not at all beautiful; her mouth is too large and her eyes big and pale. Many people say that she bears a striking likeness to her uncle, Leo X." This is the Queen whom François Clouet drew, with lines as strong and supple, with curves as crafty and elusive, as the character of his sitter. Catherine needed to wear no outward gauze. There is ever a veiled look about her face, and the colourless eyes beneath the braids of brown hair, the full, rather hanging lips, add to the mystery, the inhuman mystery, of her face. In the Catherine of 1572 and later, all these characteristics have grown excessive. The subtlety, which in earlier days, when fulfilment was still to come, could not fail to arouse curiosity, has now lost its interest; the face is more bloodless, the cheeks and jaws heavier, while the massive double chin coarsens the whole impression. Catherine, we know, grew so unwieldy with age that she could hardly walk, and we feel that her mind also grew grosser and shut itself in, and that she even lost her cunning as a player of State-chess.

The Catherine of history has been drawn for us by Clouet; Pourbus, too, has painted her as truly, and yet, perhaps, with more sense of the drama in which she played. The portrait hangs in the long passage between the Pitti Palace and the Ufizzi, and it shows us Catherine de' Medici when she was about thirty years old. The baffling eyes, the fullish lips, the long broad forehead, the rounded cheeks are all before us. Robed in rose-pink satin sown with Orient pearls, a black train flowing behind her, a jewel glowing at her breast, she stands before us as if she thought that she would endure for ever. Young, remote, relentless, pre-eminent without being great, she dominates the gallery-wall to-day as she once dominated the world of her own generation.

Great ages produce great figures—not one but many—and the few that stand forth from the rest only prove their greatness the more by rising above the high level of those around them. At such a time the general air is electric; the public, the artists, the geniuses are all bound together by the something they have in common: some ideal of beauty or conduct which makes the one understand the other. In Italy, the quattrocento painters—in Germany, the band of fifteenth and sixteenth century philosophers and reformers—in England, Shakespeare and the Elizabethan poets—show us, each group in turn, the richness of the generation that produced it. It is, in itself, the sign of a decadent period when one figure alone dominates everything; a figure with no adequate background, an exception crushing all around. Such an one exhausts, even vitiates, the air about it and increases the corruption which first favoured its own existence. For a power is bound to act powerfully, and when it meets nothing to work with it is a bad business. Such single personages were Napoleon Bonaparte and Philip of Spain; such would have been Cæsar Borgia and, perhaps, our Elizabeth, had they lived amidst poorer surroundings; and such was undoubtedly Catherine de' Medici. She, like Napoleon, used up the vitality of the soil and made it impossible for any big idea to grow there.

This was perhaps one important reason of the failure of Protestantism in France. There are many others—to be discussed in their place. But this much may be asserted: that the real growth of Huguenot beliefs came too late, when the vigour of the Renaissance was over. It is easy, it is plausible, to regard Catherine as a murderer of ideas as well as of men. But no person can kill an idea. The real assassin is the decadent tendency which makes a Catherine de' Medici possible and uses her as its agent to achieve its own terrible mission.

CHAPTER II

The Youth of Catherine de' Medici

AUTHORITIES CONSULTED

Biographical Introductions—*Le Comte de la Ferrière*.
Histoire de France—*Michelet*.
La Renaissance—*Michelet*.
History of the Papacy—*Creighton*.
Rélations de la Diplomatie Vénitienne—*Baschet*.
Histoire des choses mémorables—*Fleurange*.
Catherine de Médicis—*Henri Bouchot*.
Florence—*Herbert Gardner*.

CHAPTER II

The Youth of Catherine de' Medici

CATHERINA Maria Romola de' Medici was born in 1519. She was called Romola—the favourite Florentine name—in honour of her great-uncle, the Medici Pope, Leo X. Her father was Lorenzo of Urbino, Leo's nephew and the great-nephew of Lorenzo the Magnificent. Her mother was Madeleine de la Tour d'Auvergne, the child of Jeanne de Bourbon and of the Seigneur de Latour, a descendant of Geoffroi de Bouillon. Their wedding was one of the most sparkling that lives in the pages of the old chronicles. It took place at Amboise by moonlight, *et fut ballé le plus possible*, the Loire giving back the thousand flames of the torches and the torches firing the precious stones on the dancers' dresses, as they trod their stately pavanes, or held high revel on the terrace. It was prophetic that Amboise, so often to be Catherine's home, the place where she brought up her children, the scene of the chief plot against her, should have witnessed the marriage of her parents. She was born a year later. Medician craft and Medician sumptuousness, Bourbon arrogance and Bourbon dignity were born in her blood; the acuteness of Italians, the practical genius of the French, were her natal dower. Her mother died at her birth; her father decadent, worn out, followed his wife a few days after, and his mother, Alfonsina Orsini, took charge of her orphan grandchild. Alfonsina was a great lady, a patroness of artists, anything but a grandmother—and, at five months old, the poor infant nearly died. From her birth, Catherine was the centre of intrigues. The question of her marriage was discussed round her unquiet cradle (in which cradle, it is said, she was painted by Andrea del Sarto) and, before she was a year old, Pope Leo summoned her to Rome. *Secum fert aerumnas Danaum*,* he exclaimed when she was borne into

---

* She brings with her the calamities of the Greeks.

CATHERINE DE' MEDICI

his presence. This was quite the Renaissance Pope's conception of the way to address a baby, and he might have added with truth that, like all the people around her, he did not regard her as a child, but as a little pivot for the struggling Medician interests. He died, however, in 1521 and her grandmother a year earlier. Alfonsina's daughter, Clarissa, the wife of Philip Strozzi, took her place as the little Catherine's guardian—a stern stiff woman of the grand style, who had a religious sense of what was due to family. Her one notion of education was to give her little niece a serious idea of her high postion, to teach her from the time she could toddle that in her the great lady must come before the baby—so that from the first the child grew up in a bleak, sunless atmosphere, the tall palace walls shutting out the light. As she became older, the harshness of her education told upon her and trained her to be an adept in falsehood and in cunning. Her condition was certainly desolate. Her only close relation, her half-brother Alessandro, afterwards the infamous Duke of Florence (the illegitimate son of her father and a Moorish woman) was hardly an attractive connection. He had an unbridled temper which estranged her from him, and there was no confidence between them. Then, as later, her cousin Hippolyte, afterwards the Cardinal de' Medici, was the only person for whom she had any affection. A kind of companionship grew up between the two and they sought each other more as time went on. As for her cousin,* the second Medici Pope, Clement VII, she saw, with unchildlike clearness, that he only used her as a tool for his own ends.

* It is noteworthy that the French historians always speak of Catherine as the niece of Clement VII, whereas, she was, in reality, only his nièce à la mode de Bretagne, being his second cousin once removed, as the following table will show.

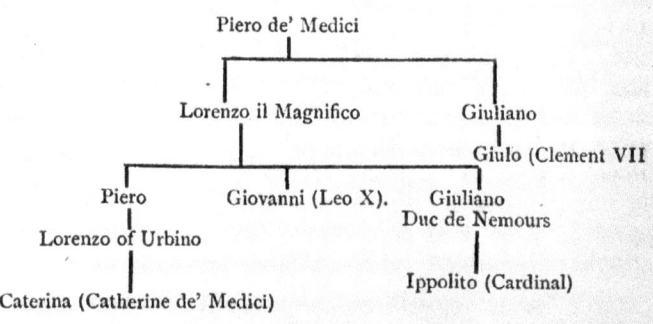

THE YOUTH OF CATHERINE DE' MEDICI

The years 1525 and 1526 were troubled ones for the Medici. There was an organized movement against them, and Catherine's presence in Rome became a peril. One day the Cardinal Passerini appeared and carried her off in a coach to the Palace of Poggio Caiano, near Prato, and thence to Florence, to the austere convent of Santa Lucia, once dear to Savonarola. But she was never long in one place. This time it was her aunt who fetched her and hastily brought her to the Medici Palace, which was then in a state of siege. Ottaviano de' Medici was defending it against the Florentines, who once more had risen against his House. The risk grew so imminent that the luckless little Princess was soon moved back again to her nunnery. In 1527, when Florence was bombarded by Pope and Emperor, Clement redemanded the girl, but she was denied to him. After this, for a space, her life was a series of flittings from one unhealthy nunnery to another, till finally she found some sort of haven with the nuns of the "Murate" Convent. It stood where now stand the "Prigioni" of Florence—not much less prison-like than they—at the end of the long narrow Tuscan street, the Via Ghibellina.

The child was given the cell to which another Catherine, the militant Catherine Sforza, had retired nearly twenty years before. The nuns made much of the "little Duchess," as she was called, and her letters and confidence in them, her desire to be with them long after she was Queen of France, make one of the few pleasant passages in her unnatural record. But even here her presence divided the convent into two camps, and the poor nuns were torn between their civic honour and their wish for peace. "These Murate Sisters taught her the art of opportune pretending," so says her distinguished biographer, M. Bouchot, and indeed, the cloistral habits imposed upon her, the compulsory quiet that surrounded her, made the place not only a refuge, but a training-school of deportment.

No wonder that she took root there in terror of the outside world, and that when the Signoria at last sent for her force had to be used to bring her to their presence. During her sojourn in the convent, the Medici had been expelled from Florence and the Republic once more ruled the city. The "Murate" had naturally become a nucleus of Medician intrigue, and during the siege of Florence by the imperial forces the Government decided to remove her. They sent a great noble, Salvestro Aldborandini, for this purpose. "When Salvestro arrived, after he had been kept waiting for some time, the little Duchess came to the *grille* of the parlour, dressed as a nun, and said that she intended to take the habit and stay for ever with these my revered Mothers . . . The poor little girl . . . was terribly frightened and cried bitterly, not knowing to what glory and felicity her life had been reserved by God and the heavens . . . But Salvestro did all he could to comfort and reassure her, and took her (once more) to the Convent of Santa Lucia, where she stayed till the war was ended." As soon as she could, however, she ran back to her beloved Murate and, in the months that followed, she decided that she had the true vocation and would herself become a nun. Vocations at eleven years old—in all ranks of life—are apt to be rather illusory, and when, within the year, the summons came to her to take her place in the world as a princess, she caught at the prospect with an eagerness not unlike that of most other little girls of her age. Ottaviano de' Medici was sent to fetch her to Rome, and she went with a goodwill.

"She has a very animated nature," says one who saw her at this time, " she is small and thin in her person, with a face that has not one distinguished feature; she has big eyes, quite the eyes of the Medici family." Such was the figure that stepped forth to meet Ottaviano, who, with a gorgeous cavalcade, awaited her at the convent door. We can imagine the scene as if it were some fresco in Florence : the endless street, the tufa palaces, the tall overshadowing houses on either side ; the glittering lords and ladies ; the pawing steeds, the scarlet trappings, embroidered on the grey background, with the chilly convent gateway in front ; the Duchessina passing the *grille*, led by the Mother Superior and divested of her habit for ever, the dark-robed white-coifed nuns crowding round her, tearful but restrained by discipline ; and then the lengthy courtesies, the holding of a stirrup, the crack of a whip, and the whole coloured procession winding like an illuminated scroll along the sober street till it vanished out of sight. We can watch it, if we will, across the brown bridge of the Trinity, onward towards the road to Rome, and as the Porta Romana rises in massive strength before us, we can almost say that the Catherine approaching is still more than half a child, but that the Catherine who issues from it on the other side is already a woman, a politician.

Who can be surprised that she entered the world armed

CATHERINE DE' MEDICI.
BY CLOUET. MUSÉE DE VERSAILLES.
From a photograph by A. Giraudon.

THE YOUTH OF CATHERINE DE' MEDICI

cap-à-pié with diplomacy ? Her experience of human nature had not been edifying. Unprotected save by monastic walls, she had always seen herself the centre of feuds and of plottings, and she knew now that her chance was to enter the arena herself and to outwit as she would certainly be outwitted. At Rome she was immediately installed as the Pope's relation—as a personage with her own attendants. Her duenna, Maria Salviati (the daughter-in-law of Caterina Sforza) was, it is true, a severe Puritan, but Catherine was no more a child to be chidden. Her quick wit matured in the midst of Court life ; princes took note of her, ambassadors were charmed with her repartees. But the only person she cared for was, as of old, her cousin Hippolyte. Whether he showed any love for her, whether her feeling for him was more than a girlish sentiment, will remain moot points. It is known that François I of France had once wished that they should marry, and stories were afloat about them in Roman circles. Such a union, however, was far from the Pope's designs. Clement VII was bent on making a splendid bargain of his kinswoman with a due regard to his own purse. Suitors in plenty appeared. There was James V of Scotland who was dismissed because Clement thought that posts to Edinburgh would be too expensive ; or Francesco Sforza, Duke of Milan, rejected as too old and too poor ; or the Duke of Mantua, whose morals were objected to. Others also were considered and discarded. But when François I despatched an embassy to open negotiations for his second son, Henri, Duc d'Orléans, matters at once became serious. The French legate saw her and reported that she was graceful and *portée à plaire*, that she showed a need to be caressed and loved. It became evident that the Pope meant business. When a fresh ambassador arrived from France the conscientious Clement sent Catherine off to Florence, nominally to escape malaria, more probably to be removed from the danger of her cousin's neighbourhood. At the same moment, Hippolyte was heaped with sudden honours ; was sent on a mission to Turkey and allowed to assume for the occasion an especially distinguished Hungarian uniform. It is in this princely dress that Titian has painted him and that he will always live for us on the walls of the Pitti Palace. The pale, presageful face, the dark eyes, the sumptuous suit of mulberry velvet, and the cap to match that sits close upon his black hair—all breathe the spirit of romance, anc the deep shadow of the background intensifies the picture. Drama is written on his face and we feel no surprise when we learn that a few years later, when he was but twenty-five, he was treacherously poisoned by Catherine's half-brother, Alessandro. Meanwhile, among the people she saw there was no one so likely to attract her. Already a power in affairs, he was quickly made a Cardinal, and his great abilities and high ambitions were well suited to her own. It is impossible not to surround these two young people with some softening romance, as M. Bouchot has already done. But the Pope cared for no sentimental considerations; Hippolyte departed to Constantinople and Catherine led a rich, a new, existence among the artists and princes of Florence. Clement was all the time proceeding to negotiate with France. The portrait of the young Duc d'Orléans was casually shown to her; envoys came and went, compliments were paid, and in 1531, the affair was settled. History has many ironies, but none perhaps more pointed than that Catherine's marriage settlement was drawn up at Anet, where François I and his Court were staying with Diane de Poitiers.

No sooner was his scheme safe in port than Clement VII began to haggle about the dowry, and the difficulties that he raised took two more years to determine. "This man is the scourge of God," said the Cardinal de Grammont impatiently. The Pope did not mean to be at much expense and Rome— to its great impoverishment—was forced to provide the dowry, the trousseau, the wedding-presents and even the bride's travelling expenses. Among the gifts thus extorted were some fabulous pearls, worth a fortune, which afterwards passed to the next Dauphine, Mary Stuart, came with her to Scotland and finally were taken without a word and worn by Queen Elizabeth. The biographies of royal jewels would make a significant volume. The French bridegroom and his father sent the bride " a sapphire tablet and a diamond cut *en dos d'âne*." Her dresses were the talk of Italy, her retinue was of the most distinguished. Hippolyte d'Este returned from Turkey to ride, grave and splendid, in her train. The Pope had demanded his presence in order to put an end to gossip, but the young noble could hardly have fancied his position. François I tried to woo him with presents, but the only one he would accept was " a fine Barbary lion," though what he did with it history does not record. Tradition clings round the names of Catherine's ladies—Maria Salviati, Caterina Cybo, Palla Rucellai, and the rest. There were some so young that they

THE YOUTH OF CATHERINE DE' MEDICI

still had governesses, among them three coloured maidens: Marie the Moor, Agnes and Margaret the Turks, all taken in an expedition against Barbary and adding to the Oriental splendour of the bridal pageant. To crown all, the Pope was to accompany the retinue and witness the wedding at Marseilles, the place insisted on by François for the meeting, as a proof of Papal deference to France. But true to himself, if to no one else, Clement temporized and dallied to the last, even to the moment of Catherine's farewell dinner at Florence, urging his age, the sun, the dust, in order to escape from more perplexities. Go he did, however, and the great cavalcade at last set off. The marriage-contract can still be read with all its stipulations. France settled an immense sum upon Catherine, and the Pope promised her a dowry of thirty thousand golden crowns; but the full sum was apparently never paid and Clement was generally supposed to have broken faith with France.

Nothing could exceed the splendour of the wedding pageants at Marseilles. The chief figure there, strange to say, was not the bridegroom—still a half-fledged lad—but his father François I, behind whose dazzling personality the prince seems to disappear. François and Clement, the astute monarch and the crafty prelate, had a regal meeting, and while they dealt in ceremonious courtesies, they sounded the depths of one another's cunning. The Pope tried to make the King promise to undertake a crusade against the Turks, and the King tried to ascertain the Pope's real intentions towards the Powers of Europe. And all the time, on carpets of gold tissue, Hymen was spouting long Latin compliments and nymphs were reciting wordy verses to the newly-married pair.

But the Pope departed, the feasting ended, and Catherine's married life began. There must at once have been cruel disappointment for this fifteen-year old bride. She, the polished princess, found herself the unwished for wife of a silent gloomy boy, who had nothing to say to her, or, for the matter of that, to anybody else. There is singularly little known about their early years together and the reason probably is because there is little to learn. They had not much individual life, moving tribally about with the Court in the strange crowded fashion of those strange days. Catherine might have found some compensation for what she missed in private life, had the public welcomed her more warmly. The marriage, however, was unpopular. Paris was disgusted at the expense it had incurred;

it turned a cold shoulder to her and her State entry there fell flat. For the country at large she was, from the first, " The Florentine "—an object of suspicion and dislike. She was, with some justice, accused of raising her Italian followers over the heads of the French, which did not help to mend matters; nor did the Pope's shabby behaviour about her dowry induce France to love her better. Two years after the marriage, the Venetian envoy reports that the match was still objected to and that only Catherine's submissiveness could make her position possible.

Even to her, the arrival at the French Court, that supreme school of etiquette, must have appeared formidable. She had written from Italy to beg François I to give her dancing lessons at Marseilles that she might not make an awkward impression on the French ladies. Her qualms were by no means unfounded. For these great personages were already jealous of the influence she would exercise over the King, and were not too well disposed towards her till they saw her portrait. Her heavy cheeks and rather unformed look reassured them and they found consolation in talking over the royal bride's impecuniosity and the over-sumptuousness of her trousseau.

Her chief lady was the friendliest. This was Mademoiselle d'Heilly, soon to be famous as Duchesse d'Estampes and as the mistress of François I. It is strange that her fellow lady-in-waiting should have been Anne de Pisseleu, otherwise Madame de Châteaubriant, the woman whom she was soon to supplant in the King's affections. Marguerite de Vendôme, a Bourbon and later Duchesse de Nevers, was also of Catherine's train; so were Charlotte Gouffier, dame de Brissac, and Anne Gouffier, dame de Montreuil, the daughters of a rich and learned family—a retinue alarming enough for a girl of fifteen. But happily the King's sister, Marguerite d'Angoulême, Queen of Navarre, took her under her protection. To this loving and powerul lady Catherine had the skill to defer. From the moment she arrived in France, she took the rôle of the humble, appealing young girl, and she had the reward she wanted in Marguerite's constant friendship and good word with the King. This, perhaps, she hardly needed, for he encouraged her at once, and from the time he received her at Marseilles to the day of his death she was his constant companion. Her quick wit, her bold tongue, her acute insight pleased him. He loved fashion, and she did all she could, she even learned Greek, to be in the fashion, and to win him. Astride her horse, she rode by his side, his chosen comrade when he hunted in the leafy forests of Fontainebleau, and he liked her courage as much as he liked her talk. He lost no time in enrolling her in his famous Petite Bande—the troop of blondes and brunettes, who followed him in the chase and dined at his table and asked him primitive riddles and, generally speaking, rejuvenated him. They accompanied him from palace to palace, from Les Tournelles in Paris to Fontainebleau, paradise of hunters; or from the river-girt Château of Amboise to the proud little city of Blois. The fair and irresponsible ghosts of the Little Band still meet us on its palace staircase, the spiral, shell-like staircase which seems made to lead aërially from one golden pleasure to another.

Every lady capable of charming the King's tired taste was of it. The Duchesse d'Estampes was the ruler of the rainbow-coloured troop and its members were bound to have her approval. No one was allowed to be squeamish and few had the inclination to be so. For the rest, a provision of high spirits and good stories, together with a hardy taste for exercise, was all that was required. The real significance of the Band was, however, beyond the King's control. It bore a leading part in Court intrigue, and was the faction of one of the two crafty queens who were trying to out-plot each other on the State chess-board. The Duchesse d'Estampes was not for long the only ruling force; the Petite Bande soon became a fighting regiment, an opposition party to the rising planet—to Diane de Poitiers and her followers.

For the curtain had already gone up and the first Act of the drama which was to occupy the reign had begun. Diane de Poitiers had taken possession of Henri II, and in 1536, three years after her marriage, Catherine found herself supplanted in the heart of her husband. The great world immediately divided into camps, one for the King and his Duchess, the other for the Prince and Diane. Father and son had never got on and now the position became strained. Everything depended on the relative power of the ladies. The Duchesse d'Estampes was the younger and enjoyed saying that she was born on Diane's wedding-day. But Diane had the stronger mind and knew best how to use it. In place of the Petite Bande, she had the Guises as her allies and also the Connétable, Montmorency. This was a grievance with Catherine, for he had at first been her staunch friend and she did not rest till, later, she got him back again. Round him and Diane, at this moment, gathered all the charmers who were not of the Petite Bande.

Nor was it long before the two hostile groups made a war-cry of religion. They began the fashion which afterwards did so much to ruin the Reformation in France. Without one religious thought, they made a party badge of the differing creeds and stifled the free growth of thought and of faith with intrigue. Diane led the Catholics, Madame d'Estampes the growing sect of the Huguenots. Thus, from the beginning, Catherine was identified with the Reforming party; though the fact then had little importance, for it impelled her to no course of action. Her adherence to Madame d'Estampes was the only intimation that she gave of any enmity towards Diane, but that, too, brought about no direct results. For at this period of her life it was Catherine's pose to efface herself and pass unnoticed. "Her rôle was not to have one, unless it were to sue for the King's favour." And the nullity of her conduct while she was Dauphine, which looked like want of character at the time, was the strongest proof of her strong will. For deliberately biding her hour, she made herself like a sheet of blank paper to the world till the light should come that would reveal the writing below the surface. Meanwhile, she had to bear neglect, even at public festivals, as well as the frank contempt of the public for her childlessness. There was a time, some ten years after her marriage, when François, actually meditated her divorce from Henri. Catherine, now Dauphine, still remained without children and, at a great family council, Diane de Poitiers persuaded the King that a separation of the husband and wife was the only wise course. The rumour of the King's resolve reached her, and the meek little diplomat knew how to play her part. Her father-in-law could not bear to see tears, and she went to him weeping bitterly. She had, she said, heard of his intention; she sacrificed herself for the good of France and would retire to a convent, or remain in his service, as he pleased. "Ma fille," said the King, "have no doubt, since God hath willed it, that you ought to be my daughter-in-law and the Dauphin's wife, and that I would not have it otherwise. Peradventure it will please Him to grant to you and to me the grace that we desire more than aught in the world." Catherine withdrew in triumph, Diane for once was defeated, and her ally, the Constable, disgraced.

Marguerite, the Queen of Navarre, wrote Catherine a letter of sympathy: "My brother," she says, "will never allow this repudiation, as evil tongues pretend. But God will give a royal line to Madame la Dauphine when she has reached the

HENRI DE VALOIS (HENRI II) IN HIS YOUTH.
BY FRANÇOIS CLOUET.   CHÂTEAU DE CHANTILLY.
From a photograph by A. Giraudon.

age at which women of the House of the Medici are wont to have children. The King and I will rejoice with you then, in spite of these wretched backbiters." So strongly did Marguerite feel on this subject that when she spoke of it to her secretary, "this charitable princess could by no means keep the tears from her eyes for the fervent love that she bore in her heart."

When at last, in 1543, a year after the scheme for the divorce, a son was born to her, it was Diane de Poitiers, in her widow's dress of black and white, who received it into the world, prescribed for the mother and constituted herself her chief attendant. For all these ignominies, received with outward affability, Catherine kept, as stands recorded, "*une plaie fort saignante au coeur*." Those around her saw but a meek and rather spiritless young woman; but to us, who know what followed, she rather appears like the panther lying low in the brushwood before it springs—passive only to hide its presence. Self-defence, at that moment, was her only possible policy. While the King lived she had at least a protector. But when he died, the case was different and no one was afraid to be her foe. Madame d'Estampes lost her power and Diane reigned unchecked. Catherine's lot was hardly to be envied when Henri II came to the throne.

Before we regard him as King, it becomes necessary to glance at Henri of Orleans while he was still Dauphin, and to see what manner of man it was who made the centre of two women's lives. It is strange to observe how his wedding and his early married life seem almost to have gone on without him; how his father, the old glamour still about him, played the chief part at the marriage festivities, and later that of protector to the Dauphine. But until the death of François, his son showed but little personality. Timid and taciturn by nature and afraid of his father, who did not care for him, he carefully hid himself except to Diane de Poitiers. And yet he made an impression upon the ambassadors at Court. "The *serenissime* Dauphin," writes Dandolo of Venice, "is twenty-three years old. He has a presence which is passing comely and he is rather tall than short, neither stout nor thin, but so well-knit that one would think he was all made of muscle. . . . Natheless he hath a nature which one cannot but call taciturn and sombre. Rarely doth he laugh or give sign of laughter, and those at Court assure me that they have not seen him laugh a single time."

Five years afterwards, when he had turned twenty-eight, Cavalli takes up the tale :

" He is of a robust constitution but of a melancholic humour and is well skilled in the use of arms. He is no *beau-diseur* in his repartees, but is most clear-cut and firm in his opinions. His intelligence is not of the readiest, and yet it is such men as he who often succeed best." Diane's work was beginning to bear fruit in this strange, slow-developing nature.

It is easy to gather from these sketches that the man they draw was no nonentity. His very silence is refreshing in that age of brilliant babble, and we feel the force that dominated Catherine. What he would become, and she also, lay in the same hand. For one person moulded the destinies and shaped the characters of both—his by subjection, hers by resistance—and that person was the Grande Sénéchale of Rouen, Diane de Poitiers.

CHAPTER III

Diane de Poitiers

AUTHORITIES CONSULTED

Correspondance de Diane de Poitiers.
Memoirs de Henri II—*Archives Curieuses*.
Lettres et poésies d'Henri II.
Lettres de Catherine de' Medici.
Rélations de la Diplomatie Vénitienne—*Baschet*.
Lettres envoyées a la Reine-Mère—*Archives Curieuses*.
Memoirs de Tavannes.
Memoirs de Vielleville.
Sur la Règne de François II—*Régnier de la Planche*.
Catherine de Mēdicis—*Bouchot*.
Les Moeurs Polies de la Cour de Henri II—*Bourciez*.
Les femmes de la Renaissance—*Maulde de la Clavière*.
Introduction to Correspondance de Diane de Poitiers—*Guiffry*.

CHAPTER III

Diane de Poitiers

DIANE DE POITIERS, Grande Sénéchale de Rouen, Duchesse de Valentinois, daughter of M. de la Vallière, wife of Louis de Bézé, was a typical woman of the French Renaissance, superb, practical, rich in vitality, a patroness of the arts, a dabbler in Plato, well versed in medicine, a busy leader of factions. Sumptuous she was, beyond belief, with a palace like a little city, a staff of servants like an army, and a poet for her Chief-Secretary.

Legend has been as busy with Diane de Poitiers as with Catherine de' Medici—as busy in the opposite direction. If the one has figured as a sensational villain, the other has been a proverbial goddess—a type of beauty and romance. But Diane, even in her youth, was not beautiful. The authentic portraits and medals of her show her to be comely and reposeful-looking, with a naturally brilliant complexion, renewed, Dian-like, by nothing less pure than cold water. These images are very different from those by which the world knows her : from Benvenuto Cellini's green bronze goddess, who with her quiver and her hounds once presided over Fontainebleau ; or Jean Goujon's Diana, cool and prone and deliciously elegant, in old days the guardian deity of Anet ; or, again, Primaticcio's fashionable Artemis, a painter-laureate's homage to a rising beauty. But these representations of Diane, long supposed to be portraits, were really no more than Court compliments, poetic variations on the name of the Greek goddess. And except for a general memory of the coiffure and the air of the great lady, they have little more to do with her likeness than had the crescent-crowned nymphs who emerged, spouting Latin poems, to greet Henri II from every pageant. The goddess of the chase was the vogue and, handled in a thousand ways, became the symbol of the favourite.

Diane de Poitiers was seventeen years older than Henri II. Age is an important factor in human intercourse, and it is

CATHERINE DE' MEDICI

enlightening to find that when he first knew her, in 1536, he was barely twenty, she a widow of nearly thirty-seven, and that their relations with one another lasted for twenty-two years, until the day of his death. She had found him a morose and tongue-tied boy, she evoked the man of force and the monarch. In this she was unique—that, from first to last, she conducted the education of a King. Perhaps no woman, before or after, has formed a ruler as completely as she formed Henri, though had Louis XIV been younger when he first met Madame de Maintenon, that great lady would have vied with her. It might even be said that few women have more completely formed any man or had a steadier hold upon him. Their alliance has become such a classic of historical scandal, is so fraught with gossip and political considerations, that its deep and enduring romance has been too much overlooked. And yet it should count as one of the rare things in biography—a passion that lasted; rarer still among royal personages, who are more apt to deal in gallant episodes than in faithful love. Henri's fervent letters, the poems that he wrote her, are no mere vents for sentiment or collections of lyric conceits, but the sincere outpourings of a human heart—very different from the rhymes and love-letters of his father, François I. Later there were lapses in Henri's devotion, but they were brief and unimportant, always followed by a speedy return to Diane. His feeling for her was strong enough to bear the natural transition from poetry into prose and their union was, in all ways, a happy marriage, save for the grimly pathetic figure of Catherine, who stood between them like the ghost of some past entanglement—anything but the lawful wife. As for the royal children, they were no bar to this strange domestic felicity, for Diane was ready to love them as if they were her own, and Anet was as much their home as Amboise. What then, we are forced to ask ourselves, was the secret of the power which this middle-aged woman exercised over a man young enough to be her son?

It was not beauty that attracted him, for we have seen that she was not beautiful, and her lover himself, in his most fervent moments, never pretended that she was so.

>   Non la beauté—qui un léger courage
>   Peut émouvoir—tant que vous me peut plaire.

So he writes to her in early days, in the full tide of his love; and *honnête* (which in those days meant comely) is the warmest epithet he finds for her face. It is curious to compare the writers of her own time, or immediately after, with one another and to discover how, with more or less evasion, they all agree about her. Brantôme, the invaluable liar to whom every grand lady was a paragon, is the only one who mentions her beauty. "I saw Madame la Duchesse de Valentinois when she was seventy, as fair of countenance and as amiable as when she was thirty"—so he says; but it was unfortunate for his veracity that she died at sixty-four. Other authors are more truthful, though they are discreet. "She came into the King's life," writes a Venetian, "when he was only Dauphin. He has loved her dearly and loves her still.... old though she be. She has, it must be said, never used paint, yet (perhaps by virtue of the minute pains she takes) she is very far from appearing as old as she is." A French historian is less considerate. "It was a grievous thing," said he, "to see a young prince adore a faded face, covered with wrinkles, and a head fast turning grey, and eyes which had grown dim and were even sometimes red." And this rather unkind description is borne out by some Latin verses written when she was thirty-eight, about eighteen months after her first meeting with Henri. *Rugosa est facies*, so they begin, not overcomplimentarily; nor, for all their elegance, do they spare either her white hair or her wrinkles. However many women, no more beautiful than she, have been so romantic by nature that they have woven a golden web around themselves, a web of glamour and of mystery. Here again legend has been at work on Diane, and here again legend is not justified. To tell the truth, Diane de Poitiers was the most matter-of-fact woman in the world—as practical as only a Frenchwoman can be and absorbed in concrete things. We need only read her letters, full of current affairs and household details and medical prescriptions and discussions of the hams of Mayence, to grasp how little sentiment or subtlety there was in her composition.

The secret of her influence is, after all, no very remote one. She was the first to find out and to draw forth the latent powers in the Prince, powers that he himself did not as yet realize, though he suffered from all the discomfort of unexpressed and unemployed energies. Diane herself was forcible enough to see that his gloom was the gloom of a concentrated nature. He was inarticulate and she taught him speech; awkward and morose from diffidence and she gave him self-confidence and success. Above all, he needed affection. His father, absorbed in his eldest son, had never liked the second. " I do not care for dreamy, sullen, sleepy children," so he once said of him. His mother, who might have found out what was in him, died while he was still a child. Diane de Poitiers was the first woman in his life, the first person to show him any tenderness, and passion leaped forth in response. While she was making a man of him, she was also making a poet.

> Plus ferme foi ne fut oncques jurée
> A nouveau prince, oh ma seule princesse,
> Que mon amour, qui vous sera sans cesse
> Contre le temps et la mort assurée.
> De fosse creuse ou de tour bien murée
> N'a point besoin de ma foi la forteresse,
> Dont je vous fis dame, reine et maîtresse,
> Pour ce qu'elle est d'éternelle durée.

So he sang in one of his poems to her, lyrics few but fervent, all written in his own delicate hand, a significant fact in a day when princes used secretaries to write even intimate letters. His short notes to her, too, are full of concentrated feeling, as different as possible from the amorous conceits, the strained images, the scrolls and flourishes of language usual in the *billets-doux* of his time. In all he writes there is the sincerity, even the note of suffering, which belongs to real passion and which we do not remember in any contemporary love-letters. " Natheless," he writes to her from camp, " I entreat thee to keep in thy remembrance him who has only known one God and one friend, and to rest assured that thou shalt never feel ashamed of giving me the name of thy Servant. Let this be my name for ever." " *Madame m'amye* "—(runs another) " I thank thee humbly for taking the trouble to send me news of thee, which is the thing on earth that best pleaseth me.... I cannot live without thee, and if thou didst but know the dearth of all enjoyment from which I suffer here, thou wouldst pity me." When he has been two days away, he " cannot live without her " ; when she is indisposed, he offers to leave all business and come to her side, on the chance of doing her service. Sometimes Diane sends him a pious present and he hastens to thank her. " I received thy letters yesterday and also the chemises of Our Lady of Chartres. They could not have come at a better time, for I intend setting off the day after to-morrow, and about the middle of August I hope to reach Montdidier, and to put mysel into such condition. . . that

I shall be worthy to wear the scarf that thou hast sent me... Remember him who has never loved, who will never love, any one but thee. I implore thee also, *m'amye*, to deign to wear this ring for the love of me." This note, like all the others, is signed with their intimate cypher, two D's back to back which formed an H in the centre and were bound together by a loop called *le lac d'amour*—the monogram that sowed itself through France, on the walls of the Louvre, on palace and on chapel, on prayer-book and on choir-stall, as if it were the monogram of the Queen and King of the land.

And so in truth it was, for though Diane made a poet of the Dauphin, it was by the way. She was much more intent on making a king; and if one source of her power lay in his need of affection, another, as potent, lay in his need for a Mentor. " To the miserable Grande Sénéchale " (writes a hostile chronicler of the day, a secretary of Marguerite of Angoulême) " the King was introduced, on the advice of favourites, as to a jewelled ring that might possibly take his fancy, and a pedagogue from whom he might learn much virtue." She taught him how to reign. His father did not take the trouble to train his son. " In his lifetime he never knocked him into shape, nor did he even summon him to his Privy Council, so that the Prince came to the throne devoid, one may say, of any notion how to govern." With a woman's insight, Diane understood her material; with an administrator's skill, she made the best of it. His heaviness was converted into dignity, his slowness into prudent policy. Diane was, it has been said, a typical Frenchwoman. No land but France has produced this race of the graceful *maîtresse-femme*, the brilliant State-housekeeper, making many ends meet while she seems to be simply amusing; kind and cruel, honest and ambitious, as lucid as a mathematician, as enigmatic as a woman. In after times, Madame de Maintenon was, as it were, the reincarnation of Diane de Poitiers. There is a likeness in the good and the bad points, in the very circumstances, of these two magnificent tutoresses. Both were widows in the grand style, both eminently respectable, both boundlessly ambitious, yet capable of disinterested scheming for the honour of their respective sovereigns; both matter-of-fact, with a genius for educating children; both making their names synonymous with the anti-Protestant party—though Diane did this on merely political grounds, while Madame de Maintenon was sincerely ecclesiastical. Both, too, grew so invaluable to their pupils that Madame de Maintenon sat in Louis XIV's Privy Council and Henri II took no decision without first holding a *tête-à-tête* Parliament with Diane de Poitiers. To say the truth, we confess that we prefer Madame de Brézé to Madame Scarron, for, whether owing to her time or to her temperament, there was something more of *bonhomie*, something warmer and more generous in her atmosphere than in that of the later and more scholastic Egeria. It is pleasurable to think of Diane, robed in her black and white satin, discussing the last Platonic book with an elegant philosopher in pearl-sown doublet, as together they pace the broad terraces and galleries of Anet—the little volume in her hand, fresh from Italy, sumptuously bound in brown and gold ; more pleasurable than to conjure up Madame de Maintenon in her famous *feuille-morte* dress, dissecting the newest treatise on theology with a black-stoled, black-capped priest, or writing her finished letters of advice (far subtler than anything of Diane's) which, masterpieces though they be, leave us chilly and dissatisfied. But each was suited to her own monarch and left an indelible mark upon his career.

Diane's contemporaries were not slow to recognize her effect on him. "The person whom, without a doubt, the King loves above all others, is Madame de Valentinois," writes one of them (five years after Henri's accession)—"She is a woman of fifty-two.... a woman of intelligence who has always been the *inspirer* of the King. She even helped him with her purse when he was Dauphin.... She is *au courant* of everything, and day by day, as a rule, the King goes to find her after dinner, and stays an hour and a half talking with her, and he tells her everything that happens." The unfledged Dauphin, with his passion for hunting and the exercise of arms, began to study art and literature, even grew to like them for her sake. But Diane had too much of a woman's genius to woo him thus educationally to her service without consulting his tastes. She made Anet and its forests into a huntsman's Eden. There was an incomparable heronry there ; rare birds and strange beasts, falcons and leopards were kept in the gallery that she built for them ; its walls were sculptured with emblems of the chase ; her own name was deftly made use of to enhance the general sense of sport. At every corner she reminded the King that she was goddess of his favourite pursuit no less than of his heart, and the imaginary statue of her as Diana guarded the approaches of her palace.

DIANE DE POITIERS.
PORTRAIT IN ENAMEL BY LÉONARD LIMOUSIN. COLLECTION SOLTIKOFF.
From a photograph by A. Giraudon.

DIANE DE POITIERS

It was not for nothing that she was his elder; she knew full well that passion is not long-lived and that a wise woman herself provides her lover with pleasures independent of her presence.

It is difficult to define Diane's attitude towards Henri. She was not passionate, or even emotional; her feeling for him was that of the artist for his work, of the statesman for his cherished idea, of the successful teacher for his disciple—with the added excitement that the teacher was a woman and the disciple a man and a king. The glamour of his royalty, of the vistas it opened before her, of the reflected splendour cast upon her by his prestige, entered into her feeling for him. Her manner to him was evidently ceremonious, for in one of his lyrics he entreats as a rare favour that he may be allowed to kiss her face; but in this she was like other Frenchwomen of the day with whom etiquette had become a religion. Now and again she worked herself into some response to his outbursts, and perhaps nothing measures the depths of her matter-of-factness so much as these more melting moments of hers. Henri is about to part from her for a space.

> Et je lui dis encore davantage
> Que la supplie de bien se souvenir
> Que n'ai joie jusqu'au revenir—

he exclaims in farewell. Diane, for once, tries her hand at answering in kind:

> Adieu délices de mon coeur,
> Adieu mon maître et mon seigneur,
> Adieu vrai estoc de noblesse!
>
> Adieu plusieurs royaux banquets,
> Adieu épicurieux mets,
> Adieu magnifiques festins!

The Muse broke down quickly and the natural sybarite asserted herself. If the love for *plusieurs royaux banquets* is not poetic, it is at least sincere, and this is a distinction in an age when every cultivated lady wrote reams of erudite doggerel and believed her many admirers when they told her she was a Sappho.

Sincere Diane was. She had the qualities of her faults—the staunch fidelity, the cult of habit, the reliable good sense of a rather cold-blooded nature. She was always a motherly wife rather than a mistress, and no doubt this suited the King. Her indulgent wisdom, her calm, her coolness as of water from the spring, refreshed his fastidious taste as no more exacting woman could have done. It was by such means that she gained her absolute power. "This lady," (exclaims Henri's chronicler) "got complete possession of his will, and every one, even the Queen, was wont to call her 'Madame.'"

With the world outside the Court she quickly grew unpopular. "*Sire, si vous laissez comme Diane fait' par trop vous gouverner, Sire, vous n'êtes plus que cire,*" wrote a daring punster of the day. The crown-jewels went to her—were flaunted in the Queen's presence; her head, instead of Catherine's, was struck with that of the King on almost every medal from the mint; she was painted in enamel riding in a crupper behind him, and gradually every benefice, every important appointment, civic or ecclesiastical, was transferred to the firm keeping of those white, grasping hands of hers. "*Dans cette cour, les femmes faisaient tout, même les géneraux et capitaines,*" grumbled the surly old soldier Tavannes. The poets were rather more polite,

>Que voulez-vous Diane bonne
>Que vous donne ?[1]
>Vous n'eûtes comme j' entends
>Jamais tant d'heur au printemps
>Qu' en automne.

So sang, not without malice, the gay Protestant poet, Clément Marot, and indeed it seemed as if fortune had withheld no gift from the Grande Sénéchale. Her despotism at all events justified the insight of François I. "Do not be subject to the will of others as I have been subject to the will of one other," he said to his son on his deathbed, little understanding the depth of that son's sensibility. There is an old tradition that François, in despair at Henri's want of deportment, himself chose Diane to be the Prince's mistress, imagining that love for such a woman would be his best education. There would have been nothing very strange in this. It was the fashion for parents formally to arrange connections such as this between a young man and a woman of the world, who was ready to train him and whose *serviteur* he became—connections which, according to circumstances, were more or less Platonic. But in this case the tradition seems mere legend. Henri's own letters to Diane disprove it. "Since in times past" (he writes) "I was not afraid to lose the favour of the late King by remaining with you, I should hardly com-

[1] Que je vous donne ?

plain of any trouble that I may have now in doing you the slightest service." The King could hardly have been displeased at the progress of this attachment, if he himself had initiated it.

It is unfortunate that this phrase in Henri's letter does not as definitely refute another tradition about Diane which seems to be equally fallacious. This is the ugly story that she had been the mistress of François I before she became the mistress of his son—a legend which was made the most of by Michelet, that most lurid of historians, and to which some romantic writers still prefer to cling. It should have been enough for them that years ago, before the modern high-tide of documentary research, Sainte-Beuve, the Pope of criticism, rejected this report by the light of his own good sense. But since his day M. Guiffry, the editor of Diane's correspondence, the expert authority upon her, has so stated her case that no fair mind will doubt her innocence. Without recapitulating his admirable essay, it may perhaps be advisable to sum up the gist of his evidence against the long-lived scandal, and also to recount the cause of the scandal itself.

In the plot which the great Connétable de Bourbon wove against François I many people were implicated, and amongst them Diane's father, M. de Saint-Vallier. The Connétable escaped but, Saint-Vallier was taken. It is alleged that Diane pleaded with the King for his life, that her request was granted at the expense of her honour, that her father was finally reprieved when already standing on the scaffold. This was in 1524. Diane had been happily wedded for eight years to the Sénéchal of Normandy, Louis de Brézé, and had given him two daughters. It was he who, in ignorance of his father-in-law's complicity, had been the means of revealing the conspiracy to François. What more natural than that he should bestir himself for the relation he had unwittingly betrayed; that his wife, who was waiting-woman to the Queen, with easy access to the King, should have gone to François to entreat for her father's pardon? That the reprieve was granted at the last moment and that this was rather an exceptional act of mercy, are the facts which are nearest testimony against her. For the rest, the whole affair is grounded on a single sentence in the contemporary *Journal d'un Bourgeois de Paris*: "And it was rumoured that the aforesaid Seigneur de Saint-Vallier, during the King's absence, had threatened to kill him for dishonouring a young girl—and in truth, if it had not been for his son-in-law, the Grand-Sénéchal of Normandy, he would have been beheaded." But Diane at twenty-three, a great lady, long a wife and mother, could hardly have been called a " young girl " ; nor does the stern dignified character of her husband, who never changed in his respect for her, make the episode more probable. It was not till forty years later, when she had innumerable enemies, that the accusation was brought up again, and then it was her chief foe, the Protestant historian, Régnier de la Planche, and the arch-gossip Brantôme, who converted the Bourgeois' tale of a father's vengeance into the current and widely different version.[1] It is noteworthy also that two reliable historians writing at the time of the event (one of them a follower of Marguerite of Angoulême) ascribe Diane's success with the King to nothing more remote than her filial prayers and tears ; that, contrary to the general belief, a whole month elapsed between Saint-Vallier's condemnation and his sensational reprieve on the scaffold ; and last, but almost first, that François, at that date, was in the heyday of his love for Madame d' Estampes and that neither woman would have brooked a rival. There is nothing in Diane's life—and this is an essential matter—to justify this charge against her. She always led the existence of a faithful wife, whether a legitimate or an illegitimate one, and the malicious gossip inseparable from a King's favourite, including the absurd report of her *liaison* with Marot, was so evidently groundless that it was never really believed. Henri himself swerved twice from his vows to her, but these aberrations were of the briefest and had nothing to do with his heart, which remained absolutely true.

It has seemed necessary to dwell thus long on this much disputed question, because upon its upshot depends our whole estimate of Diane de Poitiers and her significance in history. Had she been a light woman she would have lost half of her interest. And it is a remarkable fact that Henri should have always been supported by two such wives of stainless loyalty —who have notwithstanding gone down to posterity as types of immorality.

II.

Such were the three figures that confronted one another when the reign of Henri II opened.

The King, impressive in appearance, the only tall man of

[1] Contarini mentions the rumour as a fact in 1552, but he only ascribes the connection to the time when Diane was a widow—a report too vague to be attended to.

his family, learning as it were to speak and, when he did speak, speaking well—strong of mind, strong of feeling, given to deep depression, the very man to need a *grande passion* that would take him out of himself. Diane, the real, the uncrowned queen, superb, a little arrogant, a little cold, an able Prime-minister, an agreeable talker on art and letters, securely throned amid a throng of architects, poetasters, drawing-room metaphysicians, almoners and secretaries, all dependent on her largesse; Catherine, the crowned, the unreal queen, suave, indifferent, self-contained, sober, even religious since her father-in-law's death—a reservoir of hidden forces, of wounded dignity, and of wounded affection working deep below the surface—distributing alms with generosity, careful to employ all the artists and men of letters who had a grudge against Diane, careless as it seemed of power, yet hoarding every scrap she could lay hands on. Here is good material, straight to the hand of the great dramatist who shapes history.

It is impossible to understand this strange three-cornered household without some comprehension of the atmosphere that surrounded it. Outwardly there was nothing conspicuous in these arrangements; their significance only lay in what went on unseen by the world. Italian fashions were in vogue amongst cultivated people, and neo-Platonism, the philosophy adapted to the foibles of its professors, had spread from Rome outwards. When Marsilio Ficino and Pico della Mirandola religiously revived the study of Plato and tried to wed it with Christianity, they little foresaw to what uses later fashionable circles would put their fervent studies. Men and women, especially women, too weak to be wholly good, too good to like the knowledge that they are weak, are ingenious in finding shrines to shelter and consecrate their frailties, their love of excitement and novelty, their insurmountable fickleness. Perhaps it is a compliment to human nature that they wish to idealize their failings. Platonism asserted the unworthiness of the body, the unimportance of the marriage-bond, the all-importance of the soul. " Take care," says one of the Platonists, "not to pollute thyself in the matter of love. . . drawing thy soul away from its fair intellectual ideal to drown it in the ocean of the flesh—of base and misformed matter. For Absolute Beauty is our father and Primal Beauty is our Mother, and immense Wisdom is the land from whence we first came."

The creed of the aesthete and the creed of the ascetic—of

the man of fastidious taste and the renouncer of self—though opposed in nature, are perilously alike in their outcome, in a scornful rejection of common life. From these cloudy ethics came cloudy results. The marriage-bond, usually formed for reasons of convenience, did not count except as a dull obstacle to a spiritual existence ; while the friend-elect, chosen for his affinity of soul, counted as everything—as the embodiment of all that was noble, all that should be striven for. It was even considered bad taste for a husband and wife to love each other much. Hence many vagaries, some really immoral, some only seeming to be so. It was not the only time that this kind of casuistry obtained. Before Platonism there was chivalry ; after it, there came eighteenth century sensibility, the return to Nature, a score of different subterfuges. But this pseudo-Platonism was peculiarly suited to Italy, to the imaginative, impressionable, irreligious people, who having no real faith of their own, were prone to become enamoured of any new-fangled ideal. In practical France, however, the land of scepticism, of gay common-sense, such a high-flown creed as that of Platonism never took real root. The *esprit gaulois* preferred Rabelaisian laughter and frank immorality. It demanded lighter *galanteries* that were less of a strain upon sentiment. So it came about that the Platonists were only temporarily in vogue, nor did their fantastic tenets spread beyond high circles. Aristocratic society professed an enthusiasm for Italy and for all things Italian, and it was Marguerite d'Angoulême, herself a serious student, who first introduced the study of Plato to the Court. When in her poem she raised a temple to God and built up its pillars with books, she made the main shaft out of Plato's works, with the Gospel immediately above them. About her there was nothing of the corrupt Platonist and she might have been a disciple of Pico della Mirandola. Yet her Heptameron is full of the new sentimental Platonism and it caused her to tolerate ideas and facts of which her acceptance would otherwise bewilder us. But it must not be forgotten that with all its errors, this new Platonism, like chivalry, had a civilizing influence. It denounced coarseness ; it refined the manners of men and gave new possibilities to their intercourse with women. These were valuable results, especially in the French Court where the tone was habitually gross, and Marguerite knew how to appreciate them—and the small group of French Platonic scholars looked upon her as their centre. Two among their number attained to fame that has survived them. There was Bonaventure des Pêriers, who dedicated his translation of Plato's "Lysis" to her, and the famous Ramus who wrote that Plato's Dialogues were, "Salvation—the haven dimly seen from afar." This profounder phase of Platonism was not, however, natural to princesses and did not find another student like Marguerite; but when she died, Diane de Poitiers took her place as the leader of Renaissance fashions and the lover of Platonic sentiment. Two volumes of the "*Amadis de Gaul*," the favourite romance of the day, were dedicated to her and, like others of their kind, were stuffed full of these emotional theories. She cultivated them as assiduously at Anet as she cultivated rare shrubs, and, though transplanted from their native soil, they flourished under her care.

In this same novel, "*Amadis*," there is a strangely prophetic passage. Zahara, Queen of the Amazons, is bent on making a certain king love her, and though he is already married to a Princess of Trebizond, Zahara succeeds. "If only the king's head is as good as his heart," she says, "I should in time so win him that the queen and I should share him—she as his wife, and I as his friend." It was such notions as these, shocking to no one, that first made the attachment between Diane and Henri possible. Catherine figured as the usual representative of the unreal marriage-tie, Diane embodied the true, the higher love, and it was only the extent to which this conception was carried, and the remarkable power that Diane acquired over Catherine's destiny, that distinguished this regal trio from others less elevated in rank.

It remains to be explained why Henri II, wedded to a young, attractive and quick-witted wife, should have left her for another woman only three years after their marriage, and exposed her to the obloquy implied by desertion and neglect. The two women, alike in their signal common-sense, were unlike in all else. And there was one difference more vital than the rest. Diane was frank and direct, almost blunt, Catherine was tortuous and cunning. The Frenchwoman pursued the obvious; the Florentine preferred mystery. This crooked quality was probably one of the causes that estranged her husband from the first. He liked straight roads and was, in most ways, a simple soul, with a conscience. Nothing gives a stronger impression of this than his conduct at his coronation. The account of it comes from Dandolo, the Venetian envoy, but the original source of his knowledge was Diane herself.

"Madame la Sénéchale told her lady-in-waiting (who repeated it to me), that she had observed in what deep devoutness the King knelt absorbed at the moment of receiving the Crown, and she had asked him afterwards to tell her for whom it was that he had prayed so fervently to God. The King answered that he had prayed to no other end than this: that if the Crown he was about to accept meant good government and the welfare of his people, God would leave it to him for a long while; but if not, that God would quickly take it from him." This prayer, naïf from a king, surely came from a nature far removed from Medician craft. Had Diane, when she questioned him, a woman's conviction that the King's earnest prayers were for her? If so, she was dealing with one too sincere to tell her anything but the truth.

Catherine, at all events, could never have imagined that she was the object of his orisons. At his coronation, as on other occasions, she was completely in the background, and when the crown proved too heavy for her head, it was laid down at the feet of Diane who stood by her side. She was effaced in much the same fashion at the famous triumphal entry into Lyons on Henri's accession, and this though a colony of Florentine merchants lived there and might well have been expected to make much of her. True, the Queen's litter had precedence, but the pageants were all for Diane. It was to her that Dian's nymphs, dressed in black and white (her colours), tripped forth from costly artificial forests and recited endless Latin compliments; to her that they led rare hounds and leopards in golden leashes. Catherine sat there in state, but no poems were repeated in her honour and the sign of the Crescent prevailed in the decorations of the city.

The attitude of these two women to one another is among the problems of biography. For while the Queen hated her rival she was dependent on her for any position she possessed, as well as for countless services: "*bons et agréables services*," as Henri was pleased to define them. Never was a usurper's friendship so forced upon the deposed person, never was open enmity conducted with such impeccable amenity. "The Queen is continually with the Duchess, who, on her side, does her excellent service in gaining her the King's good opinion." So writes a matter-of-fact contemporary. It was owing to the Duchess, he adds, that the King went back to Catherine from whom since his meeting with Diane he had long lived away. This must have been more bitter to the Queen than her husband's desertion, and when at last her children were born, it was Diane who received them into the world and prescribed for their welfare—Diane who chose their nurses and their medicines. There exists a strange picture in which an attendant is proffering a new-born princeling to the Duchesse de Valentinois as if to beg her for her patronage, while in the background, almost effaced, is the figure of the Queen. Nor was it long since this same Diane had made mock of Catherine's childlessness to the King, with the intention of getting her gibes repeated to her victim. For the rest, Catherine heard many things. Listening chambers made between two ceilings were not unknown in those days of intrigue. But Catherine was more inventive. Diane's apartments were below her own and she pierced a hole in her ceiling that she might at all times watch and overhear what went on underneath her—a terrible form of self-torture for this jealous Stoic, who could get no vengeance for her wrongs, yet insisted on knowing their full extent. To the outward world, however, her behaviour was always dignified and it was only to her intimate friends that she confided her sorrows. " Madame de Valentinois," writes Diane's never-failing enemy, Tavannes, " kept the Queen out of her husband's affairs and—sith that she was not beautiful—this was not without suspicion of using witchcraft. The Queen complained to the Sieur de Tavannes, who offered to cut off the nose of Madame de Valentinois. Her Majesty objected to the infliction of such a loss ; he answered that, in truth, it would prove a pleasure to her, for that it meant the extinction of vice, and of the King's and the nation's great trouble. The Queen thanked him and made up her mind to patience." Her patience, even in public, was often tried sorely enough, for Diane never scrupled to exhibit her power and to act the triumphant wife. There was one occasion, that of the birth of Charles IX, when she lured Henri to Anet three days after his son's birth, an unparalleled proceeding in the annals of royal etiquette. And it must have been still more galling for his wife when his mistress praised his conduct as a husband. " I must tell you," she wrote to Brissac, " that the Queen has been very ill, but thank God she is much better now ! And I can assure you that the King has played the good husband capitally, for he did not desert her for a moment."

Perhaps it was as much silenced anger as silenced love that made Catherine go on behaving as if the King cared for her. " She follows him as much as she can, without a thought of fatigue," (writes Soranzo) "and when he goes to the wars, she and her ladies wear mourning." She went so far as to invent a monogram of her initial and the King's which should as closely as possible resemble Diane's chosen cipher. But she could not deceive the world. The crescent—the growing moon—was no bad symbol for Diane, who, now allied to the Guises, grew insolent in her omnipotence. She did not scruple to meddle with Catherine's religion, which she suspected of a Protestant taint. The Queen's confessor was sent about his business and an orthodox theologian put in his place. "Did she not force a doctor of the Sorbonne upon you, to corrupt your conscience, and did she not afterwards thrust him upon the King?" So, with righteous indignation, wrote one of Catherine's Huguenot correspondents. It was a diplomatic feat on Diane's part to take hold of Catherine by her weak side, politically speaking—her leaning towards the Reformers—and to present her in this light to the Court and the King, whose own tendencies that way had been shortlived.

Nothing stayed the favourite's hand. Perhaps her power reached its zenith when Henri departed to wage war against the Emperor on the German frontier and she so manœuvred that, in spite of all precedent, the full Regency was not given to the Queen. The Chancellor, Bertrandi, was appointed as her colleague and Catherine's authority was thus annulled. The motive of this deliberate insult was not far to seek. Catherine, now an experienced woman of thirty-six, would play her part admirably as sole Regent, would gain prestige with the people, probably with the King, and might endanger Diane's absolute monarchy. Nor was such a chance of a covert affront to the Queen an occasion to be neglected. That lady behaved admirably. A courtier wrote to the Constable that when her "*Brevet*" was read out, she only smiled and said that however ample the King might have made it, she would have used it soberly. She compared it with the full power which François I had given to his mother, Louise de Savoie, but she would not, she added, ask for any redress. Only she was determined not to publish the "*Brevet*," "lest it should lower her reputation with the populace."

But even Catherine occasionally lost self-control and there were dramatic moments between husband and wife. "At the opening of the reign," writes Contarini, "the Queen could not endure this love of the King for the Duchess. But later, *by reason of the urgent prayers of the King*,[1] she resigned herself, and now she bears it with patience." Her endurance turned to gall in her heart. In all her correspondence during her rival's lifetime there is only one mention of Diane's name and that is made during the single brief moment of triumph that she enjoyed over her. The Constable, jealous of Diane's power, had been plotting against her and had fanned up a flickering flame in Henri's breast for a Scotswoman, Lady Fleming, the beautiful governess of little Mary Stuart. The affair ended quickly and Henri returned to the side of Diane; but there was a scandal and Lady Fleming had to leave the Court. "The Countess," writes Catherine to Mary Stuart's mother, "took leave of me the day before yesterday, but all the same, she spent the night in this town without showing herself either to Madame de Valentinois or to me." It is easy to understand why in this contest Catherine felt no reluctance to inscribe the hated name. After Henri's death she does not make any reference to her husband's abandonment of her, excepting in two cases and those singularly interesting ones. They are among the rare fragments of autobiography which dropped from her austere pen and were written when she was an old woman and could afford to look back. Nor are they written without purpose; for the one occurs in a letter that she sent to her son-in-law, the King of Navarre, to reprove him for infidelity to his wife, and the other draws a parallel for her daughter's use between their respective marriages.

"My son" (runs the first), "I was never in my life so dumfounded as when I heard the words which Frontenac has been reporting everywhere as being those which you ordered him to convey to your wife. I should never have believed that this was true, had he not himself assured me that it was so. . . . You are not, I know, the first husband who is young and not too wise in such matters, but I believe that you are the first, and the only one, who after such events would venture on such language to his wife. I had the honour of marrying the King, my lord and your sovereign, whose daughter you have married, but the thing which vexed him most in the world was after he found out that I knew about such doings; and when Lady Fleming misbehaved herself with him, he was much pleased when she was sent away and he never showed me any temper about it, nor spoke one angry word on the matter. As for Madame de Valentinois, she,

[1] The italics are those of the present writer.

CATHERINE DE' MEDICI

like Madame d'Estampes, conducted all things honourably; but when it came to those who made a noise and scandal, he would have been very angry had I kept them anywhere near me."

There is more frankness in her second mention of Diane, made in a despatch to Belièvre, at that moment her agent in Spain.

"Let her not quote *me* as a precedent," says she, referring to Queen Margot of Navarre—" For if I made good cheer for Madame de Valentinois, it was the King that I was really entertaining, and besides I always let him know that I was acting sorely against the grain; for never did woman who loved her husband succeed in loving his mistress. One must call a spade a spade, though the term is an ugly one on the lips of *nous autres.*"

Who that reads these words can help wondering whether, as she wrote them, the wound in this strange woman's heart re-opened?

We know at least that she never brought herself to go to Anet. Once, during her widowhood, she promised that on her way to Rouen she would visit the retired Diane there, but at the last moment her resolution gave way and she turned aside. There is little wonder that she did so. For Anet had been a bewitched place for Henri—the citadel of Diane's charms. It was there that he ever loved to linger, to receive his friends and to despatch business. Thither came the ambassadors—William Pickering, the Englishman among them—to be sumptuously entertained by a generous host and hostess; here, too, the little princes and princesses ran about in the sunshine, playing at ball or at quoits on the stately terraces or on the margin of the lake. So like husband and wife did these two become that Henri permitted himself to indulge in sulky moods, and if anything went wrong with the children while they were under her care, he sometimes would not speak to her for two or three days together. But Diane's temper was impeccable; she sat at her splendid writing-table penning his letters, thanking his friends, outwitting his foes, like the faithful consort that she was. Nor did she neglect more obvious means of keeping his love fresh. The idealized portraits, the complimentary statues of herself that she was constantly ordering, her choice dresses and harmonious surroundings, were all so many means to preserve his first enchantment. Her palatial hearth was his home and there he always found happiness—while Catherine sat solitary at Amboise.

DIANE DE POITIERS

III.

Diane de Poitiers became the one avenue of approach to the King, and even the Powers of Europe were forced to acknowledge her. Charles V, when he received the French Ambassador at Brussels, pending negotiations for the Peace of 1556, asked only after her and the Constable without a word of the Queen. "He also mentioned Madame de Valentinois, but no one else, for he knew that in these two (in her and in the Constable) lay all authority and favour." No one so powerful as Diane could escape being well hated, and she did not make herself more popular by her close alliance with the detested Guises—the Duke François, the Cardinal Charles de Lorraine and their less known brother, the Cardinal de Guise—"those firebrands of mischief," as she and they together were called. The marriage of her daughter to the Duc d'Aumale, the son of François de Guise, strengthened the tie that bound her to them. This arrogant family, oppressing the poor, sowing discord among the rich, daily increasing in power, were a serious peril to the nation. They made Diane omnipotent in intrigue against Catherine and fanned the worst passions of the Roman Catholic party. With this party Madame de Valentinois identified herself, both from policy and from habit, and hence her worst detractors are to be found among the Protestants. "The more children they had, the more the King neglected the Queen," so writes one of them, . . . "and so God, in His wrath, allowed the poor prince—*intoxicated by that baggage, Diane*—to admit a young serpent into his house—the Cardinal of Lorraine." This "serpent" the chronicler continues, talked ill of the psalms with the Sénéchale, "banqueting on the verses of Horace" and kindling the King's love by "*ces beaux poètes du diable.*" "For when he (the Cardinal) saw that the aforesaid Grande Sénéchale had got a French Bible, in imitation of the Queen—with a great sign of the Cross and his hand on his heart and the deep sighs of a hypocrite—he set about decrying it and damning it and showing her how wrong it was to read it; that such reading was not seemly for women; that she had better hear Mass twice instead of once and rest contented with her Paternosters. . . . Whereupon this poor old sinner (*pauvre vieille pècheresse*) persuaded the King to believe all that he had said. . .

Règnier de la Planche, the Huguenot historian, and others of his kind, tell the same story, and it is largely owing to them that Diane's true image has been falsified. Meanwhile, she had enemies enough in her immediate circle without more from the outside. For though she had attached the Guises, she soon estranged the Constable—and this was at her peril, for the Constable was almost as omnipotent as herself. It was evident that two such powers could not remain side by side. They first came to blows over the King, for the Constable, anxious to rule unchecked, made use of Henri's love of sport to distract his attention from the State. Diane, as we know, exerted her influence in the opposite direction and Diane won the day. While she was thus occupied, the smouldering embers leaped into flame and her difference with the Constable assumed a definite form. The indefatigable Contarini recounts the quarrel at some length :

"There was one moment when we courtiers asked ourselves which of the twain the King loved best—the Constable or Madame de Valentinois, but now we all know by a great many signs that Madame de Valentinois is the best beloved.... I say this because to his Majesty's great displeasure, these two persons, the Constable and Madame, are sworn enemies. This hostility ... only broke forth openly last year when Madame the Duchess perceived that the Constable had plotted to turn the King away from the passion he had for her by making him in love with the governess of the little Queen of Scotland, a very pretty little woman.... Madame complained of this bitterly, the King had to make humble apologies, and for a long time the Constable and Madame were not even on speaking terms. At last, at his Majesty's entreaty, they patched up the semblance of a peace, but at bottom their hatred is as deep as ever. Hence have grown the two parties which are like two factions at Court ; and as the Constable is not too much beloved there, nearly all the great folk gather under the flag of Madame, and among them the House of Guise, no less because M. d' Aumale is Madame's son-in-law than because the Cardinal wished to reign alone." The Cardinal had not measured the strength of his ally. " It might at first appear strange," says another old commentator, " that considering sex and custom and the general usage of all nations, a woman should be included in this government, but facts prove that so it was." Two treaties—the "Sainte Ligue" with the Pope and the Treaty of Câteau-Cambrésis—were attributed to Diane's skill, and while she held sway even the Guises were subject to her.

Her unpopularity as a politician must have sorely troubled her *bonhomie* and she sought compensation by courting popularity as a patron—a patron, that is, of a national art and literature. Catherine, " the Florentine," though in other ways such a true Frenchwoman, naturally loved Italian influences and favoured Italian artists, with whom the hostile people identified her. Diane cleverly saw that a broad road to their favour lay in advocating all that was anti-Italian, all that was essentially French. So she gathered around her at Anet a circle of French craftsmen and French writers—poets, sculptors, and architects, rich in native genius. Olivier de Magny was her Secretary and some of his passionate sonnets were probably written at Anet, poems instinct with human feeling which defied the conventions of his day. Long before Catherine took Philibert de l' Orme to build her new Palace of the Tuileries, that great architect worked for Diane at Anet and told the world that he was her servant by his crest—an elm with the moon shining above it. Jean Goujon, too, chiselled his radiant Dian for her fountain : Jean Goujon, the exquisite stylist in marble ; the Frenchman who possessed the French gift of a natural artificialness, the poet's charm of subtle elegance and brilliant grace.

Such men as these made Anet a resplendent citadel of the French Renaissance, and Diane, the typical Frenchwoman, was well equipped to play the part she had chosen as its queen. Her palace was indeed a kind of Thelema—the home of nature and of intellect, of beauty and of ease. " *Fais-ce que voudras* " might well have stood written over its portal ; Rabelais would have wandered there content, nor would Diane have been too refined to laugh at his jokes with the true Gaulois spirit. To her, as to her fellows, gaiety was more necessary than delicacy.

It is interesting to study her at Anet apart from her intercourse with the King. Her life was one of ceaseless energy and manifold occupations. In the first place she managed her estate and superintended all the building there herself. " I can only talk about my masons," she wrote to a friend, " not a moment of my time with them is wasted and I hope that when you come here, you will find something new to give you pleasure." All this personal supervision, which must have stimulated her craftsmen, was not confined to bricks and mortar. There were, besides, her human interests to be seen to. She had married off her two daughters, Françoise and Diane, at an early age, the one to the Duc d'Aumale, the other to the Comte de Bouillon. But the care of the royal children was largely in her hands, not only when they were at Anet, but when they were elsewhere with their Gouverneur and Gouvernante, Monsieur and Madame d'Humières. And she knew how to win these two important personages to her side. " The King was wonderfully pleased at M. le Dauphin's reception of the Queen of Scotland," she wrote to M. d'Humières, " and I know it all came from your teaching. . . . How I long to have you here for two hours, if it were only to make you eat the butter and cheese made by your dairywoman of Picardy ! "

A more conscientious guardian than Diane could not have been found. She wrote the minutest instructions about the royal children's concerns, whether she had to deal with the quarrels of their maids or the treatment of the Princess Claude's cough. Her letters are like terse and lucid despatches and woe to him who misunderstood them. All this must have taken up a great deal of time, but her day, like that of other ladies of the Renaissance, seems to have consisted of forty-eight hours. She spent a great part of it over her charities and perhaps nothing gives one such a notion of these as her Will. It is a triumph of administrative power and good sense. She leaves the bulk of her property to be divided between her two daughters, but if either of them should grow quarrelsome, " or disapprove of what I have done," her share would be taken from her and revert to some Hôtel-Dieu. One does not know whether to dislike her grim insight into her children's characters, or to respect the sound, if indelicate sense which took prudential measures in good time. The sum which she tied up for her grandchildren was to be taken from them in the same way if they showed the least sign of " *la nouvelle religion*," and a like fate awaited the legacies bequeathed to her executors, if they did not at once pay her debts. "Him alone I consider my heir who findeth good my last will and testament," so concludes this remarkable document. Meanwhile, it arranges for the completion and the maintenance of a fine Hôtel-Dieu at Anet. She leaves one fund for the dowries of destitute girls, " who have not a thing in the world," another to provide alms for five poor persons daily—the almoner to cry, as he bestows them, " *Priez Dieu pour Diane de Poitiers*." She supports thirteen fortunate old bedeswomen ; she organizes and endows with admirable precision a Home for little girls who are to go there when they are seven years old and stay till they are ten, at which mature age they are to be fittingly married, with a dowry of ten francs each ; or if no husband can be found at once, they may live on there till he appears. Even if we allow for the spiritual diplomacies of a repentant great lady and her efforts to cajole Heaven by good works, a great deal of practical kindliness remains. Perhaps it strikes rather chill, as the roomy benevolence of those days is apt to do, a benevolence unwarmed by any fire of love. But Diane was not a personal woman and there was no place for intimacy in her scheme of existence.

Apart from her correspondence with Henri, the most affectionate sentence to be found among her papers is perhaps in another clause of her Will. "To my nephew, Loys de Brézé" (it runs), "for the sake of the good love which he knows that I have borne him . . . and that he may hold me in remembrance, I give a pointed diamond, set in black enamel, the largest of the pointed ones in my possession.". . . 'The largest of the pointed ones!' What a profusion of diamonds, cut in all shapes, does that one phrase suggest, helping more than any description to evoke the Diane of Anet, the woman of the Renaissance. One cannot but speculate on the nature of the nephew who had meant so much to this rather inhuman lady. For the rest, she was a good friend of sure counsel, and people were evidently accustomed to go to her for help in their difficulties. There exists an amusing letter of hers, the letter of a model duenna, about a marriage of which she disapproved for the sake of propriety.

"*Madame, ma bonne amie*—I saw your poor sister yesterday as you wished, and gave her a long, judicious lecture about her marriage. I made her see all the dangers it involves, and enforced on her that she must not expect much from a man who has never given up the company of unvirtuous women; but . . . all my words ended in smoke and the worst things I said went in at one ear and out at the other. She was so miserable that I did not persist too long, nor can there be much hope of any change of heart by such means. And so I come only to tell you that I see there is nothing to be done but to let her follow her inclinations."

Her letters of sympathy, like those of Catherine and of most Renaissance women, were full of a large philosophy, but brought no warmer consolation. Her cousin, M. Bouchage, had lost a child. "I think that you should not be vexed about it, considering that you have another and may have more," she wrote—"Besides this, worry may make you ill . . . and therefore I entreat you not to grieve any more, for really there is no use in that." There was only one occasion on which her pen showed any emotion and that was the death of Lady Jane Grey. She was writing to her friend, Madame Montaigu. "I have just been hearing the account of the poor young Queen Jane, and I could not keep myself from weeping at the sweet and resigned words she spoke to them on the scaffold. Surely never was there seen such a gentle and accomplished princess."

Usually, however, her correspondence does not dip below the brilliant surface of things, or express anything less obvious than a regal kind of high spirits. "When on earth are you coming to see me, *Madame, ma bonne amie*?" she asks a friend, "I am very anxious for a sight of you, which will be sure to cheer me up in all my troubles. . . . The messenger from England has brought me back several handsome dresses from that country, of which, if you come quickly, you also shall have a good share. Do not put me off with fine words and promises—for I want to feel both my arms round your neck."

Did the friend, one would like to know, resist this vitality and good-nature—as well as the dresses from England?

The sun did not shine every day, however. Diane was a good comrade as long as she had her will, but the person who got in her way found reason to repent. It was not only to Catherine that she was merciless. There is a notable instance of this in her conduct to the Duchesse d' Estampes. When François I died, Diane and Henri II were resolved on the downfall of Madame d'Estampes, who had long been their chief foe. They incited her husband to sue her about the arrears of his pension which they said she had kept back for herself; they accused her of plotting with Wolsey to bring the English to the walls of Paris and, not content with this, they contrived to hit her harder through one, Jarnac, her lover. An intricate scheme was laid—so intricate that only a woman could have invented it—to insult Jarnac through the lips of La Chataignerie, the most invincible swordsman of the day, and thus to bring about a duel which would end in Jarnac's certain death. All began as they wished; and the duel, about to take place, was turned into a splendid public Joust, attended by the King and Diane and by all the great of the land. But Jarnac, trained by a skilful Italian fencer, was put up to the trick of reviving a fashion of chivalry and demanding heavy armour for himself and his opponent. To the amazement of the spectators, the unerring La Chataignerie, unused to this weight, fell to the ground defeated and mortally wounded.

DIANE DE POITIERS

The custom of old Knighthood on such an occasion was for the victor to go to the King, to beg his fallen adversary's life at the royal hands, and, should he be fighting to vindicate himself, to demand his honour back from His Majesty. It was Jarnac's right to claim this privilege and he prepared to do so. All the world was watching when he approached Henri and Diane, who awaited him with lowering brows. Three times did he make his petition, three times did the King keep silence, transgressing every precedent by doing so. The enraged Jarnac turned to Diane; "Madame," he shouted, "you told me how it would be!" His cry revealed the plot to the public and the King, watched by a breathless audience, was forced at length to yield—to deal in the customary hyperbole and reluctantly to tell Jarnac that he fought like Cæsar and spoke like Aristotle. But he walked away sullenly and never went near his faithful henchman, the dying Chataignerie, who had been the cause of this disgrace. The story seems worth telling at some length because it is so characteristic of the philosophical heartlessness of the age. No one would have thought the worse of Diane for her share in it, nor did it prove that she was an especially cruel person.

There is, perhaps, nobody so hard to realize as the woman of the Renaissance. The woman of the Middle Ages, still rather primitive, with occupations and restrictions far remote from ours, is comparatively easy to grasp because she is out of reach. But the woman of the sixteenth century, robust, naïve, intellectual, pursuing interests and activities like our own, with widely different thoughts and aspirations, is almost impossible to reconstruct. There is probably no such dividing gulf as superficial likeness, and these ladies were so vivid that no pale presentation of them serves. To approach them at all we must first get rid of our notions of morality, next of our notions of society. Etiquette, then, was not our stiff manufactured wire fence, but a flowering hedge—trimmed and artificial, but marvellously picturesque; and there never was a time when grand people were so free and easy in their own circle and so encased in divinity for those outside it. If we remember this, it may help us to form some not too unreal image of Catherine de' Medici and her rival, Diane de Poitiers.

They were the last great ladies of the Renaissance, for after them practically began the modern woman. The Princess Margot, wife of Henri IV, already wrote in her own individual style, dared to be natural, created forms of her own, with a freedom far from the days of the Court of her mother, Catherine. And Diane, the Frenchwoman, even more than Catherine, the Florentine, is the epitome of her sumptuous generation: Diane the Queen, Diane "*la maîtresse-femme provide (provident) et très-avisée qui donnait ordre sans bruit.*" We close our eyes and see her, rather dim, rather distant, gracious and dominating, on a background of gold and silver tissue—the eyes smiling, the lips firmly closed. As we look, she opens them to speak and this is what her eyes and lips say to us: " I was born without the doctrine of conviction of sin and I hate the Reformation ! "

CHAPTER IV

The Court of Henri II

AUTHORITIES CONSULTED

Memoirs de Henri II.
Histoire de Lyon—*Paradin*.
Lettres de Catherine de' Medici.
Memoirs de Marguerite de Navarre.
Lettres de Marie Stuart.
Femmes Illustres—*Brantôme*.
Memoirs de Vielleville
Rélations de la Diplomatie Vénitienne—*Baschet*.
Le Siège de Metz—*Archives Curieuses*.
Mélanges de l'histoire de François I et Henri II—*Archives Curieuses*.
Lettres envoyées à la Reine-Mère—*Archives Curieuses*.
Grand et magnifique Triomphe fait au mariage de François de Valois et Marie Stuart—*Archives Curieuses*.
Trépas et obsèques de Henri II—*Archives Curieuses*.
Le Livre des Marchands.
Catherine de Médicis—*Bouchot*.
Catherine de Médicis—*Capefigue*.
Biographical Introduction to the " Lettres de Catherine de' Medici "—*Le Comte de la Ferrière*.
Les Mœurs polies de la Cour de Henri II—*Bourciez*.

CHAPTER IV

The Court of Henri II

BETWEEN 1543 and 1555 ten children were born to Catherine and her husband, three of whom—twins, and a boy Louis—died in early infancy. The remaining seven were the Dauphin François, Charles and Henri (afterwards Charles IX and Henri III), François (Duc d'Alençon), Elizabeth (wife of Philip II), Claude (who married the Duc de Lorraine), Marguerite (Queen of Navarre). With these, in spite of Diane, Catherine was constantly occupied. She was a devoted mother as long as her children could not contradict her, and her letters of minute injunctions about them vie with those of her rival, exceeding them the while in affection. " Monsieur d'Humières " (she writes to their *Gouverneur*), " I have received your letter of the first of May and was rejoiced to have news of my children, who are quite well, for the which I praise God. As to what you write to me concerning the food of my daughter, Claude, the King and I are of opinion that she be fed upon toast and water rather than anything else, since it is healthier for her than broth—wherefore pray send for some for her. I beg you, M. d'Humières, to have all my children painted for me, but let them be taken from a different side to the one from which the painter usually does them and send me the portraits the moment they are finished."

Or again to Madame d'Humières—

"To come to my little girl, I shall be very glad if you can go to her soon; I have sent the tailor who makes the bodices of the daughters of Madame la Connétable to make one for her too. I entreat you to take great care that it should be very well cut—and I pray God, Madame de Humières, to have you in His holy keeping. . . .

"Votre bonne amye,
"CATHERINE."

CATHERINE DE' MEDICI

While her children were still young, Catherine taught them a great deal herself, and later both she and the King were careful in the choice of their tutors. Henri himself appointed Danés, the illustrious Greek professor at the Collège de France, as the Dauphin's instructor. Amyot, the great Amyot, once rescued by Margaret of Angoulême from a student's starvation in a garret, now an honoured Bishop famed for his translation of Plutarch, was given as a teacher to the other princesses, who recited sonnets in public at seven years of age and were adepts in Latin, as well as in Italian and Spanish, when they had grown a few years older. But even these learned little ladies were surpassed by their cousin, Mary Queen of Scots, "la petite Sauvage," as she was called, who soon became part of the Valois family. This bewitching baby princess of six was sent by her mother, Mary,[1] to be brought up at the French Court under the protection of her maternal uncles, the omnipotent Guises, and of her cousin Henri II, destined as she was, from her first coming, to be his eldest son's bride. "*Cette petite Reinette écossaise*" (wrote Catherine), "*n'a qu'à sourire pour tourner toutes les têtes françaises,*" and her charm lay in her vivid sympathies, her need of pleasing every one from highest to lowest. There were grand preparations made for this infant Queen's arrival. "His Majesty," writes Diane de Poitiers to the Humières, "desires that Madame Isabel (Princess Elizabeth, who was then three years old) and the Queen of Scotland should be lodged together, for which reason you will choose the best room for these two and for their suite; for His Majesty wishes that from the beginning they should become closely acquainted." There were solemn arrangements too for the Dauphin's reception of his lady-love. The bethrothed couple were then six and seven respectively, but the Dauphin lost no time in becoming her devoted squire. He was a sickly, silent child, with pale cheeks and heavy manners—"like his mother in countenance," so says a Venetian envoy. But his affianced bride had always the power of putting life into him. "He dearly loveth Her Serene Highness, the little Queen of Scotland, Mary Stuart, who is destined to be his wife. She is a very pretty child . . . and it sometimes falleth out that—caressing one another the while—they are fain to retire apart, into a corner of the room, that none may overhear their little secrets."

[1] Mary of Guise, the widow of **James VI**, King of Scotland, and Regent during Mary's minority.

THE COURT OF HENRI II

It was not only the son she conquered, but the father, for Henri II adored her, as Charles de Guise, the Cardinal de Lorraine, tells her mother. "The King" (he writes) "has taken such a fancy to your daughter, the Queen, that he spends his time delightfully in talking with her by the hour, and she knows as well as any woman of twenty-five how to rivet him by her good and wise conversation." This was some four or five years after her arrival, when her gifts and intelligence were already a topic for the courtiers. Their tropes knew no end. At nine, she was Minerva—at twelve she was Venus also. Catherine taught her at first with her own children, and there still exists a Latin exercise written when she was ten and corrected by the Queen of France. Later, she and her cousins passed into the hands of tutors. St. Paul, Cicero, Aristippus, Diogenes and Plato were elaborately expounded before these precocious scholars, so that they might become models of fortitude, virtue and erudition. At thirteen, Mary Stuart created a sensation by standing up before the King and Court in the great hall of the Louvre Palace, and reciting an elegant Latin discourse of her own composition. Her mate in work and play was the little Princess Elizabeth, and one of Mary's tasks was to write themes on a given subject in the shape of letters to her comrade. One or two of these may still be read—fine embroidered samplers in writing, full of elegant twirls and flourishes on the duties of princes. "It is to incite you to read Plutarch, *ma mie* and my sweet sister, that in these my epistles I so often make mention of him. For he is a philosopher written to be heeded of princes. . . . The true grandeur and excellence of a prince, my very dear sister, is neither in rank, nor gold, nor purple, nor jewels, nor in any other pomp of fortune ; but in prudence and virtue and wisdom and knowledge. And the more the prince desireth to be different from his people in his habits and his manner of living, the further off must he be kept from the foolish opinions of the vulgar herd." This aristocratic sentiment smacks of Ronsard, who was, indeed, her poetry-master ; but it is a strange picture, that of these little girls in their stiff jewelled bodices, bending painfully over their stiff, sparkling epistles on remote royal topics to one another.

Some women are born in a tempest to evoke tempests, and more storm-winds could not have blown round Helen of Troy than blew, from the beginning, round Mary Stuart. As might be supposed, Diane de Poitiers' first move was to steal the girl away from Catherine and win her to herself, an achievement made all the easier by her alliance with the Guises. Other things helped her. The fastidious " Reinette d'Ecosse " in a naughty fit, probably after a Latin lesson with the elder Queen, called Catherine "*une fille de marchands* "— an amusing sidelight on the view that the Guises took of the Medici. The saying was promptly repeated to Catherine. From that time forward, though her outward behaviour never varied, though she treated her daughter-in-law with honour, Mary fell out of her good graces. Diane's ascendency over Mary increased accordingly. " I won't forget to tell you that my uncle, M. de Guise, and my aunt, Madame de Guise, take greater care of me and my affairs than they take of their own child. . . . I can say no less of Madame de Valentinois. I pray you, Madam, write to them all "—so she addresses her mother in Scotland. And again, rather later: " For the rest, my mother, you know how closely bound I am to Madame de Valentinois because of the love that ever more and more she showeth unto me." And she goes on to complain that she is no longer in favour with Catherine.

Everything about the girl is picturesque, even the small cares that oppress her. Mary of Guise has ordered her to give away some of her dresses to her ladies-in-waiting and one of them has misrepresented her as disobedient to these orders. She has already presented three to her ladies that they may make church draperies out of them, and she has given more to others. But she finds her things taken from her wardrobe by her treacherous accuser, so that she has nothing left for presents. " Nor has she ever credited me with giving away so much as a pin, whence I have got the name of being stingy—so much so that some people have said that I was not in the least like you." At fifteen, such minor preoccupations no more existed for her and her letters are already concerned with the making of Court marriages and other mature topics. The child, however, lived on in her beneath the stately brocade; for shortly before this, the Cardinal wrote home to her mother that she still " sometimes forgot herself and ate too much, owing to her always having such a good appetite." " But I will take greater care than ever about her diet "—so concludes this grand hierarch of a nurse. . . . " The doctors pledge me their word that she is of a temperament that will, with God's help, ensure her living as long as any of her relations."

It would be difficult to give undue prominence to Mary

THE COURT OF HENRI II

Stuart, for she had a genius for being the centre wherever she found herself, and she was long the centre of the French Court. Before she married, however, a rival younger by ten years had appeared in the shape of her cousin, the Princess Margot, as remarkable a child as herself. This astonishing little creature was a prodigy of wit and repartee. Vivid, endearing, passionate and brilliantly naughty, she soon became the life of her circle and made a willing subject of her father. The picture of the King's delight in his little girl is as refreshing as clear water on our wearisome journey through those corrupt days, and no one could portray it more prettily than did the Princess Margot herself. She will start, she says, at the first interesting, remembrance of her life:

"Like to the geographers who describe the earth, when they have reached the last boundary known to them and say—'Beyond this there are only sandy deserts, uninhabited countries and unnavigated seas '—so shall I likewise say that beyond me there stretches only the large vague plain of first childhood, where we live guided rather by nature, in like fashion to plants and animals, than as men governed by reason. And to those who brought me up at that tender age, I shall leave the superfluous research which may end in the discovery of certain childish actions, as worthy perchance to be recorded as those of the childhood of Themistocles and Alexander . . . among which may be counted the retort I made to my father, the King. . . . I was at the time some four or five years old, and he, holding me upon his knee to make me talk, told me to choose which of the two I would take as my servitor: Monsieur le Prince de Joinville (later the great and unfortunate Duc de Guise) or the Marquis of Beaupréau, son of the Prince de la Roche-sur-Yon. Both these boys were playing near my father and I was looking at them. I told him I would choose the Marquis. Quoth my father,' Wherefore? he is not as handsome as the other ' (for the Prince de Joinville was white and fair and the Marquis de Beaupréau had brown hair and a brown complexion); I replied that it was because he had a better nature and that the other could not live patiently through one day without doing a mischief to someone and must always play the master. A sure prophecy of what we saw in after days."

It may be that this was the only moral choice ever made by the "Reine Margot"; it certainly was the one moment that she did not desire the devotion of Henri de Guise, whose love she set her wayward heart upon. The Prince she was destined not to love but to marry, little Henri of Navarre, must also have been her playmate when he visited the French Court with his parents. "Wouldst thou like to become my son-in-law?" said the King one day, taking him in his arms, and the bridegroom-elect no doubt retorted gaily. The King, must have loved and attracted children, for they seem to have been always about him. These "golden boys and girls," with their fine manners and their childish grace, flit like April sunbeams across the stern page of history, and constantly recall those superb miniatures by the Clouets of kingly little personages, half children, half men, plumed caps on their heads, shining chains round their necks, standing out in their ermine and white satin against green backgrounds, so gallant, so courteous, so confident, so helpless, that we long to put out our hands and beseech them to stay where they are that they may never grow older or less innocent.

II

The world in which these children and their elders lived was a strange one, so strange that we cannot judge it. It is full of the contradictions and paradoxes, the serious frivolity and frivolous seriousness, the self-indulgence and reactionary austerities of a time of transition. Its powers of production and its absence of discrimination are alike surprising. Eternal mysteries were clearly proved by logic, while plain scientific facts were wrapped in a dense obscurity. On the one hand, men seemed to be rushing into free thought; on the other, philosophers, like Paracelsus, believed in salamanders and gnomes as an essential part of the cosmic order. Astrology, too, ranked high as a branch of knowledge. Catherine brought the two Ruggieri in her train from Italy; and, in 1556, she summoned Nostrodamus, far-famed for his skill in horoscopes, to Paris, to act as a kind of chief horoscopist to the young Princes. She went so far as to build a tower for her astrologers in Les Halles, and it may have been there that the King came to consult one of them who prophesied the manner of his death. In this time of constant discovery, this time, too, of no newspapers, everything appeared equally possible, and Pliny's "Tales" were as much believed in as the travels of Magellan and Columbus. Africa was popularly supposed to produce fire-breathing dragons, and Guillaume de Tester, who made an imaginary map of the country beyond the Ganges, peopled it

MARGUERITE DE VALOIS, REINE DE NAVARRE.
(LA REINE MARGOT.) VERS 1555.
PORTRAIT ANONYME. BIBLIOTHÈQUE NATIONALE.
From a photograph by A. Giraudon.

with pigmies fighting with cranes. The East exercised its magic spell on men's fancy. Postel, the great professor at the Collège de France, had been wandering through Syria, trying with the child-like faith of the Renaissance scholar to discover the traces of a primitive language which would prove to be the origin of all languages; had wandered and returned to teach Eastern tongues at his College. There had been a time when he had dreamed of François I as Emperor of France and of the East, and though Henri II cherished no such remote ambitions, he kept some Asiatic tastes. Oriental dress became fashionable at Court and so did Oriental masquerades. There was one of especial magnificence given by Henri at night in the Rue St. Antoine. Amidst the flash of torches, he and the Dauphin in mystic white silk robes, their followers dressed as Moors and Turks in armour or in opalescent draperies, came forth on horseback, some from the Palace of Les Tournelles, some from the Hôtel de Montmorency, and danced, centaur-like, on their horses, to the sound of weird Eastern music. Phantasmagoria such as these were perhaps partly suggested by the strange sights seen at the Court; by the wild beasts kept there and the outlandish dwarfs that gave such mysterious pleasure to the crowned heads of that day; "Augustin Romanesque," for instance, in his big turban and his velvet dress, half yellow and half grey, or "le petit Bezon," or "la Jardinière, Folle-en-tître de la Cour," all belonging to Catherine, sure of pleasing her whatever they did, and able to get what they liked from her. The world they reveal to us is constantly grotesque, but it never lacks colour. We turn our eyes indoors and find walls amply covered with Flemish tapestries and Italian pictures— or outside, and see rivers strewn with painted barges and streets pied with gaily-clad citizens; or else we may watch one of the frequent jousts in which the King's men, dressed in Diane's black and white, fight some grandee's followers in scarlet, or purple, or gold, for each noble can be recognized by the hue he has chosen as his own.

And when we seek a background to this vivid, motley life, we reconstruct the Paris of the sixteenth century. It was still half a feudal-looking city, with Renaissance ornament grafted on to warlike walls. In the centre of everything, on l'Île de France, stood, as it stands now, Notre-Dame, like the spiritual citadel of the place; the Sainte Chapelle rose there too, and still rises, definite and delicate and graceful as a French idea. On the south was the Hill of Ste. Geneviève, with its churches and colleges, its monastery-orchards and green convent-gardens, sloping steeply down to the river. The fashionable region, made up of narrow streets, shockingly paved and worse lighted, lay to the right. Here in the Rue du Temple was Diane's sombre palace, La Barbette, while close by, in the Rue St. Antoine, was the Hotel of Madame d'Estampes. The Bourbons lived opposite in the Louvre itself, still rather stern and only half concerned with the Renaissance. But the Court often lodged, as of old, in the ancient Palace of Les Tournelles: Les Tournelles, with its famous galérie des Courges where the courtiers walked—the Gallery of Angels which the Duke of Bedford had had painted more than a hundred years earlier. From its azure ceiling there descended " a legion of Angels playing on sweet instruments and singing anthems to Our Lady," and angels upholding princely blazons floated down its whole length. In past days, Queens had "passed along it to their Oratory." Catherine more probably used it for diplomatic walks with one of the Venetian ambassadors.

Perhaps nothing is more characteristic of this perplexing age, and nothing more clearly marks it as a time of transition than the position of royalty itself. Sovereigns were never farther from, or nearer to, their subjects. They still kept the remoteness of their divine right; the more so, perhaps, because there had already been faint whispers questioning the divinity of their privilege, faint tremblings of the eternal throne beneath them. And they still kept the old-fashioned feudal familiarity of a King with his people, the familiarity which looks as if it were the opposite of heaven-conferred kingship, but is, in reality, part of it. For these monarchs accepted a kind of fatherly, miracle-working godhead as belonging to their royal office, and they regarded the contact with the mob which it implied much as the Olympian gods must have regarded it. When Catherine went in and out of the Louvre, it was probably her daily duty (as it was that of Anne of Austria) to hear herself loudly addressed by the crowd, even to have her dress seized by them. Personal petitions, presented by all manner of individuals, from the fishwives upwards, were also of common occurrence and no grievance seemed too small for the ear of royalty. There was also the King's "touching" of the sick. For this function he retired to the town of St. Marcoul, the patron-saint of the scrofulous, for ten days after his coronation. And this task of his was by no means confined to the opening of his reign. He frequently fulfilled it wherever he went, and a Diarist of 1556, who witnessed the whole proceeding at Fontainebleau, has left us a picture of what he saw.

"That same day," he writes, "when every one came out from Mass in the Palace Chapel, a large number of sick people were placed in order on the Road of the Lake of Fontainebleau—a fine broad road leading to the King's palace . . . sheltered by the shade of divers great trees, that are planted in rows . . . and beneath this shade on their knees were the aforesaid invalids, who were waiting for His Majesty to come out from Mass and to touch them. The which he did very humbly, in nowise disdaining the poor sick folk, howsoever ravaged by disease, but touching their faces with his right hand, saying: 'I touch thee, may God cure thee!' Monsieur the Grand Almoner, Louis de Brézé, stood behind the poor people and, by the King's orders, he gave to each a piece of money as an alms, saying unto them, ' Pray God for the King.' This being done, His Majesty admonished them to be ever good Christians . . . devoutly serving God, the Virgin Mary and Monsieur St. Marcoul—the which we witnessed with our own eyes, being at that very time in the town of Fontainebleau."

The scene is a curious mixture of arrogance and homeliness. Catherine, with the blood of Florentine merchants in her veins, carried the homeliness a step farther, or rather she made it the cloak for curiosity and jealousy—perhaps also for her love of adventure. With all her caution she could do things that amaze us by their rashness. She used at one time to walk masked and disguised about the streets of Paris to spy upon the actions of the King. But oftener her secret wanderings had a political purpose. Sometimes she went alone, sometimes with her daughter Margot. "That very day she walked in the city with the Queen of Navarre without being recognized, and this was so that she might listen to people talking and learn what they said of the Government. The two ladies went in and out of the shops, making believe to want to buy things; and there they heard many stories against the great, even against the Queen of Navarre, who was standing there." The dignity of such doings is questionable, and they make a contrast which is almost uncouth, when compared with the buckram etiquette which Catherine imposed on her courtiers as well as on her children. She is never tired of preaching its importance to the little Queen of Spain, in the first days of her marriage, when childhood was still hardly behind her.

CATHERINE DE' MEDICI

"*Madame ma fille*" (Catherine writes) ". . . I am told by those who are about you that you do not make as much of any of your women as of Vineuf and that, in comparison with her, you take no count either of my cousin, or of Madame de Clermont . . . so that all the Spaniards and even your husband laugh at you. In truth . . . in the position which you occupy this is very unseemly, and your feasting and paying such attentions to your ladies shows that you still have the child in you. When you are alone in your room and in privacy, pass your time gaily; frolic with them and with everybody; but before people, take great notice of your cousin and of Madame de Clermont. The other young creatures can only teach you imbecilities. Do what I tell you in this respect, if you wish me to approve of you and to love you and to believe that you love me as you ought."

Rather a terrible letter for a homesick little girl to get, alone in a foreign land. But seeming absurd was ever the cardinal sin in Catherine's eyes.

Kingship in those days was not kept up without expenditure and a vast amount of picturesque effect. Many were its resources, chief among them, perhaps, the use of public pageants, a ready means to maintain Majesty as well as goodfellowship with the people. These pageants were arranged by the best artists and carried out with an almost insolent sumptuousness. The long list of birthday-feasts and weddings and funerals and processions to churches and entries into towns, with all their monotony of splendour, is fatiguing to the mind. Every occasion was made a pretext for them. If there was a drought, the Holy Chalice of Ste Geneviève had to be borne in state through Paris; if the Turks arrived at Court with handsome gifts from Soliman, Fantasias costing fortunes were invented for them. At Henri II's entry into Paris after his coronation, two thousand pages walked, each before his master, dressed in that master's colours; "and one would have said," writes old Vielleville, "that the eye looked on meadows pied with blossom, as if it were the merry month of May . . . the which was a thing most delectable and wondrous to behold."

A great deal of eating and drinking was, of course, connected with these festivities. Catherine's accounts for the banquets she gave to Paris in 1549, form an extravaganza of culinary imagination. The names of the cakes in the pastry-bill alone make the most abstemious person wish to taste them—even after reading of twenty-one swans, nine cranes, and thirty-three "*trubles à large bec*," an enigmatic bird of the past whose name seems to breathe a mystic succulence. After such solid fare, "the sum of 93 livres 7 sols tournois spent upon sweet waters for the perfuming and folding of the linen used at the said banquet"; and the "Item, in flowers, bouquets and toothpicks 47 sols," come as a graceful finish; and the entry of "musicians' wages" seems to set the whole feast dancing. The concoction of these rarities was considered to be almost as much of an art as painting or sculpture, for, even then, French cooks were a recognized dynasty. "The other Kings of Christendom, nay, even of the Universe, can in no way approach the excellency of our delicate dishes: whether it be in singular fashions of triumphant cooking at banquets, or in the dainty and cleanly dressing and disguising of viands by our officers. Whereof no other testimony is wanted than that all the foreign Princes send to France for their cooks and confectioners." The pride of France in its *chefs* went farther than this. When the Marshals Vielleville and André went to England on a deputation to Edward VI, their King forbade them and their retinue to touch English food. So they brought with them twelve horses laden with every kind of game and fruit, of such a nature that "*tous les millorts* cursed the intemperance of their climate which forbade the existence of these dainties."

France has remained the same in other and prettier ways than cooking. "It belongeth to Frenchmen alone to play the fool with a good grace," says a gentleman of the time, and "French minds" (he sagely adds) "are like the heavens themselves—to wit, in perpetual motion." But although this quality of mobile gaiety has not changed, the manner of its expression has transformed itself. There is apparently no difference so incurable as a difference in the sense of what amuses, and this it is, indeed, which makes one of the chief difficulties in reconstructing past centuries. Humour is a matter of fine shades and of intricate social relations, and in the sixteenth century the sense of humour could hardly be said to have existed. The jokes of that day fill us with a kind of despondency. Henri II entered a town of Savoy and was met by a company of a hundred men disguised as bears, who conducted him to Mass and thence to his palace, climbing along the walls of the houses and frightening the horses in the streets so much that they threw their unfortunate riders; the King only remarked that he had never seen anything so funny and gave the bears two thousand crowns. This kind of fun is hard work. Perhaps the same may be said of an occasion at Brussels, when the King of Spain, in church and having the Gospel in his hand, was solemnly ratifying the Peace of Vaucelles. He had to hold on by the altar-rail, so shaken was he by his mirth at the sight of an unseemly scramble for " Largesse " which suddenly took place. It had been organized by a French wag, in derision of Spanish stinginess, and the sight of the congregation falling hither and thither so exhilarated not only Ferdinand, but the Queen of Hungary and the French Princesses, that they laughed for a whole hour " while the comedy lasted." That day at dinner, the same wag delighted His Majesty even more by suddenly taking up two corners of the tablecloth, throwing himself the whole length of the table, seizing the remaining corners and walking off with all the delicious banquet—by no means forgetting to bow and say "*grand merci*" at the door. Other times, other manners; and when we long for the adventurousness of a past day, we must also remember its tediums and its hilarious stupidity.

The most abiding quality in human nature, the link which most unfailingly unites one generation with another, is probably the need of distraction. And this is especially the case in a decadent period like the last half of the sixteenth century—a time of restlessness following on one of large and concentrated activity—of asking " Cui bono ? " after living on convictions. " Some " comments Tavannes " set their hearts on building and gardening, on painting, or reading, or the chase; they run after an animal all day and get their faces torn in the woods; or they trot from morning till evening after a ball of wool; or they spend the day and the night at games of hazard, from which they rise without any great reluctance; or they buy arms and horses and never use them. Sadness and melancholy without a legitimate cause are their own just punishment—a failure to recognize the grace of God which has made us immortal. What honour is there, after all, in being like the million ? And must we for ever be searching the world for a thing that is not in it ? "

The passage might apply to our own day, the last words to almost any day; but they have a special meaning for the age over which Henri II reigned as King.

THE COURT OF HENRI II

III

The Henri II of thirty-two was a very different personage from the Henri II of ten years earlier. He had become a popular King and his Paris loved him. Youth was not his moment even as regards his looks, which grew striking with the advancing years, a fact by no means unimportant in the eyes of his impressionable people. "His figure . . . is a gallant one for work . . . his mien is so affable, so human, that from the first moment he takes possession of every man's heart and every man's devotion." So writes one of his subjects and chroniclers, Claude d'Aubépine. "He has vivid black eyes," says another, "a big nose, a rather common mouth and a pointed beard of two fingers' length; the whole *ensemble* of his countenance is extraordinarily winning . . . His kindliness is natural . . . he is gracious and refuses an audience to no one. At his meals there are constantly people present full of talk about their own affairs, and the King listens and answers everything in most courteous fashion. He has never been seen in ill-humour except sometimes out hunting, and he is in many ways a temperate man. When we compare him with his father, we may even call his morals pure, and there is certainly one good point about him—he does not get himself talked about, which could not be said of King François. . . . He eats and drinks most moderately. . . . It is a fact that he is considered less liberal and less magnificent than his father; that, however, may be because he gives much to the few." A changed being this from the "dreamy, drowsy, sullen boy" who was never seen to laugh and had nothing to say. Diane had done her work well. He had, it is true, none of the intangible glamour, the charm almost amounting to genius, which hung about his father, but his qualities were more solid and more stable. His faults, too, were such as his impressionable people readily forgave.

> Le peuple excuse Henri,
> Maudit Montmorency,
> Haït Diane,
> Surtout ceux de Guise aussi.

So runs a lampoon of the time and it sums up public opinion. For however bitterly Diane was hated, she lent an extra interest to the King's personality, an exalting interest of romance which he would have lacked without her. A traveller of the time then in Paris, who had the one virtue needful in a traveller, the habit of keeping a journal, tells us how he one day looked up at the palace of the Louvre and saw the King distinctly in one of the rooms giving upon the Seine. He wore a black cap with a little white feather and a gold chain round his neck. "His coat was of black damask bordered with velvet, and embroidered with two silver crescents most closely united by the embrace of the two Ds, even as are, in truth, the two souls of the two lovers." The Swiss and the Guard, says the diarist, were in the same black and silver and bore the shining crescent on the back and front of their uniforms, as well as the royal motto, "*Donec totum impleat orbem*,"[1] a picture which suggests a sober splendour, more harmonious than any regal colours.

Henri II grew grey early and looked an elderly man at thirty-five. It is amusing to find how anxious were the sovereigns of Europe about each other on this score. Charles V's enquiries concerning Henri II's appearance read like those of an elderly beauty after another and a younger lady. They were made in the midst of a critical business interview, when the French ambassadors went to Brussels to conclude the Peace of Vaucelles with the Emperor. They found him in a small house, seated on a black cloth chair, dressed very differently from their sumptuous Henri, in "a little suit of Florentine serge like that of a common citizen, cut above the knee, his arms being passed through the sleeves of a black coat made of German stuff; he had a cap trimmed with a narrow silk cord, and a chemise with a simple collar." . . . "How is the King?" he asked in the course of the conversation. "Very well, *Sire*," replied the envoy. "Hé! how glad I am!" quoth Charles, "but I am told he is already turning grey. Yet there *can* be nothing younger than he is. It seems, so to speak, only three years since he was a child in Spain, without a hair on his face." "*Sire*," answered the polite Frenchman, "in truth, the King hath two or three little white hairs." . . . "Oh! no need to wonder at that," resumed the monarch. . . . "I will tell you what happened to me when I was about his age. I was returning from a journey . . . and I stayed at Naples. You know the charm of the town, the beauty and goodly grace of its ladies. I am a man—I wished to gain their favour, like other men. The day after I arrived, in the morning, I summoned my barber to brush and frizz and perfume me . . . I am given a mirror. I look at myself, much as your King, my good brother, must

[1] Until it fill the whole world.

have done. Startled and amazed—'What is this?' I ask. 'Two or three white hairs,' says my barber. There were more than a dozen. 'Remove those hairs,' say I to my barber, 'and do not leave a single one,'—the which command he obeys. Do you know what happened to me?" (these words he addressed to all the French lords)—"A little time afterwards, wishing to look at myself again in the glass, I found that for one white hair that had been taken away, there now were three. And if I had done the same by these, in less than no time I should have become as white as a swan."

Henri II's grey hairs did not impair his energy. We have only to glance at an account of his ordinary day to be reassured on this head. It began at dawn with "Les affaires du Matin," a function which originated with him. As soon as he woke his chemise was brought to him, and all the grandees entered to salute him. The garment was then handed to him by the Prince of highest rank then present; the King dressed and prostrated himself in public before the little altar in his bedroom. When he rose every one retired, excepting those who remained for "l'Etroit," or Privy Council, which held peace and war in its hands, despatched the administrative work of the realm and organized, as well, all its naval and military arrangements. Mass followed business, then he had a frugal dinner, after which the General Council assembled to debate on such matters as appertained to legislation and to justice. This, however, was rarely attended by His Majesty, who divided the afternoon between outdoor sports and such studies as happened to be interesting him. The impassioned huntsman came first in him, the racquet-player second. In the racquet-court all ceremony was abolished. "Hardly would any one know that the King was playing," says one of his spectators; "his very mistakes are openly discussed and more than once I have heard him put in the wrong." Indoors, his chief pleasure was music, in which as he grew older he took ever greater delight. "Dearly doth he love music and he hath the best notions concerning it, asking for it nearly every day both at his *lever* and his *coucher*."

What were the delicious melodies to which he rose and slept again? What were the dying sounds of lute and horn and dulcimer, of rebec, of hautboy and of clavichord? Did he wake to some air by Goudimel whom Palestrina loved? or to Jannequin's "*Caquet des femmes*" and his "*Chant de l'Alouette?*" And was it the Dugués, that family of sweet musicians, who played him into kingly slumbers? In earlier days it would have been his chapel choristers with "flutes, spinets and viols, among which rose up their voices, in the which he took a great delight;" and they would have sung him some psalm of Marot's, or perhaps the one that he himself composed in his youth. He could hardly ever refrain from joining in these chants himself, and when he was ill, they alone refreshed his spirit. But if some music-loving guest, however humble, chanced to enter the room during a concert, the King graciously bade him approach and listen, and gave him the parts of the song which was being sung so that he might carry them away.

Other arts than music were more or less indifferent to him and, unlike his contemporaries, he had no sort of taste for jewels or tapestry or the minor crafts, or even for the larger one of building. But talk in his later years diverted him and it was his custom after early dinner to seek it in the Queen's public drawing-room. Here, together with his wife, his sister Marguerite, his little daughters and Mary Stuart, he found (to use an old flatterer's language) "a troop of human goddesses, one more beautiful than another. Here, every lord and gentleman entertained her whom he loved best, and this devising lasted for two hours. After the which he went out to enjoy divers exercises . . . the ladies for the most part following him, so that they, too, might share this pleasure." With the dusk came the stately royal supper and, until two years before his death, he spent the hours after it with Diane. But from 1557 onwards, he changed his tactics and in gratitude for the help his wife had given him while he was absent in the wars, he nightly repaired to her rooms and spent an hour there with her. The time went in talk, unless there happened to be a ball. Then he would stay to join it, or to watch the stately dances that they had then: grave and deliberate dances, "like games of chess played upon squares of carpet"—the Pavane, the Allemande, the Canaries, the Branle des Sabots, or the Branle des Torches, in which a torch was passed from one to another; or else the Branle des Lavandières, in which the dancers clapped their hands to imitate the sound made by washerwomen when they beat their linen near the Seine. "All this brilliance," says Brantôme, might be seen shining in a ball-room of the Louvre, as stars shine in the sky when the weather is serene." The evening over, there began the King's State *Coucher*. He undressed in the presence of the Court; the Chamberlain himself saw that his bed was made and, as a final ceremony, the usher brought him the official keys and put them under his pillow. This done, the King was at last allowed to go to sleep like other mortals.

The tone of the Court during his lifetime—a Court where there were three hundred ladies, French, Scotch, and Italian—is the true measure of his personality. His steady fidelity to Diane, his steady infidelity to his unpopular wife, created a peculiar kind of moral code, and Contarini tells us that from being famed for its vice the French Court became "regular enough." "King Henry loved good stories as well as the Kings, his predecessors, but he did not like at all to shock ladies by them." No courtier dared laugh at a coarse joke, and Catherine was as strict as he was about any breach of manners. Her ladies and gentlemen were summoned to her presence even if they quarrelled, and each one stood in wholesome awe of her—"for that she was the best lady in the whole world at rebuffing and astounding an offender." No doubt, in spite of her scoldings, "*les Marquis et Marquises de Bellebouche,*" as the Court scandal-mongers were called, found work enough to keep their tongues busy.

In the forefront of all mischief-making stood Charles de Guise, Cardinal de Lorraine, "who would like" (wrote Jeanne d'Albret) "to set households by the ears all over France." His brothers, though quite as arrogant, were not quite as baneful as he; the Marquis d'Elboeuf, the Cardinal de Guise, and the Duc d'Aumale (Diane's son-in-law), because they had less influence, and the omnipotent François, Duc de Guise, because he was so often absent in the wars. They all professed the same tenets and led the Roman Catholic party against every opponent, whether heretical or merely desirous to reform the existing Church. Here again the Cardinal de Lorraine was pre-eminent. He was a singular mixture of the fashionable preacher, the ambitious dandy, the art-patron, the scholarly man of letters, and the *Valet d'Etat* with an immense salary. "Ever most perfect in the science of the courtier," upstairs and downstairs and in my lady's chamber, he was equally at ease with his Horace in the library or in a Parisian pulpit, pouring forth his elegant cascades of oratory to a crowded congregation. Many accomplishments were his besides; he was a brilliant linguist, a deft theologian, and he had, according to a distinguished modern critic, "the strongest political head of his day." It was perhaps even more to his advantage that he possessed the gift of good looks, was "*de noble et grave presence,*" and won the hearts of most women. Nor had he to wait long for results; he speedily laid up treasure for himself and combined success with economy —" keeping no private table for the space of two years, but dining daily at the table of Madame de Valentinois," which must have been a sad aggravation to needy courtiers who had to provide their own dinners. For the Cardinal was decidedly avaricious, though his avarice, like his natural violence, was kept under steely control and was almost equalled by his love of luxury. He surpassed his fellow Cardinal, Wolsey, in display of mundane pomp, and, with his refined aristocratic traditions, he had many more tastes to satisfy. Indeed he had never known hardship and was made for the alcove where he usually remained. Not that he was without his more adventurous moments. In one of the campaigns against the Emperor he rode forth to battle on a grey mare, together with the French troops, dressed in a crimson velvet robe with a white cross, and wearing finely-wrought spurs affixed to his boots—all ready to help him to flight. " Whereat," observes his chronicler, " every one fell a laughing." And this was not the only occasion on which his discretion was the better part of his valour. We catch a glimpse of him in a Paris riot—an anti-Guise demonstration—when " a swarm of people, like bees after a storm, came in serried heaps to the shop into which the Lord Cardinal had retired—whence also he issued forth with some of his guard—his head hanging low, like a poppy beaten by the rain."

A very different person was his brother, the Duc François. Insolent and brutal he was of course, or he would not have been a great sixteenth century soldier; but generous and heroic also, and dignified by the sufferings and privations that war had compelled him to undergo. His qualities were sensational and, in spite of the hatred of the nation at large, he periodically became the darling of fickle Paris. But both he and his less important brothers were dramatic types rather than individuals, and though they dominated the Court, they have no fine shades with which to occupy us.

Far more interesting, as is often the case, were the leaders of the Opposition: the two Bourbon princes, Antoine, King of Navarre, and his brother, the Prince de Condé; and the three noble Châtillons, also brothers—Gaspard, the Admiral

THE THREE COLIGNYS.
THE CARDINAL DE CHÂTILLON. THE ADMIRAL. THE MARÉCHAL D'ANDELOT.
DRAWING OF THE FRENCH SCHOOL IN THE BIBLIOTHÈQUE NATIONALE.
From a photograph by A. Giraudon.

de Coligny, the Marshal d'Andelot, and the Cardinal Odet de Châtillon. These five men, especially the last three, were more or less identified with the Huguenot cause and more or less hated by the Guises. The Bourbons, as princes of the blood and therefore next, after the royal children, to the throne, were the objects of their especial enmity, but as far as principle went, their most implacable foe was Coligny.

With the name of Gaspard de Coligny we come to one of the thrilling—the morally thrilling—personages of history; to a man of bronze, a man, too, of human flesh and blood; a being of unspotted integrity; a Protestant statesman, a child of Israel, who wished to found a new Jerusalem and yet remain loyal to the Crown. His brothers were cast in much the same metal, but they had neither his initiative nor his moral genius. Perhaps the man who came nearest him in originality, though neither in force, stability, nor intellect, was the Prince de Condé, a person in many ways his opposite in character; Condé, the high-souled buccaneer of the Protestant party, the born soldier, noble, restless, ambitious, glad to swing his sword in the defence of a principle, yet serving that principle with a rather worldly devotion. The Bourbons were not strong, like the Châtillons, but Condé's fire almost served instead of strength. Unfortunately this was not so with his brother, Antoine, who through his marriage with Jeanne d'Albret became King of Navarre. "Unstable as water, thou shalt not excel," might well have been written upon his forehead, and his vacillations between Protestantism and orthodoxy were, from the first, an obstacle to the Reforming party. Their real difficulties, however, had not yet begun, nor had the hour struck for these Huguenot captains to figure as the leading actors on the stage and as the symbols of a great idea.

It was only at the end of Henri's reign that the religious question again assumed formidable proportions. We saw that earlier in the day he himself became three-quarters of a Huguenot of the Puritanical order, loving to sing Marot's Psalms and to read the Bible in the vernacular. Politically, too, he showed the same colours when, in 1552, he allied himself to the Protestant German princes against the Emperor Charles V. But this heretical state of things came to an end and orthodoxy reasserted itself. It is true that he always thought little of the Pope as a person, but he honoured him as the Head of the Church, and this tendency increased under the influence of Diane and the Guises. The wars against the

Emperor and Philip II for a time distracted the King's attention from matters of dogma, but after the peace of Câteau-Cambrésis, when he once more had leisure for thought, religious matters again began to absorb him. His attitude was none of the most clement; the years 1558 and 1559 saw bad persecutions and, considering the power of Diane and her colleagues, it is likely that worse things would have ensued had not his death intervened and put an end to all questionings.

With Henri II's foreign relations this book, which is a personal record, has but scant concern. Like most monarchs of his time, he had a passion for war and was distinguished by his military prowess, although he lacked any large military conceptions, imperial or otherwise. In the same way he had big soldiers—Guise, Montmorency, Brissac, Coligny, Tavannes —but no truly great leader; no one adequate to " *le renard*." as the Emperor Charles V was called.

What fighters there were in France had, at all events, plenty of work. For seven years of Henri's reign war was practically incessant. In 1552, the King allied himself with the German Princes and with Maurice of Saxony, their chief, who had deserted and betrayed his imperial master. The result of this campaign was the famous siege of Metz by the French, and their taking of that important place as well as of the fortified towns of Toul and Verdun. At the same time Henri had declared himself against the Pope in Italy, and his troops were fighting there as well as in Germany. His victories in the last-named country brought him considerable prestige, but the Emperor afterwards revenged himself on certain French cities in the Netherlands, and the war went on smouldering till the signing of the Peace of Vaucelles, in 1556. That same year, Charles V retired to his monastery of Yuste, leaving the imperial crown of Austria to his brother Ferdinand, and the realm of Spain, together with his possessions in Italy and the Netherlands, to his son, Philip II. Philip at once allied himself to England by his marriage with Mary Tudor; and the French saw with dismay that, with Protestant Britain only divided by a short sea-passage from the Protestant Netherlands, he had a powerful kingdom in the North as well as in the South of Europe. To prevent the establishment of his Northern rule, the French king broke the Peace at the end of the same year in which it had been inaugurated, and he sent the Duc de Guise against Alva in Italy and Montmorency against Emmanuel Philibert in the Netherlands. The result was

THE COURT OF HENRI II

disastrous in both regions. The French army was defeated near Civitella and, more signally, in Flanders, at the siege of St. Quentin (1557). The Duke of Savoy was besieging that town and Coligny, hard pressed, was inside it, when Montmorency, by an ill-advised movement, tried to come to his aid and brought his inadequate forces into contact with the enemy. He suffered total defeat and was taken prisoner with several other princes. Philip had Paris before him; but he did not follow up his advantage, and, while he dallied, the Duc de Guise was recalled from Italy, was made Lieutenant-General of the French army and at once retrieved the French fortunes. For, by a skilful stratagem, he diverted his adversaries to Luxembourg and himself recaptured Calais— a master-stroke of brilliant tactics. This was in 1558; and in that year was signed the Treaty of Câteau-Cambrésis, a treaty which was always considered an indignity to France. As it was said to be the work of Diane de Poitiers, perhaps this can hardly be wondered at. True, it assured to the French the possession of Toul, Verdun and Metz, as well as of Calais and Boulogne; but it also compelled her to barter 189 important places in Italy and the Netherlands against some insignificant Spanish possessions. "*Sire*," said Guise and Brissac to the King, "you give away in twenty-four hours what thirty years of reverses would not have taken from you." Perhaps Henri II consoled himself by thinking of the two royal marriages which were also part of the agreement—that of his sister Marguerite de Berri to the Duke of Savoy and of his little daughter, Elizabeth to Philip of Spain.

Bare outline though this be, it is enough for our present purpose, our business being not with military matters, excepting in so far as events affected Henri's life and that of Catherine. And amongst these there are two, already alluded to, which altered their relative positions. The first of these was the royal decision concerning his wife's Regency during his absence on the German campaign. It would have been the natural thing to leave Catherine as sole Regent during his absence. François I had thus empowered his mother, Louise de Savoie while he was away in the field, and after such a precedent any other arrangement amounted to an insult. In spite of which, as we have seen the King at Diane's instigation decreed that the Chancellor, Bertrandi, no especial friend of the Queen's, should be fellow-Regent with her, thus practically annulling any power to act freely on her part. No deed more firmly established the power of the Guises, or so much lowered Catherine in the eyes of the people. Had she had sway over them then, when it was important to her to gain popularity, she might have made a position for herself which would have changed their later attitude towards her. And this privation must have been the more galling as she was peculiarly fitted for the Regency and had served a serious apprenticeship in matters of the State, taking great pains to study its requirements both in peace and in war. "I assure you"—she writes (alluding to the provisioning of the army)—"that I have become a past-mistress therein." And I shall not spare any trouble till I know enough to please the King." The woman who thus expressed herself should have had full responsibility given her.

Her humiliated pride must, however, have been partially restored by the rôle that she played after the siege of St. Quentin. The news of this unexpected and unnecessary defeat flew on swift wings to Paris, and the town gave itself up to panic and showed signs of rioting, Catherine saw that the one thing to do was to stop the disturbance and to get from the State the funds necessary for continuing the war. She lost no time in proceeding to the Parlement and demanding 300,000 livres in all, 25,000 livres of which she asked for at once; after which, with consummate tact, she offered to retire so that her presence might not trammel the debate. The speedy result was a vote for a sum exceeding her request and a great sensation throughout the city. The King himself was more impressed by her because of this achievement than he had been throughout their marriage, and he showed it in his behaviour. For it was from this day, as has been told, that he changed his habit of giving the evening to Diane and spent it with Catherine instead. Nor is it without significance that now, for the first time, François Clouet struck a medal with the King's head on one side and that of the Queen on the other—a venture that could not have been made before this signal success of hers. She did not win Henri's love, but she had at least gained his respect.

What fruit all this might have borne for her will never be known, for before two years were over Henri's life was cut short. These last months of his existence were taken up with royal weddings. In 1558, Mary Stuart was married to the Dauphin; and in 1559—as had been agreed in the Treaty of Câteau-Cambrésis—Marguerite of Berri was wedded to Emmanuel Philibert, Duke of Savoy, and Princess Elizabeth of France to Philip II of Spain.

The marriage of Mary Stuart is one of the most picturesque on record, and it made so typical a pageant that to describe it is to describe the Renaissance. Great preparations went forward for it. A theatre was erected on the " Parvis," or Pavement in front of Notre Dame, and here a crowd of Princes, Bishops, grandees of all sorts, assembled; so did a multitude of minstrels, with their flutes and their viols and their citherns. Through their midst to the great West door came the bride, a shining dream of April charms : " For she was clad in a white garment, like unto a lily, fashioned so richly and so sumptuously that none can imagine it. And two young maidens bore up the train thereof, which was of a marvellous length. From her neck there hung a circlet of untold worth, made of fiery stones . . . and on her head she wore a golden crown studded with pearls and diamonds, with rubies, sapphires and emeralds . . . but above all others, in its midst there glowed a great carbuncle." The Dauphin met her and there, outside the church, gave the wedding-ring to the Cardinal de Bourbon who married them where they stood. The square was packed ; the Heralds, according to their custom, cried " Largesse " three times over ; the mob scrambled for the coin till some fainted, and some lost their cloaks and hats, and the people themselves implored the Heralds to stop throwing money. And all the while the Dukes and Lords marched along the high scaffolding into Notre Dame, where the Archbishop celebrated Mass and the wedded pair sat upon a throne beneath a canopy of cloth of gold. Then back to the Bishop's Palace, where a gorgeous ball and banquet agreeably symbolised the union of the powers temporal and spiritual. " The very Christian King danced with the Queen-Dauphine, and the King-Dauphin danced with the Queen, his mother, and the Prince de Condé with Madame Marguerite, the King's sister ; and there were present divers other princes and princesses robed in golden tissue . . . decked out with such magnificence that the Elysian Fields could not have been more lovely." These fascinating revels lasted till the reasonable hour of five in the afternoon, after which supper was served at tables of white marble, surrounded by officers of the Parlement in their robes of vivid scarlet. The meal seems to have had rather an exhilarating effect, for after it " the matrons and the maids leaped in the air for joy," and then settled down to the absurd "*balades et momeries*" which ended this extravagant day. These would be tedious to read of were not they so characteristic. Into the hall there cantered pretence horses, which were ridden by princely children and drew coaches full of pilgrims clad from head to foot in silver tissue and jewels, "the which sang melodiously and in all perfection to their instruments many sweet hymns and psalms in praise of marriage and the married pair." The pilgrims having taken themselves off with their costly paraphernalia, a fleet of ships came into sight, rolling forwards and backwards, as if on a real sea. Each gentleman of the crew chose a lady and sailed away with her—the King of Navarre, to every one's surprise, carrying off none other than his wife. "And no one knew" (concludes the chronicler) "whether the torches or the jewels gave the most light."

It seems abrupt to go straight from a pageant of life to one of death, from a royal ball to a royal funeral, but it is not abrupter than reality. The year after Mary Stuart's marriage. took place the weddings of Marguerite, Henri's sister, and Elizabeth, his thirteen-year-old daughter. The shows were as splendid as they had been twelve months earlier and lasted some days after the ceremonies. The finest of these festivities was to be a Joust, in which the King was to take part in the presence of all the great guests who had flocked to Paris for the marriages. The day (it was in midsummer) arrived. The night before, Catherine had dreamed that her husband had lost his eye, but she paid no heed to the omen. The lists were ready, the "gilded youth" of France had assembled, and "it was a boastful thing to see the magnificence of four Queens met together in this city." As the King and his adversary, Montgoméry, advanced on their horses, a boy in an upper gallery leaned forward and cried out loudly, "*Sire*, do not fight!" but he was summarily repressed, nor did he himself know why he had spoken. The fighting began ; the King and his foe had several rounds and Henri was always victorious. At last he sent word to Catherine that "he would try one more bout for the love of her," a wonderful message for her to get when we remember that it was his last. Once again the King and Montgoméry set to—once again Montgoméry made a thrust with his lance ; but this time it struck home, and Henri sank to the ground with the blade in his eye. The audience recoiled in horror ; there was a general cry, a general rush, and the King was borne out from the lists to the Palace of

MARGUERITE DE VALOIS, DUCHESSE DE SAVOIE
BY FRANÇOIS CLOUET. BIBLIOTHÈQUE NATIONALE.
From a photograph by A. Giraudon.

les Tournelles hard by. There was no hope from the first, and he died ten days afterwards.

Montgoméry was a Protestant and the suspicion of deliberate assassination fell upon him. Whether this was founded, or no, has never been proved, but Madame Marguerite, Henri's only sister, "felt a great anger towards him, for her brother and she loved one another dearly." Catherine, meanwhile, was prostrate with a profound grief. Yet her grief was not so strong as her hate. Before the breath was out of her husband's body, she had sent messengers to Diane's palace to command her to return the crown-jewels and the thousand presents that Henri had sent her, each one of which stood recorded on the tablets of the Queen's remorseless memory. When all was over, she ordered her rival to leave Paris and to hide her head at Anet. Diane lingered ten days in the hope of some assistance being offered her, but none came and she was forced to go. Nor was this the only bitter draught she had to swallow; Anet was left to her, but Chenonceaux, her dearly-loved Chenonceaux, was taken by the Queen, who compelled her to exchange it for Chaumont. If Catherine had made no figure as a royal wife, she figured sufficiently as a royal widow.

The details of her vengeance were only gradually carried into execution. For the first day after the King died she remained prone on the ground by his bedside, dazed by her sudden sorrow. "She is so unhappy still," wrote Mary Stuart to her mother some days later, "and is plunged in such grief for the loss of the late King, that I fear her misery will give her a bad illness." And this was the impression she made on others. When the Venetian ambassador paid her a State visit of condolence, he found her surrounded by sable hangings. The walls and the floor of her apartment were covered with black, and so were her vast bed and the High Altar, both standing there: the whole unlightened save by two wax tapers, which burned dimly in the general gloom. The Queen, wrapped in a veil from head to foot, wore an austere black dress, the effect deepened by the ermine collar round her neck. Beside her stood her daughters and her sister-in-law, and near them the slender Mary Stuart, all of them robed in white and making a daylight in the darkness, Catherine thanked the envoys for their sympathy in her name and that of those surrounding her; but her voice was so weak and so stifled with emotion that no one could hear what she said.

There is always a good deal of showy conventionality about the mourning of sovereigns, but the black that Catherine wore from this day onwards, and the motto, "*lachrymæ hinc, hinc dolor*," which she henceforth adopted, were no pretence on her part. Perhaps we are the readier to believe her, because in other ways she was unconventional. It had hitherto been the custom for a king's widow to remain six weeks in bed in a darkened room, seeing no one beyond her family and attendants; but Catherine broke the tradition and, soon after her loss, accompanied her son, now Charles IX, to Saint-Germain.

There were in any case enough ceremonies to go through, for there was no end to the pomps and vanities that surrounded a monarch's death. In the first place, the embalmed body lay for eighteen days in an upper room, before it was borne to a State bed in the *Salle d'honneur*, which was hung with fresh tapestries for the occasion. Here it abode for six more days, the King's waxen effigy, sumptuously clad, beneath it. The nobles entered one by one to sprinkle holy water on the corpse, and Mass was celebrated daily at various resplendent altars. Daily, too, His Majesty's dinner was served in the room as usual, the grandees waiting round the empty table, after which ghostly ceremony the meat was given to the poor. Twenty-four days being now over, the body was again moved on a high scaffolding to the next room, the *Salle de Deuil*—a vast hall of darkness hung with black, the light shut out by thick black curtains. And here, among the shadows of death, the great prelates met next day for High Mass and received the new King from Saint-Germain, in his mourning mantle of purple sown with gold fleurs-de-lys. The reception was monotonous in its solemnities. When it was at last over the young King stepped forward to sprinkle holy water on his father's form, followed first by his brothers, then by all the princes and peers, and last (two days later) by a throng of Government officials, Presidents, Provosts, and Judges. The traditional thirty days had now come to an end and the dead King was carried to Notre Dame in the midst of a winding procession —a shifting mass of gold and purple and scarlet against a black background—stopping in the cathedral for the Requiem (and also for the mourning princes' dinner hard by); filing out and onwards to St. Ladre, and thence again to St. Denis. Funeral orations were in plenty, but we cannot help a feeling of relief when we read that the King who was no more, yet was still trammelled by etiquette, was at length taken to his quiet grave. At one end sat the Cardinal de Lorraine, at the other the Connêtable de Montmorency, dominating the situation to the end. Then there sounded a cry of "*Rois d'armes, venez faire votre office!*" and the Knights-at-arms and the heralds advanced slowly, bowing low to the open grave and taking off their hats and breastplates which they laid within it. The flags and spears of other officers, handed to the Rois d'armes, were put beside the armour; the Maîtres d'Hôtel followed with their bâtons, which they themselves dropped into the trench; and the Crown and the *Main-de-Justice* made up the sum of the funeral offerings. The Constable rose from his seat, and "*Le Roi est mort!*" he called out; the "Rois d'armes" next took three steps and shouted, "*Le Roi est mort; priez Dieu tous pour son âme!*" Whereat the surging crowd knelt down and prayed "for the space of three Paternosters," after which the Constable withdrew his bâton from the grave. "*Vive le Roi!*" he cried; "*Vive le Roi!*" repeated the Rois d'armes and the princes; there was a sudden burst of music from drums and from fifes, and Henri II was left to sleep in peace.

For his heart, which was embalmed, there was a separate funeral. In the Louvre we may still see the elegant and mundane urn which the great Germain Pilon made for it to rest in. The three Graces—rather Parisian Graces with a head-dress half classical, half Valois—stand in a ring with their backs to the urn and hold it lightly poised upon their shoulders. There is no hint that they are bearing a burden; they seem rather to be on the point of dancing: dancing, maybe, down the trimmed alleys of French history with the heart of Henri II. But they evidently have no idea that it is a human heart which they carry—something which has suffered and enjoyed and moved to a disturbing measure. Or do they know what it is supposed to be and do they doubt if the legend be true? Perhaps it is our fancy that their prudent lips smile and their eyes turn from us with a question. Are they looking at their neighbour Diane, as she lies, not far off, in cool marble repose, and is it from her they seek an answer? She remains enigmatic and silent in the large halls of the Louvre.

BOOK II

Catherine and the Reformation

CHAPTER V

The Reign of François II

AUTHORITIES CONSULTED

Sur le Règne de François II—*Régnier de la Planche.*
Memoirs de Tavannes.
Memoirs du Prince de Condé.
Discours de Michel Soriano.
Lettres de Catherine de' Medici.
Eléonore de Roye—*Le Comte Delaborde.*
Histoire de France—*Michelet.*
Histoire de France—*Martin.*
Catherine de Médicis—*Capefigue.*
Biographical Introductions to the " Lettres de Catherine de' Medici "
—*Le Comte de la Ferrière.*

CHAPTER V

The Reign of François II

CATHERINE had now achieved the desire of her heart and had practically attained the Regency. For though François was sixteen years old and had therefore passed his majority, he never even played the part of King.

Heavy and indolent, he had no wish to do so and he inaugurated his reign by a formal address to his subjects bidding them obey his mother in all things. "This being the good pleasure of my Lady-Mother and I also approving of every opinion that she holdeth"—so runs the formula that he ordered to be used in state-documents.

Catherine knew well the feeble instrument on which she played and understood how to use her son as a buffer when she found herself in straits between the Guises and the Bourbons. She was fully aware that the Kingdom could get not on without her. "I believe," wrote the astute Mary Stuart to her mother, "that if her son, the King, were not so obedient to her that he does nothing except what she wishes, she would soon die, which would be the greatest disaster that could possibly happen to this poor country and to all of us." For some time the Queen Mother imagined that if she flattered the Guises enough she could keep them as her tools. She allowed François to issue another statement in which he commanded obedience to the Duke and the Cardinal, and gave to the former all the military, to the latter all the administrative honours of the realm. When his father's old servant and master, the Connétable de Montmorency, duly presented himself in the Louvre, followed by his nephews, the Châtillons, the new King taking the Seals from his hand cut short his profession of allegiance. "We are anxious," said François, "to solace thine old age, which is no longer fit to endure the toils and hardships of my service." After which the monarch proposed to relieve his faithful follower of the Seals and other offices which his ministers, the already hard-worked Guises, had consented to accept; but he begged him to retain his place in the Privy Council. This the outraged Prince refused to do. " Being old and half in my dotage," he ironically said, " my counsel can be of little or no use to you; though if some business should arise in which my presence were needful, I would give you my life and my estate." Whereupon he left the King and sought out the Queen-Regent, to whom he repeated what he had just said. But she received him very differently, covering him with reproaches for his former hostility to her and for the slanders that he had uttered, nor would she listen when he refuted her charges. The source of his disgrace was clear enough to him now and he had no alternative but to retire. Retire he did to Chantilly, " but with such a retinue that the King's train seemed small in comparison, concerning which the Princes of Guise conceived a great jealousy." Pomps and vanities were, however, poor consolation for loss of power and when the title of " Grand Maître," the highest in the kingdom, was taken from his son to whom it had been promised and given to the Duc de Guise, his cup of bitterness was full. Nor did this same son's appointment as Grand-Marshal bring any balm to the Constable; it did not restore his position, which indeed seemed hardly better than that of Diane de Poitiers. But there was this difference between the two dethroned sovereigns—Montmorency had vengeance in his hands. It was short-sighted of Catherine not to see that his alliance with her and the Guises could alone consolidate her power. She was making a dangerous foe: for although he was deprived of office, he could still throw in his lot with the Bourbon Princes and the Protestants, and become a factor in the Opposition.

With the Opposition Catherine had begun by dallying. For some time she counted the strings to her bow and was uncertain whether the Guise or Bourbon string would best suit her designs. If she chose the Guises, her sway, as she foresaw, would run great risks from their tyranny, yet, if she chose the Bourbons, she would have the awful Guises against her. Had Antoine de Navarre obeyed the Constable's summons, sent before the death of Henri II; had that shifty Prince been capable of prompt action and immediately appeared at Court, things might have been different. Meanwhile, it was upon the Guises that her choice finally fell and she trusted to her own craftiness to outwit their despotic ambition. Besides, in exalting them thus she made them her

ANTOINE DE BOURBON, ROI DE NAVARRE.
BY FRANÇOIS CLOUET. CHÂTEAU DE CHANTILLY.
From a photograph by A. Giraudon.

debtors, and she knew them to be so daring that there was nothing they would not attempt at her bidding. "For the rest, she judged wisely that supposing she caused discontent or disturbance by any enterprise of her own, the blame would be thrown rather on them than on her." She lost no time in making the Bourbons feel her decision. The Prince de Condé was sent on a safe foreign mission which removed him from perilous plottings. As for the King of Navarre, he lost many days in wondering whether or not he should visit the Court, many more in preparing a boastful train. When at last he set forth it was too late. The Guises had got hold of two of his followers who persuaded him that temporizing was his best course. Spain, they said, was spying upon his actions; caution was the wisest policy towards France; he should go to Court, certainly, but only with a few followers. Their advice was taken and he started in humble guise. It was largely on behalf of his Protestant subjects that this so-called Protestant monarch was supposed to be undertaking the expedition and many were the promises he made them before his final departure.

The King of France was at that moment at Saint-Germain. It was his custom, when an honoured guest arrived, to meet him as if by chance, out hunting. But on the day of Antoine's coming François II's sport took him and his companion, the Cardinal, in another direction and when the King of Navarre arrived unescorted at the palace, it was only to find that no apartments had been prepared for him—a Prince of the blood. The Maréchal St. André eventually gave him his room, and his suite found lodgings in the village. But insults were not at an end. When he entered the audience-chamber, the King stood still without advancing to meet him; so did the Cardinal, Antoine's inferior in rank. He embraced both without any sign from either, nor did they even invite him to take part in the Privy Council. He was, as Catherine remarked, " reduced to the position of a chamber-maid," and had to pocket the offence as best he might. Antoine de Navarre had no dignity. His only resource was to play toady to the Guises till, finding there was no more to be got, he threw up the game and retired defeated to Navarre without fulfilling a word of his promises to the Huguenots. Their disappointment was not without importance and doubtless counted for something in the religious troubles that were soon to convulse the kingdom.

Meanwhile, the Cardinal de Lorraine was, if possible, more potent and worse hated than heretofore. The measure of popular likes and dislikes is generally to be found in the current lampoons, and these were not wanting in his case. The suave and remorseless prelate, the politic dilettante, was meet food for the satirist's pen.

> On voit mathématiciens,
> Les plus doctes musiciens,
> Menestriers et sonneurs de luths
> Se donner à un Carolus.
>
> Si vous voulez, sans oiseleurs,
> Des oiseaux de toutes couleurs,
> Prendre bien mieux qu'avec la glus :
> Il ne vous faut qu'un Carolus.
> * * * *
> Les inventeurs de tous malheurs,
> Les larrons et plus grands voleurs,
> Et les gens les plus dissolus,
> Sont maintenus d'un Carolus.

So runs a topical song of the day. The making of anagrams, too, was a favourite game of the Renaissance—imitated, says a chronicler, from the Greeks—and those on his name abounded. The letters in "Charles de Lorraine" lent themselves to many an abusive epithet : "Hardi larron se cèle" (A bold thief hides himself); "Renard lasche le roi!" (Fox let go of the King!); "Raclé à l'or de Henri" (Raked up from the gold of Henri), and the like. "Carolus," indeed, lived in continual dread of assassination, the more so that a violent death had been prophesied to him. Some of the consequences of his panic were strange and would have pleased the philosopher of "Sartor Resartus." The cloaks of that moment were wide, the boots immense—excellent hiding-places for weapons. But the mode suddenly changed and cloaks and boots shrank perceptibly. One omnipotent little Prince's fear of death had transformed the ruling fashions. It would have been well had he stopped here. But he had induced Catherine to write and beg Philip II for his protection—the first of a series of such treacherous appeals—thus giving Spain a mischievous footing in France. And he had vowed to Alva and to the Duke of Savoy that he would wage war against the Protestants, a promise which he kept. He filled the prisons and kept the hangman busy. "It is impossible that this should go on longer . . ." writes Hubert Languet, the most temperate of Protestants—"the Cardinal of Lorraine is abandoned by many of his own side who dread future events." The bad harvest of 1560 and the acute want that ensued enhanced both the general discontent and the feeling against the inactive priests. Converts to Protestantism increased, and though the Cardinal had apparently suppressed the Protestant Church in Paris, he could not suppress the idea that gave it birth. He had yet to learn that authority is not the same as enduring power.

The match that set light to the faggots was the trial of Anne du Bourg, a Councillor of the Parlement. In that institution there had recently grown up a little party of so-called "Politiques," or "Moderates"—a band of cultivated men and earnest thinkers who inclined towards the "New Opinions." These Girondins of Protestantism, though they made no violent demonstration, were gradually extending their influence and were a stumbling-block to orthodox people. If the Parlement were to become a centre of heresy the peril would be extreme, and the Parlement therefore it was that the Cardinal resolved first to purify. His zeal only waited for the next person it could lay hands on. This was Anne du Bourg, one of the chief "Moderates," an ardent, book-loving man, who no doubt cherished heterodox views but was actually arrested on a false and insufficient accusation. His first trial was indecisive and he made an appeal which would have probably succeeded; but the ill-advised Huguenots chose this moment to shoot down an unjust Judge of his, the Président Ménars, and they settled the fate of du Bourg. He was summarily condemned to be burned in the Place des Grèves, a verdict quickly carried out. The Protestants, horror-stricken at this unrighteous judgment, read in it the Cardinal's intention to root them out and to destroy them. The Huguenot plot of Amboise was the direct result.

There were at this moment in France two parties among the Huguenots: "the Huguenots of Religion," who resented the persecution by the Catholics, and "the Huguenots of State," whose first motive was hostility to the Guises and loyalty to the Bourbon Princes. These political Protestants again split into two factions: that of the Monarchists—associated with Elizabeth of England—which wished to depose François II and put the Prince de Condé in his place; and the subversive democratic faction, which wanted to depose the King and set up a Republic, the true Calvinistic ideal, symbolized by their seal which was graven with a broken crown. Both groups united in their resolution to invalidate the Guises and Catherine de' Medici, whose children they declared to be illegitimate; and both, too, agreed to hand over Mary Stuart to the Scotch Covenanters. But these were secret aims. Publicly they only dared demand the dismissal of the Guises, the just distribution of offices and the convocation of the States-General—all three requests made, so they said, in the true interests of the Crown.

With these Huguenots, and especially with the more temperate among them, Catherine at first showed a good deal of sympathy. "When I see these poor folk burnt, bruised and tormented, not for thieving and marauding but simply for upholding their own opinions; when I see some of them suffer cheerfully, with a glad heart, I am moved to believe that there is something in this which transcendeth human reason."

So she wrote to Madame de Mailly, one of her Protestant ladies. There were others at her Court—Madame de Crussol, Mademoiselle de Goguier and the Duchesse de Montpensier—and the Protestants had reason to hope much from her. When she was on her way to the King's Coronation at Rheims, Coligny, Condé and Madame de Mailly begged her to see them. Nor did she refuse the interview; it served her interests to learn their secrets, whether as friends or as foes. Madame de Mailly was spokeswoman. Catherine, she said, had promised to be her friend. The Protestants looked upon their Queen as a second Esther; should they look in vain? She implored that Esther not to pollute the young King's reign with blood, "for that which had been already shed cried loudly to God who had avenged it." Catherine took this as an allusion to Henri's death. "What do your threats mean?" she asked: "what more can God do to me, since He hath taken from me that which I loved and prized the most dearly?" Then with an effort she calmed herself and pledged her word to stop the persecutions, provided the Huguenots would live in peace. Coligny and Madame de Mailly even made her promise to see and to confer with a minister of the Reformed Church. After much debate, the Consistory at Paris resolved to send one, Chandieu, a great light among them, to meet her at a village near Rheims. But when the appointed day came, the Cardinal knew well how to prevent her going and the minister kept the tryst alone. She found herself helpless in the hands of the Guises and, far from ceasing, the persecutions redoubled. After du Bourg's execution, the Protestants reminded her of her promise and warned her that God's vengeance would come

THE REIGN OF FRANÇOIS II

upon her. "They threaten me," she said, "but they have not got as far as they think." The more statesmanlike of the Huguenots saw the mistake of their fellows. "Those of the religion (*Ceux de la religion*) have exasperated the Queen-Mother who sought to moderate all things," so writes Hubert Languet, one among them : "They have menaced her with God's judgment ... and she, in her great indignation, treats them as scoundrels.... Thus it is that our people conduct affairs...." And thus it was also that the Plot of Amboise was conceived.

The nation was at that moment bound to be the prey of such conspiracies. For, apart from internal dissensions, the kingdom was sadly unsettled. In spite of all precautions, a rumour had gone abroad that the young King was suffering from a form of blood-poisoning which was bound to end fatally in a few years. The doctors recommended him the mild climate of Blois and the Court took up its residence there. On this place, therefore, the plotters concentrated their energies. There was to be a general military rising all over France and, at a given signal, troops from every direction were to march on the town of Blois, to seize the persons of the King, his mother, and his brothers, to send away the Guises and to convoke the States-General. If the King refused to become a Protestant, another King was to be set up in his stead. The nominal leader in this business was a certain Sieur de la Rénaudie who had a private grudge against the Guises. He rallied the Huguenots of Strasburg, he got the help of German mercenaries ; but, for all that, he was only a chief in name. The real heads were the Prince de Condé and, secondarily, Antoine de Navarre, to whom La Rénaudie had letters of introduction. It is true that to all seeming they promised him nothing; but none the less were they the mainsprings of the affair. Louis Prince de Condé, the would-be Louis XIII, was a man of nimble wit. He and his uncles by marriage, Coligny and d'Andelot, were in correspondence with Elizabeth, with the Scotch Covenanters, with the Flemish Anabaptists and the Swiss Calvinists, with every Nonconformist in Europe. Help was promised on all sides. Calvin alone refused to countenance a scheme so ill-advised, but, except for this, all was auspicious.

The plan was lucid enough, but it was too widespread to succeed. The English Catholics got wind of it and betrayed it to the Duc de Guise ; La Rénaudie too and his German colleague, the Jurisconsult, Francis Hotman, had allowed their tongues to be indiscreet; and the Moderates of the Parlement, who thought that violence would ruin the chances of Reform, were not behindhand in hinting that something was on foot. Catherine was as usual applied to in this strait, and as usual showed crafty resource. She summoned Coligny to come to her at once on the fictitious pretext that the English were about to attack some French ships, knowing that such a call would bring her loyal servant directly to her side. When he arrived, she put off the Queen and played the lonely woman. She begged for his advice; she entreated him not to desert the King. He replied that the Guises, who were "hated like the pest," were alone to blame for the bad state of the kingdom and he assured her that the only remedy would be an Edict of Tolerance. Catherine lost no time in passing a decree which forbade the persecution of Protestants, allowed them liberty of worship, and extended an amnesty to all offenders excepting Ministers and such as had plotted against the King, his mother, or the Guises. But this was not the moment for a temporizing policy and the Duc de Guise's presence of mind stood the throne in better stead. He promptly removed Catherine, King, and Court from the dangers of Blois to the security of Amboise. This, at all events, calmed the general panic, from which none had suffered more acutely than the Cardinal, whose sudden death had been prophesied for 1560. But the general gloom did not last long. "In three days they have forgotten all their terrors, after having made a great disturbance and guarded the Castle closely without budging from it. But now the King goes a'hunting again"—So wrote Chantonnay, the envoy—the spy—of Philip II. "The French are so little persevering," he continues, "that these good folk are already beginning to feel ashamed of making such a fuss." They had expected an attack on March 6 and that date once passed, they felt that all was safe. But on the 13th, a troop of men was met on the side of Tours and three days later more were found in a wood, most of them artizans. Some prisoners were taken and brought to Amboise. When they arrived, the King was at the window. Tutored no doubt by his mother, he only detained three or four and set the rest free, with the present of a crown-piece in their pockets. But in doing so he asked them why they had come. "To speak to the King," they replied, "and beg him to let them live according to their religion, for the salvation of their souls, or else to do as he willed with them." If they had stopped there all might have been well, but the crown-pieces made them expansive and they went on to tell his Majesty that they had been sent forth from Geneva, that their leaders had promised to join them shortly, on a fixed day when all their troops, mustering 40,000, would assemble. Search was made round about, more men were imprisoned, a band of one hundred and fifty came to Amboise and knocked at its great door. There was no answer till they retired, when they were hotly pursued and one and all taken. After that, skirmishes and arrests were continual. Every crenellation of the castle was disfigured by the heads of the slain and the conquerors took to drowning and beheading their victims. These executions, or rather wholesale massacres, went on for a month and were witnessed by the cold-hearted Court from a balcony as if they had been stage-representations. "*Ceux de Guise*," says a Chronicler, "arranged all this expressly to make some distraction for the ladies, who were, as they saw, becoming bored at staying so long in one place.... And what was worse, the King and his young brothers appeared at these performances, as if the Guises had wished to excite their nerves." Only the Duchesse de Guise (Anna d'Este, the child of the Duke of Ferrara and his French wife, Renée) showed signs of any susceptibility. She had been dragged to the dreadful spectacle against her will and she came to Catherine's room in tears. There her sobs redoubled. "What ails you," asked the Queen, "that you lament in so strange a fashion?" "I have just seen"—replied the Duchess—"the most piteous tragedy—the cruel shedding of innocent blood, the blood of the King's loyal subjects. I have not a doubt that in a little while a great disaster will fall upon our House." The Guises were duly informed of her faint-heartedness and did not forget to show it in their rough behaviour to her. Nor did the Prince de Condé, then at Amboise, fare much better at the hands of his foes, who were always trying to incriminate him. They invited him one day to go into the next room and watch a band of men being killed—"the which having for a long while refused, they at length compelled him to look through one of the palace windows. Then was his heart pierced with great bitterness. 'I am amazed,' he cried, ' that the King allows himself to be thus advised to take the life of so many honest lords and gentlemen ... when he thinks of the great service that they rendered to the late King.'"

But François II was throughout no more than a helpless

tool, negative even in good intentions and forced to look on at cruelty which he was too feeble to prevent. "Why do my people detest me so?" almost in tears, he asked the Cardinal. Then in a sudden access of anger—"They say it is because of you," he cried—"I wish you would go away and then I should know which it was that was disliked, you or I."

Even the Cardinal's own cronies grew to hate and dread him. The Chancellor Olivier was almost as bad a man as he was. "Go, you have damned us all!" he cried, when the prelate came to visit him upon his death-bed. "Damned, damned—he lies, the wicked creature!" the Duc de Guise was heard to mutter later, in an access of superstitious fear. Catherine, too, was forced to do her Minister's will. Sometimes she attempted to save a life, "trying everything she could—even seeking out these new Kings in their chambers and caressing them," but all in vain. One captive, seized with panic at the end, sent for the Queen-Mother, who went on foot to his dungeon and heard his confession of a Spanish plot. He made it, probably falsely, in the hope of a reprieve, though his scaffold was already raised and spectators were waiting outside his prison walls; but he had to do with Catherine de' Medici and his last hope was vain. Perhaps the most impressive of the prisoners was the Baron de Castelnau, a distinguished Protestant, who during his mock-trial compelled the Cardinal to hold a religious discussion with him. They talked long concerning the Eucharist and other matters of doctrine, until the Cardinal himself was forced to own his eloquence and the reasonableness of what he said. "Remember your brother's answer and that he approved of my beliefs," said Castelnau turning to the Duke. "I know nothing about disputations," replied Duke François, "but I fully understand the cutting off of heads." And with this grim retort Castelnau's fate was sealed. He was followed by a throng of fellow-sufferers until the death of Rénaudie, who was eventually shot in the forest, put the finishing touch to the victory of the Catholics and the destruction of the conspirators.

"Never was enterprise worse conceived, or more stupidly carried out," said Calvin. In a letter to Coligny—who had asked him to clear himself from wrong imputations—he writes that when he was consulted he had told "a certain one" what he thought of the scheme: that "it was not founded on God; that even from the worldly point of view it meant lightness and presumption; that it could not bear good fruit;

and that if one drop of blood were shed,* the rivers all over Europe would overflow therewith." The drop was shed: St. Bartholomew's Eve was the result.

Meanwhile Catherine found work to her hand. In violent crises she was resourceless, but after, as before them, her dallying power came into play. She required a man to embody her cooling policy of moderation and she found him in Michel l'Hôpital, who had long been the counsellor of Marguerite of Berri and Savoy and had followed her into Piedmont. Calm and intellectual, he was more than half a Protestant and was wholly an honest man. Catherine now recalled him to France and showed her wisdom in consulting him on spiritual affairs. He lost no time in publicly declaring his views. "Every man hath made a religion for himself," he said in his speech before the Parlement—"some for a good end, some from pure malice. Others desire that *their* religion should be accepted and the faith of the rest hunted down. The remedy we seek proceedeth from a greater source, even from the hand of God— by means of a General Council. Till that is arranged we must try to deal gently with one another, to invent a *modus vivendi*. For the diseases of the mind are not cured in the same fashion as the diseases of the body." The result of his intervention was the Edict of Romorantin, which left the handling of heretics to the clergy. This was a crafty decree not visibly of a Huguenot colour; but l'Hôpital knew full well that the hatred of the populace for the clergy would make them cautious in their doings and hold them back from persecution.

Moderation seemed the watchword at Court. The Cardinal himself suavely said that he "would give his life to bring these poor lost sheep back to the fold," and added that the King would no longer take proceedings against the Protestants who went to Prêches unarmed. And then there was a Council at Fontainebleau, held largely to discuss religious matters, at which Coligny suddenly rose and presented a petition to His Majesty to the effect that two equal Churches, the Catholic and the Protestant, might be allowed to exist side by side in the realm: "Whereat every one turned round and stared, all amazed," and the King, with lowering brows, ordered him to return to his place. "Every one" must also have been astonished at Catherine's speech to the Council. Two-thirds of her subjects, she said, were Protestants and so she could not use

---

* The italics are those of the present writer.

the sword to all of them. And she defended Coligny's brother, the Cardinal de Châtillon, against the Papal Nuncio, for imitating the English Ambassador and turning his back to the Altar at the elevation of the Host. The Nuncio complained angrily to the Cardinal, but the diplomatic prelate replied that, after all, it was only natural for a woman to speak more gently than a man. The Reformers' influence spread visibly. There were Huguenots in Languedoc and Périgord, among the students and others; while Hotman's blatant treatise, "The Tiger," directed against the Cardinal, enjoyed signal success. The only thing wanted was an active leader who would escape suspicion, and for the moment such an one was found.

Maligny, Condé's agent, a stirring, practical man, organized a plot to seize Lyons; and this time he got the approval of the Protestant Pope, Calvin, as well as of the minister, de Bèze, who was, so to speak, his Viceroy in France. But the plan was again betrayed to the Cardinal, and Condé's servant, La Sague, was arrested on a journey to Montmorency and was found to have letters upon him incriminating high persons. The Vidâme de Chartres was suddenly conveyed to the Bastille and confessed to his knowledge of a conspiracy. And the Constable, much caressed in public, was privately accused of other faults than the real one—of betraying the Lyons conspiracy, a charge very far from the truth. The rough, impulsive old soldier, suspecting it was Catherine who had slandered him, sought her out and dared to make a scene with her. She confessed to having given evidence against him and his tongue did not spare her. She undertook to rule the kingdom, so he told her, without knowing anything about it, and achieved nothing better than the maintenance of hated ministers. Catherine only answered by laughing heartily at "*le bon tour qu'elle avait joué a son compère.*" She knew that she would probably need his help when her son died, so she held her hand back from vengeance, suavely allowing him to scold her and retire in sulks from the Court.

Meanwhile the Bourbon Princes did not go unimpugned. Condé was suspected of being implicated in the plots both of Amboise and of Lyons. The King of Navarre received a royal mandate to bring his brother, who was staying with him, to the Court, then resident at Orleans, that he might clear himself from these charges. Condé refused to go. The King sent persuasive letters, he promised safe escort and a friendly reception to the brothers. "I beg of you to come and see the

THE REIGN OF FRANÇOIS II

King at once, as he wishes it so much," wrote Catherine . . . " and I assure you that he and I will do our best to make such good cheer for you that you will have no reason to be sorry for coming and for joining a company by whom you will be so dearly loved and esteemed." Jeanne d'Albret, the astute Queen of Navarre, and Princess Eléonore de Roye, the staunch wife and comrade of Condé, implored their husbands to stay at home—to pay no heed to fair speeches which were certain to prove mendacious. But Condé, that man of fiery mettle, deemed such hanging back a piece of cowardice and departed, carrying his brother with him. Navarre might have known what to expect. No welcome met them at the gates and they rode in silence to the palace. The Venetian ambassador, Michieli, relates how when the Princes arrived in the audience-chamber there were immediate signs of their disgrace. Though the King of Navarre humbled himself and, contrary to usage, knelt on one knee to François, that mock-sovereign did not move a step towards him and only made a sign that Antoine's first obeisance should have been to Catherine. As for Condé, no one greeted him or answered his addresses and the King did not take the trouble to uncover in his presence. All the great nobles were there; the Guises were lounging against the high stone window behind their niece, Mary Stuart, but neither Navarre nor Condé spoke to them. Presently the royal personages retired into Catherine's privy closet and, after a few minutes, Condé was bidden to enter there. No sooner had he done so than he was summarily arrested. Antoine de Navarre and his other brother, the Cardinal de Bourbon, begged to be appointed as his guard, but their request was met with a stern refusal. Condé was taken to the prison of Orleans and kept in the strictest confinement, beyond the reach of any intercourse; and later Catherine moved him to Amboise, already haunted by so many ambitious ghosts. " I have come back this morning from my journey to Amboise " (she wrote to a friend), " where I have been visiting a little gallant who has nothing in his brain but war and tempest. I assure you that whoever finds himself there will not get out again without leave, for the place is already strong and I have been adding to the fortifications. I have also had a good many doors and windows walled up and have had strong iron grating put to others. I don't think there is a place in the whole of France where the prince could be safer or better looked after."

The matter-of-course grimness of this seems to strike us

with worse terror than any lurid stage-effect, and as we read these dire words, once fresh from a woman's pen, we can almost hear the iron snap of fate shutting Condé into his trap. Directly after the news of his arrest had reached her, his wife, Eléonore, had tearfully parted from her children and set out for Orleans. There were hardships to endure, great difficulties to be overcome, but at last she entered the city—to find herself helpless against destiny. The Guises had so hemmed in the Prince that there was no step which she could take. She could get no letter, no message to him. In vain she appealed to Germany, to Elizabeth of England: Condé was condemned to die. The execution was to take place upon December 10—there was no time to be lost. On every side she found herself impeded by the pitiless Cardinal of Lorraine, who refused even now to allow her to see her husband; but no obstacle could dash either her faith or her courage. At last she succeeded in gaining an audience of the King. She implored him to permit her to visit Condé, if only "*pour lui donner courage*;" once more her entreaty was denied her. The Guises had got thorough hold of François and did not mean to let their perilous prey escape them, though his death meant danger to themselves. "No man has ever attacked the royal blood of France without finding himself the worse for it," wrote Renée of Ferrara to the Duke, but little was the heed that he paid her. The gods, however, were against them and shifted the scene. For, as we shall see later, the death of the King, four days before the date appointed for Condé's punishment, put an end to the scheme against him.

But this is to anticipate matters. In the meantime, Catherine was busy making friends with the children of unrighteousness. Despite her treachery to Condé, she won over his brother of Navarre and effected some sort of reconciliation between him and the Holy See. Her reason was not far to seek. The King was growing daily more sickly; the chance of her Regency came nearer; and as the Guises, she knew, would never allow her rule, she must have adequate support and she could only get it from Antoine. But as long as Condé with his dangerous influence was at large she could not be certain of her man, and it was to ensure Antoine that she allowed the younger Prince's confinement. While he was safe at Amboise it was easy to bribe his elder; to call him "*mon frère*;" to take his arm and walk up and down the "Salle d'Etat" with him, absorbed in agreeable conversation; to make him pledge himself to her when

THE REIGN OF FRANÇOIS II

the hour came for her to become Regent. She went so far as to patch up a peace between him and the Guises, with whom she continued to keep well, according to her provident custom. As for Condé's arrest, she laid it at the door of the poor little King whose every word and gesture were the result of her dictation; and while she was indulging in these professions, the Prince from the depths of his prison was making futile efforts to get a fair hearing and to defend himself before the world in a court of law. In vain did he kick against the pricks; the impenetrable walls remained.

The Guises, with an eye to business, saw that Navarre was gaining favour. Knowing their woman, they did not then try to influence her; but they had a niece on the throne and through Mary Stuart they could get the ear of the King. The Cardinal induced François to fall in with an elaborate plot. He was to summon Navarre to come unattended to his apartments where only the Guises and the Maréchal de Saint-André would attend him; he was next to reproach Antoine with the disturbed state of the country and then, as if in a sudden fit of rage, was to strike him with a dagger, on which the attendant trio would come forth and do the rest. Catherine heard of this scheme and, diplomat that she was, entreated her son to desist. She went farther and begged her confidante, the Duchesse de Montpensier, to warn Antoine not to respond to His Majesty's next invitation. He obeyed her injunctions and refused the royal mandate, but when the first was followed by a second one his courage was touched and he felt he could no longer keep away. He certainly knew what he was facing; for he called his favourite valet-de-chambre and made him vow that if his master were murdered he would straightway carry his shirt, with the bloodstains upon it, to his wife, the Queen of Navarre. Then he went to seek the King. When he entered the room, the Cardinal shut the door carefully behind him. François was standing behind the table in a loose robe, with a dagger in his girdle. Navarre, prepared for danger, behaved with such humility that the King could open no dispute with him. François' heart failed him at this eleventh hour and he allowed Navarre to leave his presence unharmed. "*Voilà le plus poltron cœur qui fut jamais,*" the angry Cardinal was heard to ejaculate, but he ejaculated in vain. He was not strong enough to weigh against Catherine in her son's counsels. It was she herself who told his wife, Jeanne d'Albret, the story of how she thus saved Antoine's life, and it was Jeanne who published the episode in a manifesto of 1568.

What might have happened later history does not tell, for the King's fatal illness at that moment changed the face of affairs. The doctor's prophecy was fulfilled rather sooner than they expected and it speedily became evident that His Majesty could not recover. The Guises were distraught with fear. No tyranny of theirs could do away with the fact that the Bourbon Princes were, after the royal children, nearest to the Crown and that any popular rising, such as happens when things are unsettled, would probably put one of them on the throne. In this strait, the Guises tried to persuade Catherine that her own security demanded the assassination of the Bourbons, but her good sense, supported by Michel de l'Hôpital, was against the plotters. She knew too well how profoundly they were hated and how she would inevitably become identified with them; so she got rid of them with bland prevarications and summoned Antoine de Navarre to her presence. He found the Queen-Mother alone with Madame de Montpensier and in tears. She dilated on her situation, dwelt on the youth of her nine-year old son, Charles, the next heir to the throne, and entreated her Bourbon cousin to renounce his claims to the Regency in her favour. If he did so, he should be Lieutenant-General and all edicts should be published in their joint names. If he did not, she would certainly join the side of the Guises. Antoine, warned by Madame de Montpensier that non-compliance meant his death and that of his brother, weakly did as he was bidden and so gave a blow, not only to his dignity, but to the cause of Protestantism in France. Catherine, well pleased with the effect of her tears, now re-called Montmorency. She plied the Guises with bitter honey and told Spain that "for the sake of religion" it was essential that a woman should be Regent; she kept her irons ready in the fire and, with every faculty alert, awaited the death of her son.

She only had a few days in which to exercise patience; François II died unloved and unhated on December 6, 1560. The Cardinal was by his bedside, overshadowing him to the end. He had never let him alone, nor did he do so at this solemn hour. In the tone that had ever been obeyed he dictated the boy's last prayer to him. It was a strange one : " Lord ! pardon my sins, and impute not to me, thy servant, the sin committed by my Ministers under my name and authority." The words are the only suggestion we have that the Cardinal possessed a conscience.

CHAPTER VI

The Princesse de Condé

AUTHORITIES CONSULTED

Memoirs du Prince de Condé.
Eléonore de Roye—*Le Comte Delaborde.*
Sur le Règne de François II—*Régnier de la Planche.*
Histoire de l'Eglise Réformée—*Théodore de Bèze.*
Femmes Illustres—*Brantôme.*

CHAPTER VI

The Princesse de Condé

THE Queen-Mother did not hesitate to show the colours she had chosen. She wrote to Pope Pius IV and urged him to remove from the churches the images of the Virgin and the Saints, nor did she scruple to make the heretical demand that the Communion should be administered in both kinds to the laity. The Spanish envoy, Chantonnay, was horrified. "We always have a Prêche going on in the apartments of some lord or lady of the Court, whatever hue and cry I make. The upshot of my inquiries is that no one knows anything of the matter, but that enquiry shall be made."

Catherine took little heed of Chantonnay, who caused her to rue the fact afterwards; and when the Third Estate presented her with remonstrances concerning the low morals of the clergy, she pledged herself to allow full toleration to the Reformed faith throughout France, and even declared that the King and the Princes should be brought up as Huguenots.

Meanwhile, as she had openly allied herself with her so-called convert, Antoine de Navarre, there was no longer any reason for his brother's imprisonment.

Condé had already experienced a moment of relief; he had learned the death of François II through the ingenuity of an attendant, who, while the prince was at table, made vain efforts to signal the news and then had the happy thought of dropping something by the prisoner's chair. He whispered his tidings as he stooped to pick it up from the ground, and his words set the Prince's pulses beating to a quicker tune. Soon after, his liberty was offered to him, but he refused to accept it until his honour had been publicly vindicated. As this request was only answered by half-measures, he chose to remain where he was—a high-souled decision, in which his wife unflinchingly supported him. In consideration of his failing health, however, she persuaded him to exchange his rigorous prison for less severe confinement at Ham, where she was allowed to be with him. His sojourn here was not a long one. For before much time had elapsed, his wish was fulfilled: his honour was cleared in a way that satisfied his demands and, free from any stain upon it, he was restored to his former position.

The fresh air must have tasted sweet to him and so did the sight of his little family. There is a touching contemporary account of his first meeting with them. "After '*l'action de grâce*,' they brought him his children, Monsieur the Marquis François, and Monsieur and Mademoiselle. "Mademoiselle was put upon his bed and Messieurs, his two sons, remained standing by him. . . . Suddenly they began to cry so bitterly that neither their father nor the people present could restrain their own tears. . . . And you ought to have seen the little Mademoiselle, who is a living picture of beauty, clinging round the neck of Monsieur her father and drowning his face and beard with the brooklets from her eyes, without being able to speak, excepting in broken half-words. Monsieur her father tried so hard that at last he soothed her."

This tender picture creates a desire to know more of the Condé household—of the homes of the other great Protestants. Elsewhere in France family affection seems to have died out, but in these homes it was still to be found fresh and living, and it was they that produced the spiritual flower of the country. This, however, only applies to the Huguenot aristocracy. For, as in all great revolutions, the people who made this religious movement fall under two distinct divisions—those that led and those that followed—the cultivated nobles and the people. And the results were much the same as in the French Revolution. There were the Saint-Justs—men of noble theories, blameless lives and stern ideals which made cruelty seem better than corruption: Old Testament men, like Coligny, ardent patriots, who aimed at an elaborately organised religious Republic and dreamed of a Puritan France. There were the Dantons, fierce implacable idealists; or the Robespierres of thought, the absolutists—like Calvin, and some of his subordinates—persons of unflinching logic who forgot that human nature was illogical. There were, as we have seen, the Girondins, or folk of academic mind; and (to close with) the adventurers, the men of action, the poets, the heroes of romance who plunge into any great current because it carries them with it, giving them the chance of fresh experience and of espousing the cause of the advance-guard. Such men depend more upon persons than ideas, and their motive is often vanity, of however high a strain. They are, as it were, the spoilt children—sometimes the *enfants terribles*—of a great movement, glorifying and frequently damning it. To this category belonged the Prince de Condé, and the glamour that surrounded him gave him great power with the crowd.

For below the leaders come the People, a section which admits of few fine lights and shades, but nevertheless has its differences. For it includes the skilled artizans, thinkers in their own rough way, sometimes mystics, like the weavers of Meaux, seeking in a spiritual Utopia compensation for the hardships of their lives: patient creatures under daily toil, but uneducated and uncontrolled, with passions easily roused and hard to extinguish. It includes also the unskilled workmen and the idlers—the unthinking impressionable rabble who are always on the look out for excitement and " see red " on the slightest pretext. This is the element in a nation that is equally likely to create a Reign of Terror or a big religious revival; for emotion is a primal and perilous force and, like the genius that Sindbad let loose, is not easily lured back to its box again. That the French are an emotional people, providing emotional leaders for an emotional mob, may have helped their artistic glory; but it has ruined their political power, perhaps their religious power also. It is the calm leaders who dominate and produce a lasting effect, and it would seem that, apart from Coligny, there was no forcible man to inspire the troops of the Huguenots.

But if there were not men, there were women. One remarkable fact distinguishes the Reformation in France from the Reformation in other countries: that, always excepting for the Admiral, its most effectual and distinguished chiefs were great ladies. Margaret of Angoulême, the initiator of the movement, was the first of a feminine dynasty. The precedent that she had set up was followed by her daughter Jeanne. For while the King of Navarre was nicknamed " l'Echangeur," and shifted his position like a weathercock, his Queen organized the Huguenot forces and presented a front of adamant. And if Condé, who " had the woman in him," was the victim of his own gallant vanity, his princess filled up his deficiencies. She knew how to assert her cause, effecting more things by her being than most people by their doing. What her power might have been, had she lived, it is not easy to conjecture, for when she was twenty-eight death ended her career; but even so, she was the soul—the exquisite flower—of the stern Huguenot party; tenderer and less ambitious than Jeanne d'Albret; a saint and yet a Stoic too. Jeanne, on the contrary, had nothing of the saint and everything of the ruler about her. She was a born general, more so, perhaps, than Coligny; as weighty as he was, and untiring in her cause as only a woman knows how to be. She was capable, too, of rising to any military demands, as her conduct during the siege of La Rochelle showed in subsequent years. Nor was she the only lady of ambition. As active as she, though not so great, was Louis XII's daughter, Renée, Duchess of Ferrara, who after the Duke's death left Italy for her native France and became there, as at Ferrara, the centre of religious intrigue, the politician of her sect, with a hundred wires to pull. And these women were no creatures of impulse; they had a consistent policy which they steadily pursued. To the affairs of the Reformation they brought the vitality of the Renaissance; nothing came amiss to them and there was nothing they did not venture. If we read the diaries of the day and follow the imprisonments for heresy, we shall find that it was oftenest the women of noble birth who were arrested at heretical services for listening to Huguenot preachers. These were the heroines of their cause, and the weaker sisters of their faith were naturally more numerous. It is surprising how many Court ladies who did not commit themselves openly were yet inclined to Protestant ideas, some of them Catherine's greatest friends: Jacqueline de Longwy, Duchesse de Montpensier, the Duchesse de La Rochefoucauld, the Princesse de Poitien; and others with less repute and more or less conviction.

Of all these Eléonore de Roye was the most winning, perhaps the most human; and if we want to get an idea of a well-born Huguenot lady, we cannot do better than sketch, however roughly, some outline of her and her household; even though in completing it we are bound to anticipate events and overstep the limits of strict chronology.

The grandmother of Eléonore de Roye was Louise de Montmorency, the sister of the Constable, and the wife of Monsieur de Châtillon. She belonged to the early days of the "New Opinions," the first days of Margaret of Angoûleme, when the main innovation brought by the religious movement meant no more than private study of the Bible, and Scriptural discussions with a minister—long before doctrinal heresies had come to be prominent matters. Already in her youth this primitive Protestantism attracted Louise de Montmorency, and in this faith she brought up her family—her daughter and her three splendid sons: Gaspard the Admiral, Odet the Cardinal, and d'Andelot, the soldier and the Puritan. Their simple, even stern education in the grim feudal castle, the Bible-readings with their mother, her uncompromising ideals of conduct, were no bad training for young and impulsive beings, and perhaps France never produced a finer race than these Châtillons. For their Puritanism only restrained, it did not blunt, their feelings. No stronger proof of this could be had than a letter of Coligny's to his wife, written in later years, after the loss of a child. It was sent from camp, in sight of the enemy's army.

"Although thou art right" (it ran) "to bear with sorrow the loss of our dearest son, yet am I constrained to remind thee that he belonged more to God than to us. And sith that it hath pleased Him to withdraw him to Himself, it is for thee and for me to obey His holy Will. True it is that he was already a lover of good and that we could expect great contentment from a son of so fine a strain. But remember, my well-beloved, that none can live without offending God, and that he is very happy to have died at an age when he was still free from all sin."

The sister of the man who wrote this made a good wife to M. de Roye and a good mother to her children; and we can well imagine what a hero the Admiral must have been to the little Eléonore and her sister, later Duchesse de La Rochefoucauld. They were brought up in much the same way as their mother had been before them, with perhaps something more of sweetness—a sober sweetness—in their training. But they had few pleasures; spiritual privileges were substituted for them in their young and serious lives. Grave ministers gave them pious instruction, and their mother's tenderness and the gaiety of Nature were the only indulgences they knew. Such an existence kept them fresh. Sincerity was their watchword, or rather the atmosphere they breathed; and a kind of limpid sincerity was always Eléonore's distinction. It was small wonder that she fell in love with the frank and generous Condé, whose very weaknesses were just such as needed her strength. For a long time her love, intense and faithful to the end, was equally returned by him, and, in spite of later infidelities, he always returned to her side and relied on her constant friendship. But the days that are good to read of are the early days of their marriage, before Isabelle de Limeuil and Madame de St. André had appeared to destroy illusions. Condé, the man of Courts, must have enjoyed teaching the ways of the world to this most unworldly princess. He was gay, too, and he was gallant, an adept at making love, and he taught his sober bride how to laugh.

As we read contemporary accounts of him, the man rises vividly before us : a creature of quick sympathies, something of a chameleon, with the very qualities that first fascinate and then prove a man's ruin. He was, indeed, a mixture of Cavalier and Puritan, of gravity and sparkle, such as only France could produce. Vivid rather than deep, he had none of the fanatic and something of the knight-errant about him. Like his brother, he wanted ballast, but in him a certain mettle often took the place of stability. And whatever else he may have been, he was a born intriguer. No matter what time he had lived in, he would have found some mission to flash his sword in. Not long after his marriage, the Château de Condé became the harbour of frequent guests—strange guests of different nationalities, from Switzerland and Germany—men who rode up booted to the gate, in travelling raiment and with an air of business. There were noblemen and soldiers, some dust-stained, some richly clad, the bearers of letters in cypher, or of news that could only be spoken—the men of the Amboise plot, the conspirators of Lyons, all alike entertained by the Prince and his gracious wife. Coligny came here too, so did the Princess's other uncles, d'Andelot and the Cardinal de Châtillon, and each of them looked upon Eléonore as his and as her husband's best friend. The castle walls must have listened to not a few sallies about the Guises from the ready lips of Condé ; not a few expressions of hatred for the Cardinal of Lorraine, or earnest declarations against him made by the vigilant Admiral ; and there must have been many discussions, now sanguine and now contemptuous, about the course of the Constable, the erratic Great-Uncle Montmorency ; many doubts as to whom he would finally serve, whether God or Mammon ; many oaths sworn to be kept, and some also to be broken. And with this brave soldierly company there mingled the black-robed figures of the ministers whom Eléonore loved to have about her—stern almost to harshness, conferring, reproving, exhorting. Theodore de Bèze, their chief in France, must have stayed here ; Perussel was one of her chaplains, Chandieu, Cappel, Bernadin, were among her friends, and so on, through names now unknown. They must have brought letters from their Pope, Calvin—those awful letters which every heretical lady of quality seems to have received from the uncompromising logician and indefatigably disagreeable correspondent. It is surprising how women like Marguerite of Angoûlême and Jeanne of Navarre and Renée of Ferrara were cowed by him—how they allowed him to interfere with their household arrangements, to spy upon their servants and dominate their existence. Perhaps it is one more proof of the unpalatable fact that a bully (and Calvin was one, both by nature and by principle) fascinates and rules the hearts of women, especially unconquerable women, such as Jeanne and the Duchess Renée. On the gentler Princess Eléonore de Condé he did not produce this effect, but it would have been hard, even for Calvin, to have found cause to disapprove of her.

It was a strange home, this, for children; for the three boys and the girl who by-and-bye appeared sedately amid this motley circle of guests. Perhaps, when they were alone, they played at being conspirators, and they must have woven romances round the goers-out and comers-in. The soldiers caressed them, the solemn ministers taught them, and it is not difficult to conjecture which they loved the best.

Their education was rather severe. A lady of the household describes it in a letter to "*une sienne amie, dame étrangère*": "In the morning the 'Proverbs' of Solomon and after dinner the 'Commentaries' of Julius Cæsar; from which Monsieur the Marquis, the eldest of them, has reaped such fine fruit that he is the best informed boy for his age you could see." These lessons, which belonged to nursery days, were softened to them by their mother's love and their mother's teaching. "The mother"—says one who knew them—"was very intimate with her girl. And they held divine discourse together concerning the greatness of God, His wisdom, kindness and pity; concerning the hell made by the consciences of them that did not fear Him; or they talked on the difference between pure and false service, on the certainty of faithful souls when death approached them, and the like high themes." . . . "I should be puzzled" (concludes the witness) "to say the which spoke the best."

But her first-born son, Henri, was the closest to her. "An especial bond united them." The boy was loving and impressionable, serious and very intelligent. "He had never left her; had shared her trials, had prayed and thought and felt with her, and had plighted her his boundless reverence and love." From the age of twelve he had become her best friend. For from that time onwards, his father's aberrations and infidelities made her need a steady arm to lean on. Her last words to him on her deathbed sum up their relation to one another. "Love thy two brothers and thy sister," she said, "not as a brother, but as the father thou must now be to them, since thou art the eldest and no longer a child. Talk as often as thou canst with the ministers, Perussel and d'Epine, for the good of thy soul, and believe the counsels of the gentlemen of the robe whom thou knowest that thy father and I have loved and esteemed. . . . Be a lover of the public weal, and gain it by all the just means thou canst use without offence to thy conscience. . . . As for thy Book of Solomon, never let it out of thine hands. . . . Make thy mouth the home of truth, keep thine hand open to the poor and thine house shut to flatterers. If thou dost all this, my darling, thou wilt have, like Abraham, Isaac and Jacob, the blessing of God and mine also."

The sorrowful moment for these precious counsels was happily as yet some years distant, and no foreboding of it had overshadowed Eléonore's home. Here she lived in the utmost simplicity, renouncing luxury and "keeping her hand open for the poor." Much of her property she sold on behalf of Protestantism, giving estates to the ministers as places in which to hold public services, for services were only allowed in certain districts outside towns. Private services were held in the apartments of private people and before persecution began, these "Prêches" became the fashion. Catherine set the mode of attending them, and all the grand world, even the Cardinal de Lorraine (who did it for a bet), might be found on one or other occasion crowding some palace salon to hear the preacher then in vogue.

The Condés' rooms in Paris made one of the chief centres for these "worldly-holy" functions—we had almost said entertainments—though to Eléonore and a few others they meant solemn homage to God. They took place in the Palais de Condé, when the Prince, his wife and their household were in attendance on the Court. The Princess probably dreaded Paris, for there the Guises were ever on the watch to trap her. At one time she was nearly arrested for eating meat in Lent, at another, her carriage was shot at as she was driving through the city gates.

These were Condé's best days. "At present" (he writes to a minister) "I experience and feel to the quick the presence of God's grace in me—so much do I feel it that I grow more intent on losing my life and on spilling my blood to advance the honour of God." Coligny was his hero and his chief, and the great man drew out the best in the lesser man's nature. Had he remained under him, nor sought independent adventure, his malleable temperament might have kept Coligny's impress. "I declare," said the Prince (and he meant the Guises to hear it) "that if there should be any who undertake to address themselves to Monsieur the Admiral by word or deed, or by any means but those of justice, I will make them understand that I shall resent it as much as if they attacked my own person—I being his friend . . . and he a great knight sorely needed for the service of the King." Thus the fiery Condé, whom none can help loving. It is hardly a surprise to hear that he was small: thin and sharp he must certainly have been, like a sword always out of its scabbard. His wife's power over him lay in restraint; indeed her whole power with his party was that of the moderator—a power by no means of the weakest. For she had the enthusiasm which sympathised, although she was not a born fighter, but by nature a lover of concord. It is thus that she reveals herself in a letter to Catherine de' Medici. "Besides the fact that my business as a woman is not at all with arms" (she says), "my temperament is so much inclined towards peace that I should think the end of my life happy if I could have helped to bring about in France those things which are most requisite and necessary, and hardest, apparently, to accomplish. . . . But when they are begun and the end is at least expected, then it is that the great God permitteth that they should be promptly executed."

In this Eléonore de Condé was uncommon—that her gift for tempering men's minds never weakened her convictions and she was as firm as if she had been a fanatic. At a moment when the Queen-Mother was incensed against the Huguenots, Eléonore took an opportunity to deplore their fate in her presence, and boldly reminded her that "the strange destiny which had struck down" Henri II, had overtaken him at a moment when he was planning fresh persecutions. "What!" cried the outraged Regent—"Every one says that there is no such hateful race as these Huguenots." "It is easy enough" (replied the Princess) "to impute anything in the world to us since we have no one to defend us; but if Her Highness knew us better, us and our cause, she would surely judge us very differently." Here again, in her answer, there steps forth the woman of quick tact as well as the upholder of a principle. It was one of the most interesting things about her that she was always a practical Frenchwoman, full of keen insight and swift resource. She stood by the plotters through every vicissitude as their counsellor and their comrade. In the justice of God she trusted implicitly, but she also believed in the use of worldly wisdom. If her husband had listened to her, he would never have gone to Orleans with Navarre to fall into the trap the Guises had laid for them; would not have languished in prison and wasted the time and strength that might have been serving his cause. Well would it have been for him, too, had he listened to her in other ways, but he would not. It seems the law of noble natures like hers that they should be tested by adversity. The three years from 1561 to 1564 brought only pain and grief. Condé's need for excitement would have anyhow landed him in some place below his own level—some place of degeneration; but it was the Guises who decided where it was to be.

Isabelle de Limeuil, the merry Circe who bewitched him for more than two years, was the tool of the Cardinals and also, it must be said, of Catherine. A free-lance in the Regent's "Flying Squadron," she was deliberately told off to separate Condé from his Huguenot wife and make him join the Catholic party. For the rest, she was a gay Pagan lady, and "*fort grande parleuse. . . . Jamais le bec ne lui cessa*," even in her last illness. Nor is she unknown to romance, for it was she of whom it is recorded that she had a death "*joyeuse et plaisante.*" She called her page Julien to her—"a sweet player of instruments"—and "bade him play 'The Defeat of the Swiss' till he came to the words 'All is lost.' . . . 'Play that phrase four or five times over,' she said, 'as piteously as possible.' . . . He did so, and when he came to 'All is lost' she said the words twice—and turning to the other side of the bed: 'All is lost with that chord,' quoth she, and thus she died." In these days death was yet afar and she carried everything before her. The task set her of gaining Condé could not have been an unwelcome one, but the final separation between husband and wife she could not, with all her wiles, effect. The Prince depended too much upon his wife's sympathy; she had struck too deep roots in his life. But he sank very low. Although he knew that Isabelle was acting as a kind of secret police, he did not scruple to write her letters " in which he threw restraint to the winds and trampled on all his duties as a husband." And bad became worse. Tiring of her laughter, he turned a kind of Quixote in love and became the fervent champion of the Maréchale de Saint-André, the mischievous widow of the Guises' ally, a lady of boundless ambition and boundless wealth. She, in her turn, became infatuated by Condé, and wished to renounce her fortune and give it to him and to his children. He stooped as far as to accept from her the Château de Valléry, besides other properties, and the connection threatened to be as dangerous as the last.

Calvin and Bèze wrote him letters of exhortation. Calvin could be a casuist at moments—when he feared to lose a great prince—or could at least shut his eyes to what he did not care to see. "We do not believe"—he wrote—"that any evil is going on directly offensive to God, but when we hear that you make love to ladies, we feel that it must greatly derogate from your authority and reputation. Good people will be offended by you and malicious folk will make you their laughing stock." This last thrust again shows the writer's cleverness. Not in vain had he taken refuge in Courts. He was man of the world enough to know that the one thing which might sway Condé was his dread of ridicule. But the Reformer's efforts were in vain, and Condé remained ensnared until sorrow intervened and took the scales from his eyes.

Throughout all this bitter ordeal Eléonore had never failed him. She had answered the claims of friendship with innate dignity. Her troubles were talked about by everybody but herself, and she allowed for her erratic husband's nature with all a mother's faithful patience. "God proves you now by a fresh kind of trial which is by no means new to you, for it is not the first sorrow you have suffered, and you have had heavy griefs—enough to shake the strongest men in the world," so wrote a minister in evident allusion to the Prince's conduct. And at last even her firm spirit broke, or rather it wore out her body, and that last sad illness began which brought her husband back to her side.

"So here I am" (she wrote, while still in health, to a cousin), "always on the alert, and listening to hear what it may please

God to send me." A month later she came down from her room with a radiant face. A voice had told her in a dream that death was very near, that she must prepare for it; and ever since she heard it, she "had longed for that holy separation." Straight upon this there began the terrible malady that killed her. Yet, far from being a fatalist, she did all she could to save her life. "It is not for us to desert this garrison without the leave of our Captain," so she once said, and, though she knew it was useless, she took all her food obediently. "Whatever her anguish," wrote one of her ladies, "I always saw her with dry eyes, without cries, without tears and without complaints, such as even the most courageous indulge in." Perussel, her Huguenot director, watched and prayed by her bedside, strengthening her with sober consolations. "Thou hast reached"—he said—"about the half of a mortal's age . . . oughtest not thou to thank God and bless Him in that He desireth to excuse thee the sweat of thy labour for the rest of the day, and give thee the wage thou wouldst have earned hadst thou toiled the whole day long?" Her soul, even then, ruled her body. A few days before the end, she could not find ease in either of the two beds in which she was put in turn to see if the change would bring her relief. "Almighty Lord!" she prayed, "since in all the places of this earthly manor-house, great and spacious though it be and the work of Thy hands, I cannot find with my utmost diligence one little spot of comfort . . . I quit this hired tenement . . . to return to Thee, whose arms I see outstretched towards me."

Condé had come back to her, never to leave her again. But he was such a convinced adversary of gloom that he shut his eyes to the truth. Even at this solemn time of trial his need for distraction came uppermost. "My Nephew" (runs one of his letters)—"My great wish to get news of you prompts me to write this note and at the same time to entreat that, if you can manage it, you will come to see and console your good friend and relation. Come with your setters, also with your horses and your arms, if that be possible, and I will promise to show you as fine a hunting-course here as you could know how to find. My horses and arms will arrive to-day, and I hope that if you come we shall find ways, God willing, to enjoy ourselves."

The last five words are characteristic of the man and his creed: of his inability to win heaven and his inability to give up earth. Eléonore, who knew too well his quick, susceptible character, was tender to it to the last. "Fearing to move her husband too much if she herself told him that she felt the end coming . . . she charged two intimate friends to go and seek Condé and to beg him to let her entrust him with her last wishes in an authentic form. "Tell the Prince,"—she said—"that since God is pleased so soon to separate our bodies, I have but one aspiration—that our spirits may continue to be bounden inseparably together. . . . Tell him also that (to begin my last Will) I constitute him the universal heir to the mass of love that I have vowed to my children, and that I conjure him to hold vigil in my place—henceforth both for himself and for me—so that they may be brought up in the fear of God, the which I know is the surest patrimony that I can bequeathe to them." The Prince, returning to her bedside, rose to the occasion: "God who joined us now divides us," he said—"Blessed will be the moment when He commands us to meet again in a place of eternity." He "spoke many loving things to her," and she, losing no time, "with a wonderful force and clearness" continued to exhort and encourage him in words fraught with a solemn dignity which must have lifted him to her, which lifts us even as we read them. When he had withdrawn, she bade farewell to her children. With her eldest boy she spoke apart, begging him, as we know, to act as a father to the younger ones, nor did she in any way advise him to refer to Condé. The place that she assigned her husband in the counsels of their son is also sadly significant. For she bade the boy serve the King, trust his relations, honour the Queen of Navarre, the Cardinal de Bourbon, his father, his grandmother, and his other uncles, Messieurs de Châtillon and de La Rochefoucauld, all of them Godfearing folk." And then in the sacred hush which followed her voice, she blessed the weeping little prince: "I give thee my benediction," she said, "and with it this diamond ring, which I pray thee keep for the love of me and in remembrance of my words."

The darkness fell, and at midnight she asked for her husband. "I am sure"—she said—"the Prince will not mind being awoken for this occasion, and it would not be well to wait till I could no longer declare to him the things that God has put in my heart." After he had come, there passed between them those moments from which none may raise the veil. Then she lifted her voice in prayer. "O God, my winter is past, and my spring is come.

Open to me the gate of Thy heavenly garden that I may enjoy the fruit of Thy eternal sweetness."

When the end came, she was alone with two of her ministers; Condé had withdrawn, unable to bear more. It was one of these ministers, Labrossière, who went to tell him of her death. When he entered Condé's room the Prince knew well what had happened; none the less he continued for a while to read in a prayer-book which he held in his hand, then turning his face to the minister, he asked him how his wife was now. "My lord," replied Labrossière, " she is with God, where you will one day be also."

Condé's grief was acute, and remorse lent it a fresh sting. Nothing perhaps about him touches one so much as his words to his little girl—his wife's last bequest to him—directly after Eléonore's death. "Try, my darling," he said, "to be like her, so that God may help you as He helped her . . . and that I may love you more and more, as I surely shall do if you are as she was." . . . "Girls" (he added) "are usually like their fathers, but you must try to vie with your mother's goodness. For you will be told things about your father and his life that you must not imitate, though there are other things in him you may follow; but in your mother . . . you will find nothing that should not serve as your dearly treasured ideal." His grief, for the moment, exalted him; it relieved him to express it in verse, and though there is no kind of literary worth in the lines he wrote, their impetuous sincerity, the feeling of ' too late ' that inspired them, turns them into poetry of the heart—

> C'est moi, Segneur, elle n'a fait la faute,
> Et c'est raison que la peine me suive.
> Non, je fais tort à ta prudence haute !
> À vrai parler, mort je reste, elle est vive.

Eléonore de Roye belonged to a race of saintly women who seem indigenous to France—of women who unite Evangelical fervour with Roman Catholic unction. Intense, yet full of amenity, they were *grandes dames* without being worldly and looked upon good manners as a natural part of holiness. They belonged to no time and no religion, but were now of this creed, now of that, according as one or the other embodied the most living faith; and in the time of the Condés, the Protestant religion meant the keenest spiritual life and produced the saints of that day. But the Noailles, the Liancourts, the Montagus, the Lafayettes, the Duras, the La Rochefoucaulds, those Roman Catholic martyrs of the French Revolution, belonged to the same tribe; so, in the seventeenth century, did the ladies of Port Royal; and so, in later days, did the ultramontane Ferronays and the pious Eugénie de Guérin. They represent the fine flower of sanctity and a courtesy of soul that has never been surpassed.

Nor, indeed, has it ever been changed. For not the least remarkable quality of this dynasty—their strength and their limitation—is their incapability of modification. In whatever time they lived they have been entirely unaffected by surrounding conditions, and if they could all have been gathered together, there would be no real barrier to divide them. As far as Eléonore de Roye was concerned, the Renaissance might never have existed. Yet the world about her was full of it: it was the constant topic, the mainspring, of the society at Court in which she herself had to move when in Paris. But for her the classics still slumbered; art was but the servant of a corrupt Church; learning an unimportant, often perilous, accessory of existence; and joy in life—the manifold life of mind and senses—a condition alien to her; or, if she realized it at all, it was as a temptation. Such beliefs were always common among Puritans, but she was unlike the Puritans in this, that she did not condemn others. She had too gifted a nature to be a Pharisee, and her goodness was so instinctive that she neither knew nor needed shibboleths. It would have been well for the Huguenots could her delicate spirit have guided them.

CHAPTER VII
Jeanne de Navarre

AUTHORITIES CONSULTED

Lettres d'Antoine de Bourbon et de Jeanne d'Albret.
Jeanne d'Albret—*Miss Freer*.
Lettre de Renée de Ferrare à Jean Calvin—*Archives Curieuses*.
Introductions to "Lettres de Catherine de' Medici"—*Le Comte de la Ferrière*.

CHAPTER VII

Jeanne de Navarre

IF France is distinguished for its women saints, the same may be said for its religious politicians—the dealers in " celestial politics," as Lowell once called them. They began with the Abbesses of old ; repentant ladies swelled their numbers ; Catholics, Calvinists, Frondists carried on the race through the centuries. The Protestant, Jeanne de Navarre, the Catholic Madame de Maintenon, are of the same blood spiritually, if not of the same creed. The fact is that the true Frenchwoman is essentially practical and positive, and politics, in whatever form, represent the most practical of sciences. This was as true in the sixteenth century as it is now, but in those days religion provided women with their only opportunity for statescraft. And the Protestant religion, whose votaries were in the minority, whose codes were still forming, whose tenets were still fought and plotted for, presented a fine area for feminine politicians. It could boast of many, but of none so much as of Jeanne of Navarre and of Renée of Ferrara. Jeanne was by far the most eminent of the two. Renée, though as active as she, was active in smaller ways. Unlike the Queen of Navarre, she had no large conceptions, and was little more than a conscientious intriguer. Jeanne, on the other hand, was a stateswoman, with a strong and unswerving policy and, had she lived in a later century, would have found scope in a secular field. Her family traditions, however, and her naturally austere temperament made her the fitter to devote her energies to Protestantism.

This kind of religion was quite compatible with the love of art and knowledge, and beneath the large roof of Jeanne de Navarre the Renaissance and the Reformation lived comfortably together. Less could hardly have been expected from the daughter of Marguerite of Angoulême—the Princess who had made it her mission to reconcile the " New Opinions " with the " New Learning " and to help both to flourish in an atmosphere of suavity. Jeanne did not care about suavity —in her girlhood it had irritated her as much as her mother's dreamy mysticism. For Jeanne hated vagueness; but she loved convictions and she loved the classics, and welcomed every definite attempt at scholarship. She was something of a royal bluestocking and nothing at all of a poet; and though as a sixteenth century Minerva she was bound in honour to write verses, they took the form of abnormally dull "Epistles," devoid of literary taste. And yet she delighted in Latin poets and Greek philosophers, for she herself was no mean scholar and no mean student of philosophy.

But intellectual though she was, it was character which most distinguished her and made her dominate her surroundings. A strong, clear will and a need of power, a vehement temper, the faculty of concentration—these were her endowments and had been since she was a baby. The Queen Jeanne was just the same person as the Jeanne who had spent her wayward childhood between her parents and her uncle, King François; the Jeanne who had almost ruined her mother by her extravagant love of masques and plays; who, in a naughty fit, had cut off the heads of the Saints from the tapestry in Marguerite's embroidery-frame and replaced them by the heads of foxes—a feat which may be said to show more of the Renaissance than of sanctity; the Jeanne, finally, who, at twelve, had summoned the Cardinals and prelates of Paris to the Cathedral and there formally refused the Duc de Clèves, the bridegroom her uncle had chosen for her—that omnipotent uncle whose will none but she dared resist. She knew her mind as clearly, she acted with as prompt decision, as she did in after days; and although she was whipped by her governess every day to make her submit, she bore the penalty with the same courage that later she spent upon her cause. It was not the first time that a like chastisement had been administered to her. "Well do I remember," she wrote in later years, "that long previously, the King, Monsieur my most honoured father and lord, hearing that the Queen (Marguerite d'Angoulême) was engaged in prayer in her own apartments, with the ministers, Roussel and Farel, entered and dealt her a blow on the right cheek—the ministers having contrived to escape in great perturbation—while he soundly chastised me with a rod, forbidding me to concern myself with matters of doctrine; the which treatment cost me many bitter tears, and held me in dread until his death"—the only

RENÉE DE FRANCE, DUCHESS OF FERRARA.
BY JEAN CLOUET. CHÂTEAU DE CHANTILLY.
From a photograph by A. Giraudon.

JEANNE DE NAVARRE

instance of fear which exists in the chronicles of Jeanne d'Albret. Had the princess been beaten black and blue, she would still have been the leader of the Protestants in France, all the more so because of opposition. The discipline, however, was not without its merits. Hard times produce hard characters, but they also create Stoics, and perhaps Jeanne's power of endurance would not have been the same without these buffetings and beatings.

Her father's despotism, her mother's Protestant training had thus established her vocation. But though she was the heir of her mother's creed, she was not, as we have said, the heir of her mother's ideas. Marguerite could never have been a leader—she was too literary, too amiable, too imaginative; she saw all sides and aimed at reconciling them. Jeanne, on the other hand, saw one thing clearly and made for it without any subtleties. Practical, fiery and masterful, she was born to carry out ideas, not to originate them. Of atmosphere she had little, of force she had a store, and the cause of the Reformation, then synonymous with that of liberty, was ready to her hand. And it was as the cause of liberty, not as the cause of religion, that the movement really appealed to her, however sincerely she believed that her motives were spiritual. This is important to remember because it is the key to her character. For she had not the religious temperament—was, indeed, a sceptic by nature, and a born free-lance. Had she lived in our own day, she would have been an advanced freethinker, probably a woman of science.

The same holds true of her elder comrade-at-arms, her admirer, Renée of Ferrara, who formulated her views in a remarkable letter to Calvin, in words that express Jeanne's attitude almost as well as her own. She is speaking about miracles, which she refutes. "Men's bodies, when their souls have left them, do not work these miracles, nor yet while they live in this world." Such is the way she reasons and a more matter-of-fact statement could, perhaps, hardly be found. Nor does she stop here. "For the rest" (she continues breezily), "I have never demanded or desired the services of ministers who offered to pray for me or for others. I always leave every one's prayers to his own liberty of conscience. If I asked those who have had gifts from me to pray for me, it would seem as if I wished to reward myself. . . . We all pray for one another in the prayer that the Lord has taught us. . . . Nor again am I one of those who pray, or get others to pray, for the people who are no longer in the world." All this must have pleased her omnipotent correspondent; but she had a keen eye, too, for the faults of her own side and she did not keep them to herself. Brave woman that she was, she did not hesitate to confront him with a protest against cruelty. "Monsieur Calvin," it runs, "I am sore distressed that you know not how half the world is governed in this kingdom, so that simple little women are induced to promise that they will kill and strangle with their own hands. This is not the rule that Jesus Christ and His Apostles bequeathed to us; I say this in deep sadness of heart. . . . I pray you Monsieur Calvin, to put up prayers to God that He may show you the truth of all things. . . ."

This again might have been written by Jeanne. She had inherited the traditions of her upbringing—the traditions of her mother's large heart—and her own philosophical nature pleaded of itself for tolerance. She was a woman of the Renaissance, and the humaneness of the Renaissance had passed into her.

She did not at once step forth as the chief of the Huguenots. Her letter, already quoted, shows why; the dread of her father restrained her as long as he remained alive. It was Renée who first urged her into action and hailed her as the Captain of their creed. "Maybe," she told Calvin, "that the Queen of Navarre will achieve the establishment of our faith. It seems to me she is as fit for the task as any woman I know. I bear her a mother's love and adore the grace that God has given her." This was after the death of the tyrant, Henri de Navarre, when Jeanne was herself not slow to announce her mission to the world. "At the present moment," she writes, "freed by the death two months ago of the said Monseigneur, my father, and urged by the example and exhortations of my cousin, the Duchess of Ferrara, it appears to me that reform is as reasonable as it seems necessary; so much so that I deem it disloyal cowardice towards God, towards my conscience and towards my people, to halt longer in suspense and perplexity."

The new opinions had come to her by degrees. Her youthful impatience with her mother's transcendentalism had at first rather set her against them and it was only when left to herself that they had gradually taken hold of her mind. This had happened long before she thus professed them publicly, and her Bourbon husband shared her views. For in

1548 (seven years before her father's death), Jeanne, who had then turned twenty, had married Antoine de Bourbon, Duc de Vendôme. The Duc de Guise had proposed for her, but him she had haughtily rejected. His brother, the Duc d'Aumale, had married Diane de Poitiers' daughter. "Do you wish"—she said to the King—"that the woman who ought to be my train-bearer should be my sister-in-law and that I should hobnob with the daughter of Madame de Valentinois?" Antoine de Bourbon was fortunately her own choice. One wonders if she knew how very nearly she had lost him. For at the last moment, just before the wedding, he was seized with panic lest her marriage in childhood with the Duc de Clèves (a nominal marriage long since annulled by the Pope) should not have been duly dissolved and should cause him trouble hereafter. His fears were pacified, however, and the fact would not be worth recording, were it not so characteristic of his easy-going, vacillating nature.

With so resolute a character as hers she was bound to have a weak husband, and yet, though she was always the man of the two, she kept the inconsistency of the woman and, to the end, was devoted to him. The secret was not far to seek. She was his Mentor, his support, and more than this, for many years he adored her. Not without good reason; for at the time she married him she must have been the most fascinating girl, though, like most fascinating people, she was difficult to live with. Her face was expressive, not beautiful, and needed the animation of talk. Her cool head and her stormy heart governed her in turn; her witty tongue was a vent for both. Qualities have their defects and she confounded truthfulness with rudeness, a certain brusquerie being native to her. Insincerity she never forgave. Her hatred of pretence and her high-born simplicity amounted to a moral force, and as for Court ways they altogether disgusted her. "I tell you," she wrote from Paris, "that if I had to go on in this way for a month, I should be ill. Indeed I do not know that I am not so already, for I am never at my ease here." With the cosmetics, actual and spiritual, that courtiers were wont to deal in, she would have nothing to do. "If you talk of her beauty," she says of a certain great lady, "I tell you that she helps it so much that she enrages me, for, of course, she is spoiling it. But paint is almost as common here as it is in Spain."

That Jeanne had never used it for herself, in a day when it

was almost thought improper to be natural, required no small courage on her part. And yet, in spite of her primitiveness, she belonged, we must repeat, to the Renaissance. It is a common mistake to picture her only as an austere woman given up to theological discussion. She presented a surprising number of contrasts, and was by turns serious and gay, coarse and refined, *gauloise* and pedantic, a romping hoyden and a logician of strong intellect. At one moment, we find her enjoying the play as of old and watching a farce, "a complete travesty of the ceremonies of the Church." At another, she is sitting dreaming, her ladies round her, deep melancholy in her eyes, a Virgil lying in her lap. Or she rises impetuously in her Council and pours forth a stream of unstudied eloquence which amazes, perhaps exhausts, her audience. And next, by the strangest transition, this princess of strong vitality sings a song of Béarn while her son is being born, in order to win a bet—a rich gold chain—from her father. Her spirits were exuberant even for those days, and, it must be added, unredeemed by any sense of proportion. But she was not heartless like so many of her contemporaries. There seemed to be a well of feeling hidden deep in her steadfast brown eyes.

Nothing in their early married days could exceed her husband's love for her. "Now I know full well" (he wrote) "that I can as little live without you as the body can live without the soul . . . I entreat you to come straight to Cognac, where I shall await you, so that you may find your host and your room as well prepared to welcome you as in any place you ever were in." Or again—

"I will no longer live without you! You may believe me or not, as you like, but I am terribly bored when I do not see you, much more than you can ever know. You would pity me, darling, if you saw me, for I have grown very much thinner and have no good hope of getting better till I see you and revive under your care. . . ."

The "believe me or not, as you like" suggests a little world of domestic difficulties, for Jeanne had probably begun to doubt his truth. She had also kept the temper of her girlhood, and his letters betray an amusing fear of it. "Wherefore I implore of you, dear love, not to feel vexed if things do not come about as quickly as you wish . . . with which words, darling, I will close, begging you once again not to be cross, for I swear on the faith of an honest man that to prove my love for you, I would give both my life and my estate." So he

JEANNE D'ALBRET, REINE DE NAVARRE.
BY FRANÇOIS CLOUET. BIBLIOTHÈQUE NATIONALE.
From a photograph by A. Giraudon.

wrote about some family affair which he was supposed to be settling and about which his wife had strong preconceived notions. Sometimes he tries to coax her into self-control.

"I have, my dearest," he writes, "received another letter from you all full of frettings and fumings at the way in which the Baillive and the Viscount are tormenting you. I shall write to them as you wish, and I assure you that I shall not support them or anybody else against you, but on the contrary I shall uphold you as the mistress. As a reward for this, I beg you to try and control yourself very sensibly as you promised me. You are no longer a child, but a woman, and at an age when you ought to have discretion. But indeed you possess such a good store of it, both in conducting yourself and in managing our affairs, that I shan't trouble about anything."

Antoine was evidently a diplomat, and in the early years of his marriage he exercised a strong influence over her. At that time Jeanne would have been the last person to recognize his weakness, for he was quite the man to blind her acute vision. No man is conscious that he is a light creature and Antoine had a serious side, in which, especially in youth, he believed as firmly as his wife could do. His soul was well-born and his aims were noble enough, however inadequate his power of sustaining them. "My wish to see you," he tells her, "is not a whit less than yours; but the love of honour—the desire to stand in the ranks of the men who leave their memory behind them . . . keeps me at this place" (the seat of warfare) "longer than I like to be kept." And his best self comes out again in a letter to François II—the letter he wrote when first he was summoned to Orleans. "I have been considering"—he says—"the inconstancy and changefulness of all things human, which ever incline of their own nature towards the great abyss; which would, in sooth, sink into decadence if the immense Divine Goodness did not lend us a Hand, and draw us forth from this maze of error which tires us out with mortal distress."

If this be a confession of weakness, it is also full of sincerity. Self-deception is not dishonesty, though it is often taken for it, and the fact that a man's practice does not square with his eloquence does not necessarily prove him to be a hypocrite. Antoine de Bourbon had an ardent southern nature and began by caring enough for the cause of the Reformers to be in strong sympathy with his wife. For the rest, he was a gay, easy-going soldier, handsome to look at, a brilliant man-of-arms and a good comrade, contented with what the day brought forth.

"I was never" (he writes from the camp) "better pleased than I am now, for we are splendidly looked after—M. de Nevers, M. le Maréchal de la Marche and I—and we do just as we like. We never budge from one another and we spend our days as joyously as we can contrive to do."

No man, no Frenchman even, could be more social than Antoine, or more susceptible to the companionship of women. His career as a bachelor was fraught with flowery adventures; however, when he married Jeanne he was convinced that they were all over. In a letter a year after their wedding, when his young wife was in Béarn, "I never dreamed," (he said), "that I could receive the courtship of ladies as ill as I do now; it seems to me that they have all grown ugly and boring. I know not if it be the sweet wind that blows from Béarn which is the cause of this, or if it be my eyesight which has changed so much that it can no longer deceive itself as before. I am sure that those who once made a point of informing you of my misdoings will quickly tell you of all the good I'm doing now."

And again, three years later—a long time for the fidelity of a prince of the Renaissance: "I will end my note," he says, "and assure you once more that neither the ladies of the Court, nor the ladies of anywhere else, can ever have the slightest power over me, unless it be the power which makes me hate them. . . . On the contrary, all that I possess I wish to keep for my companion, and I pray her to do the same."

"You do protest too much," Jeanne might have said, and probably did say, though she was yet far from the days of her real ordeal. Like other married couples of other days they had difficulties besides those of jealousy, and we smile as we read that the French mother-in-law already existed in 1549—the first year of their life together. "Madame my Mother"—he writes—"has written and said that she wishes very much that you would go to La Flèche with her while I am away. I entreat you to go as she wants you so badly; and if you are bored with her, return home and make the excuse that our affairs force you to take a journey and that you will come back to her as soon as ever you can. If by good luck you like being there, break up the carriage; it will be of no use, as we decided together, you and I, a little while ago."

Once more in Antoine's soothing tone we detect a certain

nervousness as to how his self-willed bride would take his suggestion. Nor is the note without significance for those who read between the lines. It is a curious little proof how, even in these early days, he misapprehended the nature of the woman he had made his wife. For to think that she would consent to get out of a discomfort by a false excuse was a fundamental blunder—and the blunder of an inferior character. In those few lines of his letter there lies the whole of a poem by Browning.

Soon after they were written, events settled her plans for her. That same year, 1549, her eldest child was born.

A bare hour's rail from Laon, there rises on a steep hill the huge castle-fortress of Coucy, the largest and the mightiest in France. Throned on its height, it looks like some ancient giant turned to stone—the Spirit of the Feudal System, Titanic yet helpless, watching the pageant of the modern world below. It was here that the birth took place. The poor baby was made over to the care of Jeanne's old governess, the Baillive de Caen, who subjected it to the treatment then given to highly-nurtured infants. It was shut out from every breath of air and kept in a dark room, in a cradle muffled in draperies. The Maréchal de Vielleville in his Memoirs tells us how he saved the life of the child of some friends of his—a creature of a few weeks old—by insisting on opening the windows, drawing the curtains and stripping its bed of every hanging. The lookers-on were horrified, but the baby recovered. This one was not so fortunate as to meet with an enlightened gentleman and, not being of the strongest, it died. So did a second boy, who followed it rather closely. The third survived these first perils, but his fate was even sadder. His nurse, a sixteenth century prince's nurse, high-born and of exuberant spirits, was dallying at a window with a courtier who was standing on the balcony below. Bethinking herself of a new form of frolic, she threw the baby to him like a ball, but as he failed to catch it, it fell to the ground. The wretched woman, panic-stricken, stilled its piercing cries, and the fact that its ribs were broken was never discovered till too late. The poor child followed the fate of his predecessors and his parents were again left without a son. "My love," wrote the husband with the inhuman philosophy of his day " . . . I pray you to let me alone bear this grief and do not torment yourself; since for one that God takes away, He can give us a dozen."

Jeanne's father, then still alive and still the one person she dreaded, did not take the matter so coolly. The loss of an heir touched him deeply and his anger with his daughter on this third occasion knew no bounds. It was all due to her neglect, he said, and should she become a mother again, he himself would undertake to rear his grandchild. He was as good as his word, and, when she once more had expectations, he made her promise that she would give the new born infant into his care. He therefore removed her to his palace at Pau in Béarn, and it was here that on December 13, 1554, the little Henri IV saw the light.

His birth was the occasion, already alluded to, of Jeanne's winning of a bet by a song. Her father, restored to good humour, was one day sitting in her company. They were talking, perhaps of the coming event and of all that it signified; of their wishes for a boy and the heritage that would be his. Henri knew full well that Jeanne felt great curiosity about his Will. Suddenly he rose and opened a coffer from which he took a long neck-chain fastened to a small gold box. "*Ma fille*," he said, " you see this box. Well, it shall be your own, with my last Will which it contains, provided that when your child is about to enter the world, you will sing me a Gascon or a Béarnais song. I do not want a peevish girl, or a drivelling boy." Jeanne was charmed and her father ordered his faithful servant, Cotin, to sleep in her dressing-room and to fetch him at the eventful moment. When it came, between two and three on a bleak winter morning, she remembered to keep her promise and despatched Cotin to her father. Not long after, she heard King Henri's step upon the stair and in a strong sweet voice she began to sing the ballad of the country-side—"*Notre Dame du bout du pont, aidez moi à cette heure*"—an invocation to the miraculous image of the Virgin, the patron-saint of matrons, which stood in the little chapel at the end of the Bridge of Pau. Henri was in time to receive the baby into his arms. With great circumspection, he wrapped it in the skirts of his robe and then conscientiously placed the gold box in his daughter's hand. "There! that is thine, my girl," he said, as he did so, "but this," pointing to the child, "is mine." With these words he carried it away to his own apartments where the nurse awaited him. But before he gave it to her, he fulfilled the old custom of Béarn and first rubbed its little lips with clove of garlic, next offered the newcomer wine in a golden cup.

JEANNE DE NAVARRE

Legend says that the precocious prince smelled the wine and raised his head joyously, with other "signs of satisfaction"—that he swallowed the rich red drops which his grandsire put upon his tongue. "*Va, tu seras un vrai Béarnais!*" exclaimed the delighted Henri. It may be that the legend tells true, if we choose to take it as an allegory; the baby was the contemporary of Gargantua who came into the world athirst, and Rabelais, the preacher of *joie de vivre*, had but lately passed away. Having thus satisfied Béarnais traditions, His Majesty of Navarre bore the boy into the crowded ante-chamber. "My Lords," he shouted, lifting him above the heads of the expectant courtiers, "lo and behold! A sheep has brought forth a lion." The poor "sheep," meanwhile, was having a bitter experience. We may be sure that no fatigue prevented her from instantly examining the precious box, the contents of which meant so much to her. What were her feelings when she found that her malicious father had not given her the key! The Will was safe enough, but her curiosity was defeated.

The whole history is alike characteristic of the father and the daughter; characteristic, too, of the times, of the vivid blending of tradition with reality, of familiarity with grandeur, of crude jokes with severity. Where Antoine was, meanwhile, we cannot tell. The husband played no part in the drama and Henri ruled omnipotent. He was determined that this time the baby's health should not suffer. He sent it away to the home of its nurse, a strong peasant-woman who brought up the prince with her own child. But she sickened with an epidemic and so did seven nurses who succeeded her. The boy was at last given over to the care of a labourer's wife, with whom he spent his infancy—his mother being permitted by the King to visit him in private when she wished. The cottage where he lived was long shown, the arms of France blazoned over its doorway, with the words, "Sauve-garde du Roy," a privilege conceded to "Jeanne Fourchade and her posterity for ever."

Six years later Henri died, and Jeanne succeeded to the throne of Béarn and Navarre. For the last two generations the inheritance was a diminished one, Spain having won from her grandfather the province known as Spanish Navarre. Of this realm Philip II had recently been proclaimed King, and the constant manœuvres to regain it formed a prominent part of the history of Jeanne and her husband. From the early days of her reign, she devoted much of her energy to the administration of her domain, seconded by Antoine, but herself the leading spirit. "God" (she writes) "has always done me the grace to preserve this little corner of the country—this Béarn—where, bit by bit, good grows and evil becomes less. The more I receive from Him, the more I owe Him." Her life was for some time a very happy one, between her husband and her son and the little girl, Catherine, who came not long afterwards. That Antoine was frequently obliged to be away in the wars only laid stress on their content, since absence refreshed their love, and the letters he wrote her at this time give a pleasant picture of their home and of their life together there.

"*Ma mie*" (to quote one of them), "I have received the letter that you sent me by this messenger asking me to tell Charles of a place to plant your mulberries in, which I will do. There seems to me no more fitting place than along the meadow slope where we play at *Barres*. Mine had better be planted at the end of the bridge over the Gave. . . . As for the high garden, if Perguade does not bring the trees do not touch it . . . but if they have come, have them planted in the middle alley."

Or he begs her to order some seeds of melons and sweet onions, "of each sort a leathern sack, about a foot high. . . . for the sowing season approaches in which, as you know, my dear, whoso wishes to eat first-fruits must not fail to work duly."

Or he comments upon the festive exchange of presents, more frequent between relations in those gracious days than now.

"I send you by the little monk, whom you know so well, a pair of hounds, the prettiest imaginable, and a linnet who kept me company while I was ill, the nicest and best-spoken that ever you saw. I commend it to you, because it loves me so much that it will reply to me and to no one else. That is why I loved it. . . . I will not tell you anything more, except that all my life I shall believe, both as an honest man and as a husband, in the things that touch us nearly. As to what you say about wishing to wear a cap this summer, you could not do more wisely, since you were the better for it last year."

He gives her a gold chain of his designing, a coach with "white horses, or grey ones," his own being white and roan. She shall choose which she likes, for "the merchant, his mare and his services are all at her command." She, in her turn,

JEANNE DE NAVARRE

sends him presents of fine linen to the camp. "Last night we slept to the sound of drums . . . but I could not be uncomfortable as I have done what I meant to do. I have received the chemise you despatched to me but I shall bring it back quite white, for a man who in this cold sleeps in his clothes does not care to undress in the morning."

Some of his notes are beyond their day in a natural grace of feeling and expression uncommon in that period of tedious and elaborate compliment. "I beg you" (runs one of them) "to excuse me for writing so badly at this moment; the reason lies in the company hanging about me. As for me, I am, I consider, a clever fellow enough when I am in touch with things, or when I am—you can guess where—on horseback, like St. George. . . I protest, *ma petite vieille*, that I am wholly at your service, saving my honour. And this is the end, dear love, of my constant assurance that you cause me many more regrets than you are worth."

Or here is another, lamenting the letters that have not reached her: "I am very sorry for two reasons—because it is a joy to you to receive them and because it is a trouble to me to write them. And I will not make this one longer, except to beg you to keep my little comrade in good condition." The "little comrade" was the toddling Henri IV—"Mignon" as he called him. He makes constant allusions to his children, for whom he longed with touching constancy. "Please" (he wrote), "as often as you can, send me news of my children, and sometimes a letter from Mignon"—and "May God have thee and the little troop in His holy keeping!" was the prayer he liked to close with.

Now and again his letters sound a deeper note and it is curious to observe the difference between the one that he sent when their child died and this other, written when she lost her father.

"I have a great fear for you because of the love which you bear him, greater than your love towards any one excepting myself; because also you deem this grief greater than any you have had. I am afraid that Nature will compel you to make violent demonstration of sorrow, and I implore you to show yourself wise and to feel sure that you have married one who will serve you as father, mother, brother and husband. For I am certain that . . . you will be none the less obedient and I promise you I will never be aught but the gentlest and most loving mate in the world."

Until the accession of François II their public life flowed on fairly smoothly. A great event was their journey to the French Court with their little son. There had been murmurs against Jeanne's growing Protestantism, and Henri II had even threatened invasion if she did not send away her heretical preachers. She parried the blow with skill by making the Cardinal d'Armagnac, a pillar of orthodoxy, the governor of Béarn. But other difficulties arose. The French monarch, for reasons of his own, desired the possession of Navarre and offered her another province in exchange. Jeanne refused with righteous indignation, but matters became so complicated that a visit to His Majesty seemed desirable. She ended by carrying the day, and that without offending the King, for when she departed homewards the match between her son and Princess Margot was practically resolved on.

It was not long after this that there were signs of a rift within the lute. Other ladies no longer seemed so "ugly and boring," to Antoine. His absences were more prolonged, his protestations more eager. Scenes were growing frequent between the pair.

"I learn by your letter"—he wrote—" the new motto that you have taken; I consider it neither à propos nor reasonable. But if you wish every one to think that our good faith and love are broken, and if this be what your heart desires, pray tell me and I too will change my wishes and my motto, that mine may accord with yours and that I may do like you. With which, my dear, I end; and I beg you to answer me by this footman and to believe that I shall follow you in everything, be it good or be it evil."

Occasionally his notes show pique and a kind of nettled longing for her presence. "If I cannot go to you, you must come to me," says one of them. . . . "I believe that you want to very much, but not as much as I do. I don't say that once upon a time you had not this advantage over me, but now I have it over you."

Directly he was tested, Jeanne was bound to find out what a poor creature he was. Anything that needed a decision found him wanting. As long as affairs were calm he kept his dignity, but when the cause of Protestantism became prominent and made increasing demands upon him, he failed her at every step. Their kingdom was soon recognized as being the stronghold of the Huguenots. Here gathered the adversaries of the Guises, and here the men who died at Amboise, the followers of Maligny, must often have discussed their designs. Jeanne inspired and reinforced them. She organized troops for the future; she held State-Councils; she chose officials and passed decrees which materially aided the Protestants. Elizabeth of England herself could not have better chosen her men and was not as originative a statesman as the Queen of Navarre. Jeanne wove, as it were, a strong web of tolerant legislation which, in a happier day, should have made an ideal kingdom. And while, single-minded, she threw herself into the movement, she tried to draw her husband after her. When she was in sight he followed, but her presence once removed, he succumbed to other influences. The Guises had bribed two of his chief Councillors to betray him, and he fell into the hands of these spies, an easy prey to their cunning. He stopped to dally and to temporize, and the enemy triumphed while he waited. Or, worse still, he acted precipitately in a sudden access of energy, such as comes to irresolute people.

Perhaps all this helped to force his wife into action and to establish her as leader of her party. It was well that at the moment of personal disappointment this great cause was absorbing her and employing all the dangerous forces which would otherwise have fed upon themselves. Like her mother, she had a generous love of protecting the oppressed, though perhaps the protection was inclined to be a trifle despotic. But she made herself the champion of young converts to the New Opinions whose families objected to their views, and amongst her ladies there were several girls whom she had rescued. The memory of beatings once endured made her kind, and some of the pleading letters that she wrote show her at her best. There is one to a cousin of hers, a certain Madame de Langey, about her daughter.

"I have, as you know, nobody whom I need obey, but if my God had so afflicted me as to let some one wish to coerce me, . . . I would rather endure death than obey the creature before the Creator. And this makes me entreat you, Cousin, to try and overcome the hatred that you bear your daughter and to give her all honest liberty. It it vexes you to keep her near you since she has a different faith from your own, I beg you to send her to me. I assure you that many girls of like fate live with me—girls of very good birth, and some, even, whose parents have opposite views to those that we profess. And yet they leave them with me, to live according to their conscience."

Or to quote another letter :
"You must not be surprised if, having heard of the way that you are supposed to have been behaving to your daughter, I, on my part, am as much offended with you as I can be. I cannot imagine how a mother who has such a good and virtuous daughter by a man of honour like your husband, can possibly show her such inhuman cruelty as rumour ascribes to you, to your marvellous discredit (*merveilleuse déréputation*). To remedy the which, Cousin, I was very willing to tell you frankly that if it is only her religion which causes you to have thus perturbed and irritated yourself, you must remember that the strong hand of God, which cuts both ways . . . separates the father from his children . . . and that there exists no religion in which cruelty and irrational inhumanity find a place."

These last words expressed a deep-rooted conviction and one which distinguished her from the narrower Puritans. Mercy was part of her creed and all persecution disgusted her. She could never have said with Rénée of Ferrara, " If I knew that the King, my father, and the Queen, my mother, and my late husband, and all my children would be disapproved of by God, I would hate them and desire hell for them." It is true that Calvin had been reproving the Duchess for lukewarmness to her enemies, but under no circumstances would Jeanne have made such a confession. Renée was anxious to shine in the implacable eyes of her Director and had evidently grown rather jealous of the Queen of Navarre's importance. She complains that Jeanne had been admitted to a great clerical Council from which she had been excluded, and is hardly mollified by receiving an *étrenne* from Calvin—an *étrenne* of the Genevan school, consisting of a gold medal inscribed with an insult to the Pope. The two ladies had a kind of rivalry, too, about their Huguenot ministers, and when they joined the Court at Blois they respectively brought their men with them and made them preach in turn. The Cardinal reproached Jeanne with infringement of the King's decrees, but she alleged the royal permission to hold " Prêches," given her long since at Lyons; whereupon Catherine again authorized the services both in her case and that of Renée, so long as they were held in the Princesses' apartments and were only attended by their people.

Catherine's temporizing, however, did not at all suit the Queen of Navarre, nor was that lady's zeal less antipathetic to the Regent. "At last, when she saw that she was hard-pressed and that I did not believe her, she began to laugh," wrote Jeanne, who was paying a visit to Catherine: "For, mark this, she never talks to me except in a bantering tone, as you will see by our conversation. She unsaid many of the things that she said to M. Biron. . . . My gentleman is at the end of his cunning; he does not know what he ought to say. On the one hand, he is afraid of the Queen, on the other, I reproach him (always with a laugh), and tell him that he has cozened me. He shrugs his shoulders and tries to invent excuses for the Queen the best way he can. . . . "

And later, in the same letter, to her friend M. de Beauvoir: "I marvel how I can bear all the trouble that the folk here have given me. They scratch me, they prick me, they flatter me, they brave me; they want to get everything out of me, without showing their game. In short, I have only one follower who walks straight, and that is Martin, in spite of his gout. And then there is M. le Comte who does me all the kind offices imaginable . . . But as for myself, by God's grace, I fortify myself from one hour to another and I assure you that I thoroughly keep in mind your injunction not to get into a rage, for they try me to the very uttermost. I show the most beautiful patience that ever you saw. But I believe that they rebuff me like this to drive me to appeal to the Judges."

Her mission to the Court concerned the matter nearest her heart—liberty of worship; she got half-way measures for her pains, but no half-way measures contented her. "The religious privileges granted us will not suffice to nourish souls aflame for heavenly food—for the which cause we have fought and wrestled the best part of our lives!" she cried; and later she bursts out to Catherine: "We will all die rather than leave our God and our religion, which we cannot maintain without worship, any more than a body can live without eating and drinking . . . I entreat you very humbly, Madam, to believe that the affairs of the soul are not conducted like those of the body, for there is but one salvation, to which there is but one road, wherefore that which we propose to you is what we *can* propose, neither more nor less."

But single-minded though Jeanne was, she did not lack the wisdom of the serpent. When three of her chief ministers were cited before the Court of Orleans for seditious opinions, she boldly refused to allow them to go and meet a probable death. At the same time she was wise enough to forbid their teaching throughout the Duchy of Albret. When the intolerant Cardinal d'Armagnac was made Inquisitor-General of that territory (an appointment which lay with the Cardinal de Lorraine as Chief Commissioner), Jeanne warily compelled her Bishops to forbid public disputations on religious matters throughout the province. This was as well, for when the Inquisitor, in the full splendour of state, halted in the streets of Oléron to give his blessing to the people, the crowd, refusing to kneel, would only laugh and bid him pass on. The Cardinal revenged himself by arresting the minister, Barran, but he reckoned without his host. The Queen of Navarre recognized that the moment for prudence had passed. She pronounced the prelate's measure to be illegal and set the prisoner at liberty. No doubt as she grew in power she also grew more exacting. "His Holiness the Pope"—writes one of Catherine's correspondents from Rome—"always defends himself by saying that the aforesaid lady (the Queen of Navarre) not content to let folly enjoy the liberty given by your Edicts, forces the conscience of her subjects." There may have been some truth in this, but, after all, Jeanne's tyranny was the tyranny of a fervent nature and, in the main, she kept up her own fine standard of freedom.

She trained her son to follow her example. For as her illusions died away and it was clearly borne in upon her that Antoine could never lead the Reformers, all her hopes and efforts centred in her boy. He should achieve the task of which his father was not worthy and she would spare no trouble to fit him for the battle. A knowledge of the world and a broad culture must form part, so she deemed, of his mental equipment, and she chose as his tutor a certain M. de Beauvoir, a forcible man who acquired great influence over her. But she herself took an active part in the prince's lessons. Every day she set him a passage to translate into Latin or Greek and to put back into the original language, and when she was away from home these exercises were sent to her for correction. By the time Henri was eight years old he had, with his mother's help, translated the greater part of Plato, and his brilliant intelligence, joined to an impressionable nature, encouraged her sanguine dreams for him. She began very early to give him insight into affairs—sometimes to refer them to him—and to make him her comrade and confidant.

"My son" (she writes to him), "I have received your letter and I am very glad that you are so well and that Pistolle has had puppies. . . . The day I got here, your cousin arrived, but he is not nearly so tall as you. I think it is because he is too much in love. . . . We celebrated Ricquète's wedding, but I confess that your absence took away half of my enjoyment. My cousin is taking me to Poitiers to see his lady-love. I send you the report that Captain Moreau brought me that you may think over it and give me your advice. . . . Above all be careful, as much for the sake of duty as example, to hear Prêches often and prayers every day, and to obey and believe in M. De Beauvoir, as you have always done so wisely; and don't fail to listen to some lessons from M. de Francourt, as you promised. Young M. Puche is dead. . . . Madame de Vaulx arrived the same day that I did. Now, my son, I have written everything that I can to you and I pray God to help you in all things.

Your good mother and friend,
JEHANNE.

And later, from the Court at Blois, whither there was talk of his coming:

" Do, pray, attend to three things—to look well to the graces of behaviour and to talk boldly, even when you are summoned to private interviews, for remember that the impression you make when you arrive will stamp the opinion that will thenceforth be held of you. . . . And train your hair to grow upwards. . . . No one here at Court can believe in your height. As for me, I think you are as tall as M. le Duc, who is about an inch shorter than the measure brought by Saint-Martin. . . . Your sister has a very bad cough and is still in bed. She drinks ass's milk and calls the little donkey her foster-brother. That is all I can tell you.

From your good mother and best friend,
JEHANNE.

What a link is tenderness, what a modern, what an ancient thing is the love of mothers! Jeanne's letter would have said the same things had it been written yesterday, or in the Middle Ages. There is always a touching note of pride when she talks of her little girl, Catherine, whom she had with her on this journey. "You cannot think" (she writes to M. de Beauvoir) " how pretty my daughter is at this Court. Every one attacks her about her religion; she holds her own against them and never gives in by a jot—and all the world loves her."

Jeanne needed her children more than ever, for Antoine was drifting far from her. His weakness grew more prominent, more tangible, and betrayed both his cause and her. From this time forward, his infidelities became public talk and a scandal to the Protestant party. Théodore de Bèze, their chief minister, wrote to tell her of his sympathy and support, though the only comfort he offered was the thought of Antoine's death. "Your letters"—he concludes—"give me more occasion than ever to sigh in my heart because I have no means of serving you, though you need it as never before. . . . But take courage, Madam, more and more, that you may overcome temptation, however grievous, by the strength and goodness of Him in Whom and by Whom all things turn into blessing and consolation."

And yet, even now, Antoine had brief returns of his love for her. " It seems to me, my dear," he wrote, a short time before Bèze's letter, " that I have felt the love I bear you more keenly through all that has been happening than I have done since first I knew you. . . . And I beg you, darling, to do what you write in your last letter. It is thus that I shall make sure of renouncing all the light behaviour which too often gives a dog a bad name. . . .

" Your very affectionate friend and most loyal husband,

"ANTOINE."

The " most loyal husband " was, at about that time, beginning his connection with La belle Rouet—the connection which completed his moral ruin. For Catherine and the Guises had sent her from out the " Flying Squadron " to bribe him back to Catholicism, just as in Condé's case they had sent Isabelle de Limeuil. It was during the Council of Poissy that these base feats of strategy took place, the assembly which drew to one place all the actors in the great religious drama. And thus it was here that Jeanne d'Albret underwent the crucial moment of her life ; for her position both as a Protestant and as a wife was strangely affected by the events she witnessed at Poissy.

CHAPTER VIII

The Council of Poissy

AUTHORITIES CONSULTED

Lettres de Catherine de' Medici.
Histoire de l'Église Réformée—*Théodore de Bèze.*
Histoire Universelle—*Agrippine d'Aubigné.*
Sur le Règne de François II—*Régnier de la Planche.*
Memoirs de Marguerite de Navarre.
Memoirs de Henri II—*Archives Curieuses.*
Memoirs du Prince de Condé.
Memoirs de Tavannes.
Rélations de la Diplomatie Vénitienne—*Baschet.*
Biographical Introductions to the "Lettres de Catherine de' Medici."
Jeanne d'Albret—*Miss Freer.*
Histoire de France—*Michelet.*
Histoire de France—*Martin.*

CHAPTER VIII

The Council of Poissy

THE accession of Charles IX, who was barely ten years old, gave Antoine de Bourbon his opportunity, and it might have been also the turning point in the fortunes of the Reformation party. Had he grasped the moment, the course of French Protestantism would have altered and he himself would probably have figured as its leader. For after the death of François II, Catherine took her resolution. Her first aim was the Regency, and this she saw she could not establish without possessing powerful allies. The choice lay between the Guises and the Bourbon Princes and, as she knew that while the Guises reigned her Regency could only be nominal, she finally decided for the Bourbons. She united herself more and more closely with the King of Navarre, making him Lieutenant-General of the kingdom. He had everything in his hands, but his hands were nerveless. "Can one"—says a contemporary—"count upon the judgment of a man who is frivolous enough to wear rings on his fingers and ear-rings like a woman, in spite of his age and his white hair?" As usual Antoine shifted to this side and to that, incapable of telling the truth to either, frightened of Spain, corresponding with Philip II, and yet at the same moment giving oaths and promises to the Huguenots. "In an important matter," says the same old writer, "he follows the advice of his sycophants and of light persons . . . and I can attest that in affairs concerning religion he has shown neither firmness nor wisdom." Flattered by Catherine and cajoled by fair words, "by hints even of a distant prospect of the French crown," "l'Échangeur," Antoine, succumbed to his love of ease and splendour and inclined more and more towards Catholicism.

Condé was more difficult to capture. When he came out of his prison, he swore that he would never hear Mass again, and his creed, at least, remained consistent. In other ways, too, he was much more dangerous than his brother, dangerous, that is to say, in the Guises' sense of the word. For he exercised an influence over Catherine possessed by no other human being. She was fascinated by him altogether; his keenness and his brilliance, his ready resource, his spirit of adventure, appealed to her effect-loving temperament. She was perhaps as near being in love with him as it lay in her nature to be. That she had immured him in a dungeon had no apparent weight with either of them. That had been part of a political necessity, by no means of their personal relations, which for the next few years made the drama of Protestantism in France. He played, as it were, the rôle of Essex to her Elizabeth, though the analogy must be taken with reservations. The character of their connection was neither warm nor decided, and, not to speak of the immense difference of nationality between the two Queens, Catherine was never the woman to give herself away. But in Condé's half interested intimacy with her; in the way he thwarted while he dominated, careless alike of her bursts of petulance and her inability to do without him; in the romantic ambitions which he cherished, indifferent to the feelings that he crushed on the road to fulfilment—in all this he reminds us of the great Adventurer-Earl, the rebel-dreamer, who used a Queen as his pawn.

Very different were her relations to Coligny. Throughout his life she respected, even when she most hated him, and there was perhaps no moment of her Regency when she did not secretly fear him. Not without reason. For he wielded a two-edged power: the primitive power of the rude soldier and the unconscious power of goodness. His goodness affected all who had intercourse with him, especially young people. Had Catherine allowed it, the little King, Charles IX, would have fallen completely beneath his sway. The boy was just ten years old. "Truth to say," writes a Protestant chronicler, "he is gifted with brilliant and lively wits, his bearing is serious and modest, his speech gentle and full of kindness; grace and gaiety meet in his countenance. . . . One may with reason found great hopes upon him, if Heaven watches over his days." With such a disposition, it was natural that he grew to love and trust the Admiral, to look on him as the only rock amid the glittering quicksands which surrounded him. And one of the most interesting things about Coligny is the fact of his passionate loyalty to the throne. Loyalty, indeed, it was which prompted his revolt against tyranny and the

THE COUNCIL OF POISSY

Guises. If he planned a religious Republic, it was in despair of otherwise attaining his ideal of a State, and could he have brought up the King as a Protestant ruler, he would have preferred it to aught else. Condé was a rebel, because he would have liked to supplant the King for the sake of his own success ; Coligny would never have usurped the throne, and if at one time he thought of himself as the President of a Commonwealth, it was as the embodiment of a principle which could be carried out in no other way. Thus, at the time of the Council of Poissy, he was still standing on the border-line : between the new King from whom he expected much, whom he wished to make the head of Protestantism—and the Cause of Protestantism, which was greater in his eyes than any monarch. Had Catherine owned one noble aim or been capable of protesting against the Guises, had she been for one hour a frank woman, she might have kept Coligny for the Crown.

For the Council of Poissy was her opportunity. The chief Catholics and Protestants were to meet and discuss their points of difference together. The whole conception of this effort at reconciliation was a big idea and belonged to her alone. It represented the best in her—that large intellectual taste for unity which, had it been backed by an adequate morality, would have made her play a splendid rôle in history. And the early days of the Council, when it kept the stamp of her first intention, before the Guises had worked their will, make the finest chapter in her life. But the attempt had no solid results and we cannot but ask ourselves why. Whatever the surface reasons, we come back to the chief cause—the want of a guiding principle by which to steer the State. This is a negative reason, but there was a more positive one connected with it. For though Catherine had no directing conviction, she had a fixed idea by which all her actions were ruled—her determination to keep the Regency. Everything bowed before this ambition ; she trimmed her sails according to its dictates. Often beginning in one set direction, her bark would suddenly veer round and shift its course, because she had sighted some possible reef in her way, or the chance of fresh assistance from an opposite quarter. But as always, when private desires are put in the place of larger aims, this resolve of hers corroded the atmosphere. No good movement, no large thought could live in it, and the Council of Poissy degenerated because it became a struggle to win the Bourbons without incensing the Guises. Of no one can we say more truly than of Catherine that the

CATHERINE DE' MEDICI

truth was not in her. She put up her own idol in the place of a God, and it was worse than if the shrine had been empty.

She had reason to be afraid, for her Regency was anything but established, in spite of many outward dignities and some privileges that it brought her—the right, for instance, to hold immediate intercourse with ambassadors, instead of through the intervention of the Cardinal. But such things meant little in the face of danger, and there was danger from within and from without. At home there was her unpopularity, which had not grown less with the years. The Regency of a woman was excessively disliked—had even been condemned by the États; and there was, moreover, the original feeling against her as a parvenue. "Perhaps," writes an old Huguenot, "it suffices to say that the Queen is a woman and, what is more, a foreign woman. Let us add that she is a Florentine, born to a private condition far from the greatness of the French Throne. And so she has neither the credit nor the authority which she might perhaps have had if she had been born to the Crown, or, at all events, come of noble stock." These hostile opinions made themselves felt. There was a moment when the States-General—*ces fols* as she called them for their pains—voted that she should not be Regent. She characteristically suspected her new ally, Navarre, of having planned this attack that he himself might gain the place she vacated. But her letter of accusation only put her in the wrong and gave him a fresh hold over her. For not only was he able to deny her charge, but to point out all that was his by right of his Bourbon blood and all that he had generously renounced for her sake. The States-General were eventually appeased by his appointment to the Lieutenancy and the coveted honour was left her, but its tenure was still insecure and she knew no peace of mind. "God first deprived me of your father," she wrote to her daughter in Spain, "and, not content with that, He has now deprived me of your brother, whom I loved you know not how much; and He has left me with three little children and a kingdom torn asunder, without a single soul I can turn to who is not possessed by party passion."

Nor was her position easier with regard to the Powers outside the kingdom. The Pope was naturally suspicious of her attitude towards the heretics. The Emperor, keen to regain Metz, was watching for a pretext of warfare. Elizabeth of England had fixed a wakeful eye upon Calais, while the Duke of Savoy had designs on certain cities in Piedmont.

THE COUNCIL OF POISSY

And Spain, the most dangerous foe of all, tied to her by marriage, divided from her by ambition—Spain, the "arbiter of Europe," whose interests agreed with hers only so long as she remained a Catholic—Spain surrounded her with spies and confronted her craft with greater cunning. There was a rumour that Philip had bribed the Duc de Guise and meant to invade France through his agency—a peril by no means fictitious, for the Guises, alarmed at the ascendancy of the Bourbons, would have stuck at nothing to keep their power. They had also an effectual friend in Chantonnay, the Envoy (more properly the detective) whom Philip sent to reside at Catherine's Court. This man, wary as a lynx and a true son of the Inquisition, was henceforth to play a leading part in her life, dogging her footsteps, knowing every detail of her days, and reporting them to his master. She, on her side, was as resolute in trying to mask her actions from him, and a great part of the next two years was taken up by the match of wits between them—the acute game of chess that this well-suited couple played together, occasionally, it would seem, for the pure enjoyment of catching one another out.

Hemmed in as Catherine was by all these risks, the course that she now adopted was as much a proof of real courage as it was a bid for the support of the Bourbons. For when, in December, 1561, she convoked the States-General, she openly espoused the policy of her noble and heretical Chancellor, Michel de l'Hôpital. The occasion was an impressive one and framed in an impressive setting. "At the feet of the King sat Monsieur de Guise on his chair, in virtue of his office as Grand Maître-d'Hôtel. By his side, but at a good distance to the right, sat Monsieur le Connétable, and on his other hand, to the left . . . Monsieur de l'Hôpital, Keeper of the Seals of France." De l'Hôpital opened the campaign by an eloquent plea for tolerance, one of those great speeches which seemed to come straight from his heart. In spite of the Catholic nobles, the tone of the House was Huguenot. The majority inclined to Coligny's proposal that the two Churches should live on equal terms, side by side. It is curious, indeed, to remark how much this view was taken as a matter of course, even by the Broad Church Party, who had not as yet joined the Reformers. "In our religion, there are two sects," spoke a certain Député from Angers, "one living in obedience to the Roman Church, the other calling itself Evangelical, and both are so numerous that it would be hard to say which counted the most adherents." Another member, the Sieur de Silly, boldly opposed the exemption of the Church from taxation and proposed that its property should be used to defray State debts. There was much debating, much bitter warfare, but the final result was l'Hôpital's "Ordinance of Orleans," a fine measure that promoted freedom of belief and adopted some of the reforms which the General Assembly had suggested. The New Opinions were preached every day in the house of the Condés, and at Court in the apartments of the Admiral. Chantonnay warned Catherine that if these doings continued he would get her sent away to Chenonceaux. The Constable—who had recently allied himself with the Guises and so become stringently orthodox—pronounced these Prêches to be intolerable; he prayed, he said, that the roof might fall in and destroy such wicked congregations. He and the Duc de Guise, on their way to hear the Court sermon, learned that the preacher was to be a certain Bishop whose tendencies were larger than they liked, and they turned back from the door. Their absence did not pass unnoticed, and when Catherine questioned Guise about its reason, he burst out upon her and said that he and his had made her Regent in order that she might defend the Faith—that were it not for this, the Princes of the Blood had a better claim. She let his anger find a vent, but later she went to visit him at Nanteuil. It was a strange interview, typical of her cautious policy. Leading the conversation to religion, "Would you"—she asked—"remain true to me, if I and my son changed our faith?" "No, I should not," he answered, "but as long as you keep to the faith of your forefathers, I would give my life in your cause."

Matters could not rest here and the Duke, strong in his alliance with the Constable, took his own measures. He, together with his brother and the Duc de Nemours, made a plot to kidnap the little Prince Henri, younger brother of Charles IX. Having got hold of him one day, they plied him with questions. The unconscious child had been romping with his playmate, the Prince de Joinville, son of the Duc de Guise, when they called him away from his game. They asked him if he were a Papist or a Huguenot. "I am of my mother's religion," he warily replied. The Duc de Nemours tried to tempt him to go away with him to Lorraine, but the Prince only said that his mother would not like him to desert the King. Meanwhile the Duc de Guise, standing with his back to the fire, was carelessly talking to his boy as if unconscious of what was happening. But young Joinville had been prepared for his part; he was to coax his friend to come with them, to dwell on the pleasures of travel, the beauties of the castle in Lorraine, the good cheer that he would find there. He would be much more petted, he was told, than ever he was at home. Joinville performed his task to perfection and spoke his words as he had learned them; but there was one thing his teacher had left out—the fact that his pupil was a boy. When Henri gaily asked him how they would go, his comrade, forgetting everything but comradeship, told him with glee that he would have to descend from a window by night and drive off in a coach that would await him. The Prince naturally confided this strange plan to his mother, who lost no time in writing a letter to Spain. With diplomatic presence of mind, she begged Philip to advise her how to deal with Nemours—" Knowing as I do the friendship that there is between us, the which must sorely displease folk of such malice as he and his, and impelleth them to ask your help under cover of religion." But Philip, well-informed, was not to be hoodwinked, and Chantonnay's ill-temper continued. There were frequent scenes, frequent explanations. In the face of all this she showed, we must repeat, a fine boldness by persisting in her path of tolerance: by writing, for instance, such letters as the following to Spain, addressed to the Archbishop of Limoges, her resident ambassador there.

" Let us come to religion; for as new accidents arise there must also be new medicaments, until we have discovered the one remedy which can work an entire cure. For twenty or thirty years now, we have tried cauterizing—attempting thus to burn out the contagion of this disease from among us; and we have seen by experience that this violence has only served to increase it. For owing to the severe punishments which have constantly been given in this kingdom, an infinite number of poor people have become confirmed in these beliefs. So that many persons of good judgment have thought that there was nothing which so prevented the destruction of these new opinions as the public execution of those who professed them, since, as every one saw, it only fortified them in their faith. . . . The ashes of the fire which has gone out are still so hot that the least spark will make them leap up into bigger flames than we have ever seen."

" The times," (she says elsewhere) " no longer permit us to

deal forth death and rigourous justice, as in the past. For the evil has grown so much . . . that the wisest thing we can do is to keep things tranquil." Nor, as she grew surer of the Bourbons, was she slow to indict the Guises. "All the trouble" (she tells her daughter Elizabeth) "is purely caused by the hatred that the country feels for the Cardinal de Lorraine and the Duc de Guise, for I find there is a general belief that I mean to restore them to power. This I have emphatically denied. For why should I do anything for them? You know how they treated me in the lifetime of the late King, your brother. I am quite resolved to be mixed up in their quarrels no longer, for I know full well that, if they could have done so, they would themselves have seized the Regency and abandoned me to my fate—the sort of thing they always do if they can reap either power or money. That is all they have in their hearts . . . and as for my love for them, they are only amazed by it." For once we can sympathize with the Guises. Who could feel otherwise than amazed at a love which took such strange forms?

Her pages on these topics do not seem to have produced much effect, if we may judge by the tartness of another note to Elizabeth of Spain. "As for what you say in your letter which your ambassador brought me this morning . . . I beg you not to trouble yourself about me, for, thank God, I begin to be so well established that no one can now do me any harm. . . . I entreat your husband to answer those who press him that, as they know no more how to govern the affairs of this country than I know how to govern those of Spain, I should be much obliged if they would be so kind as not to meddle at all."

Meanwhile, the state of affairs was growing more acute. There had been bad religious riots in the provinces; there were brawls between the two sects in the streets of Paris—for Paris was bitterly hostile to Catherine's policy of tolerance. They constantly ended in barbarous murders on both sides and Catherine saw herself defeated. She and l'Hôpital had tried every parliamentary method of appeasement—the opening of a Council at Fontainebleau—of a Clerical Convocation—of the States-General. A few days before St. John's Eve, in 1561, the King, the Queen-Mother, the Bourbon Princes, and the Châtillons met together in the great Golden Chamber of the Palais de Justice and sat there from seven in the morning till near noon, "discussing the means of restoring union between the citizens of France." In the courtyard below there had

THE COUNCIL OF POISSY

gathered a crowd of "fifteen hundred and more, among them a good sprinkling of Huguenots," who were waiting to see the royal train come out of the Palais, and hear what had been decided within. "But we were all disappointed, I with the rest, for that day I, too, was waiting about," writes a contemporary diarist. When the councillors emerged, they had resolved on nothing, and went home to dine before their afternoon sitting. In vain, however, did the throng expect their return. They never came, and when a messenger was despatched to beg them to finish their debate, they only sent word that His Majesty was ill and that the assembly was adjourned for another four months.

At that moment all the Regent's energies were badly needed at Court. The ashes, as she said, still smouldered, and the rivalry between the Guises and the Bourbons had reached alarming proportions. Navarre claimed the key of the Château of Fontainebleau as his official right: the Cardinal refused to give it him and Navarre said one of them must go. "He called for his horses and mules, had his bed *troussé* [1] and his servants booted, ready to start, for he said that he would never stay in the same place with the Duke," wrote Catherine. . . . "and for all the blandishments and prayers and remonstrances, and the other means that I used, I could do nothing. . . . Nevertheless, I have now so managed that the whole business is smoothed over." This meant that Antoine's wordy bluster had characteristically ended in his staying on, defeated; but though it was a victory for the Guises and their followers, Catherine knew how to make it sour to them. She drew nearer to the Princes every day. Chantonnay demanded that she should send away Coligny and the Cardinal de Châtillon. She refused, and straight upon this, Prêches were held in the King's apartments. Chantonnay protested angrily, but his voice was drowned in psalm-singing, while a crowd assembled outside till the guard was sent to scatter them. Chantonnay once more renewed his futile efforts against the Châtillons with no more result than heretofore. The strain was telling upon the Regent's health and she complained of her sufferings to the Envoy. He blandly retorted that he had heard her illness was the result of self-indulgence—that she nearly killed herself by the number of melons that she ate. Catherine replied with disgust that it was not the fruits of the garden which caused her pain, but the fruits of the spirit.

[1] Folded.

At length in a Convocation of the Clergy the great scheme of the Council of Poissy was brought forward as a remedy. There was hot discussion, there were a hundred difficulties, but they ended in agreement. The various Reformed Churches were to write down in due form the propositions that they wished to be discussed, to append their several signatures, send the document to Poissy and—most important of their functions —elect a deputy to debate on the points at issue with a leading prelate of the other side, in the presence of the whole Assembly. That the Cardinal de Lorraine agreed to this was a matter for surprise ; he did so, it was thought, because he counted on the differences that would arise between the Lutherans and the Calvinists to invalidate the Council and nullify its results. Both parties braced themselves for the duel, the Guises and the Constable on one side, the Bourbons and the Châtillons on the other ; while Catherine was fencing with Chantonnay and, secure in the friendship of Navarre, played fast and loose with his enemies.

II

The Monastery of Poissy was at no great distance from Saint-Germain, where the Court assembled for the Conference. At first there was some talk of Calvin as the Protestant representative, but Catherine and Coligny decided that his presence would hardly be politic and his disciple de Bèze was chosen in his stead. De Bèze arrived in the late June of 1561, with twelve attendant ministers and their families—a sober caravan descending like a flight of rooks amid the tropical plumage of the Court. " They declare themselves the enemies of luxury," says old de Raymond. . . . " Instead of hautboys and dancing, they have Bible-readings and Hymns. . . . Their women, modest in bearing and dress, appear in public like to mourning Eves."

Against this stern background stands out the more vividly the figure of their leader. Théodore de Bèze was, so to speak, the Fénelon of the Huguenot party—a much smaller and less significant Fénelon, but an understander of hearts, especially the hearts of women. Jeanne de Navarre and Eléonore de Condé were not the only ladies he directed and consoled, and his ministrations were helped by his eloquent personality. " Of a well-discoursing tongue, finely pointed by the noble and expressive French language, he also had the mien and the gestures which drew the hearts and wills of his hearers," so says a con-

THE COUNCIL OF POISSY

temporary chronicler who must often have heard him. Such a man was destined to become the fashion, and when he left for the Council "all Geneva wept for his going." One historian goes so far as to say that, without Calvin, de Bèze would have been nothing better than "a little seventh-rate Catullus"; but this did not mean much more than that he had a weakness for writing Latin verses—elaborate compositions, which he dedicated to great ladies. *Esprit élégant et souple, subtil et passionné*—such is the vivid summary of a modern critic and one which Calvin would have endorsed; for none knew better than he how to value the lighter qualities in his servants.

The twelve ministers "were better received than the Pope of Rome could have been" and found sumptuous lodgings in the houses of various grandees. The day after their arrival, de Bèze held Prêches in the Prince de Condé's apartment, which was full to overflowing. That same evening, he was summoned to Catherine's room and found her there together with Condé and the Cardinal de Lorraine, the Broad Church Cardinal de Bourbon and the heretical Madame de Crussol. Catherine gave de Bèze the most gracious reception and, after many courtly amenities, expressed her hope that the discussions about to take place might be so conducted as to bring peace to the kingdom. The Cardinal de Lorraine followed suit; he knew de Bèze already by repute and through his writings, he said, and he added with a suave irony that as he had disturbed the kingdom by his absence, he hoped he would pacify it by his presence. Whereupon there ensued one of those astonishing debates in which Catherine loved to exercise her wits,—a discussion, "*mais à armes courtoises*," concerning the Eucharist: "in the which they proceeded, yet ever with charitable purpose; for they sought the terms that made them meet, rather than the terms which divided them." De Bèze had been wisely chosen by Calvin as his delegate. If the Cardinal were to be confronted it must be by a man of the world, and de Bèze had enough of the wisdom of the serpent to parry a dangerous thrust. He took refuge in mystic definitions: "the secret of the faith" (he said) "was incomprehensible to the senses," a conclusion with which the Cardinal professed himself to be delighted. Turning to the Regent he remarked that he now felt great hopes from the Conference and then, caressing de Bèze—"I am very glad indeed to have heard you!" he exclaimed ". . . you will find that I am not so black as I am painted." Catherine withdrew with her train, but Madame de Crussol remained behind. She was a shrewd woman and she knew the Cardinal of Lorraine. "Being very free of tongue" —wrote de Bèze—" she declared that some one must fetch pen and ink and that the Cardinal must sign what he had said, for he would be sure to say the contrary to-morrow. In the which she proved to have guessed right, for the next day a report had been spread throughout the Court that the Cardinal had, from the first, confounded and conquered de Bèze. But when, at dinner, the Constable in great glee announced these tidings to the Queen, she replied in a loud voice that she herself had been present and that he was most ill-informed." The incensed Chantonnay, who had probably heard the whole affair straight from the lips of the Cardinal, was not slow to report it at headquarters. He lost no time, either, in seeking an interview with Catherine and covering her with reproaches, but she put him off with generalities. It was only one of the many stormy interviews that took place throughout the Conference. "You can hide nothing from me, Madam, I know every detail of your days," he once cried in exasperation, but his hot words only rebounded as from some polished frozen surface.

Long disputations as to modes of procedure followed the arrival of the ministers. The Catholic prelates, on occasion, came to blows, so much were they at variance with each other. Catherine summoned the Protestants to a private colloquy in the palace, that she might inculcate the need of pacification and talk over the subjects chosen for debate: Baptism, the Sacrament, the Laying on of Hands, and Ordination. And she was anxious that they should not stop at definitions, but compare their institutions with those of the Primitive Church and patiently study the causes that had led to the present separation between the Roman Church and themselves. These matters once resolved, there still remained the choice of the umpires who were to adjudicate the issues of the Synod. The ministers waited upon Catherine and begged her to let them be judged "by the Word of God alone"—to be present herself, and also to allow them two secretaries who would take down *verbatim* what they said. She agreed that in any case they should not have ecclesiastics as arbitrators, and they left her presence contented. Hardly had they gone, when they were followed by twelve Sorbonnists who angrily petitioned her to forbid disputation on the part of such heretics as did not recognize Bishops. They were angry when she opposed them; still more so, when

THE COUNCIL OF POISSY

she also refused their request to let the debates be in private.[1] The strength of the Protestants was reinforced by the arrival of Jeanne d'Albret at Saint-Germain. Wherever she passed on her journey—like some Deborah of Israel—she put new heart into the Huguenots. The report that her husband had been present at Mass had impelled her to set out for the Council, and perhaps her course was still more hastened by another rumour —that of his growing intimacy with one of Catherine's beautiful ladies.

On September 9, the first sitting of the Conference took place, in the great refectory of the Dominican Monastery of Poissy. So crowded was the room that even the Knights of the Order could not all get in. The Catholics had been arrogantly confident of their own victory because, as they thought, the ministers had few friends, but the number of Protestant nobles who accompanied the divines must have shaken this belief. The audience was chiefly of high rank. In the galleries round the hall were gathered much the same persons as some twelve months earlier had witnessed the executions at Amboise. The form of the favourite Court entertainment had changed and Protestantism was now the fashion. Here were Catherine, and the King, and his younger brother, Henri, the King and Queen of Navarre, the Duc de Guise, and their followers. Six Cardinals and thirty-six Archbishops sat below. The eleven-year-old King began proceedings by making a long oration. Michel de l'Hôpital followed him, and the bigoted Cardinal de Tournon, the leader of the orthodox party.[2] Then amid the scarlet and purple of the prelates there rose the black figure of de Bèze. He held in his hand the Protestant Confession of Faith which, after stating its substance, he deposited, as agreed on, with the Council. His speech was long and, according to his own account, eloquent. He touched unopposed upon every point in question, till he came to the Eucharist. At the words— "His Body is as far distant from the Bread and the Wine as the highest heaven is distant from the earth," the Cardinal

---

[1] Later she was obliged to yield, and the last sittings had no audience but the King, the Princes, herself and some of the Court. This was, however, towards the end of the Council.

[2] The Cardinal de Tournon's speech was printed in Paris, but so fearful was Catherine lest orthodox tenets should gain ground, that she sent a royal crier through the streets of Paris to prevent its further publication.

de Tournon started up and said that if the Regent did not silence de Bèze, he would leave the hall with all his train. Several people went out, dismayed by these heretical tenets. But Catherine did not stop him. She said afterwards that she would have done so if she had not feared a riot among the audience; but the truth was that her sympathies were with him and she had no desire to check his speech. "But he, wishing to go on, completely lost the part he had studied," wrote a Roman Catholic contemporary, "and he began to look about him, in case he might catch sight of the Holy Spirit in the form of some person or another who would kindly jog his memory. This same Holy Spirit was, however, nowhere to be found, excepting in the Queen Mother—and not perfectly even there, for she had not his part in her hand and was unable to prompt him with the words which followed those where he stumbled. All the same, she would not leave him in the lurch, but—trying to put courage into him—'Monsieur de Bèze,' quoth she, ' pluck up heart and speak out boldly. What are you afraid of? Do not get bewildered.' But, for all that, he could not pull himself together again . . . and apologized, saying that he feared he had offended the King. And the Queen . . . excusing him as well as she could, said that no one must blame him for this spiritual transport, since it was the result of shame, not of ignorance." De Bèze himself makes no mention of his breaking down. "Messieurs," according to his version, he said when the clamour had subsided—"if you wait to hear my conclusion, you will be satisfied,—whereupon he returned to his oration and went on forthwith to the end."

His discourse was followed by a cross-examination from the prelates, and his answers sum up the whole position of the Protestants. They believed, he said, in the Catholic, but not in the Roman Church; their authority came from God, the evidence thereof was in their conscience. The Cardinal de Lorraine demanded what miracles they could show to give sanction to their religion. "It is a great enough miracle that we, who a month ago were being burned and exiled, are now preaching at the Court and all over the country," was de Bèze's reply, not calculated to soothe his opponents. The Cardinal de Tournon, still smarting from his defeat, again rose up in anger. "Messieurs," he began, "this Assembly will profit us little, or rather I may say not at all. For the men we are dealing with here are beasts, obstinate in their

THE COUNCIL OF POISSY

opinions. But they are cautious and they wish to keep themselves from pitfalls.". The vexed question of the Sacrament continued, however, to be examined; and before the four weeks' Conference was over, de Bèze was feeble enough to sign a document, drawn up by his orthodox opponents, concerning the nature of the Real Presence. He doubtless read his own meaning into its wire-drawn, ambiguous phrases, but this act of religious compromise was a source of deep offence to the militant Prince de Condé and a precedent for further weakness to the King of Navarre, on whose wavering nature it had a visible effect.

In other directions the New Opinions were spreading rapidly, and a wave of Protestantism passed over Court and aristocracy. Royalty set the tone, lesser people imitated it, and there followed something very like a fashionable religious revival. The great families relentlessly expelled their private chaplains and almoners, unless they consented to become Huguenots—till the Guises and their friends, it was said, were the only nobles who kept priests. There was, too, a growing demand for everything that came from Geneva The ministers had sent for a number of their tracts and pamphlets, as well as the Psalms of de Bèze and Marot— " all the which were finely bound in red and black vellum, some among them richly gilded, and they gave them as presents to the Princes and Princesses, even to the King, while those volumes that were left were put up for sale at the Court." They were evidently bought at once, for we hear of " four more cartfuls of the aforesaid books " passing through the astonished town of Provins on their way to Saint-Germain.

Meanwhile it was well known that Catherine often took the little King to hear de Bèze preach and did her best to convert him to the New Opinions, though the Guises contrived that she should fail. They did not succeed with her next son, Henri of Anjou, a boy of ten years old, who was heard to ask his mother in public why she did not give him Lutheran teachers. He had at that time strong tendencies towards Protestantism—" the religion (so he called it) of people with understandings." It was indeed this feeling— that the new faith represented the needs of the intellectual, and orthodox Catholicism the superstition of the illiterate— which prevailed in polite circles. The treatment that the young prince was permitted to administer to another infant controversialist, his eight-year-old sister, Princess Margot, shows the full length to which heresy had been allowed to run. She has described what happened in her own convincing words, and the account is too strange to bear curtailment.

"Firm" (she wrote) "was the resistance that I made at the time of the Conference of Poissy in order to preserve my religion, when all the Court was infected with heresy and many lords and ladies there besieged me with imperious persuasion—more especially my brother of Anjou, who, from childhood upwards, had not been able to escape the impress of this miserable *Hugenotterie*. He was for ever preaching at me to make me change my creed, often throwing my prayer-book in the fire and giving me psalms and Huguenot books which he made me carry in my hand: the which, as soon as I had them, I gave to my governess, whom God in His grace had kept a Catholic. She often took me to that good man, Monsieur le Cardinal de Tournon, who strengthened me and counselled me to endure all things for the sake of my faith, and gave me back prayer-books and rosaries in the place of those that had been burnt by my brother of Anjou. And this Prince's familiar friends . . . finding them once more in my possession, abused me, saying that . . . it was evident that I had no intellect; that all people with a mind, whatever their age and sex, once having heard Christian charity preached, had renounced all the abuses of this bigotry. . . . And my brother of Anjou, adding threats to their talk, said that my Queen-Mother would have me whipped. . . . I answered his menace by bursting into tears (for as I was only seven or eight, my years were still tender) and by saying that he might have me whipped or killed if he wished, and that I would suffer the worst that could be done to me rather than damn my soul."

Protestantism held its head so high that it might have been accused at this moment of offending through carnal pride. The Cardinal de Lorraine was dismayed. He was not usually the man to show his hand, but these Huguenot triumphs which he seemed impotent to check almost made him lose his self-control.

"And you, Madam," he perorated at one of the sittings of the Council, "since this realm has delegated to you its government during the minority of the King . . . pray preserve this precious hostage for us, and give him back to us at his majority strong in the faith that he possessed when

THE COUNCIL OF POISSY

we gave him into your hands! . . . In the name of the good King Henri, your husband . . . we beg you to follow his sainted wishes that his memory be not condemned, nor that of the mighty King François, your father-in-law, *who called you to enjoy such a great and happy marriage with his son.*"[1]

The last words are almost a threat—an insolent reminder that Catherine's position was not hers by right and might easily be taken away from her. Nor was Chantonnay behindhand. He had once more sought her out and brought her to book about her conduct. She must provide him, he said, with some "*bons mots*" in which to explain matters to his master. She only answered that "things were much improved, that she had more hope than ever that in time all would come right"—on which the envoy's face lowered. "A change of religion"—he said darkly—"often brings a change of Kings."

The first weeks of the Conference were now over, and in spite of her boasted confidence, Catherine was no longer sanguine. The cause of reconciliation had not been furthered and no real knowledge had been gained. Debate had sunk into the merest hairsplitting about immaterial points, and the verbose puerility, the gross irreverence of those interminable discussions must ever amaze the mind of the bold student who looks into them. The next step seemed a matter of difficulty. The Catholics, it is true, boasted of victory, but they knew that it was only a victory of words and that their position was insecure. The Cardinal de Lorraine tried every means that strategy suggested. He sent in secret to Augsburg for four Lutheran Doctors, in the hope that they might quarrel with the Calvinists and so put an end to the Conference. He decreed that the quarrel about the Eucharist should finally be referred to the Fathers of the first five centuries after Christ; but when the conscientious ministers duly came with their arms full of tomes, they found the hostile ecclesiastics without a book to turn to, unwilling to discuss and obdurate as ever. It is hardly surprising that no conclusions were arrived at. "We are sorely grieved that this meeting hath not produced that fruit we should have wished, so needful for the love of the whole Christian Church," said Catherine towards the end of the Council; but was she aware that the chief cause of the failure lay in herself, in her double-dealings with the Guises and the Bourbons, her manoeuvres

[1] The italics are those of the present writer.

for the Regency, her plots to entrap Condé and Navarre? The Assembly had no real moral support from her, no help from a strong principle, as it would have had from Jeanne de Navarre; and wanting, as it were, a central point round which to work, it lost cohesion and came to nought. "She is a Florentine"—wrote one Languet, a leading Huguenot—"What shall I say of her? I really don't know. But of one thing I am certain: to whatever side fortune veers, the Regent's chief care is to rule, and neither the Papists nor the Reformers will make her gamble away her destiny."

Yet she continued to venture much to help the Reformers. L'Hôpital was still her adviser, and the important posts were given to men with leanings towards Protestantism, such as the son of the Connétable, the Maréchal de Montmorency, who was appointed as Governor of Paris. The Catholics, who had been exulting at the apparent defeat of their opponents, soon had their spirits dashed; for fresh decrees promoting religious liberty were " cried " to the sound of a trumpet through the streets by the King's command. Great was the wrath of the Duc de Guise. Catherine's estrangement grew so marked that he could no longer endure it, and he, together with his brother, the Duc d'Aumale, the Duc de Montpensier, the Duc de Nemours and the Maréchal de Saint-André, acted upon their offended dignity and took their departure from the Court.

Their last hope had been in the Papal Legate who, after many delays, arrived in state at Saint-Germain. This was Hippolyte d'Este, Cardinal of Ferrara, uncle to the Duchesse de Guise—a distinguished diplomat, from whose adroit manipulation much had been expected. But the foible of ecclesiastical politicians once more deceived them here. Stronger qualities than tact were needed at this juncture, and the Legate produced no real effect. The most definite thing that he achieved was perhaps hardly to his credit, for it was said that he completed the conversion of Antoine de Navarre.

III

The arrival of Jeanne d'Albret at Saint-Germain ushered in the saddest hours of her life. Her husband she found to be the centre of a great Catholic plot, in which Philip of Spain had joined the Guises, and Catherine played a double part. His brother, the Prince de Condé, was also the victim of base scheming, but though he had fallen a prey to the charms of

THE COUNCIL OF POISSY

Isabelle de Limeuil, she never succeeded in accomplishing the real object of his opponents. For charmed she never so wisely, the Prince was true to his belief and, whatever his foibles, had no latent weakness for the Church of Rome. But the Guises, knowing their man, held out more dazzling dreams to l'Échangeur than the mere attractions of a Court beauty. His relations with Mademoiselle de la Limaudière—La belle Rouet, as she was called—formed only the first stage of their plan for his future. She was but a decoy, a means of dividing him from his wife, of preparing his mind for divorcing Jeanne (a righteous divorce from a heretic) and finally for a second marriage. This match, they led the siren to believe, would be with herself, which was a sufficient lure for her ambition. But their real intention was to unite Antoine with their widowed niece, Mary Stuart, and thus make him their own. Once removed from the Queen of Navarre, Antoine would run no danger of returning to Protestantism; the less so, as Philip was bribing him with that long-coveted prize, the possession of Spanish Navarre.

Throughout these machinations Catherine acted a treacherous part. Ever keeping the establishment of her Regency in view, she was anxious to please the Guises when she could, to blind them to her plottings against them, to prevent them from fighting with, perhaps from overcoming, the Bourbons, whose support was so needful for her rule. And she nourished a secret hope that if the Guises succeeded all would turn to her profit, that Guises and Bourbons would coalesce in her support, that Spain would forgive her misdoings, and the pacification she prayed for would at last be ensured. So she let loose the " Flying Squadron " of charmers —her secret-intelligence officers—and allowed them to do the bidding of the Guises. La belle Rouet had no difficulty; she quickly gained an entire hold over Antoine's susceptible mind.

The Queen of Navarre, meanwhile, was being duped on all sides. Catherine, renewing an old arrangement, promised her the Princess Margot as a bride for her son, young Henri, at the same time that she was corresponding both with Spain and Portugal about other matches. And she covered Jeanne with caresses when the plot against her was at its thickest. " I wish God had taken the Queen of Navarre, so that her husband might marry again without delay," thus she wrote while Antoine's fate was still undecided.

The arrival of the Papal Legate meant fresh developments

of the plot. He was to attach Antoine yet more closely to the Church, and if possible to convert Jeanne; but in the probable event of his failing to do so, she was to be divorced and dethroned, and finally impeached by him as a heretic before the Court of the Inquisition. Hippolyte d'Este had travelled to France in the company of Lainez, then the General of the Jesuits, and the journey had not been in vain. The wiliest of that Order could not have paid more delicate attentions to Jeanne, and during his frequent visits and encounters with de Bèze in her rooms, he never relaxed his self-control, or made any comment on what he heard. He went farther and made a playful bargain with her—that if she would attend a Mass at which the Nuncio was to preach, he, the Cardinal, would come with her and sit through one of de Bèze's sermons. Great was the surprise at Court when he fulfilled his pact and remained through a long "Prêche" which took place in Condé's apartments. But he might have spared himself his effort, for Jeanne stood as firm as a rock and he turned his attention to Antoine. Having won over that Prince's perfidious chamberlain, it was easy for the Legate to surround his dupe with spies, chief among them a Sicilian, Lauro, who became Navarre's physician-in-ordinary. Every secret of his existence was thus made known to the Guises, and their grip of him daily grew stronger. Antoine now listened to their proposals, and d'Este promised in the Pope's name to arrange his marriage with Mary Stuart if he would definitely renounce the Calvinists. They gave him a hint that Philip would rather he were Regent than Catherine and would not be averse to deposing her. Antoine's reply showed the depth to which he had fallen. "Supposing he consented," he asked, "how could French Navarre be certainly secured to him, considering that he only reigned there by virtue of his marriage with Jeanne?" The Vatican, he was told, would see to that, and would, besides annulling his marriage, depose his wife as a heretic and give her kindgom to him. Antoine, much agitated at what he heard, demanded a few days for reflection, and these were granted him on condition that he kept strict secrecy.

Thus Jeanne became in his eyes the only obstacle to happiness and the last spark of feeling died out in him. He grew cruelly cold, sought quarrels with her for her heresies, and threatened, if she continued in them, to take away her children. Nor did he stop here. For he tried to force her to go to Mass and once when their little Henri, then a boy of ten, "flew to his mother's side with a—'Nothing will induce me, either, to go to Mass!'"—his father soundly boxed his ears and ordered his tutor to thrash him. Jeanne, remembering her early defence of her mother and the beating that she got for it, must have felt that history repeats itself. Another day, finding her "about to step into her litter and attend a Prêche, he took her by the hand and led her back," with a stern command "that she should no more attend the Calvinistic services, but outwardly conform in all things to the worship of the Roman Church." Jeanne knew that transactions had been held concerning Spanish Navarre. "I would not barter my immortal soul either for land or honours!" she cried, "nor will I ever be present at the Mass, or at any Papist ceremony." Antoine took a mean form of vengeance. He revealed the conspiracy against her and swore he would divorce her unless she did as he said. "Indignation sealed the Queen's lips for some minutes, then tears fell from her eyes. She warned him that the plot meant his own degradation and the elevation of his hereditary enemies." "My lord," she eloquently concluded, "although my fate does not move you, have pity on our two children. Your repudiation of their mother will destroy her, but it will be their ruin also." Her impressionable husband seemed affected. "If this be the case," he answered—"you had best make the step unnecessary by your prompt obedience and by making your peace with Rome and Spain." As for himself, he added, "he was still undecided which religion was the true one, but while his uncertainty lasted he was minded to follow the faith of his fathers." "Well, then," retorted his wife, who had not lost her power of irony, "if your doubts on either side are equal, I beseech you to choose the one which is likely to do you least prejudice."

Chantonnay, who must have spent his days behind keyholes, instantly reported this scene to headquarters. "Madame Jeanne" (he wrote) "has been compelled by her husband to forego her Prêches; sermons are no longer allowed in her apartments at Saint-Germain—a general cause of grief and lamentation." The poor Queen's private chaplain went away in anger and she saw herself deserted and friendless: worse than this, insulted by La belle Rouet, who allowed her coarse tongue free rein in Jeanne's presence. With great dignity she dwelt on her right to go home to Béarn with her children. Later, however, she changed her mind and stayed on, with what motive it is hard to fathom, unless, as one of her biographers suggests, she saw some last chance of saving Antoine. Her delay gave another chance to the Cardinal d'Este, who, sanguine priest that he was, had still not lost his hope of converting her and never ceased to ply her with dazzling promises of what would happen when she turned Catholic. He was meantime " doing all in his power to widen the breach " between the pair. " The King of Navarre," he said, " to show me how well-disposed he was towards religion, told me a few days ago that he meant to send the Queen, his wife, home to Béarn, on the plea that affairs required her presence there. . . . But since then things have changed their aspect and she is not going yet, whether on account of this severe weather, or because of her failing health I cannot tell. The King, nevertheless, is resolved to send her back in the early spring. For my part, I shall not fail . . . to work my utmost for the accomplishment of these designs."

Perhaps he counted too much on Antoine's weakness. That Prince had one fixed idea—the acquisition of Spanish Navarre. When he tried to persuade Spain to promise that the province would be his, he was told that " His Majesty might find opposition in his Cabinet which it would take time to overcome, but that anyhow King Philip would gratify him with Sardinia and declare that island to be a Kingdom." Chantonnay enforced the offer. If the King, said the Envoy, should, all things considered, now wish to keep Jeanne as his wife, the wonderful island of Sardinia should still be his. Sardinia was in point of fact a barren and unprofitable place ; but these casuists had no scruple in assuring him that he would possess a paradise ; their zeal led them to invent a map in which fertile districts and splendid cities, all equally imaginary, were shown him. Antoine, as was his way, resolved to think the matter over and, while he was so doing, gave in more and more to his seducers.

The Catholic party, gaining confidence, had for some time been strengthened by a league, " a formidable coalition between the Duc de Guise, the Connétable de Montmorency and the Maréchal de Saint-André, to maintain the ascendancy of the Romish faith throughout the realm." " The King of Navarre "—wrote Jeanne to her friend, the Vicomte de Gourdon—" has grown so deluded and enervated, mentally and bodily, by

THE COUNCIL OF POISSY

indolence and luxury, that he has allowed the Guises, aided by the Constable, to regain the upper hand, to his great shame and the calamity of France. . . . He has become stultified by the trickery of Rome and by the false words that it sent us through the Queen-Mother, promising to restore our kingdom which Spain so iniquitously took from us: so stultified, too, by his fear of losing what remains to us, that he will neither say nor do anything, nor yet permit me to act. Amidst all this woe my soul, sad and perplexed, yearns to be counselled and consoled by a loyal friend. Come to me here, or write what you think I ought to do."

"Your Majesty should not undertake anything in the matter of religion which goes against the will of your husband." This was all the answer she got to her forlorn appeal for comfort. Her truth-loving spirit found no one to trust or to turn to; it was stifled in the air of Saint-Germain and she resolved to leave the Court behind her. This time Antoine made no objection and allowed his wife to depart with their little girl, Catherine, to Paris. Here, in the great Hôtel of the Rue de Grenelle, where she settled, she was joined by the Prince de Condé who, deeply offended at his brother's behaviour, remained loyal to his sister-in-law. Here at least there was liberty. "The palace of the Queen of Navarre is a school for the study of the new doctrines," writes an envoy from Venice at this moment of respite for her and Condé.

Their repose was soon disturbed by a fresh insult to their creed. The King of Navarre formally joined the Catholic Triumvirate, and on Palm Sunday, 1562, he, together with the Guises, walked in solemn procession from the Constable's house through Paris and attended Mass in public at the Church of Ste Geneviève. The Constable accompanied them, riding upon a mule, an indulgence which was allowed him "by reason of his age and of his gout." The Duchesse de Valentinois wrote from out her retirement to encourage the Catholic party and exhort them to keep together—her last noteworthy action on the stage which once knew her so well. Antoine was now publicly pledged to orthodoxy, and nearly broke Jeanne's heart by confiding their son to the care of Lauro, the Jesuit.

Before we trace her fortunes any further, we must, however, go back to Poissy and follow the fate of the Council.

It had lasted only six weeks, from September 9 to October 20, 1561, and it ended, as Catherine foresaw, in little more than smoke. Towards the close of the year the Huguenots rose in the provinces and fierce riots ensued. They seized on a great many churches and indulged in deeds of violence which their enemies repaid in kind. The members of the Conference had by this time dispersed, the ministers taken their departure, but Catherine called another Assembly at Saint-Germain in the lingering hope that a final effort might discover some means of reconciliation. There was a large mustering of Councillors and Députés from the provinces. L'Hôpital began proceedings with one of his fine pleas for tolerance. He was followed by Catherine herself, who spoke with unexpected eloquence in the same spirit as the Chancellor. The speech had a signal success. Even the Papal Nuncio was forced to confess that " he had never heard an orator express himself with greater art or energy." And the Regent said she herself felt that God was dictating the words to her. If she possessed this gift, one wonders why she did not use it oftener ; but it seems more probable that the occasion was an exception and that her brilliance was due to the inspiration of the moment. The result, at least in great measure, was the important " Edict of January," which came as near a *modus vivendi* as anything the Council could contrive. On the one hand, it forbade Protestants to build churches of their own, or to use those of the Catholics ; on the other, it allowed them to assemble for public worship in certain districts outside towns. The Edict was sent in due course to the Parlement, but the Parlement refused to register it. In vain did the students of the University, of whom the majority were heretical, march armed, two and two, first to Prêches and afterwards on to the Assembly, to force it at the point of the sword to publish the decree. The Députés refused.

Catherine's anger knew no bounds : " The which lady in her wrath and rage took horse at Saint Germain-en-Laye and rode post-haste to Paris. And in sooth it was hard work to keep her from galloping straight into the Council in the Golden Chamber, that she might the better demonstrate her absolute will and see the Edict safely registered. By no means cooled from her anger, she entered the room where sat the Presidents and all the Councillors, and began to plead and to grow shrill with them, as women do when they are irritated. . . . And when they had patiently listened, they tried to remonstrate with her and to prove the evil that the Edict would do to King and kingdom, to the dishonour of God : . . . wherefore, they said, they could not receive or register it. All of which the aforesaid lady refused to hear and, persevering in her threats, she formally ordered them to accept it. . . . Seeing which the Chief President rose to go, and, as he left the Hall, he spake these words: 'Madam, you and your children will be the first to repent this; you are taking the road that will lose you crown and kingdom if nobody minds your business for you.' Saying which he went out of the room and returned sorely vexed to his house. Others of the Presidents and Councillors did the same, and there only remained with the lady the Councillors whom she had cowed, and those who rejoiced at the Edict and smelt the Huguenot rat. These she commanded to register and publish the decree . . . the which they promised to do, and afterwards she went back to the Court to tell her friend, the Prince de Condé what she had done for love of him. Messieurs of the Court of Parlement having reassembled on the morrow . . . saw to the registration of the said Edict, to which they added the words that follow: ' Published, read and registered in our Court of Parlement at Paris, by reason of the importunity of those who profess the so-called new Reformed religion—and this only provisionally, while awaiting the majority of the King.' "

After this surprising episode, the Députés dispersed and though Catherine, wishing to define matters further, summoned another Conference, she got no more satisfactory returns. " They have spent about a fortnight in quarrelling over the simplest thing," she said; " they were fighting *not to be conquered* instead of talking together with a real wish to submit themselves to truth and reason."

But broad-minded discussion was not to the taste of the Most Catholic King, and his anger, which Catherine had so long parried, had taken a serious turn. An agent whom Antoine had sent to Spain returned with a message to the Regent that unless she would change her ways, His Majesty would certainly make war upon her. This alarming threat, which put her power in serious jeopardy, filled her mind with fears. She threw herself more and more into Antoine de Bourbon's conversion in the hope of impressing Spain favourably. There was a moment when Jeanne, perhaps in sarcasm, asked her " on her conscience " to advise how she should act towards Antoine. " Conform outwardly to Rome if you wish to keep your husband and Béarn," was the Regent's counsel of expediency. " Madam," exclaimed Jeanne, " if I held my son and all the kingdoms of the world in my hand, I would hurl them to the bottom of the sea rather than imperil my soul." Catherine probably gave a light laugh—the laugh which exasperated Jeanne—at so much display of zeal, but she herself, with the dread of Spain before her eyes, turned even more emphatically to the "outward conformity" she commended. And yet, in spite of her efforts, Chantonnay did not believe her. His impression was that she still "suspected everything that came from Spain and trusted Coligny and his party." Nevertheless, her apparent acquiescence in orthodoxy made the Spanish envoy's schemes practicable. With the energetic help of the pervert Antoine, now nominal head of the Catholic League, he, the Legate and the Nuncio, succeeded in driving the great Protestants from Court. Coligny, Condé, d'Andelot, and the Cardinal de Châtillon, together with the Prince de Poitien and the Duc de la Rochefoucauld, withdrew to Orleans and to Meaux—practically forced into exile, though Catherine took the trouble to announce that they "departed of their own free will."

The Regent's position was an ugly one. She suspected not only Spain, as Chantonnay had said, but all her allies. Nor was she far wrong in doing so. Bent upon hearing the secret debates of the League (now falsely called the Triumvirate, since Navarre made a fourth in it), Catherine had a tube constructed and placed without anybody's knowledge between the wall of the Council-room and the arras hangings that hung round it, an arrangement which enabled her to overhear everything from her room above. The first words that met her ear were not encouraging—a proposal, disloyal to herself, made by the Duc de Guise. He was followed by the Maréchal de Saint-André, her constant guest and now her ally at the Court. What were her feelings when she clearly heard him suggest that the League should rid themselves of her by drowning her in the Seine! It could be accomplished, he averred, without the slightest risk of discovery. It is to Navarre's credit that he sprang to his feet and refused to have a hand in such a job, nor was it likely that Saint-André himself seriously believed in his scheme. But the mere notion that such a thing was possible filled the Regent with panic, and she lost no time in inventing a pretext for retiring with the King to Fontainebleau.

Jeanne d'Albret, left alone in Paris, fared worse at the hands of this remorseless Junto. Their design was to arrest her as a

THE COUNCIL OF POISSY

State prisoner and shut her in some fortress-dungeon, a plan to which her miserable husband, less loyal to his wife than to his Queen, gave a full, even gay consent. "*Voilà, Monseigneur un acte digne de vous! Dieu vous donne bonne vie et longue!*" exclaimed the Cardinal de Lorraine, shaking him warmly by the hand. And doubtless Antoine, also, had made the act seem possible to himself by looking upon it as a sacrifice in the cause of the true religion. The warrant for her arrest was at once put in hand, but the choice of a leader for the enterprise caused some delay and, in the interval, the affair was revealed to Jeanne. She showed no emotion when she heard of Antoine's final treachery: "But from that moment," she wrote in after years, "I closed my heart for ever against the affection which I confess I still cherish for my husband, and I devoted all the energy of love to the strict fulfilment of my duty." Such sorrow as she felt she had to stifle, for this was not the moment for sentiment. With prompt decision she resolved to set out for Béarn and made her preparations accordingly. Jeanne, who never wept, shed bitter tears when she took leave of her boy, whom she saw herself compelled to leave in the hands of his Jesuit tutor. Tenderly she clasped the sobbing child in her arms and tried her best to console him. Then returning with an effort to her strenuous mood, she took him by the hand and bade him keep firm in his faith; if ever he attended Mass, she said, she would disown and disinherit him. And with this stern farewell she tore herself away. The next day came her parting with her husband—their last parting, though neither of them knew it. With her wonted fervour, she entreated him to give up the Guises, to return to her side and to safety. But he answered her with ambiguities, and they separated—for ever.

The Huguenots of Paris, having meanwhile got wind of her danger, gathered in a crowd round her Hôtel with turbulent demonstrations of loyalty. It became evident that to arrest her in Paris would be dangerous, and the Catholics determined to wait till she reached the town of Vendôme, through which she had to pass—Antoine himself instructing the local authorities that they were not to let her leave their city. She and her little girl set out in April, 1562, escorted by a band of horse. But when she reached Vendôme Jeanne might well have said that Providence protected the Huguenots. A throng of lawless mercenaries marauding the country-side made a sudden raid upon Vendôme, and billeting themselves upon the town, so filled the thoughts of the civic powers that Jeanne was left in peace. She continued her journey as far as Caumont, where she had a Huguenot ally, but hardly had she reached its castle when secret intelligence was brought her that Monluc, the Catholic Captain, was pursuing her hard at the head of a considerable army and intended to surprise her in her stronghold. She had just time to fly. Happily she had foreseen that perils would beset her on every hand and had sent a messenger to Béarn demanding a military escort. A force of 800 cavalry under her staunch friend, the Baron d'Adrets, met her as she fled towards the frontier, and "the last of Monluc's trumpets was distinctly audible in Caumont as Jeanne's troops closed round her." She crossed the boundary-line and found herself safe in her kingdom, whence she could sight Monluc's banner floating from the tower that she had left. She had not been a moment too soon and Monluc was left to fume at leisure. "Heaven knows," he wrote in later days, "the grudge that the Queen of Navarre bore me and how she reviled me afterwards . . . but she was a woman and so she could enjoy her immunity from personal combat." He evidently did not know Jeanne, who would greatly have enjoyed a duel. But the whole incident had more than a passing significance. It was one of the first strokes in the terrible religious war that was now to convulse the nation.

CHAPTER IX

The Huguenots

AUTHORITIES CONSULTED

Journal de Claude Hâton.
Memoirs du Duc de Guise.
Memoirs de Tavannes.
Memoirs de Jean Philippi.
Memoirs du Prince de Condé.
Memoirs de Henri II—*Archives Curieuses.*
Journal de l'an 1562—*Revue Rétrospective.*
Histoire de France—*Martin.*
Rélations de la Diplomatie Vénitienne—*Baschet.*

CHAPTER IX

The Huguenots

EARLY in 1562, there occurred the awful massacre of the Huguenots at Vassy, a little town in Champagne, not far from Joinville, the great family seat of the Guises. Vassy had rapidly become a centre of heresy. For a Protestant Church had been established there soon after the Council of Poissy, the congregation increasing in three months from 120 to 1,200. The Guises had already made two futile attempts to scatter this earnest congregation, but the Bishop of the diocese himself (the mundane Bishop of Châlons) was foiled in his encounter with the minister and obliged to retire discomfited. The Guises promised themselves vengeance. They intended, it was said, to execute their plan at Christmas, when near a thousand communicants were to take the Lord's Supper. A solemn warning was sent them, but they bravely continued in their course, and the Guises, busy elsewhere for the moment, did not fulfil their designs. None the less did they nourish them, and when, in the spring, the Duke returned from the German frontier, the first question he put was whether the Huguenots of Vassy "*faisaient toujours Prêches*." His mother, Antoinette de Bourbon, the grim dowager of orthodoxy, told him that they grew worse every day. "On the which he straight began to mutter and to wax hot in his courage, biting his beard, as was his custom when he felt greatly irritated." Whoever knows François Clouet's virile miniature of the Duke, an epigram of brute force and superb courage, will be able to see him as he stood there biting that terrible beard of his, so prominent in the picture that it seems the very seat of revengeful power. His schemes were soon matured. Together with his brother, the Cardinal de Guise,[1] he set out one Sunday with an armed escort (no unwonted appanage of his state), intending, so he gave forth, to dine at a village which lay just beyond

[1] Not to be confused with his greater brother, the Cardinal de Lorraine.

Vassy. The bells of that devout place were calling the Huguenots to worship, and the Duke did not fail to ask why they were ringing so loud. Suddenly diverting his course, he turned off the road to his destination and, taking the turning to Vassy, he rode to the empty parish church, the Prêches being held, as he discovered, in a rough barn a hundred yards off. Thither he despatched a messenger, who ordered the minister to stop the service, as the Duke wished Mass to be celebrated in the church hard by. The minister replied that "the Duke was only a man—that he could not overrule the Word of God to hear the which they had met . . . nor should they dream of leaving off." This was enough. A shot through the open door was Guise's only retort, and when the defenceless congregation tried to shut their enemies out, the troops rushed in pell-mell and slaughtered to the right and to the left. That the whole affair was premeditated there can be no sort of doubt, for the soldiers whom Guise brought with him were reinforced by others whom he had lodged in the neighbourhood. The cruelties are piteous to read of, sickening to recall. The minister went on preaching till the pulpit was brought down under him and he himself, covered with wounds, was taken prisoner. Men, women, children, were massacred wholesale to the sound of the Duke's trumpets, while he stood in the barn, sword in hand, urging his soldiers to kill. His wife, who had followed this strange expedition in her litter—the same poor lady who had wept at the horrors of Amboise—prevailed on him to spare a few women; some of the more fortunate Huguenots escaped by the roof, but otherwise the murder was wholesale.

"*Seigneur Dieu!*" cried the hapless victims; "*Seigneur Diable!*" retorted their foes. The Cardinal, meanwhile, remained outside, leaning on the churchyard wall and watching his men as they pursued their relentless work. "Presently the Duke went into the barn and found a Bible there. 'Look here, brother,' said he, 'look at the title of this Huguenot book.' Quoth the Cardinal when he saw it, 'There is no harm there: these are the Holy Scriptures.' At the which the Duke feeling himself confounded, fell into a greater rage than heretofore: 'Sblood! and what do you mean?' quoth he, 'when you say the Holy Scriptures? Fifteen hundred years have passed since the Passion and the death of Jesus Christ, and this book was only published a year ago. . How can you call this the Gospel?' . . . His excessive fury displeased the Cardinal. 'My brother is wrong,' he was heard to say—but the Duke paced up and down the barn, foaming with anger and pulling his beard as he walked." The Duke François' ignorance was no less amazing than his cruelty. It is hard to believe in a person who destroyed others for studying a book he had never seen, and yet this momentary flash of portraiture which reveals his primitiveness of intellect shows us the man more surely than any detailed history of his doings. He did not know what remorse meant. "For hereupon," says his chronicler, "he mounted his horse and departed from that town of Vassy with his brother the Cardinal, the Duchess his wife, and two or three of their closest comrades—and they went to dine at Ettancourt at the house of one, Jean Collesson."

Huguenot revolts quickly followed on this disaster at Vassy, and Montargis, Guienne, Meaux and Montpellier witnessed great carnage on either side. But although it was the Catholics who, at Vassy, first gave provocation, this was far from being always the case. There is nothing more delusive than to imagine that the persecutors were all diabolical, the persecuted angels of light; and though drama, fiction and tradition have combined to glorify the Huguenots, to give them no blame but for austerity, the truth is that they were, for the most part, a rude and tactless society, irreverent and coarse of tongue, uncultured and undisciplined, trampling on tradition, constantly offending the taste of the high-bred Catholics, and taking the line of aggression quite as often as their adversaries.

A movement, we must repeat, consists both of those who lead and those who are led, and in the case of the French Reformation the line of demarcation was sharper than it need be. For the leaders were aristocrats, and they, as we have seen, were spirits touched to fine issues. The Protestant ministers, too, the spiritual captains of the band, were heroes in thought and deed; but beneath them came the majority, the unthinking, energetic mob, dependent on the presence of their chiefs, swayed by every impulse in their absence. If we can picture the impression that violent religious revivalists would make upon a student or an æsthete, we may get some nearer conception of the effect produced by this new sect upon the old noblesse of France. The deeds perpetrated by the Huguenots were often as offensive as those of their oppressors. "Now it was very easy for people to be Huguenots in those days, for all that was needful was to murder, to rob churches, to slander the Pope, to give the Host as provender to dogs and cattle, to grease boots and shoes with the Holy Oil." They thought nothing of dragging the image of the Virgin tied to a string through the mud, and one of their favourite pastimes was to mock the Host—"*Jehan le Blanc*," as they called it—when the priest bore it through the streets. Not unfrequently they committed worse sacrilege. A certain man rode one day into church on a horse "which was all accoutred in bright armour," and galloped up to the High Altar, shouting "Rob! come let us rob everything." Sometimes they forced their way into the churches and, driving out the congregation, began services of their own; and it was their constant habit to hold Prêches just outside the church-door, so that the noise of their psalm-singing might disturb the celebration of the Mass. They were wont to go to these ceremonies with loaded pistols in their hands, and they returned through the streets singing loudly the psalms of de Bèze or Marot; while if it were a Friday or a fast-day, they took good care to be seen eating meat in the public places. This was as they grew bolder. In the early days they met in secret by night, and only twice a month, at different houses of the community. One of the most important—the property of the University of Paris—was in the Rue St. Jacques, and the long grey street with its high-built, sober houses still recalls those Puritan figures walking swiftly to their "supper-parties," as they cautiously called these meetings. The Prêches they held on these occasions were simple enough, and though they varied slightly in detail, their main form was the same. They sang, or sometimes read, the Commandments; they prayed to the Holy Spirit; they had two Lessons, one of them from Exodus or Deuteronomy, and three times during the service the psalms of Marot were sung, "*en chant de musique lourde et pesante . . . pour émouvoir les cœurs d'entre eux.*" "After which," an old chronicler tells us, "the men and women, who till then had sat apart, were permitted to approach one another and to hold intercourse together as they wished, and after they had fondly saluted one another, the minister, or the preacher who took his place, declared aloud the charity that they owed to one another, reminding them likewise that all their possessions were in common, so that the faith might be upheld. Then, blowing out the candles in front of him, he spake these words: 'In the name of God, fulfil all brotherly charity, and may each one among you delight in the love of each.'" Many were the great ladies, some of them tied to Catholic lords, who "giving the slip to their husbands (the which took no note of what they did)," stole out to these mystic suppers and "took with them their maids or their daughters to prevent any suspicion." The Huguenots belonged to their times, and perhaps we can hardly be surprised that these ceremonies were abused and resulted in a good deal of scandal. Huguenot men forbade their womenkind to go to them and the midnight services got a bad name. Such evils arose from no special creed. The Renaissance invented Neo-Platonism, the Reformation its own forms of mysticism, and both satisfied a need and were alike capable of corruption.

The leading Huguenots did their best to remedy all these evils and to modify at least the manners of their more plebeian brethren. Renée of Ferrara, more especially, made great efforts at pacification, and attempted to turn the Prêches at Montargis into a private rite. But even she did not scruple to lay hands on the Catholic churchyard and enclose it in her private grounds, an action which led to a grievous riot in the city. For the orthodox party, taking fire, drove her workmen with stones from their task and the consequence was a pitched battle, with a sad waste of life for either faction.

However objectionable the new Dissenters were, one thing must always be remembered—that if they had been left alone they would have given no offence. The Catholics were the persecutors, the Huguenots the persecuted. Their failings and their virtues were alike created by their circumstances, and it is with the Catholics that the guilt from first to last must rest. "Arquebuses," said a contemporary, "were the church-bells of the Protestants," and it was their enemies who rang them. The brutality of these enemies was unrelenting. With every wish not to be sensational, the chronicler can hardly exaggerate the enormity of their deeds. The slightest pretext sufficed to provoke them and a spark at once became a bonfire. A lady of rank who was travelling towards Nogent did not stop her litter at a roadside shrine to the Virgin. In an instant a crowd collected, her escort was attacked, and the angry throng seized her litter and threw it into the Seine, unwitting that she had meantime slipped out and escaped in the general hubbub. Sacrilege was nothing to them. At the funeral of a certain Huguenot the Catholics dug up the body, and when the mourners again tried to bury it, they again exposed it and put it in the midst of the muddy high-road. The atmosphere was charged with suspicion. Spies were set to watch doubtful persons on their walks, and if any pious genuflexion was omitted, any ambiguous word dropped in conversation, any smile observed, however remote its cause, while some priestly procession was filing by, the unconscious victims were at once attacked and haled to their destruction. Sometimes they were hacked to pieces, sometimes they were drowned in the river, once a well was found full of them; and perhaps the most revolting symptom in all these persecutions is the fact that the children of Paris were allowed to mutilate the bodies. Morality cannot sink to a lower depth than the deliberate perversion of childhood, and the direct result of these enormities was the generation of Henri III.

The Protestant children were at any rate more edifying than their foes. Of their own accord they gathered together and held services in the open air, " singing the Psalms of David " with clear young voices, while one among them was chosen to preach and pray.

Paris, throughout these agitations, was the chief scene of persecution. The Sorbonne, the University, above all, the cruel Paris crowd, set themselves against innovation with the same implacable hatred. " God has not forgotten the people of Paris ! " was their war-cry, and they followed it with slaughter so horrible that the English Ambassador asked permission to withdraw. "All the towns of the kingdom put together"—cried Catherine—"would not bring me one half of the evils that I endure from Paris alone ! " The city personally resented her moderate Edicts; the Parlement refused to register them, the people to obey them. In the hope of checking these enormities, she issued a decree forbidding the punishment of heretics except officially by magistrates, but the Parisians paid no attention and continued to take justice into their own hands. And when she made a fresh attempt to promote some sort of toleration, they presented a formal petition, asking her—should the new measure pass—to let them leave France for some country where they would be allowed to live at peace in the Catholic faith. The clergy, too, actually rebelled when commanded to publish these Edicts from the pulpit. " Do they wish me to tell you "—cried a preacher—" that the cats and the rats are to live in peace together and not to do harm to one another ? . . . I am not a town-crier, or a city-trumpeter that I should make such proclamations ! " "And for a long time afterwards, the priests could talk of nothing in their sermons but of Ahab and

THE HUGUENOTS

Jezebel . . . the King of Navarre and the Queen-Mother"
—so notes an old diarist who must often have listened to these homilies. Louder and louder grew the complaints that the Court always favoured the Huguenots and put their opponents in the wrong—" Constraining the poor Catholics to be as patient as sheep." It is one of their number who thus comments, but their likeness to those meek animals seems rather far to seek. Although they may have had to suffer occasional injustice from the Regent, they took good care that their fortunes should not be substantially injured.

" The Huguenots "—said Tavannes—" were intent on establishing a democracy,"[1] and though, by now, the idea has become a platitude, it is strange to find a contemporary— especially a rude old soldier—already conscious of its meaning. Apart from doctrinal revolution and intellectual claims, the Reformation was [a movement suited to popular energies. And the central object of the Reformers' first campaign was a truly democratic one—the luxury and immorality of the priests. It was, thinks Claude Hâton, the sudden increase of this class—of these parasites who exhausted the community —which sharpened men's desire for reform; it was also their boorishness and ignorance. " For in a time of peace such village labourers as had three or four boys were delighted to send one to the Schools to make a priest of him, however vicious the life of his fellow-scholars." No wonder that the results were evil. Every history of the time abounds in details of clerical self-indulgence. " They are " (thus runs one account), " so befrizzed and besponged and bescented that they are in good sooth more like lovers, or the priests of Venus than the priests of Jesus Christ." The Council of Poissy passed a peremptory decree forbidding the clergy to wear " silk garments or slashed hose," but as no such measure could touch the wealth which was the source of the evil, all remained much as before. Ecclesiastical avarice had reached its climax. " No baby is baptized without money; no priest is ordained without money; no man and woman can marry without giving sums of money to the clergyman. These churchmen sell benches to their congregations at seven or eight crowns each ; . . . they will not put up prayers in the Temple of God unless they are handsomely paid . . . and they will not allow the burial of the dead without charging for opening up the

---
[1] He adds that it was a democracy imbued with the aristocratic element.

earth ... so much so that in some churches they ask ten pounds a corpse." Nor were they less ribald than grasping. "The first folk in brawls were always the priests, their swords in their hands; they were the first, too, at dances ... at fencing-matches, at taverns; and they reeled about the streets all night with the greatest scoundrels in the land." This is the testimony of a Catholic, and as such can hardly be rejected. And the worst part of these excesses was the immunity of those who committed them, for even supposing they were prosecuted, they always had a means of escape. This was "the postern gate, the false doorway of Justice, the Court of the Spiritual Power; hither resorted every kind of tonsured miscreant: homicides, parricides, thieves, false coiners ... as to a free haven from their crimes, where no one was too wicked to find salvation." And yet the majority of these men did not seem phenomena of vice to their contemporaries, nor did they often sink below the line of current morality; when they did, and when Protestant standards began to leaven public opinion, an outcry at once arose against them. French irony awoke to a sense of the situation, and from the days of Rabelais to those of Voltaire, French irony has been a potent weapon, swift to destroy shams. A shrewd spectator of the time sums up the whole matter: "Those"—he says—"who are not 'in religion' are the only religious people, for they have more troubles and more work for soul and body than the monks, who are well nicknamed 'Sans souci,' and never lose one hour of their pleasures. ... This advantage they enjoy, too, over laymen—that they do not have a single worry. ... That is why the Jesuits are more deserving; at any rate they work, and teach, and preach to the Infidels and are useful." Words such as these ring a knell announcing that the day of despot priests and of criminal prelates was over.

Against the sumptuous pride of such men, the sobriety of the Huguenot ministers stood out in striking contrast. The pomp and the pageant of the Mass, the blaze of candles and of vestments, were to pale before the simplicity of Prêches, which demanded nothing but a bare room, or a summer grass-plot. "As for the preacher, he held the service beneath a walnut-tree—he the while sitting in a chair, with a little table in front of him covered with a cloth that the Huguenots had brought with them, and upon the table there was only an open Bible." The author of this passage was a Papist, evidently stirred, in spite of himself, by what he saw. He also gives a moving account of a Huguenot funeral, which stands out in strong relief against the costly mourning processions so often described in the annals of the Catholic aristocracy. A Protestant nobleman had lost his wife. " He entered the church with the preacher. When the coffin was placed near the grave, before it was let down into the trench, the husband struck the bier three times with his foot, saying ' Sleep, Charlotte, sleep, until the Lord awaken thee.' These words he said twice, and then he went down into the trench. The preacher gave a funeral sermon, and every one sang some psalms of Marot's—the psalms that this sect calls its own."

The grave intensity that distinguished these proceedings went deeper than mere form. The ministers, as we have said, together with a few choice spirits, were the salt of the whole movement. The consistency of their life with their ideals gave them a strong hold upon their flocks, for consistency appeals to the *gros bons sens* of the people. It gave them, too, a solid advantage over the priests, and nothing is more surprising than the freedom which these Reformers used in theological discussion with prelates. There was one occasion when the Bishop of Châlons was sent to Vassy, accompanied by a monk famous for his eloquence, to try and check the growing heresy of the place. The Bishop begged the chief clergy to urge their parishioners to come and hear this friar, but was courteously told that they would not listen to false prophets, nor would the townspeople do so. But if the Bishop, they said, would come and hear *their* service, he would find that they proclaimed nothing that was not contained in the Gospel. The Bishop, to their great surprise, consented, and came in great state to the church with his monk and an attendant train. He tried his best, however, to keep off the congregation and he stopped the church-bells from ringing, but the Protestants gave their secret signal " *de main en main*," to one another, and the congregation gathered in silence. We can picture the curious scene : the people, like a swarm of bees, settling on their benches, the prelate in his purple and gold tissue, the prosperous monk by his side, the stern minister by the altar. He was saying a prayer to the Holy Spirit when the Bishop first interrupted him. But the minister, not allowing him to finish, took up the word. " ' As I was first in the pulpit,' he said, ' it is right that I should speak first. If you find anything to object to in my doctrine, you can say so afterwards.' The Bishop would only repeat the same words as before. 'Very well then,' exclaimed the minister at length, 'if you wish so much to talk, do so, not in your quality of Bishop but only as a private individual, for we do not recognize you as anything else.' 'Why is this?' asked the Bishop, 'since my office has come to me through the laying on of hands.' 'Because'—responded the minister—'a Bishop must preach the Word of God in truth. . . . But *you*, when have you fed your flock with the pasture of life? When have you administered the Sacraments or done the least thing required by your position?' 'How do you know that I don't preach?' demanded the Bishop. 'Yesterday,' quoth the minister, 'you yourself said that you could not preach and that the fact vexed you sorely.' 'And where'—persisted the Bishop—' is it written that Bishops must preach?' 'In Chapter vi of the Acts,' replied the minister, ' and also in Chapter i of Timothy.' (But we must not forget to say, in passing, that the minister, studying his sermon that very morning, had by God's Providence happed upon these two passages in searching for something else, and so it was easy for him to answer thus promptly, his memory being quite fresh.) The Bishop saw that he was trapped : ' Oh,' he said, ' I preach by my Vicars.' " There ensued a wordy quarrel about their respective rights, the minister contending that the Bishop was no Bishop, since the people had not elected him. The prelate looked over his shoulder. "I appeal to the Provost!" he exclaimed in a rage, but that functionary did not support him. " ' You must all of you be off,' cried the Bishop. ' I see clearly that madness governs everything here.' ' No, no,' answered the other, ' we are governed by the same holy zeal which inspired the Apostles to tell your predecessors it was better to obey God than man.' Whereupon the Bishop retired with his shame, nor was he so well attended as when he entered. . . . But when the people saw him withdraw with his monk who had never dared utter a word . . . many of them shouted ' After the wolf! after the fox! after the donkey! Go to school! Out with you, out!' " The ignominious couple repaired to the parish church, where the monk got up into the pulpit and preached to his master and the retinue; but hearing some slight sound, he thought he was being pursued and fled down the pulpit stairs, leaving his slipper behind him, and neither he nor the Bishop stopped till they had escaped from the church.

It was doubtless scenes like these that made persecution

more bitter. They also stirred the shrewd humour of the populace and helped the growth of the Protestant doctrines. These spread with amazing rapidity. Twenty years before the Council of Poissy, the new faith only numbered a few great names and the "*simples gens mécaniques et artisans*": such humble folk as wandered from one town or province to another, some of whom had lived in Geneva, others in Germany. "*Femmes, fols et enfants*," is a mordant contemporary summary of these early converts to Protestantism, and the number was increased by twelve hundred, through the influence of the German mercenaries in the employ of France who so long pervaded the country. But in the decade after 1550, not only the quantity but the quality of proselytes was changed. Where there had been one, there were now six, and whereas the provincial cities had formerly boasted twice as many Huguenots among the artizans as there were among the educated people, the statistics of 1560 showed that most of the bourgeois and gentlemen had gone over to the Reformed religion. The results of these conversions were strange, bordering on a kind of Christian Socialism—a superficial and exotic Socialism, not unlike that of modern drawing-rooms. For "the gentlefolk and the Justices, notwithstanding they were richly clad, made room next them for the labourers and mechanics—working-men of every kind—and importuned each one, even the cowman and the swineherd, to sit close to them, in their coarse smocks and coats of linsey-woolsey; and so as to give them courage to turn round, they offered them delicate meats, and wine in silver cups, all of which they brought to Prêches."

Such doings did not only mean a grotesque deterioration from due reverence, but were dangerous because of the attention that they attracted, and they brought about several arrests.

Throughout these developments Catherine preserved much the same demeanour. She still dallied with orthodoxy, but showed that her sympathies were Protestant. A party at Court, numbering many of her ladies, supported her. There was also another set of people who arrived at the same tolerant conclusions by directly opposite roads—men who, like Tavannes, thought that "there never was a disease of the brain so ill thought out as that of Calvinism; wherefore, instead of lighting faggots, or using abnormal remedies, it is better to let Nature have her course." And thus, between the sceptics and the heretics, it was easy to maintain an atmosphere of moderation round the throne as long as there was no conflict with the country. There is no stranger record of the Regent's heterodoxy than the tale of a Catholic preacher who was at this time exciting Paris. He was a monk of about thirty, famed for his fervour and eloquence, and both Papists and Protestants flocked to his church to hear him. Rumours of the sensation he was making reached the ears of Catherine at Saint-Germain, and taking fright at his success, she sent delegates to Paris—" *hommes curieux et de bon esprit* "—to listen to his sermons and report to her. This they did in glowing terms. Catherine, who never lost time, straightway despatched five hundred foot and horses to seize the too popular monk and bring him to her to be judged. The capture was impossible by day for fear of a revolt in the city, but when night came, a band of armed men entered the preacher's room and roused him from his sleep. In vain did he shout for assistance; a few helpless neighbours put out their heads and, hearing some pistol shots, withdrew them again. The reluctant monk was taken and brought down the Seine in a little boat to Saint-Germain, where he was summoned before the King and his mother. They cross-examined him, they tried to confound him, they commanded a Protestant minister to hold a theological dispute with him. But for once the monk came off victorious; in spite of which the Constable was ordered to conduct him to the kitchen and have him thrashed by the lackeys there. This ignominious charge may have been Catherine's vengeance on the Catholic Constable for joining the three-fold League against her, a vengeance which failed as far as the priest was concerned. " For when they undressed him, they found a coarse hair-shirt next to his skin . . . the which moved the spectators to compassion. And the aforesaid Sieur Connétable . . . forbade any person to injure him by word or deed." A deputation had ere this arrived from Paris to beg that their preacher might be restored to them, and the King, giving his consent, sent him safely back to the city.

Catherine's fear of an eloquent priest was anything but groundless. A Catholic revival at that moment meant a Catholic insurrection which would not have been easy to quell; but how far this dread was mixed up with her natural taste for heterodoxy it is difficult to say. She attempted to avoid the risk of public display on either side. The Huguenot party, meanwhile, perceiving their precarious situation, did

THE HUGUENOTS

their utmost to sue for her favour. Jealous of the impression created by the wealth and show of their adversaries, and fearful lest their humble trappings should draw down contempt upon their cause, they tried a little innocent strategy. On a solemn occasion when they were to file in procession past her windows, on their way to some function, they went so far as to doff their black and hire grand suits of clothes and fashionable tippets, that she might be dazzled by delusions of their opulence. But when they walked past the palace in this childish and ungodly guise, she was not there to see, and their money, which had come out of the common purse, was found to have been spent in vain.

Her absence was probably deliberate—as much an act of policy on her part as the quelling of the Catholic preacher. It was gradually being borne in upon her that her own security would demand a renunciation of the Protestants; that Spain was too strong for her, the King of Navarre too weak a prop to counterbalance its hostility, and the time not far off when she must stand forth as the champion of the Catholics. Disintegrating influences were at work in her mind, but she was too wary to let any sign of them appear in her outward behaviour. If a storm were brewing, men only knew that this was so by the stillness of the air.

Old writers give two derivations of the word Huguenot. Some say it came from a corruption of the German noun "Eidgenossen," or "confederates"; others attribute it to "Hugues," an old ghost of Tours. In the deserted place that he was supposed to haunt, the heretics held their Prêches by night, and, so says legend, the folk of the country-side learned to call them the Huguenots, or followers of Hugues. Modern readers may choose whichever derivation they please; accuracy may perhaps demand the first, but allegory prefers the second. For the Huguenots were surely the ghosts who haunted the hidden places in the life of Catherine de' Medici.

CHAPTER X

Catherine and the Prince de Condé

AUTHORITIES CONSULTED

Memoirs du Prince de Condé.
Journal de l'an 1562—*Revue Rétrospective.*
Memoirs de Henri II—*Archives Curieuses.*
Memoirs de Tavannes.
Biographical Introductions to " Lettres de Catherine de' Medici."
Histoire de France—*Michelet.*
Histoire de France—*Martin.*
Rélations de la Diplomatie Vénitienne—*Baschet.*
Jeanne d'Albret—*Miss Freer.*

CHAPTER X

Catherine and the Prince de Condé

THE Venetian ambassador, Michieli, has left us a portrait of Catherine in this same year of 1562, when she was forty-three years old.

"Her intelligence" (he says) "is all alive—she is affable, capable in affairs, diplomatic before all things. . . . She never loses the King from sight, nor allows any one but herself to sleep in his room. She knows that there is a grudge against her because she is a foreigner . . . but she holds everything in the hollow of her hand . . . including the royal seals. In the Council Chamber she lets others speak first, but her opinion is their final Court of Appeal. . . . In her way of living— materially speaking—she shows very little rule. Her appetite is enormous; she is assiduous in taking exercise, walking much, riding hard . . . hunting with the King, her son, pushing him into the midst of tangled thickets, following him with an intrepid courage such as one rarely sees . . . While she walks or eats she always talks about affairs with somebody or other. She turns her mind not only to things political, but to so many others that I don't know how she can face all these manifold interests. And she is quite the woman to undertake six important buildings at the very moment when all these thoughts are preoccupying her. . . . Nor does she lack means to find money. . . Her allowance of 300,000 francs a year is double that of any other Queen-Dowager and she spends largely and liberally. . . . Her complexion is olive-coloured and she is already a stout woman."

This olive-coloured woman (a pendant to the "sea-green" Robespierre) was still playing high for power. "For she was stealthy and of such a crafty malice that she delighted in setting the Princes by the ears." Men began to call her "Madame la Rouyne," instead of "Madame la Royne (Reine)," and "Madame le Serpent," was another favourite nickname for her. "The Huguenots say that she cheated them by sweet words and by her air of deceiving kindness, while all the time she was plotting their destruction with the Catholic King. The Catholics, on the other hand, say that if the Queen had not encouraged the Huguenots, they would not have gone so far." Thus the Venetian ambassador, who well knew the woman he was writing about. Catherine continued to try prevarication and to stave off decision as long as she could. "This business needs other counsel than that of force," she writes, "for I don't want to make matters worse, still less to have trouble abroad, and my only wish is to let time pass, if possible, without spoiling anything irremediably until my son comes of age. . . . Those who are seriously ill are excusable if, when their pain grows unbearable, they use every kind of herb to soothe it while they are waiting for the doctor's arrival. . . . For to imagine that this kingdom can continue in obedience and concord, while men's spirits are so much bruised and tossed with divers opinions, why, there is not a soul alive who does not know this to be impossible."

But she found that a stronger medicine was needful, and her policy of self-preservation forced her to turn even more distinctly towards the Catholic party.

"Monsieur de Limoges" (she says this year to her Ambassador in Spain), "I should like all my lords to write to the King of Spain and tell him how I stand with regard to religion . . . because of the lies that have been spread concerning me. . . . For neither in will, nor deed, nor in my way of living, have I changed my religion—and I have held it these forty-three years and was baptized and brought up therein, and I am not at all sure that most people can say as much. And no one must be surprised that I am annoyed, for this falsehood has lasted too long for mortal patience ; and when one has a clean conscience it wounds one sorely that those who have none should talk so boldly of this matter. Show this letter to the Duke of Alva and to the King, for I do not wish him to think that I am begging for a testimonial merely because all my life I have kept a straight road. I am writing because I can no longer bear to receive people's suffrage as a charity, and because I want to shut the mouths of those who have hitherto taken pains to put me out of the favour of His Majesty, my son-in-law, which I treasure more dearly than my own life."

She founded her hopes of a reconciliation with Spain upon

LOUIS DE BOURBON, PRINCE DE CONDÉ,
VERS 1565.
PORTRAIT ANONYME. BIBLIOTHÈQUE NATIONALE.
From a photograph by A. Giraudon.

the possible abolition of the mischief-making Guises. The injuries done her, she tells Limoges, all come "from the same shop." "There are those" (she says) "who want to prove that nothing marches well without the Guises . . . But instead of my thinking that all will go to ruin if the Cardinal is no longer here, I assure you that it would be this event alone which would give me the means of putting everything to rights again." Jeanne d'Albret herself writes to warn her foe of the Guises' double-dealing and to tell her of a letter from the Cardinal which had fortunately been intercepted on its way to Alva, in Spain. "Whatever assurance the Queen-Mother makes me," so the wily prelate had written, "I cannot believe in the least that (supposing a certain person were not in existence), she would not let herself go completely. She is such a dissembler that when she says one thing, she thinks another. Her one aim is to rule—as she does. As for the rest, I know that it does not trouble her." The writer of this note was not far wrong, for at that very time she was making pathetic appeals to Antoine of Navarre to protect the royal widow and orphans—an appeal, as usual, only answered with fair words.

Meanwhile the Guises, powerful though they were, had grown thoroughly alarmed at the increasing power of the Protestants. They knew that Catherine was wavering and that their only course was to excite her suspicions. And they had good ground to go upon, for they had discovered indications of a Huguenot conspiracy of which they warned the King and the Regent. Yet de Bèze, who had preached throughout Lent, was allowed to continue his sermons, while the Puritans filed through the streets chanting the Lamentations of Jeremiah. The strain throughout the city was intense and everybody felt that a crisis was fast approaching. On Easter Monday "the Papists and the Huguenots came and went all together, the first to 'Pardon,' the others to 'Prêches.' And they looked at each other and neither spake a word." These few lines, written by a citizen in his journal probably straight on his return from witnessing the scene, fill us with a strangely vivid dread, and the silence of these grim processions is more ominous than speech. Soon after, a letter from a minister which was intercepted on its way, brought the Guises the news that the Huguenots were planning a wholesale massacre of the Catholics, having first learned, they said, that the Catholics had meant to do the same by them. "And he cited the example of Gideon and Judith and wrote that he felt in his spirit a God-sent vocation to do this deed "—so reports the same citizen, who had just seen the fatal document. The Duc de Guise took instant action. He armed fifteen hundred of his men who swore that they would die in his service; and, determined to play the King in Paris and produce an indelible impression, he summoned Corporation and Parlement to attend him at his Hôtel du Temple, where with much arrogant ceremony he made them swear fealty to him. The orthodox of Paris mustered strong; they lighted a great bonfire in the Rue St. Jacques and for three hours burned all the Bibles they could lay hands on. The churches of the city were crowded; and when the Cardinal preached on the Real Presence, St. Germain l'Auxerrois was thronged to overflowing with the fashion and the learning of the capital. The Prêches, on the contrary, had grown emptier: it was easy to see, says a spectator, that the Prince de Condé had departed.

For the Prince had been warned that Paris was no longer a safe abode for him and he left it suddenly in secret. His adversaries said that he had meant to seize Paris, but finding that his scheme was discovered he had thrown it up in despair. However that may be, he now proceeded to Meaux. His programme was to muster the Protestant leaders and to await help from the Regent who was with the King at Fontainebleau. Catherine, terrified at the turn affairs had taken, at the imminence of war and the re-established supremacy of the Guises, had foreseen that she would fall into their power, and again changed front. She suspected—and events proved her right—that they meant to remove her by force with the King to Paris, where they could watch all her movements. At Fontainebleau she had free play and opportunity to correspond with Condé. She knew this state of things could not last, and she threw herself and her son upon that gallant Prince's protection—confided her fears and woes to him—entreated his instant succour. Condé replied that, before all else, she should make herself mistress of Orleans and place Charles IX there in safety. There followed those letters from Catherine which became of such signal importance because Condé used them as a justification for making war. Catherine, on her side, protested with a great show of frankness that he had misrepresented her meaning, that she had begged him only to protect the King, not to take the side of his enemies; and that, the purposes of loyalty once fulfilled, she had wished the Prince

CATHERINE AND THE PRINCE DE CONDÉ

to lay down arms. Her letters, of which for a long time only fragments were given, have now been discovered and re-published, and the three which bear on the point in question are worth quoting here whole, if only as a specimen of the suave casuistry by which the Regent wrought such havoc.

" My Cousin " (runs the first of these)—

" I have spoken to Ivoy as freely as if he had been yourself, because I am sure that he is faithful and will say nothing to any one but you, and that you will never quote me and will have no other thought than the safety of the children and their mother—as befits one whom this concerns, one, too, who may be certain that he will never be forgotten. Burn this letter at once.

" Votre bonne cousine,
" CATHERINE."

This was closely followed by:
" My Cousin—

" Thank you for the trouble you give yourself in sending me such constant news of you and, as I hope to see you so soon, I will not now write a long letter. I will only pray you to feel sure that I shall never forget what you are doing for me; and if I die before I am able to acknowledge it as I wish, I shall leave instructions to my children. I have ordered the bearer of this to tell you something which I beg you to believe; and I feel confident that you will know that everything I do is done to restore peace and repose—a consummation which I know you desire as much as

" Votre bonne cousine,
" CATHERINE."

" If you please give my compliments to your wife and your mother-in-law and your uncle."

Soon after, came the last of the three:
" My Cousin—

" I see so many things which vex me, that if it were not for my faith in God and my conviction that you will help me to keep this kingdom safe and to serve my son, the King, in spite of those who wish for universal ruin, I should be yet more vexed; but I hope we shall still remedy all things with your good counsel and aid. And as I have told my mind at length to the bearer of this, I will not repeat it here, but will beg you to believe all that he says to you both, on behalf of

" Votre bonne cousine,
" CATHERINE."

The Regent's fears were now to be justified. The Duc de Guise, followed by Navarre and Saint-André, arrived without warning at Fontainebleau and, listening to no remonstrance, compelled the King and his mother to return, well guarded, to Paris. Dressed in black, as if in mourning, they entered the city without state and remained there for a short time, till their tyrants removed them to Melun. Here, though treated with great courtesy, they were practically the prisoners of the Guises, cut off from outside communication and dependent upon continual intrigue for any letters that they sent or received.

Meanwhile, Condé lingered at Meaux awaiting the support that Catherine's letters had led him to expect, and here Coligny joined him. Neither of them objected to the delay, for both alike were anxious to stave off the horrors of civil war. It was after they had removed to Saint-Cloud that news reached them of the Guises' *coup de main* and of their carrying off the King and Regent. This put a new face on matters; the time for hesitation was passed and they moved with armed troops towards Orleans. They advanced slowly, because Condé was still hoping to hear from the Queen-Mother; but what was his surprise when a messenger arrived with a letter from her peremptorily ordering him to lay down arms and come to Paris. At the same time he had tidings that part of the Duc de Guise's army was also marching upon Orleans. Condé was only six leagues off the city, but there was no time to be lost and the crisis called forth all his brilliance. He made a sudden rush with his troops, surprised the place, forced the hand of the Governor, and entered it in triumph amidst shouts of welcome and of " Vive l'Évangile " from the populace. Coligny, d'Andelot, La Rochefoucauld, were with him; so was Montgoméry, the man whose lance had killed Henri II, and who had figured since then as an important person among the Huguenots—and there was nothing wanting to make the town what it now became, the centre of the Protestant party. Hence the Prince wrote to Geneva, to Austria, to every minister throughout France, the while he incited the townsfolk to work and fight for their faith, so that when the enemy arrived to attack Orleans, he found an organized resistance. Other cities followed suit. Within three months from the outbreak of war, Blois, Tours, Poitiers, La Rochelle, Agen, Montauban, Béziers, Nîmes, Montpellier, Lyons, Valence, Caen, Dieppe, Bayeux, and twelve other less important places had declared for the Protestants. "When any one inquired what towns the Huguenots had reduced, the reply was, 'You should rather inquire the names of the places which they do not hold.'"

Navarre covered Catherine with reproaches and told her that she was the cause of all the troubles of France, that she had set the Bourbons against the Guises and treated the princes of the blood "worse than she treated the lowest Italian of her suite." Catherine, beset by fear on all sides, wrote to the Cardinal de Châtillon and begged him to mediate between her and Condé, but she took good care to give her own version of the letters she had written to him from Fontainebleau. She had meant, she said, to write nothing more to the Prince de Condé; but he, having asked her permission to wear arms for the sake of his own preservation and the service of herself and the King, she sent a note allowing him to do so, on condition that he would disarm the moment she told him she wished it. "And after the King of Navarre and all the lords had arrived at Fontainebleau, I sent my valet to the Prince and wrote that I begged him to lay down arms and to bid the rest do the same. But this he would not do, saying that his honour was at stake. . . . And seeing that he also told me that he wanted to keep his army, so that no one might diminish my authority, or take my children away from me . . . I wanted to show him that I was not using force, and I sent Serlan to him to entreat him, as he loved me, to lay down arms. . . . But Serlan returned with the same answer that the valet had already brought me." . . . "And not content" (she writes elsewhere) "with breaking his promise to disarm, when I begged and commanded him to do so, he wrongs me afresh by proclaiming throughout the realm that it was I who made him resort to arms and I who wished him to occupy the towns that have been taken in his name. . . . I would, in sooth, pledge my life to see the realm at peace as I desire, and as I pray God that it may be."

"We give you plenty of material for history"—Catherine might well have used these words, jotted down by a nameless chronicler in his diary of 1562. For as event followed event, the drama grew ever more entangled. The country was ablaze with civil war. Condé remained obstinate, alleging that Catherine had bidden him defend her and the King, and that he would not come to terms while the Guises kept them prisoners. If there was anything sincere about Catherine it was her desire for peace—a desire which in all her tortuous course never ceased to stand out clear and unaltered; and in order to promote this end, she now persuaded the Guises to allow her to remove to Monceaux, that Condé might see that she was no captive. The tyrants at the same time caused the King to publish a manifesto declaring that he had full liberty, but neither Condé nor the nation were deceived by this evident falsehood. Distrust reigned everywhere, and Chantonnay wrote that even now no one knew to which party the Regent belonged. She was outwardly submitting to the Guises, and secretly writing to Marguerite de Savoie to help the Huguenots of Lyons and Provence.

A country so distraught and so rudderless was an easy prey for other nations. Spain, England, Savoy, had each their own ambitions to fulfil and found easy means of gaining influence, since each of them was necessary to Catherine. For when she was a Catholic she needed Spain against the Guises, and when she was a Protestant she needed England; Savoy, bordering on France, was ever an invaluable ally. The constant possibility of interference from the outside was a serious peril at this moment, and Catherine's only hope lay in the likelihood that one power would exasperate the other. Elizabeth alone had the skill to dignify the word interference, and create the policy of intervention, a very important departure in the field of international politics. She intervened, it is true, in the nominal interests of the Protestants, but her real motive was either to win back Calais or, failing that, to take some port in Normandy and thus get a firm hold upon the French. Just now she was in constant correspondence both with Coligny and Condé, and had Catherine resolutely courted her friendship, she might still have offered a strong resistance to Philip II as well as to the Guises. But her fear of Spain, as always, held her back, and she lost her chance of evoking a large and closely-knitted Protestant party.

Not even her fear of Spain, however, quite accounts for her choppings and changings at this eventful juncture—for the vacillating tactics which injured her in the eyes of the Guises and of every other faction. Any conduct on the part of the Regent which did not serve her self-interest makes us stop to wonder and to think, and over these particular months of her life there doubtless hangs a certain mystery. There is one hypothesis which explains it, but a mere hypothesis it remains, in spite of the rumours which supported it. For scandal was beginning to be busy about her and the Prince de Condé, and it soon became the talk of the town that she meant to make him her husband. Some tongues went further, as Claude Hâton writes in his diary : "For" (says he) "the aforesaid lady was taxed with dishonour by the common people, as well as by folk of repute ... And the general opinion ran that she was in love—madly in love—with him, (*amoureuse d'un fol amour*) but this I don't believe," so adds the shrewd commentator. Yet although he was probably right to disbelieve in a *grande passion*, so much smoke most likely meant some fire, and it is more than possible that the kind of emotional fascination which Condé exercised over her had a good deal to do with her strange behaviour during his rebellion.

The great Catholic force was divided into three sections—the first at Estampes, led by the King of Navarre ; the second in the neighbourhood of Rouen, led by the Duc d'Aumale ; the third at Lyons, led by the Duc de Nemours ; and against these the Prince de Condé continued to make gallant resistance. In despair of a solution, Catherine summoned Antoine de Navarre, who went to her under strong remonstrance ; for the Guises, knowing l'Échangeur too well, dreaded the heretical effect that her personal influence might have on him. Her move was a skilful one, for Navarre at last succeeded in making Condé consent to hold an interview with her. When the news of this was brought to her " she had a transport of joy," so said the Cardinal of Ferrara who happened to be with her at the time and could not have shared her rejoicings. She and Antoine travelled together to meet Condé, as he had appointed, at a little place called Toury, not far from Estampes, but the erratic Prince never appeared. He came the next day, excusing himself on the plea that he had waited for a stronger escort. Catherine was warm in her welcome, but his bearing to her was cold and he lost no time in coming to business. He wanted, he said firmly, the maintenance of the Edict of January and the removal of all the Catholic leaders. Catherine, on her side, prevaricated. She would grant, she said, liberty of conscience, but not of public worship, a clause which was a partial repeal of the Edict that not six months before she had forced upon the Parlement of Paris. They parted without coming to any agreement and a second interview, proposed by himself, did not bring more definite results. In vain she made an attempt to induce the leading Catholics to retire, and everything seemed at a standstill. But Condé was thawing beneath her spell—and in the course of two more meetings he practically submitted. To the dismay of his colleagues, who must have thought that he was bewitched, he suddenly betrayed every principle that he and they had cherished, and pledged his word that all the Protestant leaders should withdraw and remain in seclusion until the King reached his majority.

Upon receiving the news of this agreement, Coligny asked leave once more to see the Regent and bid her a reluctant farewell, as not only, he said, was he going to retire to his house according to the treaty, but he, together with d'Andelot, intended to go away from France until the King should come of age. Catherine consented and travelled in Condé's company to the place that was fixed upon for the meeting. The Prince, who had gone so far towards peace as to sleep the night before with his brother of Navarre, hardly so much as took leave of him, so firmly had he resolved to return again with the Regent. When he and she reached their destination, Coligny kept them waiting for a long time; and when he did appear, his arrival did not savour of a truce, for he brought with him two thousand foot and no less than four hundred horse. The fact was that he had a good memory and the thought of the arrest of Condé at Orleans kept him on the look-out for treachery. Catherine prudently made no comment, "but, like a wise princess, she thought the more," and, receiving his salute with all honour, she kissed him upon the lips, as was her custom when she welcomed grandees. She expressed deep regret at his departure, promised to respect his property, and allowed him to take his leave. But what was her dismay when Condé suddenly announced his intention of accompanying the Admiral on his journey, instead of going back with Catherine as he had promised. She knew too well what it meant: Coligny had refused to accept the conditions to which Condé had acceded; Condé did not dare to tell the Regent that he had broken his word; he got out of the difficulty by flight, and civil war again became imminent.

Catherine did not know where to turn. Her so-called espousal of the Catholic cause had done very little for her, and she complained bitterly to Chantonnay that Philip had not given her the help that he had promised, adding that if he did not do so, her son, when he came of age, would act in all matters of religion exactly as it pleased him. Whereupon the Envoy, taking alarm, warned Philip that unless he sent support to the Regent, she would throw in her lot with the Huguenots—a conclusion which was the more likely since Paris, unappeased, was rising against her and she wished to reconcile England, which at that moment had an eye upon Havre. But the turn that events now took removed this immediate anxiety. The Catholics had a signal victory when they entered the town of Bourges. Montargis was the next place to be taken and, in the summer, Antoine de Navarre had moved from Estampes and begun to lay siege to Rouen.

In the months that had passed, Antoine had been playing a sorry part. His character had not grown more stable. *Caillette* (a little quail whose coat changes colour) became the popular nick-name for him, and "*Caillette qui tourne sa jaquette*" was the refrain of a topical song in great vogue among the Huguenot soldiers. To them he was "Julian the Apostate" and their opponents were scarcely more respectful. "L'Échangeur understands nothing and perceives nothing"—wrote Catherine's secretary to her ambassador in Spain—"It is not possible for any man to conduct himself worse than he does. He does not know to what Saint to bow and in all this business he is turned by every wind. . . . To-day when we were debating whether or no we should accept 10,000 men and 3,000 horse from His Majesty, the Queen-Mother said that to do so would be to proclaim the Catholic King, King of France. L'Échangeur went off straighway and reported the Queen's words to Chantonnay, at which she feels much vexed, for she has no doubt that the ambassador will carry her remark to His Majesty."

Antoine's confidences to Philip were by no means unmotived, and on June 20 of this year, the King of Spain, anxious to make sure of him, granted him his long-cherished desire—Spanish Navarre. This must have been a bitter pill to his wife, since it was to her that the province should by rights have been restored. But she took no note of her husband and busied herself with home affairs and with the formal establishment of the Reformed religion in Béarn. Antoine, greatly angered by the help she had given to Condé, now sent a Commission there to rout the Protestants and establish the orthodox Church, but Jeanne coolly arrested his chief emissary and allowed her husband's name to be erased from the Liturgy used in her kingdom. "It is high time" (she said) "to quit the land of Egypt, to traverse the Red Sea, and to rescue the Church of Christ from amid the ruins of Babylon."

Antoine took a mean vengeance upon his wife. Their little son, Henri, who was at Saint-Germain, under no better care than that of La belle Rouet, fell dangerously ill of smallpox, and his mother entreated Catherine to allow her to nurse the child. But the Regent and the King of Navarre knew too well that if they gave up the Prince they would lose the only hold they had upon her; and all that she could gain was the Regent's permission to send the boy to Renée of Ferrara—who, Protestant though she was, was also the mother of the Duchesse de Guise and so, by a strange inconsistency, was allowed to be the young Henri's guardian. The boy recovered and the affair would remain unnoticed, were it not that this passage about their child was practically the last that took place between the King and Queen of Navarre. For at the siege of Rouen which followed it, King Antoine met with his death.

The siege, begun in the summer, lasted till the end of October. The Protestants inside the town were reinforced by Elizabeth, who lent them help and promised them money on condition that they should give her Havre. The condition was granted and Havre was sold to the English. The Huguenots were to triumph still further. In mid-October, while Antoine was still before Rouen, he was severely wounded. La belle Rouet, who was with him, nursed him with the utmost devotion and he had the services of skilful doctors—one, the Jesuit Lauro, the other (characteristically enough) a Huguenot of some repute. Catherine was then with the besieging party which she had come to inspect, and her first letters give no indication that his condition showed cause for serious anxiety. He would not, however, obey his doctors, or take the rest that they prescribed. All the gayest and most ribald of the Regent's attendant dandies gathered in his sick-room to amuse him with the latest scandals from Court, while he listened and laughed, stretched upon a low couch, with La belle Rouet by his side. Or companies of boys and girls danced before him to the music of timbrels and satisfied his insatiate need for noise and distraction. When the news came that his army had at last taken Rouen, he persisted in making a triumphal entry into the town in his litter, and was carried back in a fainting-fit. He rallied to enjoy fresh licence and fresh laughter, but there was now no doubt that his days were numbered,

CATHERINE AND THE PRINCE DE CONDÉ

and his Huguenot doctor begged a certain great prelate, who was there, to tell him so. Antoine heard the verdict with unruffled calm, but he sent the crowd away from his room and begged to be alone with La belle Rouet.

His mind now veered again towards religion and all his old waverings came back. He was, he owned, a Catholic by profession, yet his heart returned to the Protestant faith. Lauro, seeing the King's peril, at once brought a priest to his bedside and Antoine yielded and confessed, but his doing so was followed by despondency. That evening, Catherine came to visit him and to bid him a last farewell before she left Rouen for Vincennes. "Brother," said she when she observed his melancholy, "you should get somebody to read to you." "Madam," he answered with hesitation, "the people around me are now mostly Huguenots." "They are no less your servants, Monseigneur," was the Regent's ambiguous retort. When she had left him, he ordered one of these Protestant attendants to read aloud the Book of Job, to which he listened devoutly. "Ah, Raphael," he presently exclaimed, "here are you who have served me these twenty years and it is only now that you warn me about the miserable mistakes of my life;" whereupon he confessed his sins aloud and swore that if he recovered, he would send forth Lutheran missionaries to preach the Gospel throughout France. Nor was this mood only of the moment. The remembrance of his wife haunted him, and more than once he said that he was surprised at her not coming to see him in his illness. One evening when the same "Raphael" was reading out from St. Paul and came to the words, "Wives, obey your husbands," Antoine impetuously stopped him. "You see"—he broke in—"that God Himself commands women to give obedience to their husbands." "True, *Sire*," replied the bold Raphael, "but the Scriptures also say, 'husbands love your wives.'"

Shortly before the end, he bade his attendants tell every one that he had once more become a Huguenot. "Never mind if they believe it or not," he said, "for I am firmly resolved to live—or die—in accordance with the Confession of Luther." In the middle of November his friends agreed to move him. He was carried by night to a boat and taken down the Seine towards Saint-Maur, his brother, the Cardinal de Bourbon, and the Prince de Roche-sur-Yon being with him. The movement of the boat greatly increased his sufferings, and towards morning he begged his faithful Raphael to repeat the

Huguenot prayers for those in extremity. All the people on board knelt round him, taking part in the solemn service, except the Cardinal and the Prince, who did not uncover their heads but stood aside in protest. Yet when the prayers were ended, the Cardinal de Bourbon was heard to mutter to himself —"These are, indeed, true orisons and not what I supposed; they believe as we do." Notwithstanding, he had no hesitation in sending for a Jacobin priest to preside over the last scene of all.

The King had been carried on shore, for his consciousness was fast ebbing. He had been lying for some time with his eyes closed, and when he opened them he found a strange monk bending over him. "Who are you that thus address me?" he asked—"I die as a sincere Christian." But the monk prayed on uninterrupted and when he had done, Antoine said "Amen." Thus he passed away, while he was still in his prime, for he was barely thirty-four years of age. He died as he had lived, between two religions, playing with both, convinced of neither, sentimental, irresolute, unblest, the sport of unresisted fate.

The Catholics made the most of the Jacobin monk and described Antoine's death in rapturous terms. "Our Lord called him to Himself, but so great was his knowledge of God and so deep his repentance that he may be said to have had the most beautiful and holy death possible," so runs a letter from Charles IX, which the Guises had evidently dictated. But such words duped no one of importance, and death itself could not dignify Antoine de Navarre.

What Jeanne felt when she learned that she was a widow—what bitter pangs of remembered happiness—history does not record. Within seven months afterwards, Chantonnay was trying to arrange her marriage with the mad Don Carlos; or, failing him, with Don John of Austria, the illegitimate son of Charles V. For all answer, Jeanne interdicted the exercise of the Roman faith in her realm, confiscated the property of the Church, and used it for the benefit of the Protestants and the foundation of colleges and schools; while a permanent Council of Nine was established by her "to settle the affairs of religion and administer these newly acquired revenues." She kept nothing for herself or for any private person. All churches with insufficient congregations were to be given over to the Reformers, and in places where the two sects were equally balanced, the church, she decreed, should be the common property of both. In vain did Pope Paul IV excommunicate her. She burnt the images of the Saints round every shrine, had the High Altar removed from the cathedral of Lescar, and was present with great solemnity at the first Huguenot service that was held there. Little recked she of Papal Bulls; she saw one thing before her and accomplished the task that she had set herself.

The Cardinal d'Armagnac threatened her with the enmity of France and Spain. "Assure yourself, Madam," he wrote, "that it is impossible for you to plant a new religion in your narrow territories, surrounded as you are by such potent kings and not having, like the realm of England, the great ocean as a rampart." "I well know the Kings, my neighbours"—she retorted—" The one hates the religion I profess and I also abhor his faith. . . . The other is the root of my race, from which it is my greatest honour to be an offshoot." And she continues to give the Cardinal her views in words that could not be accused of any Jesuitical tendency. "As to what you observe"—she says—" about the early Fathers of the Church, I hear them constantly quoted by our ministers . . . but I own that I am not as learned as I ought to be in this matter. I do not believe, however, that you are more competent than myself, for I remark you have always applied yourself more to the study of politics than of divinity. . . . Turn to the 22nd chapter of St. Luke's Gospel, and learn for the future to comprehend a passage before you quote it: an error of the kind, nevertheless, would be excusable in a woman, such as I am, but, *certes, mon cousin*, to see an old Cardinal like yourself so ignorant kindles shame . . . I know not where you have learned that there are so many diversities of sects among our ministers; though, at the Colloque de Poissy I became very sensible of your own divisions in doctrine and practice. We have one God, one faith, one law . . . I thank the Lord that I know, without the aid of your teaching, how to serve and please Him, and the King my sovereign lord, and all other Princes . . . all of whom I appreciate better than you can do. I also know how to bring up my son, so that hereafter he may be great and revered. . . . You request me not to think it strange or to take in bad part what you have written. Strange—I set no value on your words, considering of what order you are; but as to taking them in bad part, that I do as much as is possible in this world. . . . I bid you keep your tears to deplore your own errors; to the which, out of charity, I will add my own; putting up, at the same time, the most fervent prayer that ever left my lips, that you may be restored to the true fold, and become a faithful shepherd instead of a hireling . . . and likewise I desire that your useless letter may be the last of its kind. . . . From her who knows not how to subscribe herself; being fearful of signing herself your friend, and who ever doubts her relationship to you; but whom, in the day of your penitent repentance, you will find

"Votre bonne cousine et amye,
"Jehanne."

This letter is not a triumph of diplomacy, but Jeanne could be persuasive when she chose, and Catherine now wrote begging her to make the Prince de Condé listen to reason. No truce, however, was yet possible, and the month of Navarre's death was a fatal one in all ways for Catherine, and completed a disastrous record. The Protestants were signally victorious, and after wresting from her first Havre, and then Rouen, two of her most important places, they proceeded towards Paris. Their cruelties, horrible to read of, were helping to depopulate the country and one of their leaders, the barbarous Baron d'Adrets, by himself had near a thousand men massacred, besides four hundred and sixty women and eighty innocent children. The Catholic army was no better; while, added to the horrors of war, a bitter cold summer of persistent fog and rain, and a winter of unusual severity brought famine and pestilence in their train and made appalling devastations—eighty thousand poor people dying in the Hôtel-Dieu at Paris alone. The trenchant pen of Ronsard has described the general ruin in his "Discours des misères de ce temps."

> Dès longtemps les écrits des antiques prophètes,
> Les songes ménaçants, les hideuses comètes,
> Avaient assez prédit que l'année soixante et deux
> Rendrait de tous côtés les Français malheureux . .
> . . . Le ciel qui a pleuré tout le long de l'année,
> Et Seine qui courait d'une vague effrénée,
> Et bêtail, et pasteurs, et maisons ravissait,
> De son malheur futur Paris avertissait . . .
> . . . L'artisan par ce monstre a laissé sa boutique,
> Le pasteur ses brebis, l'avocat sa prâtique . . .

It was through a sadly stricken country that Condé and his men had to march before they reached their destination and prepared to besiege Paris. The Duc de Guise, with his force, followed close upon his enemy's heels, expecting to be joined by the Spanish troops that Philip had promised. These, however, did not appear, and the Duke found himself in a perilous position, at the head of a dispirited army eager to pillage and slaughter. "Notwithstanding," says their frivolous chronicler, "fresh courage was put into all the soldiers, for that they were marching towards the good wines of France and away from the cider of Normandy."

History, we are bound to own, provides other reasons for their final success. Catherine's diplomacy came to the rescue and she again induced Condé to meet her outside the walls of Paris and to hold a conference with her at the riverside Mill of Chantilly. "The Queen"—says Claude Hâton's diary—"started for this interview with a very small retinue. I do not think she asked the King's leave to go; still less did she consult the Constable, the Duc de Guise, or the Maréchal de Saint-André. For she wished to take this journey solely on her own authority, on the pretext of negotiating peace and of saving my Lord the Prince from more rebellion. With whom she remained deep in conversation for the space of five hours, quite alone with him in his tent without being seen by anyone. And of that which they did, said, and determined no man knew a word. . . . But this journey of hers and this conference gave rise to much suspicion among all conditions of people, wherether they were princes or lords, or only the citizens of Paris."

The interview lasted so late that Catherine went back by torchlight. It was followed by a second one at St. Marceau, and after the lapse of a day (during which, as a chronicler tells us, the Regent *was ill with the whooping cough*) they met again for the third time. After talking with him for a space, she retired to the Constable at Écouen, to hold a private Council with him. But Condé had grown wary and did not mean to let her slip. During the colloquy there arrived a present from him—a noble white horse, led by a trumpeter, which stood pawing the ground outside the palace. "The which horse could not endure that other horses should come near it, but kicked them whenever they approached." A horse so conscious of aristocratic privilege was worthy of its Bourbon donor and its royal recipient, but its diplomatic purpose was unfulfilled.

Whatever truth there was in current rumours, there was another reason for these interviews and one which soon became evident. For while Catherine held Condé fast in discussion, the long-expected help from Spain arrived and the Duc de Guise was enabled to enter Paris in triumph.

A pitched battle now became inevitable, and on the 19th of December, the two armies met at Dreux, between Paris and Rouen. At dawn on that day, the solemn sound of prayer arose from the Huguenot camp. The ministers, mounted on horseback, were holding their Prêches and singing Marot's psalms in French, "each one for his own regiment. . . . And they sang with so loud a voice that the King's camp heard them most clearly. . . . But, from the early morning, the Duke, Monsieur de Guise, had caused Mass to be sung by his army, at the which every soldier was present. And when it was over, the general Absolution was given to the whole Catholic host by the priest who had sung the Mass." After which memorable preface, Catholics and Huguenots, alike, rushed upon each other in the field. The fight was long and fierce; Saint-André lost his life, the Constable was taken prisoner; but in spite of these Protestant triumphs, the day ended with a great victory for the Catholics, who could boast that if their foes had caught the Constable, they themselves had won as captive no less a prize than Condé. In the meantime, while they were rejoicing, a false rumour had travelled to Paris and a breathless soldier—one who must have fled from the field when he saw that the Constable was taken—galloped into Paris on a horse without a bridle and announced with tears in his eyes that Montmorency was slain and that the Protestants had gained the day. This was on a Sunday morning. Paris was filled with anguish, while the Huguenots walked about showing their joy upon their faces. But their day of pride was a short one, for Monday, which brought the true tidings, filled all their houses with sorrow and turned the Guises' mourning to rejoicing. The King and Catherine attended a splendid service of thanksgiving; processions wound through the streets and all the bells of Paris rang solemnly.

From this time until the month of March, negotiations for peace went on continuously. Condé was imprisoned at Chartres, the Constable at Orleans, and transactions for the exchange of the prisoners were the easiest part of the business. Amid the festivities none knew better than Catherine that victory had not brought a solution any nearer, or ameliorated the condition of the country.

"I do not think" (she wrote a little later) "that there is anybody in this world who feels more misery or cankering care

ANNE DE MONTMORENCY.
BY JEAN CLOUET. CHÂTEAU DE CHANTILLY.
From a photograph by A. Giraudon.

at the . . . execrable evils wrought by the mercenaries than I, who shall die of it—standing. . . . If those who set the war going had had the patience to let us complete what we had begun at Saint-Germain, we should not be in the straits in which we are now about making a good peace—which, after all, when it *is* made, cannot be more advantageous than the old Edict of January. . . . If things had been worse than they are after all this war, they might have blamed the government of a woman; but if they are honest, they should blame nothing but the government of the men who want to play the part of kings. Henceforward, if I am not further trammelled, I hope it will be known that women have a sincerer love for the kingdom than those who have plunged it into the state to which it is now reduced. And pray show this to all those who talk about the matter to you—for this is the truth, pronounced by the mother of the King."

It would have needed a very strong woman to face the calamities which overwhelmed France at this moment. The February of 1563 witnessed one of the most dramatic among the many tragedies in the history of the Reformation—an episode so fatal to the Catholics that their party could hardly recover from it. François, Duc de Guise, was besieging the suburbs of Orleans and lodging in a castle hard by. One evening, after making a tour of inspection in the trenches, he was riding home to his wife, "having doffed his coat of mail, the which he had not done since the opening of the siege," while his page walked a few steps in front of him, when a sudden shot from behind a hedge felled him, wounded and senseless, to the ground. The assassin had time to turn and flee before help was fetched by the page, and Guise was borne back to the castle. Catherine got the news at Blois and at once bade the Cardinal send surgeons. "Although"—she writes—"they have assured me that the blow is not fatal, I am, in spite of my joy, so troubled that I know not what I do. But I assure you that I would give all that I possess in the world to have vengeance, and I am certain that God will forgive me."

Nothing, however, could save the Duke and a few days later he died.

As for the man who had killed him, "God so troubled his mind that although he galloped all the night upon his good horse and thought that he had made good way, the morning found him but one short league from the King's camp, so weary . . . that he could go no farther." This assassin, one

Poltrot de Méray, was duly brought before Catherine and stated that Coligny had hired him for a large sum to do the deed [1]—that he had not wished to obey—that de Bèze had assured him he would win heaven by the murder—that Coligny was sending forth emissaries to kill other Catholic leaders—that Catherine herself was included and the royal children were not safe. The Regent wrote to Coligny, then at Caen, who lost no time in replying and refuting her charges on his honour, article by article. He said that he had twice given money to Poltrot, once for a horse, once for some other quite unimportant purpose, but never for the reasons averred. It was true, he frankly owned, that he had overheard this man discussing the assassination of Guise, and although he had taken no part in the scheme, he had also done nothing to prevent it. But he had, in compensation, warned the Duchess more than once of various plots against her husband's life—and even that was against his conscience. "For think not, Madam," he concluded, "that the words which I utter in self-defence are said out of any regret for the death of M. de Guise. Fortune can deal no better stroke for the good of the kingdom and the Church of God, and most especially it is good for myself and all my House." He begged the King to delay the execution of Poltrot, but Paris in its fierce Catholicism had by now made an idol of Guise, and the instant punishment of the criminal was the only means of staving off riots.

Long and ceremonious was the lying-in-state of the Duke—his gloved hands folded upon his breast; sumptuous was the pomp of burial, and eloquent the Funeral Oration. "*Dur à la fatigue, d'une grande expérience dans la conduite des armées*," was the verdict of one who did not love him. Whatever Catherine's hatred for the tyrant who had subdued her to his will, the Duc de Guise was a force, and as such the deserted Regent missed him.

"At the very moment"—she wrote to her sister-in-law, the Duchess of Savoy—"when I had made every one good friends with me and when every one wished for a happy kingdom, God has again seen fit to strike me, and with me this poor

---

[1] A Catholic writer of the day assures us that Coligny had, before this, commissioned Poltrot de Méray to murder Guise, but that Poltrot, after following the Duke about for some time, had returned to the Admiral and refused to do the job—only yielding to the offer of the large sum that his employer offered if he would make another attempt. There does not seem to be any foundation for this malicious story.

CATHERINE AND THE PRINCE DE CONDÉ

country. For by the most miserable of deaths, He has taken from me the man who stood out alone and devoted himself to the King. . . . So that, in sooth, you may see how that very virtuous person (the Admiral), who professes to do nothing except for the sake of religion, desires to despatch us by its means, in spite of which I shall still try to make a nation. . . . But indeed we must face the truth that a heavy loss is ours. This gentleman was the greatest captain now existing in our realm, and I do not know how affairs will march without him if the war is going to last. . . . Meanwhile it is I who will have to take command and play the captain, and I leave you to imagine how much at my ease I feel."

The real import of the Duke's murder was not the disappearance of a military leader. His death had unforeseen results in the years that were as yet distant; it was the terrible dragon's tooth from which a harvest of armed men was to spring. For it began that deadly feud between the Guises and Coligny which could only be satisfied by blood—which ended, nine years later, on the Eve of St. Bartholomew.

The Duke's last counsel to Catherine had been that she should bring about peace. Condé, too, now seemed anxious for it, and communications with him were re-opened. They resulted in a general decision that the two great prisoners, the Prince and the Constable, should meet and discuss the situation. The interview took place at Amboise when the spring-time of Touraine was just beginning. A pavilioned boat had been prepared for the princes on the Loire, and Catherine rowed across to it with Condé; but he preferred to return to land and pace the river-bank with the Constable, deep in most earnest conversation. For two hours Catherine watched them, as she sat at some distance with her train. Next day the conference was renewed, but it was significant that this time the Prince de Condé appeared with his sword—a sign that he was no longer a prisoner. On this occasion, too, Catherine was allowed to be present. She told no tales on her return, but men augured well of what had happened, for as she went home that evening "she laughed loudly for joy and danced with the Duc d'Aumale," as if she could hardly contain herself with triumph at the certainty now hers. For Condé, tired of the war, more tired still perhaps of discussion with the two-and-seventy ministers with whom he had been allowed to confer at Orleans, at last yielded to her and the Constable. Had the Admiral been there, this weakness would never have been allowed; but Coligny was in Normandy, and though he hastened at once to the scene of action, he arrived too late to be of use. The peace of Amboise was already signed. Condé had had free play and had given away his party altogether.

The Treaty permitted the private performance of the Protestant service in noble families, but forbade the holding of Prêches in public, except in the towns which had been allowed to hold them before March 7, 1562, and the suburbs of one town in every district. These clauses, while they flattered the aristocrats, dealt a terrible blow to the popular cause of Protestantism, in spite of the suave wording in which they were framed. "It was easy to foresee that all must go wrong; that the great lords separated from the life of the towns, could henceforth no longer defend themselves, that the Papal and Spanish influence would win all along the line." Beside such stipulations, the minor articles of this fatal agreement lose prominence. But they, too, were strokes of compromise. Condé, now Catherine's man, was to be Lieutenant-General; foreigners were to leave the country; there was a show of soothing religious dissension by the hopes which were now held out of a General Council, to be convened in the near future. Such a compact could satisfy no one and Condé's colleagues were in despair. "Monseigneur," said the Admiral sternly, "you have taken upon yourself to play the part of God; with one stroke of your pen you have ruined more churches than could have been destroyed in ten years. And as for the Noblesse, the only class whose liberty you have guaranteed, its members themselves would confess that the towns first set them an example. The poor have walked in front of the rich and showed them the right road."

So much for the establishment of home affairs. But a Treaty with England was a matter of more protracted negotiations. Elizabeth could not be brought to terms. She was anxious to keep Havre and to regain Calais, while Coligny and Condé justly remarked that, as she had espoused the war from religious motives and taken Havre in the Protestant cause, it would look far from well if she now made a point of keeping it for her private profit. Elizabeth retorted that the Huguenots had broken their word to her, and the difficulty seemed incapable of solution till the French cut the knot by retaking the city of Havre. This was a fresh blow for the Protestants, but it was not nearly so disastrous as the Peace of Amboise, which reduced Protestantism to a private intrigue and gave an easy opening to the ever watchful Philip II.

This much had Catherine brought about by the strength of her negative policy. " To wish to maintain peace by means of division is to try and make white black . . . and the term ' politic ' was invented for those who prefer the repose of the kingdom, or their private ease, to the salvation of their souls and to religion; those, in short, who would rather that the realm were at peace without God, than at war for Him." So comments the marksman, Tavannes, who always hits the eye of the target, and there could be no completer summing up of the philosophy of Catherine de' Medici.

CHAPTER XI

Why the Reformation failed in France

CHAPTER XI

Why the Reformation failed in France

THAT the Reformation struck root in England and Germany, while it found no lasting home in Italy or in France, is a fact that gives material for reflection. Generalizations are dangerous, but this much may perhaps safely be hazarded : the people of Italy and France were more or less materialists by nature ; the Italians of the Renaissance, easy-going, beauty-loving, seeking after new things, subject to the first enchantment of the classic revival, were thoroughly Pagan. It was this Pagan atmosphere which made possible such persons as the Borgias and the Medici, such Popes as Leo X, Julius II, Clement VII ; and it was not, as has often been thought, the persons who produced the atmosphere. They doubtless reacted on their evil surroundings, but they were never the cause of the malady. In such a soil as this it was impossible for Protestantism to grow, impossible, indeed, for any religion, except one of mere observance, to live. The favourite quality of the Renaissance was good taste, that of the Reformation was energy acting upon conviction, but energy and taste are often at variance and Luther had nothing to say to æsthetics.

If the School of the Reconcilers, of those who wished to reform the Church already there—the School of Erasmus and his followers—had been strong enough to serve the moment, its suave wisdom and scholarly irony might have produced a large following. The lights of the Broad Church—such as Cardinal Pole in his earlier days, the poetic Vittoria Colonna, the scientific lecturer, Olympia Morata, or the beautiful ladies, Isabella of Ischia and Giulia Gonzaga—made centres of spiritual life which became the source of real influence. But for them and their kind the day was past, and the new wine was too strong for the old bottles. The other form of mysticism which found a response in Italy was the strange Neo-Platonism, the garbled and emotional philosophy which grew to be so prevalent among cultivated Italians and resulted from the rediscovery of Plato. His new expounders, Marsilio Ficino and Pico della Mirandola, were earnest, high-souled men who made (to use Picino's words) " a misty effort to set forth the image of Plato as closely resembling the truth of Christ "—and their message found many to receive it, embodying, as it did, the search after unity which was the favourite theory of the Renaissance. But the Platonic creed, like the Broad Church tenets of Erasmus, represented the beliefs of the cultured class, not of the nation at large; and they rotted or snapped like thin planks, destroyed by the forces of Paganism. Meanwhile the real outbursts of Protestantism in Italy were isolated and resulted in no school. The men who made them, from Savonarola downwards, were protestors against things as they were, rather than initiators of something that was to be. There were certain cities—Lucca, Naples, Ferrara—that were the citadels of heterodoxy; there were glowing preachers of the New Opinions, like that interesting man, Fra Ochino of Siena, or his friend, Peter Martyr Vermigli who came to the Council of Poissy; there were the enthusiasts—Flaminio, the friend of Cardinal Pole, and that fine spirit, Carnesechi, who was burnt for his convictions—but none of these were strong enough to make a general movement, nor could they have found sufficient numbers to lead forth into the field. What ought to have been an army resolved itself into scattered groups that clustered round some central figure, and the facts of history bore out the saying that " You might be able to de-Christianize Italy, but you could never Calvinize it."

In France, where the Reformation movement assumed such large proportions, where it filled men's thoughts for so long and produced such conspicuous results, where every woman of importance, from Margaret of Angoulême downwards, was occupied with the new religion—either as friend or foe—the failure of Protestantism is more striking than it was in Italy. But the main reason was the same in both countries and lay in the national character. If the Italians were born Pagans, the French were born Sceptics, and the sceptical temperament was as unfriendly to the growth of Protestantism as the easy materialism of Rome. For the sceptical temperament is the practical temperament—the temperament of common-sense—unmitigated by imagination—which clings to the present and the attainable and cares little for big vistas. It produced practical women, not romantic ones; and practical

WHY REFORMATION FAILED IN FRANCE

women demand action, the need to move in affairs, they soon develop into political women. The only politics possible for the women of the sixteenth century were provided by religion, and it was to religion, therefore, that these powerful ladies turned as an outlet for their energies. Many of them, like Jeanne de Navarre, were theologians. But theologians live by logic—by the practical temperament applied to ideas—and theology gave these feminine Calvinists a new field for their natural abilities. They were literal, and they made for absolute conclusions and the neatest fitting in of beliefs, nor did they care to leave room for the spiritual imagination. The preoccupation of Frenchwomen with religious affairs cannot therefore be taken as evidence of the religious nature of the people, and the truth remains that then—and since—France has not been a pious country.

But it has been the country of decorum, and in no other land has religious etiquette been made into such a fine art. It is, at first sight, hard to understand why so unmystical a nation as the French should have kept such a markedly ritualistic faith as that of Roman Catholicism. But they have kept it just because it need only be a matter of ritual and observance; for the sceptical temperament likes the decency of form and the restraint of a conventional creed. There were, of course, exceptional people who reacted against this artificial code: the choice race of saintly spirits to whom we have already alluded, the devout thinkers and scholars whose names are the world's property. But in discussing the character of a nation the question is, not whether it possesses these personalities, but how much it has been affected by them, and when we come to France, we shall find that their influence had no permanence. There are other fervent characters, too, to be found in the annals of French history; votaries of strange and spasmodic doctrines—Returns to Nature, Worship of Humanity, Universal Health (as in the time of Mesmer) and the like—superstitions which from time to time have taken hold of the French people. Such superstitions have always been a transitory refuge for matter-of-fact races—whether the French of the past or the Americans of to-day—who do not possess the touchstone of true religious imagination. But transitory they remain, and the real conviction of France is not represented by these, but by the Court religion of a Guise or of a Richelieu, and, if we desire a later instance, by the Concordat of Napoleon. The inability of the

Huguenots to gain their country might well have been a foregone conclusion.

It is common to ascribe such disasters to individuals; to say that Alexander VI and his successors killed Protestantism in Italy, that Catherine de' Medici and the Guises destroyed it in France. But these people are the tools of Fate, not its creators; they are the result of their age and by no means responsible for it. It is true that Catherine, half French, half Italian, half Pagan, half Sceptic, was the worst person for her place; but truth is stronger than persons, and though individuals can accelerate or impede its progress, they have no power to destroy it. Had the horrors of St. Bartholomew's Eve really put an end to Protestantism, we should have had sufficient proof that the principle of life was not in it. Had Catherine never existed, the massacre never happened, the conclusion would be the same and the Huguenots would still stand defeated.

Other minor causes there are which, if they did not give rise, at least contributed to the failure. There was no union among the Protestants. Old Tavannes observes that if the Constable, the Bourbons, and the Châtillons could but have remained at one, they would have made front against the Guises and would have probably carried the day. They did not accomplish this, and the reason lies again in French character. For France is always personal. The French Revolution destroyed itself by disputes between individuals; by breaking up into groups which circled round some single figure. And this is precisely what happened in the case of the French Reformation. Here we have a Prince de Condé, who exercises a personal spell and makes his party depend upon his private relations with Catherine and upon his boundless ambition for himself; there we find Antoine de Navarre, who shapes his shifting policy merely upon self-indulgence; or, in the earlier days, the Constable, who fights for his own hand. And in the midst of these faction-mongers stands great Coligny—"the man of bronze"—as much hampered in his single-minded aim by the selfish desires of his colleagues as he was by the wiles of his opponents.

This state of affairs was largely due to the constitution of France, to a government which admitted so many Kings in one kingdom. On the one hand were the reigning Guises, much wealthier than the Regent and her son; on the other, were the King of Navarre, and Condé who was trying to be

King; and the Constable who meant to depose the Guises, till he found out that he could not and went over to them. So many big powers could not live side by side and co-operate. They made unity impossible; they prevented a concentrated policy; but they tied the hands of their General so that effectual action became impracticable. For if the Protestants lacked a closely-knitted party, they also lacked that other necessity—one leader to dominate the rest. The conditions that we have been reviewing seem to make his existence hardly possible. His road would certainly have been beset with difficulties which genius alone could overcome. But Coligny was not a genius. He was strong—he was not originative; and the man who was needed at that moment was a being of creative force, an innovator—not only a high-souled hero of great military talent. And while Coligny was insufficient for the post, the other person who might have led forth the Huguenots was a woman—Jeanne de Navarre—whose sex stood in the way of her success.

But if the leaders are important, no less so are those who are led. "I do not know what to call *l'état Huguenot*," writes a contemporary: "it is not entirely popular, not entirely aristocratic . . . It is a democracy garbled by aristocracy, a republic in a monarchy . . . and the Huguenot aristocracy was backed by the Queen until the Council of Poissy." This is an interesting summary of what had been—what was still—in its essence a democratic movement. And the commentator partly hits the truth, for there had been throughout its course an effort to unite two incongruous powers. The attempt had begun in the days when Marguerite d'Angoulême tried to convert her Court; when her director, Bishop Briçonnet, made that society of mystics at Meaux of which she and her friends formed the upper, and the Protestant weavers the lower end.

Unfortunately these extremes remained apart, impotent because of their isolation—all for want of a fusing element. For France possessed no real middle-class, the class which mediates and disseminates; and the lack of this "entre-deux" had a great deal to do with the failure of the new doctrines.

Such a statement must needs be relative. We use the word "middle-class" in its largest sense, as meaning that division of a nation which includes the lowest of the higher, and the highest of the lower circles and thus links the noble to the artizan. England and Germany, each in its own measure, possessed this advantage, but in France the case was different. There was a middle-class in the literal sense of the term, a growing Third Estate made up of well-to-do bourgeois. But it can hardly be said to have consisted of more than one "order," for it was rather the superior artificers than the artizans that had access to it—men who merged with the artists, with the architects, the painters and the sculptors. For the rest it was mainly constituted out of merchants, doctors, lawyers, citizens, with a sprinkling of writers and poets, who were dependent on the Court or on great patrons. Many of these people, especially the merchants, made fortunes and rose into the aristocratic circles, often through financing King and nobles. But though this made a bond betwixt Court and bourgeois, it had no effect on the masses, who remained as much disconnected with the noblesse as if no third "order" had existed; and though the Reformation doctrines, which were first received by the Court and by the poor, were gradually taken up by the educated citizens, this had no effect on the other classes.

When the people are led by one of themselves, anarchy is likely to ensue, as it did in the French Revolution; when they are led by aristocratic leaders, as they were in the French Reformation, the movement is apt to end in incoherence. The old feudal relations assert themselves, and the difference of rank is too great to allow of any real tie between the captains and their followers; for the chiefs, though they may fight for truth and liberty, are not fighting for the needs of the people, which they neither know nor understand. That people demands a leader above it, but not far above it. Luther, Zwinglius, John Knox, Oliver Cromwell, were all men of the middle-class, who fully grasped the wants of the populace whom they represented.

Moreover, the religion of the cultivated classes can never be the religion of the people, or the religion which directs a revolution. Refinement, thought, and love of learning educate, but are not originative. Yet in France, as in Italy, it was the Broad Church of the Reconcilers which proved the best one. The finest spirits belonged to it and it included, at first, both the "*Catholiques ébranlés*" (as a contemporary called them), and the men who afterwards went forth and formed a body of their own. It is difficult for us to remember that these Dissenters, whom we think of as being always the conscious creators of a new religion, began with no notion of separation and only desired to introduce certain changes and hold certain advanced beliefs within the pale. They were much in the same position as the extreme Broad Churchmen of our day who still find it possible to remain in the Church of England. But when the Reformers realized that the accustomed forms were incapable of holding their doctrines, they saw themselves obliged to leave the fold and found a Church for themselves, thus greatly diminishing the vitality of the party they had abandoned. It was a party which was by no means strong enough to prevail at this critical moment, but if it could but have triumphed, the French might have been a very different nation.

The "ifs" of history, however idle a theme for contemplation, provide us with fascinating problems. Perhaps one of the most interesting is the question as to what France would have become had Catherine been a whole-hearted Huguenot and possessed the courage of her opinions. Spain, allied to the Guises, would almost certainly have made war on her, while she, helped by England, Holland and the Protestant Princes of Germany, could have made a strong resistance. Even if the Reformed faith had found no permanent footing, the history of France would have been nobler, the good effect upon its moral sense enduring. But Catherine was devoid of sincerity and our shadowy wonderings are vain.

After the Peace of Amboise, another chapter in her life begins. The terrible war had borne in upon her the whole political import of her Protestant tendencies and all the risks that they involved. She deliberately assumed a new part, and thenceforward, with few variations and in spite of underhand transactions, appeared upon the stage as the avowed enemy of the Huguenots. Every now and then an act of indulgence towards them proved that her inclination for their tenets retained its old vitality. But politics demanded a change of front, and from this time onwards she treated them as rebels. To Catherine, the friend of the Reformers, the leader of the Council of Poissy, we say farewell in 1562.

CHAPTER XII

Ronsard and the Pleïade

AUTHORITIES CONSULTED

Vie de Ronsard—*Claude Binet.*
Biographical Introduction to Oeuvres de Ronsard—*Blanchemain.*
Biographical Introduction to Oeuvres Choisies de Ronsard—*Sainte-Beuve.*
Biographical Introduction to Oeuvres de Joachim Du Bellay—*Marty-Laveaux.*
Biographical Introduction to Oeuvres Choisies de Joachim Du Bellay —*Becq de Fouquières.*
Tableau du seizième siècle—*Sainte-Beuve.*
Causeries du lundi—*Sainte-Beuve.*
Manuel de l'histoire de la littérature Française—*Brunetière*
L'Art Poétique—*Ronsard.*
Oeuvres Poétiques de Ronsard.
Illustration de la Poésie Française—*Joachim Du Bellay.*
Oeuvres Poétiques de Joachim Du Bellay.
Lettres au Cardinal Du Bellay, etc.—*Joachim Du Bellay*
Poèmes de Charles IX.
Histoire de France—*Michelet.*
Histoire de France—*Martin.*

CHAPTER XII

Ronsard and the Pleïade

THE great French literary movement between 1550 and 1580—the movement created by the Poets of the Pleïade—was practically unaffected by the Reformation. Ronsard, Du Bellay and their colleagues were the children of the Renaissance alone, and in France the Renaissance of Letters and the Reformation ran, as it were, on parallel lines: both in one direction, towards freedom—ever alongside, never meeting. In England the case was very different. You can hardly open a book of Elizabethan poetry without perceiving the signs of an intense religious activity. If we compare the work of Ronsard, Du Bellay and the lesser lights, with that of Spenser, Sidney, Raleigh, Campion, Shirley, Drummond of Hawthornden, the difference at once becomes apparent. It is not a matter of the creed professed by the men of either nationality. Ronsard wrote in defence of the Papacy, and both he and Du Bellay were orthodox Catholics under Court patronage; few of the English poets were men of Protestant tendencies. But in the one case, the spirit of poetry was Pagan, in the other instinct with spiritual fervour. Listen to Ronsard himself on the new faith, in a poem dedicated to Catherine de' Medici—

> On dit que Jupiter, fâché contre la race
> Des hommes, qui voulaient par curieuse audace
> Envoyer leur raisons jusqu'au ciel, pour savoir
> Les hauts secrets divins que l'homme ne doit voir,
> Un jour étant gaillard, choisit pour son amie
> Dame Présomption, la voyant endormie
> Au pied du mont Olympe ; et la baisant soudain
> Conçut l'Opinion, peste du genre humain . .
>
> De Bèze, je te prie, écoute ma parole,
> Que tu estimeras d'une personne folle,
> S'il te plait toutes fois de juger sainement
> Apres m'avoir ouï, tu diras autrement, . . .
> . . . Ne prêche plus en France une Evangile armée,
> Un Christ empistolé tout noirci de fumée . . .

CATHERINE DE' MEDICI

> Certes il vaudrait mieux à Lausanne relire
> Du grand fils de Thétis les promesses et l'ire,
> Faire combattre Ajax, faire parler Nestor,
> Ou reblesser Vénus, ou retuer Hector . . .
> Certes il vaudrait mieux célébrer ta Candide,
> Et, comme tu faisais, tenir encore la bride
> Des cygnes Paphians, ou près d'un antre au soir
> Tout seul dans le giron des neuf Muses t'asseoir,
> Que reprendre l'Église, ou pour être vu sage,
> Amender en St. Paul je ne sais quel passage.
> De Bèze, mon ami, tout cela ne vaut pas
> Que la France pour toi fasse tant de combats,
> Ni qu'un Prince royal pour ta cause t'empêche.

Nothing can be more conventional than the religious phrases of this passage—nothing more full of enjoyment than the recommendation to retire to a cave and read mythology.

The very aims of the Pleïade made against fervour. "Without eloquence," writes Joachim du Bellay, "all things are futile, like a blade always covered by its scabbard; without metaphors, allegories, similes and many other figures and ornaments, both oratory and poetry remain naked and weak." This occurs in his "Illustration de la langue francaise," which was, as it were, the manifesto of the Pleïade, and he goes on to speak of the Romans. "The noblest work of their State," says he, "even that of the days of Augustus—even their Capitol and their Thermæ—could not hold out against the blows of Time without the aid of their language, for the which alone we praise, we admire, we adore them. Are we then less than Greeks or Romans that we make so little of our own tongue ? . . . Why are we thus hostile to ourselves ? Why do we use foreign languages as if we were ashamed of our own ? . . . True it is that the wide plains of Greece and Rome are already so full that little empty space is left. But, great God, what an infinity of sea there still remains before we can anchor in port ! . . . And now, supposing us, thanks be to Him, safe at last in our haven, many perils passed, many strange waters left behind us. We have escaped out of the midst of the Greeks and with the help of the Roman squadrons we have penetrated into the very heart of this long desired France. March then, courageously, ye Frenchmen, towards that superb Roman city . . . yield yourselves to this fictitious Greece and sow there, I pray ye, a fresh crop—the famous race of the Gallo-Greeks. Pillage without conscience the sacred treasures of the Delphic Temple . . . and do not fear the dumb Apollo, his false Oracles, his blunted arrows."

RONSARD AND THE PLEÏADE

The passion for form which, from Ronsard to Verlaine, has characterized the French, the pursuit of the right word which has distinguished them, are not wanting here. But the language was in the making, and it was with that language, as yet so incomplete, that the Pleïade were concerned, not with the expression of ideas. They were still fashioning their crystal goblet, nor did they care about the wine which it was not yet fit to hold. But in England this was not so. The English tongue was already a complete and richly wrought vessel, finished yet flexible, so that men were free to use it first and foremost as a vehicle for thought and feeling. English words, as has been truly said, " still had the dew upon them," and there arose a great unconscious poetry, in which beauty of form and beauty of idea became one, each intensifying and inseparable from the other. Yet there was always a central conception which had a life apart from language and gave the language its vitality. Thus while in England thought grew spontaneously out of language, language out of thought, and art was large and natural, in France it was from the first elaborate—the expression of a love of form for form's sake—and language grew artificially out of the ingenuity of men.

Before considering in this light some of the poems of either country, it will be well to know a little more about the two French poets who so powerfully affected their day—the two chief stars of the brilliant Pleïade which they created.

The youth of Pierre de Ronsard and Joachim du Bellay belongs to the reign of François I and has been chronicled in another volume.[1] It will therefore be unnecessary to give more than the briefest summary of the early life of both men, only just so much as will help to the understanding of their later careers. Both were aristocratic—both driven to the study of the classics by physical infirmity—both, curiously enough, were deaf, and wrote sonnets to one another's deafness.

Pierre de Ronsard was born in the Vendômois in 1524. He was, as his accurate historian tells us, seventeenth cousin to Queen Elizabeth, who sent him a diamond ring as a symbol of his brilliant and indestructible poetry. He himself, in an autobiographical poem, retraces his family to Thrace and the banks of the Danube—not perhaps without some private comparison of himself to the other lyrist, Orpheus—and the Marquis of Thrace was the elegant nickname which his contemporaries loved to give him: a nickname in no way unworthy of the

[1] "Women and Men of the French Renaissance."

pseudo-classics of the future, so much cultivated at the Hôtel Rambouillet. The boy went to school at nine years old, but he did not like it and left it for good in a year. His father had accompanied the little sons of François I when they went as hostages to Spain and, perhaps in consequence of this, his Pierre, at ten years old, was made page to the Duke of Orleans. Young Ronsard went twice to Scotland, and spent six months in England. The first time he crossed the sea, it was as the page of the Scotch King, James V; that monarch had just married Henri II's daughter, the Princess Madeleine, whose piteous death in the arms of her young husband the lad witnessed not long afterwards. When he came back, he resumed his post at the French Court. It was after his second return, when he was about fifteen, that there occurred the great event of his life; he fell in with Virgil. One day—probably in the royal stables where his work lay—he met a Court groom, a groom of the Renaissance, reading a little gold-tooled volume, and thenceforward he made Virgil his own. He had found a friend in Olympus; he studied him at every spare moment, all other pleasures became distasteful to him; and what makes both Ronsard and his literary attempt really interesting is the fact that it was founded on this natural affinity and upon no forced revival. Soon after this, emancipated from the state of servitude, he started for the Diet of Speyer, in company with the learned Maître des Requêtes, Lazare Baïf, and later he went to Piedmont with the famous Guillaume du Bellay. When he came back he followed the Court to Blois, and there he met with his first love—the first among many—Cassandre, to whom for ten years he wrote several scores of odes and sonnets. About this time, too, when he was some seventeen years old, he was first attacked by the deafness which never left him, and this—perhaps also his tender passion —disgusted him with Court life. After much discussion, he persuaded his father to allow him to desert "*les armes*" and take to letters in good earnest, but his request was only granted on condition that he should never become a poet, or be found with a French book in his hand. It was lucky that his father died soon afterwards and that Ronsard had no objections to forswearing himself—"For in sooth" (as his friend and historian says), "a spirit such as his, which from its birth had received the infusion—the fatal impress—of poesy, could not be turned from its course, or bound by other laws than its own." He now returned to Paris and, crossing the Seine from Les

RONSARD AND THE PLEIADE

Tournelles, took up his abode in the house of Baïf and studied Greek there with his son, Jean Antoine. Under this roof, too, he found the man who was to stamp his whole career, Jean Dorat, a pedagogue poet of the old school and a scholar of the new, absorbed in developing an original system of classical education. " By him was Ronsard bewitched with the philtre of noble literature," and, quick to discover his pupil's gifts, he invited the boy to come and join him at his recently started Collège de Coqueret. Here, for seven years, he steeped him in the knowledge of the classics—him and the chosen few whom Dorat adopted as his pupils. Young Baïf followed his beloved Ronsard thither and shared his room, helping him with Greek, in exchange for Latin lessons. The two friends worked in turn all night, for they could only afford one candle, and when Ronsard had had his half of the precious hours, Baïf would rise from bed and the fellow students changed places, " nor did they ever allow the chair to grow cold." Rémy Belleau was another of the scholars—the comrade to whom in after days Ronsard sang that the years

> Ne cèlent[1] que Belleau et Ronsard n'étaient qu'un
> Et que tous deux avaient un même cœur commun.

Dorat taught his eager disciples to imitate Horace and Pindar, to act Aristophanes, to plunge into the deeps of philosophy. He read the " Prometheus " of Æschylus in a French translation with Ronsard—" all at one full flight." " Oh, master," said the poet, " why have you hidden these riches from me so long ? " These revelations had a strong effect upon him. Gradually " he began to ponder upon great designs for leading his language out of childhood," and a band of his colleagues gathered round him. It was at this time, about the year 1548 or 1549, that Ronsard, returning from a journey, met a chance traveller in a wayside tavern—a young lawyer who had come from the Legal School of Poitiers. They drank wine together ; some casual remark made them enter into conversation, and perhaps the lawyer was charmed by the golden-haired French Apollo. The talk fell on letters and on poetry, and before they mounted their horses, the stranger, Joachim du Bellay, had thrown up the law and agreed to live with Ronsard. He was to return with him at once to Paris and take up his abode at the College, so that without delay they might pursue their aims together. For Du Bellay was also a poet

[1] Do not hide.

and, in his studious solitude, he had all this time been maturing much the same ideas about poetry as Ronsard in his distant College—in the leisure forced upon him by illness, which laid him by, poor and lonely, "nailed (as he said) to a bed of pain" for two long years of his youth.

Joachim du Bellay was born a year after Ronsard, in 1525, on the family estate, at the Angevin town of Liré. His parents, who were related to the great Du Bellays, died early and he was left in the tutelage of a harsh brother, who opposed his inclination for letters and brought him up roughly as a soldier. "Cultivation" (he wrote) "was not for me. . . . I was like a flower in a green garden which no ripple refreshes and no hand cherishes." The brother, too, died, and left an embarrassed estate and the care of his son to Joachim, himself little more than a boy. Poverty and domestic cares formed fresh barriers in his way and he had no time for literature. His illness followed and the skies cleared; he was helped by his kinsman, the literary Cardinal du Bellay, was sent to take up law at Poitiers, and met his fate by the wayside.

Both men agreed that the French language was poverty-stricken, that the way to enrich it was to use it and to substitute it for Latin—the common medium of literature. To write in French was, they saw rightly, the one essential condition of a great French literature, and in order to do this they must improve the instrument, they must invent and import new words. They borrowed largely from Greek and Latin; they consorted with craftsmen of all sorts so that they might discover unknown terms; they dived into the provincial patois and brought forth long-forgotten substantives. "You must know"—Ronsard writes to his disciples—"how to choose and adapt to your work the most significant words from the dialects of our France; and you must not care whether the vowels are Gascon, Poitevin, Norman, or Lyonnais, provided they are good and appropriate to your meaning. Nor must you too much affect the speech of the Court, the which is sometimes very bad, for that it is the language of fine ladies and young gentlemen. And note that the Greek tongue would never have been so fertile and abundant in dialects and words, without the large number of republics that flourished in that day. There is, in sooth, no doubt that if France still boasted Dukes of Burgundy, of Picardy, of Normandy, of Brittany, of Champagne, of Gascony, they, of their nobility, would certainly desire their subjects to write in their native language."

RONSARD AND THE PLEÏADE

The result of all this verbal research was naturally a good deal of affectation and a kind of earnest euphuism, but their practical treatment of their mother-tongue is difficult to overvalue. The only poets who had hitherto used it freely were those of the National, or Country School, the enemies of the classical spirit, led by Clément Marot and Mélin Saint-Gelais. But they were far too crude and informal for the innovators. What the Pleïade demanded was polish, precision, a form like a clean-cut intaglio. They introduced classical metres, they imitated Anacreon and Horace; they may almost be said to have created the quality of delicacy in French poetry. Around them, in a short time, there clustered those minor constellations who, with them, made up the Pleïade—so called after a group of seven Greek poets under the Ptolemies. Besides Belleau and Baïf, there were Amadis Jamyn, Ronsard's page ("who was also his page in poetry"), and Etienne Jodelle, lyrist and playwright, and Pontus de Thiard, the Bishop of Châlons— or, for a variant on these last, Scévole de Sainte-Marthe and Muret. The Pleïade threw down the gauntlet in 1550, when Joachim du Bellay published his "Illustration de la Langue francaise," which set forth their tenets to the world. But although Du Bellay was the mouth-piece—although he was also practically the pioneer of the sonnet in France—Ronsard, as Sainte-Beuve points out, ever remained the leader.

> Amy que sans tache d'envie
> J'aimais quand je vivais comme ma propre vie,
> Qui premier me poussa et me forma la voie—

So the confident Ronsard makes Joachim address him in a poem written after his friend's death, and his voice was the voice of Du Bellay.

The appearance of the "Illustration" brought a hornet's nest about their ears and Ronsard's first volume of verse, which came out a year later, did not soothe public opinion. The old school of national poets, with Mélin Saint-Gelais at their head, rose angrily and jeered; the courtiers read the book aloud in parodying tones to the King, purposely misrepresenting the newly-invented words. Ronsard wished in vain that he had lived in the days of the lettered François I. But he and his comrades found a champion in the noble-minded Michel de l'Hôpital, still at that early date the right hand of Madame Marguerite, the sister of Henri II. He wrote a learned satire in their favour and filled the ears of his mistress

CATHERINE DE' MEDICI

with their praises. From this time onwards, the Princess was their tutelary spirit, their "*Perle des perles la plus claire*," their "*Âme hospitalière des Muses*." Joachim du Bellay's sentiment for her began by being a mere Court convention, but later it deepened into something more—a real and tender feeling for the woman who had held out a hand to him; and her departure from France at her marriage, and his grief when he failed to bid her farewell and to look on her face once again drew from him, so he tells us, "les plus vraies larmes que je pleurai jamais," and added another touch of sadness to his last suffering days. This lady was the least interesting of the three Marguerites de Valois. She was little more than the niece of her aunt, Marguerite d'Angoulême, or rather she tried to take her place; and though she was inferior, and considerably more of a blue-stocking, she had great literary influence in her day. Corneille de Lyon's portrait of her at Chantilly shows her just as she was—a singular mixture of kindness and pedantry—a trim, befurred little figure in a small hunting-cap with a fountain-like aigrette perched on one side of her golden peruke—the modish Muse of the Pleïade. They wrote her a great many poems and she answered them in rather stilted verses which they were never tired of extolling. In return, she did them solid service by spreading their reputation. Ronsard became literary tutor to the little Scotch Queen, Mary Stuart. He gave her, like the rest of the Court, a poetic devotion, which she answered with romantic friendship; when she left France, his heart was broken—for some days—nor did she forget him in Scotland. She sent him in after years a noble sum of money, besides another costly trifle—a precious "*Buffet*," surmounted by Parnassus with Pegasus at the top. When her fate became sombre, his poetry cheered her imprisonment; but she did not go so far as Châtelard, who, at the last solemn hour, brought out his volume of Ronsard and read the "Hymne à la Mort"—a lucid, philosophic eulogy of Death, the deliverer from human misery—chilly comfort, so it seems to us, for such a moment.

Meanwhile, Charles IX had come to the throne of France and he took such an affection for Ronsard that he could hardly do without him, so that "Mon Ronsard," as he called him, seldom left the Court. From the time the King was fourteen years old, he wrote verses to the poet, adoring his Muse, longing for his intellect, vaunting the royalty of poetry when put beside the royalty of thrones.

RONSARD AND THE PLEIADE

> Tous deux également nous portons des couronnes ;
> Mais, roi, je la reçus ; poète, tu la donnes :
> Ta lyre, qui ravit par de si doux accords,
> Te soumet les esprits, dont je n'ai que les corps ;
> Elle amollit les cœurs et soumet la beauté.
> Je puis donner la mort, toi l'immortalité.

Charles IX had inherited his father's poetic gift, though he did not trust it far. He was unlike most kings in underrating his pretty talent, and when first he had a tender passion for the Court lady, Mademoiselle d'Atrie, he used to employ Ronsard to write love-poems for him. Ronsard's success in this vicarious wooing did not diminish his prestige in royal circles. Catherine lavished favours upon him, and, for his sake, quarrelled with her favourite architect, Philibert de l'Orme—scolding him in public for his spite in shutting the Tuileries one day against the mocking Ronsard, who wrote a biting epigram on the offending door. De l'Orme was no match for Ronsard's irony or for his social success. He had grown rich as well as powerful. Fat abbeys were conferred upon him, according to the fashion of the day, though, as he himself assures us,[1] he was never ordained as a priest. He wrote in defence of the Faith, and Pope Pius V sent him a formal letter of thanks ; while the Huguenots made him still more popular by printing wordy pages against him. The Cardinal de Lorraine and the Cardinal de Châtillon were his friends, so was the Cardinal du Bellay. The great world was at his feet, and the world of letters followed ; for a versifier, one Guillaume d'Autels, a friend of both factions among the poets, acted as mediator between him and Saint-Gélais and healed the quarrel between them. They wrote each other elegant sonnets to assure the world of their mutual love, and now all the singers, both of the old school and the new, with a remarkable absence of jealousy, were added to Ronsard's admirers. Jean Goujon[2] carved Fame upon the Louvre blowing a trumpet in the great man's honour ; and the Court of Love at Toulouse, which awarded three prizes—a branch of eglantine, a daisy and a violet—to the three best poets that presented themselves, outdid themselves in his praise and sent him a silver Minerva. Never did prophet enjoy greater honour in his own country ; indeed he was over-lauded, and

---

[1] Du Bellay's "Louange de la France."
[2] Binet, in his "Vie de Ronsard" speaks of Lescot as having carved this figure. But Lescot was the architect of the Louvre, and employed Goujon to do all the sculpture.

the men of a later time could hardly see his achievement for his laurels.

Yet, though he loved elegance, his tastes always remained simple. He himself has described his ordinary day with the candid grace which distinguished him.

> Après je sors du lit, et quand je suis vêtu,
> Je me range a l'étude et apprends la vertu—
> Composant et lisant, suivant ma destinée
> Qui s'est dès mon enfance aux Muses enclinée :
> Quatre ou cinq heures seul je m'arrête enfermé,
> Puis sentant mon esprit de trop lire assommé,
> J'abandonne le livre et m'en vais à l'Église.
> Au retour, pour plaisir, une heure je devise ;
> De là je viens dîner, faisant sobre repas.
> Je rends graces à Dieu ; au reste je m'ébas,[1]
> . . . Mais quand le ciel est triste et tout noir d'épaisseur
> Et qu'il ne fait aux champs ni plaisant, ni bien sûr,
> Je cherche compagnie ou je joue à la Prime ;
> Je voltige ou je saute, ou je lutte, ou j'escrime ;
> Je dis le mot pour rire, et à la verité,
> Je ne loge chez moi trop de sévérité. . . .
> Au reste je ne suis ni mutin, ni méchant,
> Qui[2] fait croire ma loi par le glaïve tranchant :
> Voilà comme je vis, et si ta vie est meilleure,
> Je n'en suis envieux, et soit à la bonne heure !

His favourite home was in the country, either at his Priory of St. Cosme—*l'œillet de Touraine*—where Catherine and her sons visited him ; or at Bourgueuil, where he kept his " finest hawks " and the hounds which Charles had given him, for hunting was one of his chief pleasures. Or, if he liked anything better, it was to go to his other Priory of Croixval and wander on the banks of the Loire, or in the solitary Forest of Gastine. Here he would lie on the brim of the Fontaine d'Hélène, which had power to quench the thirst of poets, and think of the nymph, his mistress, who bore the same name as the spring ; or he would listen to the cool splash of the other forest fountain of Bellerie, " oftentimes alone, but ever in the company of the Muses." And sometimes he had a companion—

> Là devisant sur l'herbe avec un mien amy
> Je me suis par les fleurs bien souvent endormi ;
> A l'ombrage d'un saule, ou lisant dans un livre,
> J'ai cherché le moyen de me faire revivre.

He loved, too, his garden at St. Cosme, for " *il savait beaucoup de beaux secrets pour le jardinage*," and was skilful in

[1] Frolic.   [2] Ni un homme qui.

growing rich fruit, which he sent to Charles IX. His exigent Majesty grew rather jealous of all such rural occupations.

> Donc ne t'amuse plus à faire ton ménage ;
> Maintenant il n'est plus temps de faire jardinage ...
> Et, crois, si tu ne viens me trouver à Amboise,
> Qu'entre nous adviendra une bien grande noise.[1]

Happily the Court had wherewithal to console the poet for his flower-beds. For Ronsard loved the arts—painting and sculpture, but, above the rest, music, "the elder sister of poetry." "The man," he says, "who when he hears sweet harmony of instruments does not rejoice, is not stirred ... and—how I know not—gently ravished and taken out of himself, gives a sure sign of a crooked and depraved soul and we must beware of him as of one of who is not of happy birth." Such was Ronsard's version of the "man who hath no music in himself"—of the strange Platonic notion of music, bound up with the melody of the spheres. Perhaps, with pardonable vanity, the poet most enjoyed the airs set to his own verses which he sang to the sound of his lute.

He never married, but he was always in love, and his successive *grandes passions* were—for his time—long-lived. He had been faithful to Cassandre of Blois for ten years; his devotion to Marie, a humble beauty of Bourgueuil, lasted for several more, and was only cut short by her tragic death while she was still on the threshold of life. Then, after an interval of Astrée, or Mademoiselle d'Estrées, he indulged, when he was already old, in a more or less Platonic emotion for Helène de Surgères, one of Catherine's ladies, whom he courted with stately sentiment in the trim green alleys of the Tuileries.

> Adieu belle Cassandre, et vous belle Marie
> Pour qui je fus trois ans en servage en Bourgueuil :
> L'une vît, l'autre est morte, et ores de son œil
> Le Ciel se réjouit, dont la terre est marrie ...
> Maintenant en Automne, encore malheureux,
> Je vis, comme au Printemps, de nature amoureux,
> Afin que tout mon âge aille au gré de la peine.
> Et or'que je dusse être affranchi du harnois,
> Mon Colonel m'envoie à grands coups de carquois,
> Rassiéger Ilion pour conquérir Helène.

But love never filled so large a place as friendship in his life. There are poems of his inscribed to numbers of new friends,

---

[1] This word—the same as our "noise"—literally translated, means "a row."

and his intercourse with the old ones—with Belleau, Du Bellay, Jamyn and the rest—remained unbroken. When he was living in Paris, he would often fly from the fashion to breathe at his neighbouring Tour de Meudon, an abode which the Cardinal du Bellay had given him for his own; and here Joachim du Bellay sometimes joined him and both together passed their time in making mock of the Curé of the Parish, one, François Rabelais, who was not slow to return the compliment in kind. He had already opposed their innovations, and their satire was founded on real hatred; for was not he the chief of the great naturalistic school of writing which offended all their canons, as well as the professor of eccentric opinions which were hardly less objectionable to them? It is curious to think of these poets, with their air of princely distinction, meeting the mighty democratic thinker, as they must so often have done in their walks abroad—meeting him, nor ever dreaming that the royal blood of the immortals was in his veins.

The friendship of Ronsard and Du Bellay was cemented still more closely by a quarrel. Close upon Ronsard's volume of Odes appeared Du Bellay's "Olive," a series of Platonic sonnets addressed to his ideal love, Mademoiselle de Viole, on whose harmonious surname his title was an anagram. He was making his own footing in poetry as well as in prose. But while Ronsard had been preparing his Odes for the press, Du Bellay happened to see them and took the opportunity of writing another volume of his own, in close imitation of them. There was a rupture—there was talk of a lawsuit—but the affair ended in a general reconciliation, Ronsard himself encouraging his comrade to go on with the same sort of work. "Their friendship redoubled in force . . . for the Muses cannot dwell alone, but live ever in company"— and no more clouds troubled their intercourse.

Their less illustrious colleagues were almost as much made of as themselves—Etienne Jodelle, with his "Gallo-Greek" tragedy, "Cleopatra," was hailed as if he had been Æschylus. After it had been first performed at Court, the poets "*honorant son esprit gaillard et bien appris*," fêted him joyously at Arceuil. A banquet was spread on a green lawn; the company composed classic verses after the Greek "Bacchanalia"; a buck—*le père du troupeau . . . des Tragiques* "*le prix*" was led up to the victorious Jodelle, its head wreathed with flowers:

RONSARD AND THE PLEIADE

Le bouquet sur l'oreille, et bien fier se sentait
De quoy telle jeunesse ainsi le présentait.

The Huguenots made capital out of this festivity and proclaimed that the Pleïade had sacrificed a buck to Bacchus, but Ronsard, whom they were trying to hit, ends his delicious description of the Anacreontic feast with a half laughing, half indignant denial, and he and Du Bellay went on their way, unharmed by Calvinistic jeers.

About the same time as these doings, in the year 1552, when Joachim du Bellay was twenty-seven years old, his patron and relation, the Cardinal, took him to Rome (as eighteen years before he had taken Rabelais) and thus gave a new turn to Joachim's thoughts and to his work. He remained there for more than four years as the Cardinal's secretary; he saw a great deal of the world and moved among men and affairs; he watched proceedings at the Papal Courts of Julius III and Paul IV; he was present at ecclesiastical Councils and in the confidence of almighty Cardinals. The Roman drama of splendour and corruption was played out before his vigilant eyes and deepened the bitterness of mood that was all too natural to him. It found vent in his verse and he made the world his confidant—" car, poète, on pense toujours un peu à ce monde pour qui l'on n'é'crit pas," as Sainte-Beuve points out with gentle malice. In turns, he sang the vanity and the beauty of the Rome in which he lived, now with satire, now with sadness, now in French and now in Latin. For no one was more susceptible than Joachim to the subtle influences of place, and the champion of his native language had become subject to the atmosphere of Rome and the fascination of the Latin tongue. It was, moreover, his only means of communication with such of his Italian friends as did not understand French, and the most convenient medium for his modern sarcasms à l'antique. His sarcasms unfortunately stood him in no good stead, for after he had left Rome, they were made the basis of some charges that were brought against him to the Cardinal. What these charges exactly were and whether he was accused of libelling his patron or no, history does not record, but there still exists a letter that he wrote to his master in self-exoneration—a document too vague to instruct us. The prelate evidently forgave him, for some time after this correspondence, he showed Joachim marks of his favour.

These days were, however, still far off and the poet was as yet in Rome. He was a moody and intense being; the melancholy and the pride of the city of the Cæsars pleased him. His fastidious senses were soothed, his imagination excited. For he was there at a time when the Tiber and the palace-gardens were still yielding their buried marbles; when Michael Angelo was working; when the first painters and scholars of the day prepared gorgeous pageants for the populace. The poet enjoyed the electric atmosphere; the man was all the time discontented, suffering from the insolence of office, imagining himself most unhappy. He yearned for France and home; he was invaded by luxurious melancholy amid the imperial ruins. All these emotions are expressed in his French poems, "Les Antiquités de Rome" and "Les Regrets"—the series of sonnets that he set down from day to day as a record of his passing mood. His art had grown richer and fuller for his abode in Rome. It had made him at once more classical and more modern, or perhaps we should say more personal; and the intimate note in the classic form gives his poems a peculiar distinction. The most exquisite of them, "Les Vanneurs," occurs in a later series: "Les Jeux Rustiques," in which we still feel the spell of his old Roman memories—of crumbling villas, groves of cypress, broken statues and carpets of violets—but we choose three sonnets from "Les Regrets," so as to give some echo of his feeling while yet he dwelt near St. Peter's.

> Je ne veux point fouiller au sein de la nature,
>   Je ne veux point chercher l'esprit de l'univers,
>   Je ne veux point sonder les abysmes couvers
>   Ny dessiner du ciel la belle architecture.
> Je ne peins mes tableaux de si riche peinture,
>   Et si hauts argumens ne recherche à mes vers :
>   Mais suivant de ce lieu les accidents divers,
>   Soit de bien, soit de mal, j'écris à l'aventure.
> Je me plains à mes vers, si j'ai quelque regret :
>   Je me ris avec eux, je leur dis mon secret,
>   Comme étants de mon cœur les plus sûrs secrétaires.
> Aussi ne veux-je tant les peigner et friser,
>   Et de plus braves noms ne les veux déguiser,
>   Que de papiers journaux, ou bien de commentaires.

> Comte, qui ne fis onques compte de la grandeur,
>   Ton Du Bellay n'est plus : ce n'est plus qu'une souche
>   Qui dessus un ruisseau d'un dos courbé se couche,
>   Et n'a plus rien de vif, qu'un petit de verdeur.

RONSARD AND THE PLEÏADE

Si j'écris quelquefois, je n'écris point d'ardeur,
    J'écris naïvement tout ce qu'au cœur me touche,
    Soit de bien, soit de mal, comme il vient à la bouche,
    En un stile aussi lent que lente est ma froideur.
Vous autres cependant, peintres de la nature,
    Dont l'art n'est pas enclos dans une portraiture,
    Contrefaites des vieux les ouvrages plus beaux.
Quant à moi je n'aspire à si haute louange,
    Et ne sont mes portraits auprès de vos tableaux,
    Non plus qu'est un Janet auprès d'un Michel Ange.

Heureux qui, comme Ulysse, a fait un beau voyage,
    Ou comme celui-là qui conquit la toison,
    Et puis est retourné, plein d'usage et raison,
    Vivre entre ses parents le reste de son âge !
Quand revoirai-je, hélas, de mon petit village
    Fumer la cheminée : et en quelle saison
    Revoirai-je le clos de ma pauvre maison,
    Qui m'est une province, et beaucoup davantage ?
Plus me plaît le séjour qu'ont bâti mes aïeux,
    Que des palais Romains le front audacieux :
    Plus que le marbre dur me plaît l'ardoise fine,
Plus mon Loire Gaulois, que le Tibre Latin,
    Plus mon petit Liré, que le mont Palatin
    Et plus que l'air marin la douceur Angevine.

His weariness of spirit, his desire for Anjou, all vanished at the end of his third year in Rome. For the first time in his life, at some thirty years old, he fell passionately in love—with no cold ideal cult, as in the case of "Olive," but with a very human vehemence. The poetry that he wrote about her is very different from what preceded it, though not so accessible to the ordinary reader, for his "Amour de Faustine" was written in Latin and it is thus that she must have read it. The romance is not a pleasant one. His Faustine, or Colomba, or Colombelle, as he called her, was an Italian lady, young, beautiful—and married. Her husband, who was old and jealous, discovered the secret of the pair and removed her to safe confinement—eventually in a convent. There were tears, there was despair, there were sonnets—and then, suddenly, without word of explanation, we find her restored to her poet. How the adventure ended and what became of the husband, no chronicle tells us, but Du Bellay, with the boldness of the Renaissance, could doubtless have proved from texts in Plato that his own conduct was the highest-souled imaginable. It could hardly have been as a reward for this passage in his history that, after Joachim's return to France, his patron offered to make him Archbishop of Bordeaux in his stead. But nothing is too strange for a day when clerical honours were promiscuously distributed as rewards—when Ronsard and De l'Orme and Lescot were Canons of Notre Dame, and artists were certainly as clerical in character as established dignitaries of the Church. Joachim, it is true, was not appointed, but the Cardinal's intention is none the less characteristic.

His secretary's love affair was probably cut off in the middle, for the prelate despatched him rather suddenly to see after some business in France. The moment so much longed for by the poet had come—the moment of release from office, of return to his own country. But already when he stayed at Lyons on his homeward journey, his spirit had flown back to Italy, and he wrote as one overcome by regret for what he had left behind.

The rest of his story is a sad one—a record of ill-health and family cares and growing distress of mind, his increasing deafness cutting him off more and more from society. His best poetic work was done, and, at thirty-five, he talked of himself as an old man. It was when he had reached this age, in the year 1560, that, coming home one night from a supper-party, he was seized by a fit of apoplexy and died. One of the biggest stars in the Pléiade had gone out—"*L'esprit réuni à son éternité*"—to use Du Bellay's own words, and he left no other to fill his particular place. Death was not dreaded by him:

> De mourir ne suis en émoi
> Selon la loi du sort humain,
> Car la meilleure part de moi
> Ne craint point la fatale main :
> Craigne la Mort, la Fortune et l'Ennuie,
> A qui les Dieux n'ont donné qu'une vie.

Such is his courageous challenge to immortality.

Du Bellay was a profounder man than Ronsard and not so complete. His thoughts dive deeper and rise higher, his touch is more warm, more intimate, but he is not so perfect an artist, nor so exquisite a master of form. And yet just because of his incompleteness, he is more suggestive and closer to us. His melancholy—delicate, elusive—sometimes reminds us of another French artist who lived two centuries after: of the

RONSARD AND THE PLEIADE

pictures of Antoine Watteau, where the grassy banquets are full of sad grace, and huntsmen dream regretfully of what they have missed, and lovers sing songs about the end of things. But Du Bellay was a classic touched by romance, and Watteau was a romantic touched by classicism—a Theocritan classicism of the eighteenth century. The gulf of time, too, stretches between them and to many, who care for both, the analogy may sound fantastic.

Ronsard, the prosperous poet, had a quarter of a century still to live. He went on publishing poems, he went on being acclaimed. He was a born laureate and sang the virtues of royalty, or celebrated the events of the day with natural finish and felicity. His poems were dedicated to Catherine, to the King, to Jeanne d'Albret, to every great personage at Court, but it was perhaps his "Franciade" which put him on the pinnacle of fame. His reputation had grown great in other countries, and when Tasso came to France, in 1571, he was eager to read his "Godefroi" to Ronsard. And though on Henri III's accession he was rather put into the shade and younger singers were preferred, when the King wished to found a kind of private *Académie* to be held in his own apartments, he summoned the old poet from his retreat and begged him to speak at the assembly.

The most lovable part of Ronsard's success was his attitude towards young men. " He incited those who went to see him—more especially such as he judged to be of gentle nature and apt to bear good fruit in poesy—to write well, above all to write less." . . . "As for me," says his faithful historian, Binet, "I shall always mark the day with blessèd chalk when I went to see him, young in years and in experience (being barely sixteen years old), but having tasted in some sort the honey stored in his writings. Not only did he welcome the first-fruits of my Muse, but he spurred me on to continue, and also to visit him often; nor was he ever chary in confiding those heavenly secrets with the which, the first of all men, he kindled my love of poesy."

Binet was one of a group of young poets formed more or less by the Pleiade, men whose names are long since forgotten, though their world believed them to be immortal. "*La France d'Homères est pleine*," so had Ronsard sung in all good faith. There was, however, no flattery in the instructions that he gave them. "You must be careful—" he said—
"to read good poets and you must learn them by heart as

much as possible. Spare no labour in correcting and polishing your verses and do not forgive them any more than a good gardener forgives his graft when he sees it loaded with useless branches. . . . Hold sweet and honest converse with the poets of your time . . . and show them what you write; for you should never let any work see the light unless it has first been seen, and seen again, by the friends whom you deem most skilful in this business"—a precept which himself he always practised, diligently pruning and perfecting his poems according to the counsels he received. What he resented was mediocrity —" *médoicrité qui est extrême vice* "—and the buzzing race of minor poets, as active then as in all times, excited his worst severity, especially when they pretended to be like him. " Their spirit "—he once said to a friend—" is turbulent . . . more violent than keen, like the winter torrents, which get as much mud as clear water from the hills. In their desire to avoid common language, they encumber themselves with words, and with hard, fantastic mannerisms which are apt to mean mere windy impressions rather than the true Virgilian majesty—for it is one thing to be grave and majestic, and another to swell out your style and make it burst." Poetry, he added, was the language of the gods, and men should not dare be its interpreters " if they had not been anointed from their birth and dedicated to this ministry."

For the rest, he was of a sociable turn, " *fort facile* " in conversation with those he cared about and not too fastidious about his company. " He liked men who were studious, of a clear conscience, open and simple," as he was himself, " for his countenance, his manners and his writings bore ever in their forefront I know not what stamp of nobility, and in all his actions one could feel the quality of a true French gentleman." The last journey he took was to see his crony, Galland, his second soul, as he called him.

> Heureux qui peut trouver pour passer l'aventure
> De ce monde, un amy de gentille nature,
> Comme tu es Galland, en qui les cieux ont mis
> Tout le parfait requis aux plus parfaits amis.
> Jà mon soir s'embrunit, et déjà ma journée
> Fuit, vers son Occident à demy retournée.

Thus he wrote of his friend towards the close, and it was at Galland's house, " *le Parnasse de Paris*," where he often stayed with such enjoyment, that his last illness overtook him. He sent for a coach and started for home, carrying with him his Galland, from whom he would not consent to separate. "I fear—" he wrote from Croixval—"that the autumn leaves will see me fall with them." He was right. In December, 1585, came the end. He had risen and dressed to take Communion; it displeased him to take it otherwise. All through his nights of pain, he had steadily gone on writing verses which he dictated in the morning to Galland. Often they are cries of distress—

> Miséricorde ô Dieu ! ô Dieu ne me consume
> A faute d'endormir . . .
> Heureux, cent fois heureux, animaux qui dormez
> Demi an en vos trous, sous la terre enfermés.

Or he shows us the path of Death, in colours more sombre and more natural than any he had yet used.

> C'est un chemin fâcheux, borné de peu d'espace,
> Tracé de peu de gens, que la ronce pava,
> Où le chardon poignant ses têtes éleva ;
> Prends courage pourtant, et ne quitte la place.

There was little in the outside world to cheer his courageous spirit. He talked constantly about the trouble that threatened his country, "*d'un discours bel et grave*," and with almost his old fire. At the last, he longed for change and moved to Tours, staying at his own Priory and summoning one of the monks there to attend him. "The monk asked him professionally in what religion he died. "Who has told you to say that, my good friend ?" replied Ronsard—"Do you doubt of my good faith ? I wish to die in the Catholic religion, like my fathers and my grandfathers to the third generation." After this, he was possessed by a desire to get new poems written down, and just before his death he dictated his last two sonnets, inciting his soul to set forth and seek its Christ. When he passed away, it was as if he slept, and those around the bed only knew that it was over, because the hands that he had lifted upwards suddenly dropped.[1]

---

[1] Mr. Hilaire Belloc, whose recently published book, *Avril*, I have read since my own was completed, makes much of Ronsard's Roman Catholicism and would fain have us believe that it denoted religious ardour. But it is difficult for those who read with unbiassed minds to blind themselves to the utter conventionality of the poet's religion. We cannot do better than quote the report of Ronsard's dying speeches, cited by Mr. Belloc in his volume and constituting his main piece of evidence.

"He said that he had swerved like other men and perhaps more than

Ronsard was buried at Tours, but the great funeral service at Paris did not take place till two months later. "It was sung by all the children of the Muses." Cardinals, Senate, Parlement and University were all of them present, and the crowd was so great that the Cardinal de Bourbon himself was obliged to turn back from the church. The Oraison Funèbre, pronouncd after dinner by the Bishop-Poet, Du Perron, was followed by enthusiastic applause and, that over, an Eclogue was acted, composed by Ronsard's literary executors. It seemed that the chief of the Pleïade had carried his success beyond the grave.

"*L'Intellect, qui comme un grand Capitaine du haut d'un rempart, commande à ses soldâts*"—these his own words might well serve as his epitaph. He had perhaps more intellect than imagination, but, however that may be, he had (to use another of his princely phrases) "travelled far on the green path that leads men into remembrance."

It is difficult to assign to Ronsard his right place in Olympus. The Immortals by no means form a republic, and there are many different ranks among them. Ronsard does not belong to the first rank, nor could so insistent an artificer belong to the greatest of the artists. He and his school must be counted rather with Cellini and the master-goldsmiths—with the exquisite sculptors *in petto*, the fastidious chasers of jewelled vases—than with the bigger creators. The work of the Pleïade was, if the phrase be allowable, naturally artificial; its grace was studied and made no pretence to be otherwise. But in the sixteenth century, artificialness could still be naïf; it had a cooling freshness, besides a subtle piquancy to charm the intellect as well as the eye. And another interesting result was due to Ronsard and his colleagues. They, first in France,

most; that his senses had led him away by their charm, and that he had not repressed or constrained them as he should; *but none the less he had always held that Faith which the men of his line had left him ;* he had always clasped close the creed and the unity of the Catholic Church; that in fine, he had laid a sure foundation, but he had built thereon with wood, with hay, with straw. As for the light and worthless things he had built upon it, he had trust in the mercy of the Saviour that they would be burnt in the fire of His love. And now he begged them all to believe hard as he had believed; but not to live as he had lived."

Whoever is accustomed to the deathbed language of kings and great personages of those days will recognize the conventional strain of these words and their absence of individuality. And when he compares it with the Pagan tone of Ronsard's poetry, he will easily perceive which meant the real man. The words which I have underlined in the quotation strike the keynote of tradition on which Ronsard's faith was based.

began the race of conscious artists. "For the secret of saying things perfectly does not lie in the abundance, or the pell-mell profusion of all flowers, but in the rejection of some and the choice and ordering of the loveliest—just as in the course of our life many things present themselves whereof few please us, and fewer still engender that surpassing content which ravisheth our enchanted spirits." So wrote one of the school. They foreshadowed the theory of art for art's sake which recent days have worn so thin. For whereas the great men of the Renaissance have always spoken of their work in the most matter-of-fact way, these men began to talk of art imaginatively. Du Bellay compares one kind with another, discusses the merits of historian and poet, and finds analogies for both in painting and sculpture.

> Tel que ce premier-là (the historian) est votre Janet [1] Sire ;
> Et tel que le second (the poet), Michel Ange on peut dire.

The writer of this couplet had eaten of the tree of Criticism and his recognition of the poetry that breathed in the marbles of Michael Angelo sounded a modern note which had hitherto been unknown. As yet, however, he and his school had no notion of separating art and artist. If the standard of morality in the Renaissance was a great deal laxer than ours, the standard of "*honnêteté*"—that untranslatable word including truth and amenity—was higher than it is now. "For because—" writes Ronsard—"the Muses will not dwell in a spirit that is not kind and holy, take care to have a good nature, neither gloomy nor malicious nor niggardly. . . . And above all, nourish fair and lofty conceptions—such as do not drag upon the earth."

It remains to consider the precise work that Ronsard achieved, not as an Immortal, but as a Frenchman ; the permanent mark which he left upon the literature of his country. It would be folly to plagiarize or repeat, when Sainte-Beuve—Judge in the High Court of Appeal of Letters—has already pronounced a verdict ; nor can we do better than close a chapter on the Pleïade with his own adequate summary.

"When Ronsard appeared, the study of antiquity, freed from the obstacles that first impeded it, was in all its brilliance and its glory. At the beginning, the only labour had been to decipher manuscripts, to re-establish texts and publish

---

[1] The other name for Clouet, which was the surname of the famous family of portrait-painters.

editions with commentaries. Translations did not suit the literary taste of the scholars who were the men of letters of that day, and if they deigned to give an occasional thought to their mother-tongue, it was to regret that it did not of itself make some freer attempt in the paths of antiquity. Ronsard felt the need and responded to it marvellously. An admirer of the ancients, with a certain independence of mind, he initiated, instead of translating them; all his originality, all his audacity, is to have been the first to imitate. Modelling his sonnets upon those of Petrarch, his odes upon those of Pindar and Horace, his songs upon Anacreon, his elegies upon Tibullus, his " Franciade " upon the Æneid, he set within this borrowed framework a force that was living enough to earn infinite gratitude. It was the first time that the physiognomy of the past lived again in our common idiom, and the world of letters hailed the poet with that sort of indulgence—almost of weakness—that is felt for the man who reproduces, or recalls the face that we have reverenced . . .

". . . While we cease to read or to relish Ronsard, can we reproach him with anything worse than the misfortune of arriving too soon and the fault of marching too quickly? A large vocabulary to choose from did not exist in France. Ronsard saw the want and set himself to improvise one. He created new words; he rejuvenated old ones; and as for those already in use among the people, he tried to dignify them by fresh alliances. The system was conceived on the grand scale, and the success it obtained proves that it was skilfully executed. Enlightened people welcomed it, exalted it; it seemed that the French language had again found its title-deeds and yielded to none the rights of precedence. Into this joy of triumph there glided something of the intoxication of the parvenu and the vanity of the man who has just risen. Unfortunately this splendour could not last long, because it lacked the strong support of the nation."

The attempt of the Pleïade, like that of the French Reformation, was too aristocratic, too far removed from the people, to be capable of lasting success. But it has dropped more than one choice flower on the long straight roads of France, and some exist still who love their faint cold fragrance.

CHAPTER XIII

Ronsard and the Elizabethans

AUTHORITIES CONSULTED

Oeuvres Poétiques de Ronsard.
Oeuvres Poétiques de Joachim Du Bellay.
Oeuvres Choisies de Ronsard—*Sainte-Beuve*.
Oeuvres de Rémy Belleau.
French Lyrics—*Saintsbury*.

CHAPTER XIII

Ronsard and the Elizabethans

NO one—not Shakespeare in his Sonnets—believed in his own immortality more firmly than Ronsard. His lyre is constantly celebrating his fame with more or less melody. He describes how people turn round to look at him in the streets, he bids the Muses bring laurels to wreathe his brow.

>C'est fait, j'ai dévidé le cours de mes destins,
>   J'ai vécu, j'ai rendu mon âme assez insigne ;
>   Ma plume vole au ciel pour être quelque signe,
>   Loin des appas mondains qui trompent les plus fins.
>   *   *   *   *
>   Toujours, toujours, sans que jamais je meure
>   Je volerai tout vif par l'univers,
>   Éternisant les champs où je demeure.

Ronsard lacked the quality that ensures immortality—the moral insight which our Elizabethan poets possessed. This it was, joined to his genius for expression, which gave Shakespeare, the epitome of them all, his supremacy among the Olympians, his hold upon the hearts of men. For as one of his most distinguished critics [1] points out, "it was owing to that surefooted step of his in things moral that he left us in the end satisfied." And this may be said in a lesser degree of his contemporaries, of Spenser and Sidney and Fulke Greville, of Raleigh and Drummond of Hawthornden, and the many other stars in that glorious company which has shed its lustre upon England.

There were certain elements of the Renaissance which were common to every country. In all nations there was a noble and naïf curiosity, a generous spirit of intellectual adventure, a stir of the Spring at the roots of things, so that every creature, from the least to the greatest, was filled with impetuous vitality. The mind had thrown open its gates and nothing was impossible. Thought was an emotion and became poetry; science was a magnificent romance, and universal knowledge

---

[1] Canon Ainger : *Lecture on the Ethics of Shakespeare.*

the El Dorado to which all captains steered their vessels. But each country had its own particular power which distinguished its Renaissance from that of other lands. In Italy, a triumphant sense of beauty prevailed; Germany contributed the intellectual faculty which helped to evolve the Reformation—the metaphysical tendency, the genius for abstract thought which seems embodied in Dürer's Melancholia. In France we find the sceptical and practical quality which engendered the shrewd daily philosophy of a Rabelais and a Montaigne, and created the great palaces that turned into comfortable homes; the forcible discrimination which has, in later days, made the French the past-masters of criticism. And when we come to England, it is the moral genius which is its strength; the profound perception of moral issues and situations, the knowledge of hidden motives and of the human heart, which, encountering, as it did, a golden tide of language, evoked our drama and our poetry.

The Drama and Poetry have this advantage: they make a border-land upon which the rival forces, æsthetic and spiritual—Renaissance and Reformation—can meet. For the distinctive gift of each people mingled with that great wave of beauty which flowed from Italy, inundating and fertilizing the earth; and in England, where the æsthetic sense was weakest and slowest of development, national painting and architecture were practically non-existent,[1] and all the energy of the Renaissance poured itself into our literature. Perhaps it is hardly to be wondered at that such a current should make its single channel a deep one, and more congenial to the soul than the contemporary literature of other countries.

> The nobler part
> Of all the house here is the heart.

Such is the gist of English poetry among the singers who correspond to the Pleïade.[2]

Very different was the outcome of the verse written by the French Anacreons. Their note is one of subtle regret. Let us eat and drink, let us crown our heads with roses, and love

---

[1] The only painters of note at that date were disciples of Holbein's school; while, as Mr. Blomfield points out, the Renaissance in architecture did not begin until nearly a century later (*Renaissance in Architecture*).

[2] Many of them lived a decade or so later than the Pleïade, but each group represented the Renaissance of Poetry, and the one answered to the other.

for the fleeting moment, for to-morrow we die—this is the burden of their song. They make life seem even shorter than it is; they leave the taste of dust upon our lips—dust from the slopes of Parnassus, but, none the less, mortal diet.

> Et je dois bientôt en cendre
> Aux Champs Elysées descendre,
> Sans qu'il reste rien de moi
> Qu'un petit je ne sais quoi
> Qu'un petit vase de pierre
> Cachera dessous la terre.

Such is the cry against fate which makes Ronsard's constant refrain. The cry may be a true one, but he does not get beyond it, and there is all the difference between this and George Peele's

> Beauty, strength, youth, are flowers but fading seen;
> Duty, faith, love are roots and ever green.

—lines equally characteristic of the school they represent.

Nowhere do we feel more strongly the spiritual difference between the poetry of England and of France, than in their conceptions of love. With Ronsard, Du Bellay, and their followers, love is ever the matter of a song and a summer day, of a Lesbia or a Chloe, as light and as passing as the south wind. The summer day may prolong itself, the song may be sung to a silvery lyre; and yet, for all its sweetness, it expresses nothing but a graceful materialism—now gay, now luxuriously melancholy, now bursting through the flowery meshes. Such music was no new thing; Anacreon and Pindar and Horace, the Ancients who inspired the Frenchmen, sang the same strain before them. But the Elizabethans of England cherished that large and sane idea of love which has been the glory of English poetry from their day to that of Robert Browning: a noble reconcilement of soul and body, an equal companionship, a passion for beauty and for something else besides, a tender loyalty and devotion lasting when passion is over.

The nearest English counterpart of the Pleïade is to be found later on in Herrick, the unclerical Horatian clergyman who played his Golden Numbers—his songs to Julia and Amaryllis—upon dulcet pan-pipes of antique form. Or else, we have Ronsard's equivalent in the Cavalier singers, light of soul and sweet of tongue, and the writers of the Restoration who frankly imitated the French. Herrick himself had most likely read Ronsard and Du Bellay, and had been in some measure affected by them. But when these men lived, the struggle of the Reformation was over, nor could they any longer feel its influence. And nothing more clearly brings out the temperament of a nation than the effect of a great movement upon its life and literature. To some readers, the stately march of Elizabethan verse may at times seem rather ponderous after the sinuous grace, the delicate motion of Ronsard and his circle. But it must in honesty be added that their master-pieces of grace are frequently hidden in a mass of wordy dullness. Ronsard can hardly be read without selection, and the flatness of his long poems must always prevent their being known. The Elizabethans, in compensation for being so massive, give us fewer pages of tedium, and the bulk of language and of feeling which distinguishes their work turns their very weight into dignity.

It is interesting, after any consideration of poetry, to take a few poems upon like subjects from either literature and to set them side by side. We will quote almost exclusively from Ronsard, because he gave voice to the thoughts of his colleagues and expressed them with the greatest beauty. He is, for instance, mourning his loved and lost Marie.

SUR LA MORT DE MARIE

Espérant luy conter un jour
L'impatience de l'amour
Qui m'a fait des peines sans nombre,
La mort soudaine m'a déçu,
Pour le vray le faux j'ai reçu,
Et pour le corps seulement l'ombre. . .

Hélas ! où est ce doux parler,
Ce voir, cet ouïr, cet aller,
Ce ris qui me faisoit apprendre
Que c'est qu'aimer ? Ha ! doux refus !
Ha ! doux dédains, vous n'êtes plus.
Vous n'êtes plus qu'un peu de cendre !

Hélas ! où est cette beauté,
Ce printemps, cette nouveauté
Qui n'aura jamais de seconde ?
Du ciel tous les dons elle avait ;
Aussi parfaite ne devait
Longtemps demeurer en ce monde. . . .

Le sort doit tousjours être égal.
Si j'ai pour toi souffert du mal,
Tu me dois part de ta lumière ;
Mais, franche du mortel lien,
Tu as seule emporté le bien
Ne me laissant que la misère.

RONSARD AND THE ELIZABETHANS

> En ton âge le plus gaillard
> Tu as seul laissé ton Ronsard,
> Dans le ciel trop tôt retournée,
> Perdant beauté, grâce et couleur,
> Tout ainsi qu'une belle fleur
> Qui ne vit qu'une matinée.
>
> En mourant tu m'as su fermer
> Si bien tout argument d'aimer
> Et toute nouvelle entreprise,
> Que rien à mon gré je ne vois,
> Et tout cela qui n'est pas toi
> Me déplaît et je les méprise.
>
> Si tu veux, Amour, que je sois
> Encore un coup dessous tes lois,
> M'ordonnant un nouveau service,
> Il te faut sous la terre aller
> Flatter Pluton et rappeller
> En lumière mon Eurydice.
>
> Ou bien, va-t'en là-haut crier
> A la Nature, et la prier
> D'en faire une aussi admirable ;
> Mais j'ai grand peur qu'elle rompît
> La moule alors qu'elle la fit,
> Pour n'en tracer plus de semblable. . . .
>
> Soit que tu vives près de Dieu,
> Ou aux Champs Élysées, adieu,
> Adieu, cent fois, adieu, Marie ;
> Jamais Ronsard ne t'oubliera,
> Jamais la mort ne délira
> Le nœud dont ta beauté me lie.

Drummond of Hawthornden also lost his love in the early days of manhood.

> Sweet soul, which in the April of thy years,
>   For to enrich the heaven mad'st poor this round,
>   And now, with flaming rays of glory crown'd,
> Most blest abides above the sphere of spheres ;
>   If heavenly laws, alas ! have not thee bound
> From looking to this globe that all up-bears,
>   If ruth and pity there above be found,
> O deign to lend a look unto these tears :
> Do not disdain (dear ghost) this sacrifice ;
>   And though I raise not pillars to thy praise,
> My off'rings take, let this for me suffice,
>   My heart a living pyramid I'll raise :
> And whilst kings' tombs with laurels flourish green,
> Thine shall with myrtles and these flowers be seen.

Lord Herbert of Cherbury only dreamed that he had lost his lady.

CATHERINE DE' MEDICI

O no, Belov'd : I am most sure
   These virtuous habits we acquire
   As being with the soul entire
Must with it evermore endure.

Else should our souls in vain elect ;
   And vainer yet were Heaven's laws,
   When to an everlasting cause
They give a perishing effect.

These eyes again thine eyes shall see,
   These hands again thine hand enfold,
   And all chaste blessings can be told
Shall with us everlasting be.

And if ev'ry imperfect mind
   Make love the end of knowledge here,
   How perfect will our love be where
All imperfection is refined !

So when from hence we shall be gone,
   And be no more nor you or I,
   As one another's mystery
Each shall be both, yet both but one.

Ronsard was not much given to acquiring virtuous habits, or wishing them to endure. Here are two of his most characteristic poems.

   Quand je suis vingt ou trente mois
Sans retourner en Vendômois,
Plein de pensées vagabondes,
Plein d'un remords et d'un souci,
Aux rochers je me plains ainsi,
Aux bois, aux antres, et aux ondes :

   Rochers, bien que soyez âgés
De trois mille ans, vous ne changez
Jamais ny d'état ni de forme ;
Mais toujours ma jeunesse fuit,
Et la viellesse qui me suit
De jeune en vieillard me transforme.

   Ondes, sans fin vous promenez,
Et vous menez et ramenez
Vos flots d'un cours qui ne séjourne ;
Et moi, sans faire long séjour,
Je m'en vais de nuit et de jour,
Au lieu d'où plus on ne retourne.

   Si est-ce que je ne voudrais
Avoir été ni roc ni bois,
Antre ni onde, pour défendre
Mon corps contre l'âge emplumé :
Car, ainsi dur, je n'eusse aimé
Toi qui m'as fait vieillir, Cassandre.

RONSARD AND THE ELIZABETHANS

Celui qui est mort aujourd'hui
Est aussi bien mort que celui
Qui mourut au jour du déluge.
Autant vaut aller le premier
Que de séjourner le dernier
Devant le parquet du grand juge.

Incontinent que l'homme est mort,
Pour jamais ou longtemps il dort
Au creux d'une tombe enfouie,
Sans plus parler, ouïr ne voir ;
Hé, quel bien saurait-on avoir
En perdant les yeux et l'ouïe ?

Or, l'âme selon le bienfait
Qu'hôtesse du corps elle a fait,
Monte au ciel, sa maison natale ;
Mais le corps, nourriture à vers,
Dissoût de veines et de nerfs,
N'est plus qu'une ombre sépulcrale.

Il n'a plus esprit ni raison,
Emboiture ni liaison,
Artère, pouls, ni veine tendre ;
Cheveu en tête ne luy tient,
Et, qui plus est, ne lui souvient
D'avoir jadis aimé Cassandre.

Le mort ne désire plus rien ;
Donc, cependant que j'ai le bien
De désirer, vif, je demande
Être tousjours sain et dispos ;
Puis, quand je n'auray que les os,
Le reste à Dieu je recommende.

Homère est mort, Anacréon,
Pindare, Hésiode et Bion,
Et plus n'ont souci de s'enquerre
Du bien et du mal qu'on dit d'eux ;
Ainsi, après un siècle ou deux,
Plus ne sentirai rien sous terre.

Mais de quoi sert le désirer
Sinon pour l'homme martirer ?
Le désir n'est rien que martire ;
Content ne vit le désireux,
Et l'homme mort est bien-heureux.
Heureux qui plus rien ne désire !

The next lines were written on his death-bed.

Âmelette, Ronsardelette,
Mignonnelette, doucelette,
Tres-chère hôtesse de mon corps,
Tu descends là-bas faiblelette,
Pâle, maigrelette, seulette,
Dans le froid royaume des morts ;

CATHERINE DE' MEDICI

> Toutesfois simple, sans remords
> De meurtre, poison, et rancune,
> Méprisant faveurs et trésors
> Tant enviés par la commune.
> Passant, j'ai dit ; suis ta fortune,
> Ne trouble mon repos : je dors !

To return to life : here is Ronsard's deliciously cool answer to the problems of existence.

> J'ai l'esprit tout ennuyé
> D'avoir trop étudié
> Les Phénomènes d'Arate :
> Il est temps que je m'ébâte,
> Et que j'aille aux champs jouer.
> Bons Dieux ! qui voudrait louer
> Ceux qui, collés sur un livre,
> N'ont jamais souci de vivre ?
>
> Que nous sert l'étudier,
> Sinon de nous ennuyer,
> Et soin dessus, soin accrêtre—
> A nous qui serons, peut-être,
> Ou ce matin, ou ce soir,
> Victime de l'Orque noir ?
> De l'Orque qui ne pardonne,
> Tant il est fier, à personne ?
>
> Corydon, marche devant,
> Sache où le bon vin se vend :
> Fais refrèschir ma bouteille,
> Cherche une feuilleuse treille
> Et des fleurs pour me coucher.
> Ne m'achête point de chair,
> Car tant soit elle friande,
> L'été je haïs la viande.
>
> Ores que je suis dispos,
> Je veux rire sans repos,
> De peur que la maladie
> Un de ces jours ne me die :
> Je t'ai maintenant vaincu,
> Meurs, galant, c'est trop vécu.

The voice of this poet, who sang " Vanitas vanitatum " so merrily, with such gay mockery, could only have been heard in France. And what Frenchman, on the other hand, could have said with Sir Walter Raleigh—

> Give me my scallop-shell of quiet,
>   My staff of faith to walk upon,
> My scrip of joy, immortal diet,
>   My bottle of salvation,
> My gown of glory, hope's true gage ;
> And thus I'll take my pilgrimage.

> Blood must be my body's balmer;
> No other balm will there be given;
> Whilst my soul, like quiet palmer,
> Travelleth toward the land of heaven;
> Over the silver mountains,
> Where spring the nectar fountains:
> There will I kiss
> The bowl of bliss,
> And drink mine everlasting fill
> Upon every milken hill.
> My soul will be a-dry before;
> But after it will thirst no more.

Or with Fulke Greville—

> The chief use then in Man of that he knows
> Is his painstaking for the good of all;
> Not fleshly weeping for our own made woes,
> Not laughing from a melancholy gall,
> Not hating from a soul that overflows
> With bitterness, breathed out from inward thrall:
> But sweetly rather to ease, loose or bind,
> As need requires, this frail, fall'n human kind.

Or, again, with Campion—

> Good thoughts his only friends,
> His wealth a well-spent age,
> The earth his sober inn
> And quiet pilgrimage.

Ronsard and his Pleïade would not have been at all happy in a "sober inn," and but for the austerity which scholarship required—the intellectual discipline, the vigils, the poverty which they so well understood—they were all of them convinced Epicureans. Not that they lack passages of a high and solemn strain. They are scattered here and there throughout the pages of Ronsard, hidden often in lengthy poems, too tedious for the ordinary reader. This quotation from his "Hymne à la Mort," which consoled Châtelard on the scaffold, shows him perhaps at his loftiest.

> Que ta puissance, ô Mort, est grande et admirable!
> Rien au monde par toi ne se dit perdurable,
> Mais tout ainsi que l'onde, à val des ruisseaux, fuit
> Le pressant coulement de l'autre qui la suit;
> Ainsi le temps se coule, et le présent fait place
> Au futur importun qui les talons lui trace.
> Ce qui fut se refait; tout coule comme une eau,
> Et rien dessous le ciel ne se voit de nouveau;
> Mais la forme se change en une autre nouvelle,
> Et ce changement-là, "vivre," au monde s'appelle,
> Et "mourir" quand la forme en une autre s'en va;

CATHERINE DE' MEDICI

> Ainsi avec Vénus la Nature trouva
> Moyen de ranimer par longs et divers changes
> La matière restant, tout cela que tu manges ;
> Mais notre âme immortelle est toujours en un lieu,
> Au change non sujette, assise auprès de Dieu,
> Citoyenne à jamais de la ville éthérée.

And as a corollary to this thought we may add—

> Que l'homme est malheureux qui au monde se fie.
> O Dieu ! que véritable est la philosophie
> Qui dit que toute chose à la fin périra
> Et qu'en changeant de forme une autre vêtira.
>
> De Tempé la vallée un jour sera montagne
> Et la cime d'Athos une large campagne ;
> Neptune quelquefois de blé sera couvert :
> La matière demeure et la forme se perd.

It is not without interest to compare with this an English poem containing much the same idea.

> Nothing is constant but in constant change.
>   What's done still is undone, and when undone
> Into some other fashion doth it range ;
>   Thus goes the floating world beneath the moon :
> Wherefore, my mind, above time, motion, place,
> Rise up and steps unknown to Nature trace.

This is Drummond of Hawthornden's, and his again is what follows—

> Beneath a sable veil, and shadows deep
>   Of inaccessible and dimming light,
>   In silence, ebon clouds more black than night,
> The world's great Mind His secrets hid doth keep : . . .
>
> O Sun invisible, that dost abide
>   Within thy bright abysms, most fair, most dark,
> Where with thy proper rays thou dost thee hide,
>   O ever-shining, never full-seen mark,
> To guide me in life's night, thy light me show ;
> The more I search of thee the less I know. . .
>
> Light is thy curtain : thou art Light of light ;
> An ever-waking eye still shining bright. . . .
>
> Never not working, ever yet in rest.

This last poem brings us to final causes, and to the ultimate reason of the divergences we have attempted to discuss. The idea of God—the God of the sixteenth century—was widely different in either nation. To the English poets of the age, He represented mystery—the Force who harmonized intellect, passion and virtue—the Unity of all things, after which the

Renaissance sought with persistent fervour. To the French Classics, He was either a natural force, or an aristocratic First Person—definite, accurate, remote, clad, not in clouds, but in dogma. Ronsard, when he has spoken of the misery and labour of man, of the incessant toil of Nature, thus concludes—

> Ainsi Dieu l'a voulu, afin que seul il vive
> Affranchi du labeur que la race chétive
> Des humains va rongeant de soucis langoureux.

—words which in themselves seem to call forth a French Revolution. Joachim du Bellay, with greater depth and faultier form, can sound a nobler strain than Ronsard, but a Pagan strain it still remains.

> Là est le bien que tout esprit désire,
> Là le repos où tout le monde aspire . . .
> Là, oh mon âme, au plus haut ciel guidée,
> Tu y pourras reconnaître l'idée
> De la beauté qu'en ce monde j'adore.

Absolute Beauty, a Hellenic god, was Du Bellay's ideal. He hated "le vulgaire," he believed in the supremacy of the Intellect, but he got no higher than this.

If we want a French counterpart to the Deity of Drummond and his compeers, we must seek it not in verse, but in prose—in the pages of François Rabelais. "That intellectual Sphere," he says, "whose centre is everywhere, whose circumference is nowhere, and whom we call God. The Egyptians hailed their Sovereign Deity as the Abstruse—the Hidden One. And because they invoked Him by this name, entreating Him to reveal Himself to them, He widened their knowledge of Himself and His creatures, guiding them by His bright lantern." Here we find warmth and light, and that treasure of spiritual wealth which the Pleïade were not born to give us.

II

It is time to leave comparisons and only to dwell upon the charm possessed by Ronsard and his school. If they were not made to produce grandeur of conception, they excelled in exquisiteness of detail, and they give enchanting pictures of trees and flowers and water—especially of water. For in this, the poet Ronsard was like the sculptor, Jean Goujon. Fountains and forest-springs seemed to exercise the same spell upon both, and there is hardly one of Ronsard's best-wrought poems that does not make mention of them. Nor was he at any time so happy as when he lay " in a green shade " by the water's brim, drawing sweet suggestion from the plashing music of the fountain in the woods of Gastine.

Perhaps the easiest way to give his work its full effect is to put together a few of his most perfect poems—clear-cut gems of many flashing facets—and to let them speak for themselves.

A LA FONTAINE BELLERIE

Ecoute-moi, Fontaine vive,
  En qui j'ay rebu si souvent,
Couché tout plat dessus ta rive,
  Oisif, à la fraîcheur du vent,

Quand l'Eté ménager moissonne
  Le sein de Cérès dévêtu,
Et l'air par compas ressonne,
  Gémissant sous le blé battu.

Ainsi tousjours puisses-tu être
  En religion à tous ceux
Qui te boiront, ou feront paître
  Tes verts rivages à leurs bœufs !

Ainsi tousjours la Lune claire
  Voie à minuit au fond d'un val
Les Nymphes près de ton repaire
  A mille bonds mener le bal ;

Comme je désire, Fontaine,
  De plus ne songer boire en toi
L'Été, lors que la fièvre amène
  La Mort, déspité contre moi.

ÉLÉGIE

  Mais adieu, Fontaine, adieu !
Tressaillante par ce lieu
Vous courrez perpetuelle
D'une course pérennelle,
Vive sans jamais tarir ;
Et je dois bientôt mourir
Et je dois bientôt en cendre
Aux Champs Élysées descendre,
Sans qu'il reste rien de moi
Qu'un petit je ne sais quoi
Qu'un petit vase de pierre
Cachera dessous la terre.
  Toutefois, ains que mes yeux
Quittent le beau jour des cieux
Je vous pri', ma Fontelette,
Ma doucelette ondelette,

RONSARD AND THE ELIZABETHANS

Je vous pri', n'oubliez pas
Dès le jour de mon trépas,
Contre vos rives de dire
Que Ronsard dessus sa lyre
N'a votre nom dédaigné,
Et que Cassandre a baigné
Sa belle peau doucelette
En vostre claire ondelette.

A LA FORÊT DE GASTINE

Couché sous tes ombrages verts,
  Gastine, je te chante
Autant que les Grecs, par leurs vers,
  La forêt d'Érymanthe :
Car, malin, céler je ne puis
  A la race future
De combien obligé je suis
  A ta belle verdure.
Toi qui, sous l'abri de tes bois,
  Ravi d'esprit m'amuses ;
Toi qui fais qu'à toutes les fois
  Me répondent les Muses ;
Toi par qui de l'importun soin
  Tout franc je me délivre,
Lors qu'en toi je me perds bien loin,
  Parlant avec un livre ;
Tes bocages soient tousjours pleins
  D'amoureuses brigades—
De Satyres et de Sylvains,
  La crainte des Naïades !
En toi habite désormais
  Des Muses le collège,
Et ton bois ne sente jamais
  La flamme sacrilège !

A FRAGMENT FROM
CONTRE LES BUCHERONS DE LA FORÊT DE GASTINE

Adieu, vieille Forêt, adieu têtes sacrées,
De tableaux et de fleurs en tout temps recouvrées,
Maintenant le dédain des passans altèrès—
Qui brûlez en l'Été des rayons éthérés,
Sans plus trouver le frais de tes douces verdures ;
Accuse tes meurtriers, et leur dis injures !

Adieu chênes, couronne aux vaillans citoyens,
Arbres de Jupiter, germes Dodonéens,
Qui premiers aux humains donnâtes à repaître ;
Peuples vraiement ingrats, qui n'ont su reconnaître
Les biens reçus de vous ; peuples vraiement grossiers,
De massacrer ainsi leurs pères nourriciers !

CATHERINE DE' MEDICI

ODE

Mignonne, allons voir si la Rose,
Qui ce matin avait déclose
    Sa robe de pourpre au Soleil,
A point perdu cette vêprée
Les plis de sa robe pourprée,
    Et son teint au vôtre pareil.

Las ! voyez comme en un peu d'espace,
Mignonne, elle a dessus la place
    Las, las, ses beautés laissé choir !
O vraiement marâtre Nature,
Puisqu' une telle fleur ne dure
    Que du matin jusqu' au soir !

Donc, si vous me croyez, Mignonne,
Tandis que vostre âge fleuronne
    En sa plus verte nouveauté,
Cueillez, cueillez votre jeunesse :
Comme à cette fleur, la vieillesse
    Fera ternir votre beauté.

L'AUBÉPIN

Bel Aubépin fleurissant,
    Verdissant
Le long de ce beau rivage,
Tu es vêtu jusqu'au bas
    Des longs bras
D'un lambrunche sauvage.

Deux camps de rouges fourmis
    Se sont mis
En garnison sous ta souche :
Dans les pertuis [2] de ton tronc
    Tout du long
Les avettes ont leur couche.

Le chantre Rossignolet
    Nouvelet,
Courtisant sa bien-aimée,
Pour ses amours alléger,
    Vient loger
Tous les ans en ta ramée.

Sur ta cime il fait son nid
    Tout uni
De mousse et de fine soie,
Où ses petits éclorront,
    Qui seront
De mes mains la douce proie.

---

[1] Wild vine.   [2] Holes.

Or vis, gentil Aubépin,
   Vis sans fin,
Vis sans que jamais tonnerre,
Ou la coignée, ou les vents,
   Ou les temps
Te puissent ruer par terre.

LA ROSE

Dieu te gard l'honneur printemps,
   Qui étends
Tes beaux trésors sur la branche,
Et qui découvres au soleil
   Le vermeil
De ta beauté naïve et franche. . . .

Près de toi, sentant ton odeur,
   Plein d'ardeur,
Je façonne un vers dont la grâce
Maugré les tristes Sœurs vivra,
   Et suivra
Le long vol des ailes d'Horace.

Les uns chanteront les œillets
   Vermeillets,
Ou du lis la fleur argentée,
Ou celle qui s'est par les prés
   Diaprés
Du sang des princes enfantée.

Mais moi, tant que chanter pourrai,
   Je louerai
Tousjours en mes Odes la rose
D'autant qu'elle porte le nom
   De renom
De celle où ma vie est enclose.

A CASSANDRE [1]

La lune est coûtumière
   Renaître tous les mois ;
Mais, quand notre lumière
   Sera morte une fois,
Longtemps sans reveiller
Nous faudra sommeiller.
Tandis que vivons ores,
   Un baiser donne-moi ;
Donne-m'en mille encores ;
   Amour n'a point de loi ;
A sa grand' déité
Convient l'infinité.

---

[1] This is an example of Ronsard's adaptation from the classics, and is imitated from Catullus.

CATHERINE DE' MEDICI

LA QUENOUILLE [1]

Quenouille, de Pallas la compagne et l'amie,
Cher présent que je porte à ma chère Marie,
Afin de soulager l'ennui qu'ell'a de moi,
Disant quelque chanson en filant dessur toi,[2]
Faisant piroüetter à son huïs,[3] amusée,
Tout le jour son rouet et sa grosse fusée—

Quenouille, je te mène où je suis arrêté,
Je voudrais racheter par toi ma liberté.
Tu ne viendras és mains d'une mignonne oisive,
Qui ne fait qu'attifer[4] sa perruque lascive
Et qui perd tout son temps à mirer et farder
Sa face, à celle fin qu'on l'aille regarder ;
Mais bien entre les mains d'une dispose[5] fille,
Qui dévide, qui coûd, qui ménage et qui file
Avec ses deux sœurs pour tromper ses ennuis,
L'Hiver devant le feu, l'Été devant son huïs.

Aussi je ne voudrais que toi, Quenouille, faite
En notre Vendômois (où le peuple regrette
Le jour qui passe en vain) allasses en Anjou
Pour demeurer oisive et te rouiller au clou.
Je te puis assurer que sa main délicate
Filera dougément[6] quelque drap d'écarlate,
Qui si fin et si soüef[7] en sa laine sera,
Que pour un jour de fête un Roi le vêtira.

Suis-moi donc, tu seras la plus que bien-venue,
Quenouille, des deux bouts et grêlette et menue,[8]
Un peu grosse au milieu où la filace tient,
Étreinte d'un ruban qui de Montoire[9] vient,
Aime-laine, aime-fil, aime-étaim,[10] maisonnière,
Longue, Palladienne, enflée, chansonnière ;
Suis-moi, laisse Coûture, et allons a Bourgueil,
Où, Quenouille, on te doit recevoir d'un bon œil :
Car le petit présent qu'un loyal ami donne,
Passe des puissants Rois le Sceptre et la Couronne.

DE L'EPITAPHE D'ANDRÉ BLONDET

Mais par-sur-tous l'homme, qui est semblable . . .
D'esprit aux Dieux, est le plus misérable ;
Et la raison qui vient divinement,
Lui est vendue un peu trop chèrement ;
Car nous l'avons à condition d'être
Tres-malheureux dès l'heure de nôtre être. . . .
Bref, mal sur mal nous vient de tous côtés,
Et seulement nous ne sommes pas domptés . . .
À tout le moins si nature honorable

---

[1] This is also an adaptation from Theocritus
[2] On thee, [3] house-door, [4] prink out, [5] deft, [6] delicately, [7] soft, [8] thin and slender, [9] a place in the Vendômois, [10] carded wool.

Eût ordonné d'arrêt irrévocable
Que les méchants mourraient tant seulement,
Vivants les bons perpetuellement,
Quelque comfort aurait nôtre misère,
Et la nature à bon droit serait mère.
Mais quand on voit les méchants si longtemps
Vivre gaillards au terme de cent ans
Sans amender leur malice première,
Et quand on voit les bons ne vivre guère,
L'humanité de l'homme, soucieux
De s'enquérir, en accuse les cieux.
   Las ! qui verrait dans un gras labourage
Tomber du ciel le malheureux orage,
Qui d'une grêle et d'un vent jusqu'au fond
Perdrait les blés qui, jà grandets, se font
Tous hérissés d'épis, où la sémence
A se former à quatre rangs commence
Et laisserait seulement dans les champs
La noire yvraye, et les chardons tranchants,
La ronce aigüe, et la mordante épine
Qui sur le blé misérable domine ;
Qui est celui, tant soit constant de cœur,
Qui n'accusât la céleste rigueur,
Et ne branlât contre le ciel la tête,
D'avoir rué une telle tempête ?

DE L'HYMNE À LA MORT

Moi donc, Masures cher, qui de longtemps sais bien
Qu'au sommet de Parnasse on ne trouve plus rien
Pour étancher la soif d'une gorge altérée,
Je m'en vais découvrir quelque source sacrée
D'un ruisseau non touché, qui murmurant s'enfuit
Dedans un beau verger loin de gens et de bruit ;
Source que le soleil n'aura jamais connue,
Que les oiseaux du ciel de leur bouche cornue
N'auront jamais souillée, et où les pastoureaux
N'auront jamais conduit les pieds de leurs taureaux.
Je boirai tout mon saoul de cette onde pucelle,
Et puis je chanterai quelque chanson nouvelle,
Dont les accords seront peut-être si très-doux
Que les siècles voudront les redire après nous . . .
Car il me plaît pour toi de faire ici ramer
Mes propres avirons dessus ma propre mer,
Et de voler au ciel par une voie étrange,
Te chantant de la Mort la non-dite louange.

ÉLÉGIE

Six ans etaient coulés, et la septième année
Était presque entière en ses pas retournée,
Quand loin d'affection, de désir et d'amour,
En pure liberté je passais tout le jour,
Et franc de tout souci qui les âmes dévore,

CATHERINE DE' MEDICI

Je dormais dès le soir jusqu'au point de l'Aurore :
Car seul maître de moi j'allais, plein de loisir,
Où le pied me portait, conduit de mon désir,
Ayant tousjours és mains, pour me servir de guide,
Aristote ou Platon, ou le docte Euripide,
Mes bons hôtes muets qui ne fâchent jamais :
Ainsi que je les prends, ainsi je les remets ;
O douce compagnie et utile et honnête !
Un autre en caquetant m'étourdirait la tête.

Puis du livre énnuyé, je regardais les fleurs,
Fucilles, tiges, rameaux, éspèces, et couleurs,
Et l'entrecoupement de leurs formes diverses,
Peintes de cent façons, jaunes, rouges et perses,
Ne me pouvant saouler, ainsi qu'en un tableau,
D'admirer la Nature et ce qu'elle a de beau ;
Et de dire en parlant aux fleurettes écloses :
Celui est presque Dieu qui connaît toutes choses,
Eloigné du vulgaire, et loin des courtisans,
De fraude et de malice, impudents artisans.
Tantôt j'errais seulet par les forêts sauvages
Sur les bords enjonchés des peinturés rivages.
Tantôt par les rochers reculés et déserts,
Tantôt par les taillis, verte maison des cerfs

J'aimais le cours suivi d'une longue rivière,
Et voir onde sur onde allonger sa carrière,
Et flot à l'autre flot en roulant s'attacher,
Et, pendu sur le bord, me plaisoit d'y pêcher ;
Étant plus réjoui d'une chasse muette
Troubler des écaillés la demeure secrette,
Tirer avec la ligne, en tremblant emporté,
Le credule poisson pris à l'haim apâté,
Qu'un grand Prince n'est aise ayant pris à la chasse
Un cerf, qu'en haletant tout un jour il pourchasse. . . .

Or le plus de mon bien pour decevoir ma peine,
C'est de boire à longs traits les eaux de la fontaine
Qui de vostre beau nom se brave, et, en courant
Par les prés, vos honneurs va tousjours murmurant,
Et la Reine se dit des eaux de la contrée :
Tant vaut le gentil soin d'une Muse sacrée,
Qui peut vaincre la Mort et les sorts inconstants
Sinon pour jamais, au moins pour un longtemps.

Là couché dessus l'herbe, en mes discours je pense
Que pour aimer beaucoup j'ai peu de récompense,
Et que mettre son cœur aux Dames si avant,
C'est vouloir peindre en l'onde et arrêter le vent ;
M'assurant toutefois, qu'alors que le vieil âge
Aura comme un sorcier changé votre visage,
Et lorsque vos cheveux deviendront argentés,
Et que vos yeux d'Amour ne seront plus hantés,
Que toujours vous aurez, si quelque soin vous touche,
En l'esprit mes écrits, mon nom en votre bouche.

RONSARD AND THE ELIZABETHANS

LE TOMBEAU DE MARGUERITE DE VALOIS

Comme les herbes fleuries
Sont les honneurs des prairies,
Et des prés les ruisselets,
De l'orme la vigne aimée,
Des bocages la ramée,
Des champs les blés nouvelets,

Ainsi tu fus, ô Princesse
(Ainsi plustôt, ô Déesse),
Tu fus la perle et l'honneur
Des Princesses de notre âge,
Soit en force de courage
Ou soit en royal bonheur.

Il ne faut point qu'on te fasse
Un sépulchre qui embrasse
Mille termes en un rond
Pompeux d'ouvrages antiques,
Et brave en piliers doriques . . .

Vous, Pasteurs, que la Garonne
D'un demi-tour environne,
Au milieu de vos prés verts,
Faites sa tombe nouvelle,
Et gravez l'herbe sus elle
Du long cercle de ces vers :

Icy la Reine sommeille,
Des Reines la nonpareille,
Qui si doucement chanta ;
C'est la Reine Marguerite,
La plus belle fleur d'élite
Qu'onques l'Aurore enfanta.

Puis sonnez vos cornemuses,
Et menez au bal les Muses
En un cerne tout-autour,
Soit aux jours de la froidure,
Ou quand la jeune verdure
Fera son nouveau retour.

Aux rais connus de la Lune
Assemblez sous la nuit brune
Vos Naïades et vos Dieux,
Et avec vos Dryades
Donnez-lui dix mille aubades
Du flageol mélodieux. . . .

Dites à vos brebettes :
Fuyez-vous-en, camusettes,
Gagnez l'ombre de ces bois ;
Ne broutez en cette prée,
Toute l'herbe en est sacrée
A la Nymphe de Valois.

CATHERINE DE' MEDICI

Dites-leur : Troupes mignonnes,
Que vos liqueurs seraient bonnes
Si leur douceur égalait
La douceur de sa parole,
Lors que sa voix douce et molle
Plus douce que miel coulait ! . . .

Ombragez d'herbes la terre,
Tapissez-la de lierre,
Plantez un cyprès aussi ;
Et notez dedans à force
Sur la noüailleuse écorce
Derechef ces vers ici. . . .

Semez après mille roses,
Mille fleurettes décloses ;
Versez du miel et du lait ;
Et pour annuel office,
Répandez en sacrifice
Le sang d'un blanc agnelet. . . .

Faites encore à sa gloire
(Pour allonger sa mémoire)
Mille jeux et mille ébats :
Vostre Reine sainte et grande
Du haut Ciel vous le commande,
Pasteurs, n'y faillez donc pas.

Iô, Iô, Marguerite,
Soit que ton esprit habite
Sur la nue, ou dans les champs
Que le long oubli couronne—
Oy ma Lyre qui te sonne,
Et favorise mes chants !

We will add to these poems of Ronsard's a few of Joachim Du Bellay's, and one example of Rémy Belleau. The most exquisite of Du Bellay's verses, "Les Vanneurs," has been cited in another volume,[1] and was, long ago, made known to us by Pater in his "Essays on the Renaissance". It therefore seems redundant to repeat it. But the same qualities, the same silvery atmosphere by which it delights us, give the tone to the rest of his work. The sweep and the swirl of the scythe, the swaying and rippling of ripe corn before the wind, all the sights and sounds of the harvest, possess the same charm for Du Bellay as water possessed for Ronsard. The sower, the gleaner, the reaper, and the images they evoke, constantly recur in his pages, even when he is writing about old Rome— as in this Sonnet from "Les Antiquités."

[1] "Women and Men of the French Renaissance."

RONSARD AND THE ELIZABETHANS

> Comme le champ semé en verdure foisonne,
> De verdure se hausse en tuyau verdissant,
> De tuyau se hérisse en épi florissant ;
> D'épi jaunit en grain que le chaud assaisonne ;
> Et comme en la saison le rustique moissonne
> Les ondoyants cheveux du sillon blondissant,
> Les met d'ordre en javelle, et du blé jaunissant
> Sur le champs dépouillé mille gerbes façonne ;
> Ainsi de peu à peu crût l'Empire Romain,
> Tant qu'il fut dépouillé par la Barbare main,
> Qui ne laissa de lui que ces marques antiques,
> Que chacun va pillant : comme on voit le glaneur
> Cheminant pas à pas recueillir les reliques
> De ce que va tombant après le moissonneur.

The dominant note of Du Bellay's poetry is an elegant simplicity. His elegance is more natural than Ronsard's, whether he is writing about the ruins of the Past, or, as here, about the emotions of the Present—

> Votre douceur, votre humble privauté,
> Et votre esprit plus beau que la beauté,
> Perfections d'un chacun estimées,
> Mais plus de moi que tout autre aimées,
> Par un instinct naturel qui me fait
> Connaître en vous de vous le plus parfait.

What can be more harmonious than this, written to a fellow-poet—

> L'amour se nourrit de pleurs
> Et les abeilles de fleurs ;
> Les prés aiment la rosée,
> Phébus aime les neuf Sœurs,
> Et nous aimons les douceurs
> Dont ta Muse est arrosée.

But his gift is at its best when he is describing what is homely and familiar and lending it a kind of classic grace—for instance, in his epitaph on his little dead dog who lives again in his verse—

> ÉPITAPHE D'UN PETIT CHIEN
>
> Dessous cette motte[1] verte,
> De lis et roses couverte,
> Gît le petit Peloton—
> De qui le poil foleton
> Frisait d'une toison blanche
> Le dos, le ventre, et la hanche.
> Son nez camard, ses gros yeux

---

[1] Heap.

CATHERINE DE' MEDICI

Qui n'étaient point chassieux,
Sa longue oreille velue
D'une soie crêpelue,
Sa queue au petit floquet
Semblant un petit bouquet. . . .
Son exercice ordinaire
Étoit de japper et braire,
Courir en haut et en bas,
Et faire cent mille ébats
Tous étranges et farouches,
Et n'avait guerre qu'aux mouches,
Qui luy faisaient maint tourment.
Mais Peloton dextrement
Leur rendait bien la pareille. . . .
   Peloton ne caressait
Sinon ceux qu'il connaissait,
Et n'eût pas voulu repaître
D'autre main que de son maître,
Qu'il allait tousjours suivant :
Quelquefois marchait devant,
Faisant ne sais quelle fête
D'un gai branlement de tête.
   Mon Dieu, quel plaisir c'était,
Quand Peloton se grattait,
Faisant tinter sa sonnette
Avec sa tête folette !
Quel plaisir, quand Peloton
Cheminait sur un bâton,
Ou coiffé d'un petit linge,
Assis comme un petit singe,
Se tenait mignardelet
D'un maintien damoiselet !
Las ! mais ce doux passetemps
Ne nous dura pas longtemps :
Car la mort, ayant envie
Sur l'aise de notre vie,
Envoya devers Pluton
Notre petit Peloton,
Qui maintenant se pourmène
Parmi ceste ombreuse plaine
Dont nul ne revient vers nous.

Let us close with Rémy Belleau's "Avril," for it is like a light farewell from the Graces. Before we can salute them they have gone, floated past us on a shining shower, and left us regretful behind them.

Avril, l'honneur et des bois
   Et des mois :
Avril, la douce espérance
Des fruits qui, sous le coton
   Du bouton,
Nourrissent leur jeune enfance ;

Avril, l'honneur des prés verts
       Jaunes, pers,
Qui d'une humeur bigarrée,
Émaillent de mille fleurs
       De couleurs,
Leur parure diaprée ; . . .

Avril, c'est ta douce main
       Qui, du sein
De la nature, desserre
Une moisson de senteurs
       Et de fleurs,
Embaumant l'air et la terre ; . . .

Avril la grâce, et le ris
       De Cypris,
Le flair et la douce haleine ;
Avril, le parfum des dieux,
       Qui, des cieux,
Sentent l'odeur de la plaine ;

C'est toi, courtois et gentil,
       Qui d'exil
Retires ces passagères,
Ces hirondelles qui vont,
       Et qui sont
Du printemps les messagères.

L'aubépine et l'aiglantin,
       Et le thym,
L'œillet, le lis, et les roses,
En ceste belle saison,
       À foison,
Montrent leurs robes écloses. . . .

Tu vois, en ce temps nouveau
       L'essaim beau
De ces pillardes avettes[1]
Voleter de fleur en fleur
       Pour l'odeur
Qu'ils mussent en leurs cuissettes.[2]

Mai vantera ses fraîcheurs,
       Ses fruits mûrs,
Et la seconde rosée,
La manne et le sucre doux,
       Le miel roux,
Dont sa grace est arrosée.

Mais moi je donne ma voix
       A ce mois
Qui prend le surnom de celle
Qui, de l'écumeuse mer,
       Vit germer
Sa naissance maternelle.

---
[1] Bees.   [2] Store in their little thighs.

CATHERINE DE' MEDICI

Belleau's lines were to have been the last of those here spoken by the Pleïade. And yet as we write them, Ronsard's spirit, courtly and confident, rises up in protest. He is right —the final word should be his. Where is he ? In that woodland grave—the " *sépulchre* " which he chose for himself and begged posterity to make for him ?

> Et vous forêts et ondes
> Par ces prés vagabondes,
> Et vous rives et bois,
>   Oyez ma voix. . . .
>
> Je défends quon me rompe
> Le marbre, pour la pompe
> De vouloir mon Tombeau
>   Bâtir plus beau.
>
> Mais bien je veux q'un arbre
> M'ombrage au lieu d'un marbre—
> Arbre qui soit couvert
>   Toujours de vert.
>
> Tout à l'entour l'emmure
> L'herbe et l'eau qui murmure,
> L'un toujours verdoyant,
>   L'autre ondoyant. . . .
>
> Dessus moi, qui à l'heure
> Serai par la demeure
> Où les heureux Esprits
>   Ont leur pourpris.[1]

There, in that Isle of the Blest, which they were so well fitted to inhabit, let us leave the happy shades of Ronsard and the Pleïade. Supreme grace was the gift that the gods had given them. And by that grace they will live—not only in the meadows of Elysium.

[1] Dwelling-place.

CHAPTER XIV

Catherine and the Arts

AUTHORITIES CONSULTED

The French Renaissance—*Mrs. Pattison.*
Vie de Philibert de l'Orme—*Vachon.*
Philibert de l'Orme—*Reginald Blomfield.*
Biographical Preface to Œuvres de Palissy—*Anatole France.*
Lettres de Catherine de' Medici.
Histoire Universelle—*D'Aubigné.*
Memoirs de Tavannes.
Journal de Pierre l'Estoille.
Journal de l'an 1562—*Revue Rétrospective.*
Le Fort inexpugnable de l'honneur féminin—*François Billon.*
Femmes illustres—*Brantôme.*
Femmes de la Renaissance—*Maulde de la Clavière.*
Catherine de Médicis—*Henri Bouchot.*
Histoire de France—*Martin.*

CHAPTER XIV

Catherine and the Arts

"IN sooth he sorely needeth spectacles who asserteth that, in this valley of shadows, men without women would ever meet with any kind of friendship." So writes the old Euphuist, Billon, whose "Inexpugnable Fort de l'honneur du sexe féminin," a strange mixture of ingenuity, sound sense, and hyperbole, was dedicated to the women at whose lives we have been looking—Catherine de' Medici, Jeanne de Navarre, Marguerite de Berri et Savoie. From the literary point of view the book is little more than a curious Court toy, but its real interest lies in the unconscious testimony it bears to the change in the position of women. Anne de Bretagne may be said to have marked the end of the old order of the mediæval woman—and Marguerite d'Angoulême may equally be called the initiator of the new order, the first of the modern women. Under the code of the past, there was practically no alternative between marriage and a nunnery; the unmarried woman, outside convent walls, was a disgraced creature. But Billon already informs us that the unmarried state "can only be excellently praiseworthy, and, indeed, surpasses all other." He inveighs against the sin of parents in arranging marriages for their daughters with "*quelque gros animal comme un Porc, seulement vêtu de soie*"; he tells us ecstatically that every invention is due to womankind, from the days when Minerva invented oil and a lady "of the Ancients" invented riddles, seven hundred and forty years before Christ—"the Divine Man who answered the Riddle of Life once and for all." It must be added that these Renaissance reflections are followed by the riddle itself, and that it does not add any great glory to the sex. "Who," it asks, "was the parent possessing twelve deformed children, mortal and yet immortal?" And the answer, which even a man might guess, is "Time, the father of the months." But the insistence on the importance of woman, the modern note of Billon's utterance, is no mere formula of sycophancy, but the expression of a significant fact. Woman had always been there; women now came into existence, and modern society was born. There was, in the sixteenth century in France, a movement for Women's Rights not unlike that in our own day, though expressed in more primitive language. Young women urged each other not to be over-domestic, to cultivate their minds, and to be no longer subject to men. A certain erudite lady called Hélisienne of Picardy confuted "*aussi plaisammement*" the "*ironiques raisons*" of a Conservative gentleman who laid down the law that women ought to meddle with nothing but spinning. Heavy repartees, charged with learning, flew between the two camps, and women tried to prove their claims by their achievements. They wrote rhymes, not so much, says Billon, " to taste the fruit of honour, but to make dunderheads understand that woman's mind and her intellectual gifts in no way proceed from man—souls being neither masculine nor feminine." The fact that she had a brain and could be educated at all was new to the world, and each fresh bluestocking was a prodigy. Anne Tallon of Macon wrote letters "more than Ciceronian." Madame de Martinhuile was a peerless musician and composer; Madame d'Estampes "knew all the history of France by heart," and Billon adds that this was what especially attracted François I, though he had the grace to conclude with " *Ici je vous attends, Causeurs*," as if he knew how preposterous was his statement. As for the ladies of Lyons and their little côterie of blue-stockings, the world had never seen such poetesses. "Oh daughter of the very Christian Phoenix!" was one author's most moderate mode of addressing a well-educated princess, and his Euphuistic ecstasy at the growing fame of women was only the voice of his generation.

Their increasing importance had considerable effect upon the arts, their especial domain. Their taste, their patronage, even their vanity and love of novelty, gave a fresh impetus to sculpture and architecture and painting—particularly the painting of their portraits. And the minor arts may be said to have been created by them. For social needs demanded fresh luxuries and refinements. Castles became dwelling-houses; new habits required new appliances, more elegant ornamentation; and the need felt by one great lady to outshine another provided the stimulus of competition as well as of handsome payment. Perhaps such a state of things promoted the decadence of art which prevailed in the time of Catherine, or perhaps the greater traditions of the earlier days had exhausted themselves and the reign of the crafts had in due course begun. Be that as it may, the last half of the century was debased; ingenuity was substituted for ideas and art was degenerating into artifice; was becoming a rich mass of detail, bewildering in its perfection. " The end of the world is threatened when the period and perfection of all the arts is reached. It seems as if nothing could be added to man's inventions." So says a critic of that age whose words do not only apply to his own time. He hits the nail on the head. The art of the day lacked the dignity of imagination and consisted of elaborate inventions allowing no vistas for the spirit.

And it was an art which lent itself to be imitated. Another writer of the period foresaw the danger, and towards the end of the century already complains of cheap reproductions—lamenting because the figures carefully wrought by sculptors now " fell into the hands of tradesmen who cast them into moulds and turned them out in such quantities that eventually no one recognized either the creator or his work." In those happy days, a pedlar was imprisoned and whipped because he had hawked a basket of common crucifixes *all of one pattern* through the streets of Toulouse. " It were better that one man, or a very few, made their livelihood by some art, working honestly, than a great number of men, who injure one another so much by competition that they cannot earn their daily bread except by profaning the arts, and leaving things half finished." Thus did machinery and commerce cast their sordid shadows before them.

The one art which demands mathematical definiteness, which corresponded also to the social developments of the time, was the only big art which flourished. Architecture seemed to be the expression of all that was then best aesthetically. As women became prominent and intercourse more civilized, the feudal castle grew impossible and an adequate house a necessity. When talk and study became ends in themselves, drawing-rooms and libraries were requisite; and when walls served for more varied purposes than for shelter and seclusion, when the display of men's prowess, so long the main diversion of women, was replaced by music and play-acting, all manner of embellishments and ingenuities were needful. An enthusiasm for building possessed France: " *la maladie de bâtir,*" old Tavannes calls it. He says that it ought to be controlled; that its fashions changed every day because "the French were as much bent on change in their houses as in their dresses;" that many sighed in vain to have their money back and rebuild their mansions more modishly. It is curious to find how the Châteaux of François I, so much admired by their own age and by ours, were condemned by the connoisseurs who lived thirty years after their construction. "Fontainebleau"—says one of these—"is a confusion, and its only beautiful feature is the great Courtyard; the second Court has no architecture, the third part is oval, triangular, square, altogether imperfect." What would Philibert de l'Orme, once Master of the Works there, have said to such an indictment, or to the same critic's condemnation of the Tuileries, which the world regarded as his masterpiece? And what would the makers of the Louvre, Pierre Lescot and Bullant, have rejoined?

Architecture was the one art about which Catherine de' Medici was keen. This may seem a bold thing to say in face of the common belief in her strong æsthetic tastes—her heritage from the Medici. But a love of luxury can look wonderfully like a love of beauty. Catherine cared much for ingenuity, for novelty, for the possession of things that were unique, but she had not the feelings of an artist, no real conception to guide her. She wished more for ornament and splendour, for pottery, for enamels, for jewellery, than for any larger work of art. She also liked to have many pictures of herself, and when, in middle age, she returned to Lyons, where she had gone in her youth at the time of her husband's coronation, she visited the studio of Corneille de la Haye and looked at the portraits he had then taken of her and all her family. But it was not for art's sake that she did so. "So delighted was she with the painting that she could not take her eyes off it." "Cousin," she said to the Duc de Nemours who was with her, "I think that you can well remember the time when this was done, and you can judge better than anyone in this company, you who saw me thus, if I was considered to be what you report, and if I was like the woman here." Nor was there much question of beauty when she sent her commands to Court painters and sculptors. Sometimes they are contained in curt business notes, like the one to her ambassador at Rome, in which she bids him take care that her orders to Michael Angelo for a statue of Henri II are executed without delay. "Please see to it," she writes, "the more so as I hear that he who has made it is very subject to apoplexy, and supposing he had another attack and died, I am told that there is no man in Christendom who could execute his design." Her letters dictate every detail of his work to the artist in the arrogant fashion of those days. She is annoyed that the effigies of her husband and son have not yet been set up. "Be sure" (she says to their creator) "that you make them as much like Nature as you can—in the royal robes as is the custom—and I should like to remind you to take heed and do what is usual in the case of warlike and conquering kings—the which always lie with their hands upraised to show that they have not been idle. Of all this you will please send me pictures at once." Even where architecture was concerned, she showed no real taste and spoiled De l'Orme's fine original design for the Château of St. Maur-les-Fossés by demanding a graceless and monotonous façade, disfigured by an exaggerated pediment.

Like all her contemporaries, she was a collector—more from competition with others than from the love of what she collected. "I hear"—she says to Cardinal Tournon—"that the Doctor who has that lovely Adonis is very anxious to sell it and cannot find a purchaser. Pray manage to put out feelers as if on your own behalf and discover if he really wishes to sell it and for how much. And he told me that there was some benefice he wanted. Find out all about it without his knowing that you are doing so for us." The merchant's daughter came out in the hard bargains that she drove, of which this was no single instance. When her cousin, the great book-collector, the Maréchal Strozzi, died, she at once made a bid for his precious library and antiquities, and she went off with the treasure promising his son ample payment. But he never received a penny from her, and he could not get any compensation. Nor did the heirs of her cousin, Hippolyte d'Este, the love of her first youth, fare much better at her hands; she sued them for his inheritance twenty-two years after his death, and came off victorious with twenty thousand crowns and all his stones and jewels. There was, indeed, no length to which her love of luxury did not run. She had heard that the wife of her Treasurer possessed the most sumptuous furniture, and making a pretext of the lady's illness, she went to pay her a visit. But while she dispensed sympathy, her eye fell upon a seat with a crimson covering embroidered with golden lilies, richer than any of her own.

CATHERINE DE' MEDICI

She departed with many suave courtesies—and lost no time in charging the unconscious lady's husband with official dishonesty, for which he was condemned to death.

The magnificence of the Court gave a false impression of good taste. Numbers of painters, jewellers, goldsmiths and other craftsmen lived and worked upon the premises and formed guilds, each governed by adamantine laws. The first artists designed the Court dresses, and as Catherine kept near fifty ladies and paid all their expenses, her bills for their wardrobe must have been high. The best ones were wrought with gold and precious stones; and so heavy were they on state occasions that brides had to be carried to Church and princesses could often hardly stand for the monumental robes that walled them in. We have an account of the Princess Margot, bowed beneath a weight of real gold tissue, a golden wig upon her head, to provide which two fair-haired lackeys were shorn every week. And we can evoke Catherine herself, bewigged, perfumed, sumptuous yet austere, in her persistent widow's black relieved by costly furs and jewels, as she holds a court levée, or receives her Lords and Captains according to accepted etiquette—kissing the greater gentlemen on the cheek while she puts her arm round their necks, and touching the lesser ones on the shoulder. Universal embracing became the fashion and manners were as extravagant as dress. "Look at us," says Tavannes, "we mock barbarians and savages for their customs, without reflecting that we have habits which are quite as absurd and inane. We should think it barbarous in other nations if they went forth to murder for a foolish word, just as we do in France. What folly that we have to kiss all the women that we meet, and that they kiss everyone indifferently! . . . Nor are our clothes and ornaments less ridiculous; the square caps of the lawyers, the slashes, the dress-pads, the wigs, and numberless other imbecilities."

All this meant affectation, a demoralizing atmosphere for art. It also meant a growing and elaborate society. The arts that really flourished then were social. The only school of painting worth considering at this late epoch was the school of portrait-painters—of François Clouet and Corneille de Lyon (or de la Haye), of Dumoustier and Scipion, and of all their atelier imitators, men and women, who made duplicates of their productions. But the masterpieces of Clouet, in his day, were not only considered as works of art, they were looked on in great measure as a social necessity, at a time when personal communication was difficult and cheap reproductions were undreamed of. Many of the royal portraits, too, were essential for political purposes—for marriages, for compliment, for diplomacy—and were judged by their practical importance. As far as sculpture was concerned, the case was much the same. So long as the artist devoted himself to busts or to statues for tombs, the result was admirable and life-like. Germain Pilon's bust of Henri II, his "*gisant*" (or dead figure) of the same monarch, his monument of Birague; Barthélmy Prieur's bust of De Thou, his sepulchral statues of the Chabots, are vital pieces of work. But as soon as imagination comes into play, it is a different matter. Germain Pilon was the most esteemed sculptor of his day, but he is little more than a sculptor-laureate, graceful, heartless, complimentary. His three Graces upholding the urn destined to contain the King's heart is a delicious piece of courtly distinction, an elegantly turned Latin distich translated into stone. The Graces are conscious Court beauties with the germ of decadence in their very charm. The Queen's *Coiffeur* has arranged the carelessness of their hair, a State *Costumière* their classical folds, and we sympathize with the good old eighteenth-century Prior of Bessé who threw down into a well a copy of this work, then in the possession of his Priory, because he found existence disturbed by the presence of these mundane charmers. It was not for nothing that Pilon had worked at Anet and felt the sway of Primaticcio; that he had toiled at Paris in "the Chapel of the Jewellers" at "piercing open-work friezes of chestnut wood, to be formed out of coronals, cups and lilies, enlaced with palms and other enrichments." He was, indeed, a master of ornamentation, whether he were working upon "the Great Clock of Paris," for which in the true Renaissance spirit he carved "a Holy Ghost crowned with laurels;" or helping Ronsard to arrange a pageant for Charles IX's coronation. And when that monarch made him Coiner to the Crown, he provided Pilon with the delicate work that exactly suited his fancy. For his art was not a great art, an art with an outlook. It was rather the end of a tradition that had lost its sap and its strength. Here, when you ask for imagination you get conceits, and if you brush aside the fantastic furbelows, you find there is no human form beneath. It is, we must repeat, by their skill in portraiture that men like Germain Pilon live.

We have already glanced at Architecture and seen how

its growth corresponded to social development. And the other arts which prospered were the minor ones, attendant on the greater—the arts of ornamentation which should be classed as crafts. The two great ornamentors of Catherine's time are Léonard Limousin and Bernard Palissy. Limousin was a generic name for Léonard and Martin, who first bore it, and then for their collaborators, the family of Pénicaud and that of the Courts (who included a craftswoman, Suzanne) and for other artificers of Limoges, who produced their wonderful irridescent plates and vessels, blazoned with accurate portraits, or with subjects from the fashionable Court mythology. These men guarded the secret of their enamel as jealously as the Della Robbias guarded theirs, and expended all their energy in improving it. Their lives lay in their achievements; they are written in the Galerie d'Apollon in the Louvre, in countless other collections of their ware, evoking, as we stand and look at it, an atmosphere of wealth and ceremony, a vision of Catherine amid her Squadron of fictitious Junos and Minervas. It affects us precisely as Brantôme does, by a kind of remote curiosity, in turn amused and repelled—by anything, in short, but our sympathies. It seems to us splendid yet joyless, an art without blood in it—the fitting emblem of a pleasure-loving but indifferent generation.

Bernard Palissy is a different matter. He was a great thinker, a strenuous seeker, who tried to compel Nature's secrets from her and translated them into terms of art. He imitated her forms—her insects, her fish, her reptiles, her stones—as closely as naturalist or geologist could wish for the purposes of study. He collected fossils and investigated chemical laws; he evolved a new system of agriculture; he made his own persistent researches about the properties of earth and water; he was, as it were, consumed by a passion for Nature—as patient as that of Darwin, as vehement as a soldier in battle. Bent upon discovering processes, he thought he was working for art when he was really toiling for science. The results of his labour—his pottery and fish and plants and reptiles in enamel, are indeed rather curious than pleasing, their very character depending upon a kind of accurate realism; and they prove him to be not an artist but—what he really was—a man of science.

And this brings us to the truth, it gives us the key of his generation. It was not artistic, but scientific. Its atmosphere is dry and scintillating; it was critical and not creative, full of active curiosity, devoid of enthusiasm. In so far it was like our own age, that there was much appreciation of great Art without the power of producing it. The Renaissance had reacted upon itself; it had sent men back to Nature, and they brought a fresh eye for her significance; it gave them a thirst for positive knowledge of every kind. Catherine herself, we must repeat, was an *esprit positif*, a clever mathematician, essentially the woman of science, impartial yet full of curiosity, with a mind that stuck at no consequences. She was, it is true, superstitious, and cherished a firm belief in the black arts. As for her faith in astrologers, that was part of her faith in science, of which astrology was then an acknowledged branch. But she did not stop here. She consulted sorcerers and alchemists, and acted on their prognostications. It was to the house of one of these men that she repaired when she was anxious about the Dauphin François' health, and here that she breathlessly watched a doll, dressed like the prince, walk once round a table and then fall—by which sign she knew that her son had but twelve months to live. Nor was she making any pretence when, at the advent of his last illness, she accused the Guises of causing the calamity by magic. But such superstitions were of her generation, perhaps of her Italian blood, and they did not really affect her strong scientific tendencies.

Wherever we turn, we are confronted by the same facts. Art was still the natural language by which men expressed thought and knowledge, because science was as yet only half-born; but if we look into their lives, it was the scientific spirit that governed them and made their art unsatisfactory. Limousin and his fellow-craftsmen were all concentrated upon processes, upon making fresh discoveries. And Philibert de l'Orme, as his biographer, Mr. Blomfield, points out, was, if we go beneath the surface, a greater engineer than artist. "His strength, in fact" (says this writer) "lay in mechanical invention;" there was "too much reliance on knowledge rather than imagination." And he instances De l'Orme's introduction of the built-up framing of roofs, or of the "French order" of pillars, the joints of whose shafts were covered with bands of ornamentation, an ingenious and unbeautiful conception, worthier of a mechanician than an artist. One of his greatest triumphs was as Superintendent of the Royal Fortifications, when he saved the besieged port of Brest by placing imitation wooden cannons and numbers of men without pikes well in sight of the foe. And his book "l'Architecture" is illumined by his love of nature and minute observation of her ways, by his remarks upon the architecture of shells, his reverence before all her works. He and Palissy may be taken as typical men of their time, though Palissy, both in thought and character, was a stronger type than De l'Orme. And it is a striking fact that both of them were of the Huguenots. This is no accidental coincidence. If Protestantism made against art and all the temptations of beauty, it was not so with science. Scientific thought was really the logical outcome of a religion that went to the roots of things, that referred to original sources and tried to abolish superstition. In later days, science and religion parted company, but in those early times, before they had discovered they were hostile, the Huguenot atmosphere was favourable to the acquisition of truth and the assertion of any form of human responsibility.

We have chronicled elsewhere the chief events in the life of Philibert de l'Orme,[1] which, indeed, consisted mainly of the various changes in his work. He was the son of fairly well-to-do tradespeople at Lyons. As a boy he went to Rome, and at fifteen years old he had two hundred men working under him. His good fortune began one day when he was making some excavations and a certain Bishop, passing by, stopped to watch and became interested in him. Paul III gave him a commission in Calabria, but in 1536, the Du Bellays persuaded him to return to France. He worked in Lyons, he was made Superintendent of Architecture in Brittany, and then, in 1545, Superintendent of the Royal Fortifications. In this office he was bitterly disliked, because he constantly exposed and tried to reform the abuses that had hitherto been practised. Perhaps an overbearing personality had also something to do with it, for wherever he went he had quarrels and created an atmosphere of agitation. He constructed the fine tomb of the Valois (now destroyed), but his time for this kind of task grew scarce. Henri II made him his architect, which meant the superintendence of the works at Fontainebleau, St. Germain, and of all the royal buildings, as well as the "Tapisseries" at Fontainebleau. He led a life of constant riding across country, and with some dozen horses in his stables, this must have been pleasant enough. But he had

[1] "Women and Men of the French Renaissance."

CATHERINE AND THE ARTS

to board all the building-tradesmen employed by the King, a race on whom he lavished contempt; and constant quarrels with officials, besides rivalries with Primaticcio, or Serlio of the "Tapisseries," again chequered his career. In 1548, Diane employed him at Anet, where he designed the stately gardens at the back of the house, the two pavilions, the orangery, the heronry, the terrace overlooking the greensward and—his greatest triumph of all—the crescent-shaped stairway between the two. At Chenonceau, too, he worked for her, making the famous bridge and gallery; and also at Écouen, for the Constable, whose palace-portals were guarded by the two mighty slaves of Michael Angelo. With Henri II's death, De l'Orme's luck turned. That event took place on July 10. On the 12th, a royal decree appointed Primaticcio as De l'Orme's successor—a first attempt of the Guises to assert their supremacy at Court. Now that his patron, the King, was no longer there to support Philibert, the general dislike of him broke out, and a good deal of clamour ensued. But not for long. Catherine adopted him as her own, and in the decade between 1560 and 1570, he built her palace of the Tuileries—connected, as she wished, by a long gallery with the unfinished, growing mass of the Louvre, the incomplete work of Pierre Lescot. De l'Orme did not bring peace with him. There were the usual quarrels—with architects, with workmen, with artists, with courtiers, with Bernard Palissy and with Ronsard. This last was a more serious dispute, for Ronsard brought charges of corruption and wrote a poem "La Truelle crossée," to repeat his accusations. De l'Orme had certainly received fat rewards for his services: he was Abbé of Noyon and of Ivry, Chanoine of Notre Dame, King's Almoner, and Privy Councillor. But his position at Ivry was probably his payment from Diane, and as for the rest of his gains, he replied that he took them as compensation for the vast sums, never repaid, which he had spent in the course of his work. The Tuileries, still unfinished at his death, was his last important task, and we know little more of him, except that he escaped on St. Bartholomew's Eve, forewarned, as legend tells us, by Catherine.

But the finer and the deeper character, the more interesting type of his day, is, as we have said, Bernard Palissy, of whose life some short sketch is necessary in any record of his times.

CHAPTER XV
Bernard Palissy

AUTHORITIES CONSULTED

Récepte Véritable—*Bernard Palissy.*
Discours Admirables—*Bernard Palissy.*
Journal de Pierre l'Estoilles.
Histoire Universelle.—*Agrippine d'Aubigné.*
Biographical Introduction to Œuvres de Palissy—*Anatole France.*
The French Renaissance—*Mrs. Pattison.*
Histoire de France—*Martin.*
Manuel de l'histoire de la littèrature française—*Brunetière.*

CHAPTER XV

Bernard Palissy

" I DESIRE in no way to be the imitator of my predecessors, unless it be in what they have done well, according to the ordinance of God. For all round me I see abuses of the arts, while every man trots in the accustomed groove and follows the footmarks of those who went before him."

In these words of his own we have the keynote to Bernard Palissy. His wish to be " in no wise the imitator of his predecessors " expresses the whole man—the austere Protestant, the ardent follower of science, the fearless innovator in every branch of knowledge that he touched. There was not a vestige of tradition about him, no one was freer from swaddling-bands. "I entered into myself," he writes in another place, " so that I might search among the secrets of my heart and dive into my conscience." This power of introspection was part of his rough sincerity, his inability to acquiesce in any sort of platitude. A trenchant originality is felt in each word that he utters.

" All men "—says he in his writings—" toil at cultivating the land without the remotest philosophy . . . without considering the nature of substances for the real good of agriculture." "To hear you speak," replies his imaginary interlocutor, " one would think that a field-labourer needed philosophy—*chose que je trouve étrange*."

" I tell you "—breaks forth Palissy again—" that to pursue agriculture without philosophy is no better than a daily robbing of the earth. . . . And I marvel that the earth and her fruits do not cry vengeance against certain murderers, ignorant and ungrateful, who day by day do nothing but waste and spoil trees and plants." Fervent, patient, irritable, many-sided, forcible, strong of body, stronger of will, his intellect dominating all things, Bernard Palissy was essentially the thinker of the Renaissance. But—it must be repeated—

he was not an artist, although, strangely enough, it is an artist that the world has considered him. The artistic sense, indeed, seemed the only sense that he lacked. The pottery upon which his fame rests is a feat of invention, not of art; it depended on the discovery of a particular white paste which would take colour better than any substance hitherto known; and the heavily painted vases which we have all tried respectfully to admire were the results of his painful researches. But they were not the greatest of his achievements. In perfecting his material, in finding out the right clay to pulverise, the right furnace for heating and cleansing, the requisite chemicals, the laws of cooling and of hardening—all the means that had to be flawless before he attained his end—he discovered a great many things that were more significant than enamel. The secrets of earth and water lay hidden by the way—the properties of salt, the right treatment of trees, the economics of Nature, in short, what he would call " *les natures des choses.*" He possessed two invaluable powers: the desire for usefulness and the self-confidence of the Reformer. Nothing was too big or too small for him, and he was equally keen, whether he was regenerating the system of fortification in France, or constructing a model dunghill. He planned out a scheme which would revolutionize current methods of agriculture and greatly enrich his country, and he may almost be said to have initiated the modern science of geology. We catch a touching glimpse of him, in his own record, in a certain monastery at Tours, the Abbot of which was a mineralogist, bending keen and absorbed over the old man's cabinet of specimens—a rare possession in those days. And to hear him speak of fossils is to hear a poet speaking of poetry; he cannot mention them without something like a thrill of emotion.

It appears strange, at first sight, that a man so richly dowered with scientific genius should have devoted his energies to what seems a mere matter of detail. But his discoveries could not be tested without enormous expenditure; they were in advance of his age and could appeal to few of his generation. He published them in his books, but that was nearly all that he could do, whereas the achievement on which he set his heart was well within his compass. He could bring it to completion with his own hands; it would be welcomed at once by his contemporaries. Considerations such as these restricted his energies, while his intellect ranged unfettered over creation.

Palissy was a man of thought, but by no means a man of

cultivation. His tendencies were profoundly democratic, and he came of artizan stock devoid of æsthetic or scholarly traditions. That he was unlettered turned to his advantage. Not only did it lend his style a racy vernacular, a strong, almost rude simplicity, and a lucidity far removed from the lingo of the schools, but it added a fresh intensity to his life. And the noblest weapon in his armoury was his faith. For undaunted reasoner and apostle of science though he was, he was penetrated by the sense of the immanence of God. In his awe of the Universe, in his manifold discoveries, and in his scorn of ignorant stupidity, he often reminds us of Goethe; while his dignified persistence in his path of experiment in the face of every failure for eighteen years of poverty and distress, and the large and humble religion that sustained him, constantly recall a great Frenchman of recent years—Louis Pasteur. But Bernard lacked the poetic genius of Goethe and the modern specialist's concentration of Pasteur, and he did not leave to the world such important results as either of his successors. Perhaps he arrived too soon for the scientific genius that possessed him.

He was born near Saintes, in Saintonge, between 1500 and 1510, of a family of rural artizans. The craft he chose was that of a glass-painter, or *verrier* (to be distinguished from that of the *vitrier*, or glazier) and his work consisted in painting figures on separate pieces of glass. His apprenticeship once over, he went on a journey all round France, observing men and things and especially such as affected his own work. His keen professional eye noticed that the glass of the church windows which he saw was here and there worn away. "The moonlight does it," said the peasants. "The rain does it," said Palissy. When he returned to Saintes he established his own glass business—but it did not pay, and as he had meanwhile married, he turned to a more lucrative occupation. As a land-surveyor and maker of land-maps, or "*pourtraicts*," he managed to earn the necessities of life for his quickly increasing family. The tide, however, was to turn. Fame was to blow her fateful trumpet in his ear and comfort to take wing and fly away. Ronsard was sixteen when he met Virgil, and when Palissy met his fate he must have been nearly thirty. His fate was an earthenware cup of which he caught sight one day, delicately painted, enamelled in white, coming as some say from Castel Durante, though later critics think that it was French. This goblet took possession of Palissy's brain, not on account of any beauty that it boasted, but because he saw that the whitish paste of which it was made was an excellent ground for colours, and it struck him that if he could succeed in fabricating pure white enamel, he might obtain wonderful effects and reproduce the hues of all things living. He set his brain to work and " from that time forward applied himself to pounding everything that could be pounded, in the firm persuasion that if he put the whole of Nature in his mortar, he would one day behold all that he desired—white enamel." He tried every kind of powder, he changed his furnace, but for some time nothing came of it. Workmen he could not afford to employ—every penny went on his materials; he was his own mason, he tempered his own mortar, and carried the materials for his work, unaided, upon his back. When the toil of baking the pots in the fire was over, there came a terrible four weeks' labour, night and day, of grinding the paste. After three years and the expenditure of all his fortune, the mortar of his stove cracked and everything was spoiled. Ruin stared him in the face. By this time, he " always had," as he reports, " one or two children out at nurse, for whom he could never pay "; he could not afford to wait and was obliged to resume his land surveying. The advent of the King's Commissioners, who came to levy the salt tax at Saintes, gave him his chance, for they employed him on a map of the salt-marshes which put a round sum in his pocket. No sooner had he got it than the hope which had never deserted him reasserted itself, and back he went to his kiln. Then began a long drama of the will—a victory for his spirit, but a tragedy for his wife and little children. The difficulties he surmounted, the hardships he underwent for some sixteen years more, are almost past belief. The glassy powders gave him trouble—he became a master-glazier. His furnaces went wrong—he turned a professional furnace-maker. If the furnace went out, the work of all those years would be spoiled, so he sat up through the nights, wet or fine, and for a month " his clothes dried upon him." Sometimes he went to bed—" at midnight," as he tells us, " or at break of day, accoutred like to one who had been dragged through all the mire of the town; and as I thus withdrew, I walked stumbling, without a candle, and reeling from side to side like a man drunk with wine—for I was filled with great sorrows, the more so since I knew that all my long labour was wasted." " *J'étais,*" he writes elsewhere, " *dans une telle angoisse que je ne saurais dire.*" At last he engaged a potter to make his vases, but after six months he had no money for him and was compelled to send him away, giving him his own clothes as salary. Again he did all himself, hurting his unresting hands in the process. "My fingers" —he says—"were cut in so many places that I was forced to eat my soup with my hands bound up in rags." He had no more fuel for his fire; starvation pinched him, his wife and children were crying for bread—for all answer he broke up the tables and chairs and piled them on his Moloch-like oven. There is no creature so cruel as a man with a fixed idea, for he sees nothing else—common humanity deserts him and he is nothing but an unrelenting Will. Perhaps, at the best of times, Palissy was not a creature of human affections. It is strange that in his pages there is no allusion to wife or child except as factors in his suffering—no mention of an intimate friendship—no warmth but for knowledge and ideas. He went on his way, indifferent to everything but the fulfilment of his aim. His relations cursed him, his poor wife tormented him when he retired to rest. "There was nothing in the house but reproaches," he comments with pathetic bitterness. He was mocked at in the town for a madman. "Serve him right if he dies of hunger," said the citizens, "since he has deserted his profession." A report ran that he was trying to find out how to make false coins, and dishonour was added to his sufferings. "I walked with bowed head through the streets," he writes, "like one who is ashamed . . . Then I asked my soul, 'what is it that casteth thee down, seeing that thou art finding what thou seekest' . . . And when I had stayed some time in bed and had considered within myself that if a man fell into a ditch, his duty would be to try to get up again, I set myself to make some paintings and by divers other means I tried hard to earn a little money. And the desire that I had to reach my goal made me do things which I should have thought were impossible."

When success seemed near at hand, he found that his open furnace spoiled all and with difficulty he made a covered one. Another time when the actual compound seemed to be before him, some flaw in the kiln let in a shower of ashes and the delicate substance was ruined. Yet his spirit remained unbroken. "Many a time," he said, "when people came to see me, I made an effort to laugh so that they might be amused, but my heart was very heavy." It is a relief to hear of good moments, however brief. Once when he had formed some white material which seemed to approach the right kind, he "felt as if he had been born again," but the usual disappointment ensued. Then he tried a new experiment—the use of a grinding-mill which he turned alone with both his arms, though, in the ordinary course, two men could only move it with difficulty. Again he produced a substance which only just failed, but he refused an offer for a vase that he had made out of it and proudly broke it into bits : "*le soif de la perfection oblige*," might have been his motto.

At last, somewhere about 1550, the great day came and the last secret of the long-sought process was found. Fruition came to a family almost too crushed to receive it. He himself was nearly wasted away. His muscles, he tells us, had shrunk, and the garters with which he tied up his stockings fell down with them to his heels. Prosperity was at hand in pleasant places, but before we follow him there, we must first go back in his history.

Palissy was born for Protestantism—of the Covenanting sort. In 1546, some French monks who, under the sway of German Reformers had attacked the abuses they saw in their midst, were forced to fly from their monasteries. Some of them came to the district of Saintes and by degrees made themselves known to the people. Luckily for them, the Grand Vicar there had heretical tendencies and allowed them his pulpit to preach from. One of them, the saintly Philibert Hamelin, became a close friend of Palissy, to whom, born Puritan that he was, the new faith was a revelation. Hamelin, whose teaching he sought eagerly, took a garret in the town and there held Bible readings to an ever-increasing congregation, which became the nucleus of the Reformed Church of Saintes, the Church of which "Maître Bernard" was thenceforward a zealous member. In the midst of these proceedings came suddenly to Saintonge a demand for the payment of the salt-tax, or *gabelle*. The country all round revolted. The peasants took Saintes, broke open the prisons, hanged the tax-collectors, and burned the registers of the *gabelle*. Strange to say, this riot was the beginning of Palissy's fortune, for the Connétable de Montmorency was sent to settle matters with the rebels. The town of Saintes itself got off easily, through a good governor who knew how to tackle the fierce Constable. To that grandee Maître Bernard was now introduced as an able craftsman, by some of the local noblemen. Montmorency, who was always keen to surpass King and Court in magnificence, welcomed any new artist and was very gracious to Palissy. From that moment, he became his patron. He had a studio built for him upon the city ramparts and gave him work to do at Écouen—glass-painting and enamelling—which must have helped to keep him alive during his long struggle. When the famous secret was found and at the Constable's service, he became that Prince's "*Inventeur des rustiques figulins*"—a fantastic-sounding office, suggesting some fairy-laureateship and not ill-suited to the many-hued grotesques that emanated from the wizard's workshop. A great grotto at Écouen, in accordance with the fashion fresh from Italy, established his "eternal" fame. It was formed like an immense sea-cave with inner rooms and terraces and doorways and rocky pillars, and he filled its clefts with creatures in enamel, undistinguishable from real ones—cray-fish and tortoises and shells and strange ferns, all of the most brilliant colours. It sounds more like a naturalist's cabinet than any place of beauty; but it delighted the connoisseurs of the day and suited their desire for what was curious. In later times, he and Catherine de' Medici delighted in placing these earthenware animals of his—toads, snakes, reptiles of all sorts—among the plants and flower-beds of the Tuileries, not to speak of life-sized men, curiously attired; and both alike prided themselves on making a permanent contribution to the beauty of the world.

Palissy made a fundamental mistake in his whole conception of art. He confused æsthetics with Nature and mistook ingenuity for beauty. "The works"—he says—" of our sovereign God, the First Builder, must be worthier of honour than the work of human builders. Thou knowest that a portrait copied from another portrait . . . can never be as valuable as the original from which it is taken; wherefore columns of stone can never be as glorious as the columns that stand in the forest."

Unfortunately he applied the same standard to all that he accomplished. His ideal garden was to be laid out according to the 104th Psalm, because he had had a vision of "certain virgins" sitting in the shade and singing this Psalm, with voices "*douces et accordantes*"—which music led him to resolve that he would paint a picture of the "beautiful landscapes sung by the Prophet in this canticle." But then he reflected that pictures soon perish and that a garden designed after the Psalmist's words would last longer, though as the Psalm describes nothing smaller than the wonders of the Universe, it is hard to understand where the "garden" comes in. Harder still is it, perhaps, to trace the source of inspiration in the model that he designed. It was to contain "an amphitheatre of refuge" for exiled Christians, besides eight enamel "cabinets" (a species of Renaissance bungalow) full of his zoological master-pieces and scientifically constructed fountains; it had a model system of irrigation suggested by experiments with salic substances; but there is never a mention of a green alley or a flower, and we cannot imagine anyone, unless it were an engineer, being happy in it. Fortunately his plans were impossible of execution. "I know," said he, "that there are some foes to virtue and some slanderers who say that the design of this garden is a mere dream, and can only be compared to the vision of Polyphilius."

"Le songe de Polyphile" was a fashionable allegorical romance translated from the Italian, the hero of which dreams rather tediously of ornate grottoes, and it was almost the only book beside the Bible that Palissy ever read. His knowledge did not come from books but from his own observation. One can fancy him in his evening walks among the fields, or along the banks of the river Charente, to-day half starved and miserable, to-morrow alert and hopeful, but through all fortunes, faithfully, closely observant. "And straightway I began to bend my head downwards, as I walked along the road, so as to see nothing which would keep me from my inward imaginings as to what was the cause of the phenomenon, and being in this travail of mind, I then thought out the thing that I still believe, in the full conviction that it is true." Thus he wrote when he was investigating the nature of fossils, but the words apply to his method at any moment of his life. His model system of fortification was based upon his constant study of the lairs of wild animals; his model system of agriculture upon his noticing the slovenly construction of the country-side dunghills and also by his finding out the conserving properties of salt. When he went for a leisurely stroll, his eye took in each detail of the surrounding landscape. He knew which plant was diseased, which tree was wrongly lopped, which field could be made more fertile, and his brain did not rest till it had discovered the remedy.

In his most random remarks there is ever the same spirit. "I went for a walk in the direction of the east wind," thus he writes in one of those rare moments of enjoyment which flash like winter sunshine across his sombre pages, "and while I strolled beneath the fruit-trees, I felt a great contentment and many joyous sensations, for I saw the squirrels picking the fruit and leaping from bough to bough, with divers charming attitudes and gestures. In another place I watched the crows gathering nuts and enjoying the dinner they made of them. Elsewhere again, beneath the apple-trees, I found certain hedgehogs, who had rolled themselves up in a round ball and, having stuck their prickles into the apples, were moving off, thus heavily loaded. . . . I noted also a piece of cunning which a fox carried through in my presence—the finest and the subtlest of which ever I heard tell : for finding himself without any victuals, and considering that dinner-time was near and that he had nothing ready, he went to lie down in a field close by, adjoining the spur of a wood, and once prone on the ground, he stiffened his legs and shut his eyes and looked as if he had been thrown down, thus counterfeiting death . . . . Whence it happened that a crow, who also had nothing for dinner, being convinced that the fox was dead, came and perched upon his body. . . . But she was nicely trapped, for at the first peck of her beak, the fox with sudden quickness seized hold of the crow, who could not think of anything to do except to emit caws. And this is how the clever fox took his dinner at the expense of her who wished to eat him."

We almost expect La Fontaine to rise as we read, and to point a spicy moral to the tale.

Sometimes he reaches a higher plane and draws his own moral from the Universe. " I know full well "—he says—" that God created all things in six days and rested the seventh day ; nevertheless, God did not create these things so as leave them idle—and each of them performs its duty according to God's commands. The stars and the planets are not idle ; the sea rolls from one side to another and travails to produce things profitable ; the earth is apparently unresting ; that which is naturally consumed inside her she renews and re-forms on the instant, and if it is not of one kind, she makes it of another. And this is why you must put your dunghills in the ground, so that the earth may take back the substance that she gave."

The Puritan and Scriptural tone pervades his writings. " Above all else," he says, " prithee remember a passage in Holy Writ, there where St. Paul says that according as each man has received gifts from God, he must distribute them to others. Therefore I beg thee to teach the labourers, since they are not lettered, that they may carefully study natural philosophy in pursuance of my counsels." Such is the note of his discourses, and such the motive of his labour, whatever form it took.

Meanwhile, his religious experiences had been by no means calm ones. The Protestant minister, Hamelin, on a visit to the Church which he had established at Saintes, was arrested for heresy and imprisoned. Bernard dared to protest in the presence of the town authorities, but he could not prevent the removal of Hamelin to Bordeaux, where he speedily suffered death. Saintes was now left in peace for two years, until the massacre of Vassy kindled revolt in all the provinces. Luckily the Duc de la Rochefoucauld, whom Condé had sent to Saintonge, took charge of Palissy's welfare and gave him a safe-conduct to Bordeaux, where he set up a workshop. Patronage notwithstanding, he was seized one night and taken to prison; but the omnipotent Constable once more intervened, interceded with Catherine on his behalf, and, with the help of his title of "*Inventeur des rustiques figulins du Roi et Monseigneur le Duc de Montmorency,*" was enabled to set him at liberty. Palissy proceeded to La Rochelle, the stronghold of the Protestants, where he published his "Récepte Veritable par laquelle tous les hommes de la France pourront apprendre à multiplier et augmenter leurs trésors." Nearly twenty years later, there came out his other work—"Discours admirables de la nature des eaux et fontaines, tant naturelles qu'artificielles, des métaux, des sels et salines, des pierres, des terres, du feu et des émaux, avec plusieurs autres excellents secrets des choses naturelles—plus un Traité de la Marine fort utile et nécessaire à ceux qui se mèlent de l'agriculture "—a volume the very title of which is almost as comprehensive as an Encyclopedia. The colloquial dialogues it contains, between Theory, the advocate of current opinions, and Practice, who always refutes them, are, like all his writing, a boldly-woven tissue of surprising intuition and quaint hypotheses.

Soon after the appearance of his first book, he courageously returned to work at Saintes. In 1564, luck came his way. Catherine and Charles IX stayed in the town for a few days, and Bernard, the foremost craftsman of his city, found himself under the eyes of the Queen-Mother. He presented her with his enamels, he drew out a plan for a grotto, and two years later his labours bore fruit, for she summoned him to Paris to work at her new palace of the Tuileries. In its buildings "Maître Bernard des Tuileries," as he soon became, had his workshop; and there,

BERNARD PALISSY

in its grounds, not long ago, were discovered a potter's kiln and some pieces of enamel. At last he lived and toiled in comfort, undisturbed in the exercise either of his craft or of his creed, and if he was not rich, he was happy. One cannot but wish that there were some record of his wife and her enjoyment of this belated prosperity, after her long ordeal. If she survived it, who can say? For the chronicle of her husband's life in Paris makes no mention of kith or kin, unless it be of two young men, Nicholas and Mathurin Palissy, who worked in his studio; but whether they were his sons, or only pupils who had adopted his name, still remains a doubtful question. The Court showed its influence upon him; he gave up his crayfish and lizards, and took to enamelling Nymphs and Naïads; he studied antique gems and was swayed by Primaticcio and Cellini; he saw designs from Florence and it is more than probable that he came into contact with Girolamo della Robbia, who was constantly employed in Paris.

St. Bartholomew's Eve found him away in the Ardennes, where the Duc de Bouillon favoured the Protestants; he had probably fled, forewarned of danger and horrified at the national calamity. It left him broken and dispirited, but, with the Peace, he returned to Paris and went on with his work in his studio there, visited by Catherine and patronised by princes and by scholars. As time went on, he resolved to present the fruit of his researches to the world, and the year 1575 inaugurated a new epoch in his life—he gave his three famous lectures.

They were advertised at every crossing in Paris, and in order, as Palissy says, "to scare away the ignorant and the frivolous," a crown was charged for admission, though, with his customary daring, Maître Bernard offered four crowns to any person who could refute him. The benches were packed with men of fashion, of science, of the arts. The Huguenot, Ambrose Paré, the great surgeon of Henri II; Choisnin, Jeanne d'Albret's physician; Barthélmy Prieur, the sculptor, were among the celebrities in the audience. "Thanks be to my God," wrote Bernard, "never a man contradicted me with a single word." The lecturer's vogue was immense and the lectures were constantly repeated until 1584, four years after their publication in the volume of "Discours Admirables." Their success was well deserved. "We are dumbfoundered by all that this potter discovered in physics, in chemistry, in geology—that is to say, in sciences, then, even in name, non-existent. He knew that heat causes water to increase in volume and he divined the principle of dilatation; he saw that springs were due to the infiltration of rain; he observed that water tends constantly to re-ascend to the level of its source and deduced from this law a rational method for the piercing of Artesian wells; he had some conception of the weight of air; he affirmed that metals were changeless—which is true if taken in his sense, to wit that one metal cannot be transmuted into another; about the formation of ice in rivers, he emitted a theory which can still be maintained; of the rainbow, he gave such a happy explanation that it actually foreshadows our modern theory of the decomposition of light; he made experiments on saltpetre which make the basis of our knowledge of crystals; he had a confused but persistent notion of attraction; he indicated the action of metallic oxygen in the colouring of stones; he explained the varying solidity of chalky formations; he founded geology upon observations of unalterable certainty, studied the action of the sea upon the coast and understood the real origin of petrified shells. "They were"—he says—" engendered on the spot where they lay, while the rocks were still no more than water and mud, the which became petrified with the aforesaid fish." [1]

"Bernard," (says Anatole France) "never read the manuscript of Leonardo da Vinci, and yet Leonardo had said that 'the shells which one finds piled up in different strata have, by necessity of Nature, lived in the same place that the sea once occupied. ... That which has been the bottom of the sea has become the summit of the mountains.'" These statements are doubly interesting when we compare them with the already quoted passages from Ronsard in which the same idea is expressed. Very likely he had it from Palissy—possibly from one of these lectures—for when the rank and fashion of Paris were present, it is improbable that Ronsard would be absent.

Maître Bernard did not confine himself to Nature. He took the audience into his confidence and spoke about his craft as a potter, his arduous experiences, his bitter disappointments. He told them everything except his final secret, and his reserve upon this point he was not slow to explain. "My art and its secrets are not like others," he said, "I know full well that a remedy for the Plague or any other deadly illness ought not to be withheld. The secrets of agriculture ought not to be

[1] Anatole France. Preface to Œuvres de Bernard Palissy.

withheld. The knowledge of the risks and perils of navigation ought not to be withheld. The Word of God ought not to be withheld. The sciences which serve the common weal ought not to be withheld. But with my art of earthenware, and with other arts also, this is not the case. There are many goodly inventions the which are despised because they have been made common to men, and many things are exalted in the houses of princes and noblemen which, if they were in common use, would be no more esteemed than old saucepans. . . . The blunders that I made in my final process taught me more than the things which went well; wherefore I am of opinion that you should work to find the secret as hard as I did—else your knowledge will be too cheaply bought and that may cause you to despise it."

Palissy was never tired of teaching, and begged all who were in search of knowledge to come and see him in his lodgings at any hour of the day or night. Unlike other men of learning, he received them in a room devoid of books; for beyond a second-hand acquaintance with Paracelsus, a mention of Cardan's volume on him, and an allusion to the " Roman de la Rose," his literary repertory still seemed restricted to the "Songe de Polyphile." " I am not "—he says—" a Greek, or a Jew, or a poet, or a rhetorician, but a simple artizan, very poorly versed in letters; notwithstanding the which reasons, the work that I achieve has not less virtue than if it proceeded from a more eloquent man. I would rather tell the truth in my plain peasant's language than a falsehood in that of an orator." The peasant was always strong in him and his choice of invective was a rich one. We wonder if he apostrophized his audience with as little ceremony as he used towards " Réponse," in his " Récepte Véritable." " *Je t'assure que je ne connus onques une si grande bête que toi*," or " *Je ne vis onques homme de si dure cervelle que toi*," or " *Tu es aussi grann bête aujourdhui comme hier*," and the like modes of address, give much spontaneity to his style, but would hardly have ingratiated an audience. He was, to say the least, anti-classical. " Nothing ever seems good to you that does not come from the Latins," he exclaims with irritation. But the best arguments that he uses are his own robust words which, in his finer moments, can rise to a level of solid grandeur. " The coming of the sea "—he writes—" seemeth like unto a great army which advanceth against the land to combat her. And its vanguard, like the vanguard in battle, hurls itself so impetuously against the rocks and boundaries of the land, making so furious a din, that it seemeth as if all must be destroyed." He delights, too, in the wind and in the rain—" the which being gathered in the air and formed into big clouds, rush forth from one side and the other, like unto the heralds sent by God."

The lectures are full of passages such as these, and Palissy's rugged conviction must have given them an added eloquence. His success did not abate, and this happy state of things lasted till he was near eighty and Henri III was on the throne. The Ligue, that Cabal of Sixteen, ruled all things; a wave of reactionary fanaticism swept over the country; there began a fresh persecution of the Protestants, and Palissy did not escape it.

The curtain rose on the last tragic Act of his life. He was seized and put in the Bastille. Public execution would have been his speedy fate, had it not been for the interference of the Duc de Mayenne, the son of François, Duc de Guise. There is a story told by the Huguenot historian, D'Aubigné, of a visit paid him in prison by the King, who entreated him to abjure the new fath. "Otherwise," said he, "I shall be forced to leave you in the hands of your enemies." "*Sire*," answered Bernard, "I was willing to give my life for the glory of God, and if I had felt any regret, it would have been extinguished when I heard my great Sovereign speak the words, 'I am forced,' for neither you nor those who force you can force me, since I know how to die." His age protected him from the gallows, but he was left to a worse fate—a slow death in his prison. Within two years came the end. "In this same year" (1590), writes a diarist, "there died in the dungeons of the Bastille, Maître Bernard Palissy, a prisoner on account of his religion, aged eighty years, and he died of misery and want and ill-treatment. . . . The aunt of this good man having gone to enquire how he was, found that he had died, and Bussi (the gaoler) told her that if she wished to see him, she would find him with the dogs upon the ramparts, where he had caused him to be thrown like the dog that he was."

So perished one who defined his aim in life as an attempt " to incite all men upon the earth to become lovers of goodness and just labour," and so passes the wise man from the world. But his wisdom does not share his mortality.

" Ce *bonhomme* "—notes the same diarist—" left me, when he was dying, a stone which he always called his philosopher's stone. He said it was the head of a dead man, which time had turned to stone. Also another, which had served to help him in his work: the which two stones are in my cabinet, and I love and treasure them greatly, in memory of the old man whom I loved and relieved in his need, not as I desired, but as I could."

Well might Bernard pronounce that grim head to be the philosopher's stone. For to him it represented Knowledge, and Knowledge had brought content to his spirit—had solved for him the riddle of existence. "*Or*," he says, "*Dieu est sapience : l'on ne peut donc aimer sapience sans aimer Dieu.*"

* * * * *

Bernard Palissy represented, as it were, the hope of the future—he stood forth as the symbol of modern science and forged the first link of an infinite chain. With the moral degeneration of the time his stern religious nature had no concern, while his very powers were a hindrance to his sense of beauty. His generation, we must repeat, was scientific, not artistic. And science demands the critical mind; for enthusiasm, though it may make men of science the happier, forms no necessary part of their baggage. Art, on the other hand, requires hope—there cannot be a great art without joy, and a joy not restricted to the few. But any period of decadence is apt to despise the happiness which is common to many, and the age was an age of pessimism, of restlessness, when distraction took the place of enjoyment. There were writers of that day who were conscious that health and spirits were degenerating and that men were living upon excitement. "For in vain"—says one of these commentators—"do we seek for gladness if our bodies are compact of melancholy humours. Hence comes it that many are sad in the midst of pleasure, without being able to say wherefore. . . . He who has heard the nightingale will have nothing to do with him who imitates its song. Everything passes in a moment; the remembrance of the pleasures we have had is not as strong as that of the misfortunes we have avoided."

The last sentence might stand as an epitaph on the grave of the age we have been recording. Catherine de' Medici, for all her Italian animation, was its tutelary genius. Her mind was very large, but it had no rudder. It was like a big ship doomed to strew the sea with wreckage when it reached difficult places.

Nor were her faults such as grew better with time, and the last half of her life might serve as a moral tale. The woman of the next twenty-seven years, lax by taste and a bigot by policy, is not pleasant to read of. But she is always interesting as a human document. The story of this Catherine de' Medici, the colleague of Alva, the Catherine of St. Bartholomew's Eve and of the Ligue, still remains to be written if we would complete the record of an enigmatic and abnormal personality.

INDEX

A

Adrets, Baron d', 186, 220
Alava, Spanish Envoy, 19
Albret, Jeanne d'. *See* Jeanne de Navarre
Aldobrandini, Salvestro, 31
Alençon, Duc d', 14
Alexander VI, 234
Allessandro, Duke of Florence, 30
Alva, 18, 23, 90
Amboise, Catherine de' Medici married at, 29
— Condé imprisoned at, 113
— executions at, 109, 171
— Huguenot plot of, 105-7
— peace of, 226, 237
Amyot, Bishop, 72
Anabaptists, Flemish, 107
Andelot, Maréchal d', 89, 123, 184, 210
Anet, 48, 57, 60, 95, 301
Angoulême, Bastard of, 9
— *See* Marguerite d'Angoulême
Anjou, Henri, Duke of, 10, 174
Anne of Austria, 78
— de Bretagne, 291
Antoine de Navarre, character of, 102-3, 141, 143, 150, 159, 215
——appearance, 144
— attitude to religion, 143, 154, 159, 179, 215
— married life, 141, 142-5, 148-51, 156
— letters to his wife, 142-5, 148-50, 156
— feeling for her, 142, 185, 217
— journey to Orleans, 113
— behaviour there, 115
— conduct at Poissy, 173, 181
— relations with Catherine, 156, 177, 183-4
— connection with la Belle Rouet, 156, 177-9, 216-17
— joins the Triumvirate, 181, 184
— siege of Rouen, 216
— illness and death, 217-18
Arquebuses, church-bells of Protestants, 193
Architecture, Catherine de' Medici and, 294

Armagnac, Cardinal d', Governor of Béarn, 150, 154, 219
Astrology, 11, 67, 299
Aubépine, Claude d', Henri II. described by, 83
Augsburg, 175
Aumale, Duc d', 61, 63, 87, 225
Auvergne, Madeleine de la Tour d', daughter of Jeanne de Bourbon and the Seigneur de Latour, and mother of Catherine de' Medici, 29

B

Baïf, Lazare, Maître des Requêtes, 244
— Jean Antoine, 245
Baillive de Caen as nurse to royal children of Navarre, 145
Banquets, 81
Barbette, La, 78
Bastille, Vidâme de Chartres taken to the, 112
— death of Palissy in the, 318
Béarn, 144, 148, 150, 180, 183, 185
Beaupréau, Marquis de, 75
Beauvoir, M. de, tutor to Henri IV., 153-5
Belièvre, Catherine de' Medici's letter to, 60
Belle Rouet, La, 156, 177, 179, 216
Belleau, Rémy, 245
— poem by, 286
Belloc, Hilaire, attitude to Ronsard of, 259 (Note)
Bertrandi, Chancellor, Catherine de' Medici appointed co-regent with, 91
Berri, *see* Marguerite de
Bèze, Théodore de, Catherine de' Medici and, 22
— Plot to take Lyons approved by, 112
— letter to Condé from, 129
— — Jeanne de Navarre from, 156
— and the Huguenot party, 168-72
Billon, 291-2
Binet, 257
Biron, 153

INDEX

Blois, 11, 36, 107, 155, 223, 244
Bordeaux, Palissy's workshop at, 314
Borgias, 8, 18, 25, 231
Bouchage, letter from Diane de Poitiers to, 65
Bouchot, biographer of Catherine de' Medici, 31, 33
Bouillon, Comte de, 63
— Duc de, 315
— Geoffroi de, maternal ancestor of Catherine de' Medici, 159
Boulogne, 91
Bourbon Princes, 88, 105, 112, 116, 159
— Antoine de, Duc de Vendôme, see Antoine de Navarre
— Antoinette de, 189
— Cardinal de, 93, 113, 169, 217, 259
— Connétable de, plots against François I, 51
Bourbons, 18, 29, 105, 116, 163
Bourg, Anne du, trial and execution of, 105
Brantôme, 45, 52, 86
Brézé, Louis de, Sénéchal of Normandy, 51, 65
Brézé, Loys de, 79
Briçonnet, Bishop, 235
Brissac, 91
— letter from Diane de Poitiers to, 57
— Dame de, 36
Brussels, French Ambassadors at, 84
Bussi, 318

C

Calais, 91, 162, 226
Calvin, 21–2, 167, 169
— letter of to Coligny, 110
— plot to seize Lyons approved by, 112
— influence of over women, 125
— letter to Condé from, 129
— letters from Renée, of Ferrara, to, 139–40
— decision of Catherine de' Medici and Coligny against his presence at Poissy, 168
Calvinism, 199, 232
Calvinists, 107, 168, 233
Campion, quotation from poem of, 273
Castelnau, Baron de, 110
Câteau-Cambrésis, peace of, 90
— treaty of, 62, 91
Catherine de' Medici, birth of, 29
— childhood, 30–2

Catherine de' Medici, suitors, 33
— negotiations for her marriage, 33
— marriage with Henri II of France, 35
— reception at the French Court, 35–6
— friendship with François I, 36–8
— plan for divorce, 38
— relations with Henri II, 16, 37, 92, 94
— — with Diane de Poitiers, 37–8, 44, 53, 55–60, 62
— letters mentioning her, 16, 59, 60
— coronation, 50
— birth of children, 71
— her letters about them, 17, 71
— her relations to them, 14
— — to François II, 101
— — to Charles IX, 173
— — to Elizabeth of Spain, 17, 79, 80, 166
— — to Princess Margot, 7
— her widowhood and mourning, 94–6
— her relations to Spain, 20, 22–3, 119, 162–7, 170, 175, 184, 212, 214
— — to England, 105, 162, 212, 215, 226
— — to the Guises, 18, 159, 177, 207–8, 224
— — to the Bourbons, 18, 29, 103, 116, 159
— — to the Prince de Condé, 213
— — to Coligny, 108, 160
— — to Montmorency, 13, 16
— accession of François II, 101
— her conduct during the Amboise conspiracy, 105–11
— — to Condé and Antoine de Navarre, 113
— — at François II's death and her assumption of the Regency, 116
— States-General and conferences preceding Council of Poissy, 166–8
— Council of Poissy, 171–6, 181–3
— — of Fontainebleau, 166
— attitude to people of Paris, 166–194
— struggle with Guises, 176, 184
— correspondence with Condé, 209
— her conduct during Civil Wars, 91–2
— letter on murder of Duc de Guise, 223
— conclusion of peace, 226

INDEX

Catherine de' Medici, letters of, 9, 10, 13, 14, 16, 17, 59, 60, 71, 80, 112-13, 165-7, 177, 206, 209, 211, 222-5, 294-5
— letters about, 6-8, 11-13, 18, 19, 21-2, 24, 32, 38, 57-9, 60, 62, 95, 101-2, 107, 153, 174, 205-7, 213, 221
— personal appearance of, 24, 32, 36, 205
— general character of, 4-19
— jealousy, 16, 37, 57-60, 62
— good sense, 116
— tolerance, 111, 166
— attitude to religion, to Protestantism and the Huguenots, 20-3, 37, 106, 162-3, 111, 172, 234
— — to the Pope and the Catholics, 20, 114, 162, 164, 183, 201, 214
— slanders about her—how far justified, 5, 6, 8, 213
— attitude to art, 294-5
— — to science, 299
— her luxury, 296
— relations to Philibert de l'Orme, 249, 295, 301
— — to Bernard Palissy, 314-15
Catherine de Navarre, 148, 155, 181
Catholic League, 180
— plot, 176
Catholics, cruelties of, 193-4
— complaints of, 195
— proposed massacre of, 208
Cavalli, 39
Châlons, Bishop of, 189
——— at Protestant service, 197-8
Chantilly, Mill of, interview of Catherine de' Medici with Condé, 221
Chantonnay, Envoy of Spain, 108
— complaints of " Prêches " by, 119
— Catherine de' Medici warned by, 164
— demands of refused by Catherine de' Medici, 167
— stormy interview of Catherine de' Medici with, 170, 175
— letter of, 179
— schemes of, 184
— on religious views of Catherine de' Medici, 212, 214
— attempts of to arrange marriage of Jeanne de Navarre, 218
Châteaubriant, Madame de, 36
Châtelard, 248, 273
Châtillons, training of the, 123
Châtillon, Cardinal de, 89, 111, 167, 184, 211, 249

Châtillon, M. de, 122
Charles V, 10, 84-5, 90
Charles IX, 14, 96, 100, 116, 297, 314
— Prêches in apartments of, 167
— oration at Council of Poissy, 171
— religious attitude of, 173
— letter of, 218
— affection of for Ronsard, 248
— poetic talent of, 249
Chartres, Condé imprisoned at, 222
Chaudieu, 106
Chaumont, 95
Chenonceaux, 95, 164
Choisnin, physician to Jeanne de Navarre, 315
Church, corruption of, 195
Civitella, defeat of French army near, 91
Clement VII, Pope, 30, 33-5, 231
Clergy, convocation of the, 166, 168
Clèves, Duc de, 138
Clouet, François, 22, 92, 189, 296
Coligny, Gaspard, Amiral de, character of, 89
— letter to his wife on loss of their child, 123
— aims of, 161
— his plea for equality of both religions, 111
— relations to Catherine de' Medici, 108, 160
— — to the Guises, 108
— — to the Crown, 160-1
— — to Charles IX, 160
— meeting with Condé and his troops, 210
— interview with Catherine de' Medici, 214
— attitude toward the murder of the Duc de Guise, 224
Collège de France, 77
Collesson, Jean, 191
Colonna, Vittoria, 231
Condé, Prince de, character, of, 89, 107, 121, 123-4, 127
— appearance of, 127
— attitude to religion, 127, 169
— attitude to wife, 124, 130
— — to children, 120, 125-6
— — to Isabelle de Limeuil, 128-9
— — to Coligny, 127, 184 214,
— plot of Amboise—protest against cruelty, 109
— journey to Orleans, arrest, and imprisonment, 113
— liberation and acquittal, 120
— at Poissy, 169
— with Jeanne d'Albret in Paris, 208

INDEX

Condé, Prince de, correspondence with Catherine de' Medici, 209
— relations with her, 21, 160, 213–14
— conduct during Civil War, 213, 221
— taken prisoner at Dreux, 222
— negotiations for peace, 225
— peace of Amboise, 226
Condé, Princesse de, Eléonore de Roye, character of, 123, 129, 132
— abilities, 127–8
— parentage and early education, 122–3
— relations to husband, 113, 129, 131
— — to children, 125, 131
— — to Protestant ministers, 124
— — to Catherine de' Medici, 127
— illness and death, 129–32
Contarini, 58, 62, 87
Correr, 17
Cotin, 146
Coucy, Castle of, 145
Court of Henri II, moral tone of the, 87
Creighton, Bishop, 8
Cromwell, Oliver, 236
Crussol, Madame de, 106, 169

D

Dandolo, Venetian Ambassador, 39
Danés, tutor of François II, 72
Dauphin, Henri II as, 39
Diane de Poitiers, her character and abilities, 43, 48–9, 52, 66
— her tastes, 53–5
— her Platonism, 53
— attitude to religion, 58
— relations to and power over Henri II, 44–5, 47–9, 58, 61
— letters of, 64–6
— poems of, 49
— relations to Catherine de' Medici, 56–8
— — to the Royal children, 57, 64
— — to Montmorency, 62
— — to the Guises, 61–2
— her appearance, 43–5, 48
— her position as patroness of art and letters, 63
— her disgrace, 95
— her subsequent life, 63
— her Will, 64–5
Dorat, Jean, 245
Dreux, 222
Drummond of Hawthornden, poems of, 269, 274
Du Bellay, Cardinal, 246, 249, 253
— Guillaume, 244

Du Bellay, Joachim, his youth, 243, 246
— his illness and poetic aims, 242, 245–6
— his meeting with Ronsard, 246
— his position in the Pleïade, 247
— his "*Illustration de la Langue française*," 247
— poetic work, 247, 254–6, 285–6
— quarrel with Ronsard, 252
— stay in Rome and effect upon him, 253–4
— love-affairs, 248, 252, 255
— honours, 255
— attitude to religion, 241, 256
— disappointment and death, 256
— comparison with Elizabethans, 241, 268
Dumas, 4
Du Perron, 259
Dwarfs, Court, 77

E

Edict of January, 182–3, 213
— — Romorantin, 111
— — Tolerance, 108
" Eidgenossen," supposed derivation of " Huguenot," 201
Elboeuf, Marquis d', 87
Elizabeth, Queen of England, Tavannes' remarks on, 18
— Mary Stuart's pearls worn by, 34
— French Protestants and, 105
— Jeanne de Navarre compared with, 151
— designs of, on Calais, 162
— intervention of, 212
— negotiations with, 226
— Princesse de Condé's appeal to, 114
Elizabeth, Queen of Spain, Catherine's letters to, 16, 80, 166
— death of, 15
Ellancourt, 191
Emmanuel Philibert, Duke of Savoy, 90, 104
England, 237
— sale of Havre to, 216
— treaty with, 226
Erasmus, 231
Estampes, Duchesse d', 36–7, 60, 66, 78
Este, Hippolyte d', Cardinal de' Medici and Papal Legate, 32–4, 176–8, 180

F

Ferdinand of Austria, 90
Ferrara, *see* Renée of
Ficino, Marsilio, 53
Fleming, Lady, 59, 62

324

INDEX

"Flying Squadron," 16, 28, 156, 177, 298
Fontainebleau, "Touching" of the sick at, 79
— Council at, 166
— Château of, dispute concerning key of 1067
— Charles IX compelled to leave for Paris, 210
— description of, 294
Fourchade, Jeanne, 147
France, 4
François I, Catherine de' Medici's friendship with, 36, 38, 51, 91
François II, betrothal of, 72
— behaviour of to Montmorency, 101
— weak character of, 14, 110
— health of, 107
— political Protestants and, 105
— reception of Antoine de Navarre by, 113, 115
— death of, 116

G

Galland, 258
General Assembly, reforms suggested by, 164
Geneva, 199
Gonzaga, Giulia, 231
Gouffier, Charlotte, Dame de Brissac, 36
— Anne, Dame de Montreuil, 36
Goujon, Jean, 63, 249
Grammont, Cardinal de, 34
Grand-Maître, 102, 163
Greville, Fulke, Poems of, 273
Grey, Lady Jane, 66
Guienne, Huguenot revolt at, 191
Guiffry, 51
Guise, Cardinal de, 87, 189
Guise, Charles de, see Lorraine
Guise, Duc de, 6, 21, 23, 87–8
— Lieutenant-General of French Army, 91
— plan for abduction of Prince Henri, 164
— Catholic League and, 180
— cruelty of at Vassy, 189–91
— disloyal proposal of, 184
— strong measures of in Paris, 208
— at Dreux, 222
— assassination of, 223
Guise, Duchesse de (Anna d'Este), 109
Guises, the, 61, 102, 113, 115–16, 151, 163, 167, 177, 185, 207, 212, 234

H

Hamelin, 314
Hâton, Claude, 195, 221

Havre, sale of, to England, 216
— retaken, 226
Heilly, Mademoiselle de, see Duchesse d'Estampes
Henri II of France, character as a boy, 46
— marriage, 34–5
— relations to his wife, 35, 86, 92
— — to Diane de Poitiers, 45, 48
— his letters to her, 46–7
— his love-poems, 44, 46, 49
— accession, 52, 56
— ambassador's description of him, 39
— tastes, abilities and character, 39, 45, 47–8, 77, 83, 87
— love of children, 73, 75–6
— his ordinary day, 85
— his attitude to Protestantism and religion, 89–90
— his death, 95
— his funeral ceremonies, 96–7
Henri III, 15, 164–5
Henri, King of Navarre, 46–7
Henri IV, Prince of Navarre, 146, 155, 185
Herbert, Lord, of Cherbury, poems of, 270
Herrick, 267
Holland, 237
Hotman, Francis, 107
Huguenot conspiracy, 21
— funeral, 197
— riots in provinces, 182
— triumphs, 174
— tone of Council of Poissy, 164
— cruelties, 220
Huguenots, their children's services, 194
— De Raymond's description of, 168
— massacre of, 189
— — Catholics planned by, 207
— notable women of the, 122
— pledge of toleration to, 119
— posts given to, 176
— puerile show of, 201
— scandal from midnight services of, 193
— secret arms of, 106
— secret signal of, 197
— various parties of, 120–1
— violence of, 192
Humières, M. d', letter to, 64
— Madame de, letter to, 71

I

Isabelle of Ischia, 231

INDEX

J

James V of Scotland, 33
Jamyn, Amadis, 247
Jarnac, 66
Jeanne d'Albret, Queen of Navarre, character of, 137–42
— attitude to religion, 39–40, 121, 152–3, 179
— summary of girlhood, 138–9
— married life, 141–2
— birth of children, 145–6
— relations to her son, 154, 185
— feeling for her husband and disappointment in him, 105, 156, 176, 179, 185
— arrival and stay at Poissy, 171, 176
— departure for Paris, 176
— flight thence to Béarn, 185
— relations to Catherine de' Medici and letters to her, 153, 183
— letters to son, 154–5
— other letters, 138, 140, 152–3, 185
— government of her kingdom, 122, 151
Jodelle, Étienne, 252
Joinville, home of the Guises, 189
— Prince de, 75, 165
Julius II, Pope, 231

K

Knox, John, 236

L

Labrossière, Condé informed of his wife's death by, 132
La Chataignerie, 66
Langey, Madame de, letter from Jeanne de Navarre to, 151
Languedoc, Huguenots in, 112
Languet, Hubert, 104, 107, 176
Laon, 145
La Rénaudie, Sieur de, 107–8
La Rochelle, siege of, 122; Protestant stronghold, 315
Latour, Seigneur de, grandfather of Catherine de' Medici, 29
Lauro, 178, 181, 216
L'Hôpital, Michel de, Chancellor, 23, 111, 116
— Keeper of the Seals, 162
— opening speech of at States-General (1561), 182
— and the Pleïade, 247
Leo X, Pope, 29
Lescot, Pierre, 301

Les Tournelles, Palace of, 94
Lignerolles, 9
Limaudière, Mademoiselle de la, "La Belle Rouet," 177
Limeuil, Isabelle de, 124, 128
Limoges, Archbishop of, letters from Catherine de' Medici to, 17, 165, 206
Longwy, Jacqueline de, 122
Lorraine, Cardinal de, Charles de Guise, 61, 73
— abusive anagrams on his name, 104
— his attendance at "Prêches," 126
— at Poissy, 169, 175
— character of, 87–8
— Chief Commissioner, 154
— his friendship with Ronsard, 249
— his harshness to Princesse de Condé, 114
— his presence at funeral of Henri II, 97
— prayer by, 116
Lorraine, Duchesse de, 14
Louis XIV, 44
Louvre, 47, 97, 101, 301
Luther, 231, 236
Lutheran doctors sent for by Cardinal de Lorraine, 175
Lutherans in Council, 169
Luxembourg, 91
Lying in state, Henri II, 96
— Duc de Guise, 224
Lyons, plot of, 112

M

Machiavelli, 8
Magny, Olivier de, Secretary to Diane de Poitiers, 63
Mailly, Madame de, letter to, from Catherine de' Medici, 106
Maintenon, Madame de, 44, 47–8, 137
Maligny, agent of Condé, 10, 112
Mantua, Duke of, 33
Marche, Maréchal de la, 144
Margot, Princess, 7, 14, 22, 67, 75, 174, 296
Marguerite d'Angoulême and Navarre, 8, 21, 52, 232, 235
— introduces Platonism to the French Court by, 54
— as initiator of Reformation, 121–2
— rough treatment of, 138
— letter to Catherine de' Medici from, 38
Marguerite de Berri and Savoie, 92–4, 111, 212, 224, 248
Marguerite de Vendôme, 36

INDEX

Marot, Clément, 247; his psalms, 20, 86, 89, 192, 197, 220
Marseilles, wedding of Catherine de' Medici at, 35
Mary Stuart, Queen of Scots, 34, 113, 115
— education of, 72-3
— letters of, 73-4, 101
— marriage of, 93-4
— proposed marriage with Antoine de Navarre, 178
— Ronsard's relations with, 248
Mary Tudor, 90
Masquerades, 77
Mass on battle-field, 222
Maurice of Saxony, 90
Mayenne, Duc de, 318
Meaux, 210
— fighting, at, 191
Medici, Ottaviano de', 32
Melun, 210
Ménars, Président, 105
Metz, siege of, 90
Michael Angelo, 260
Michelet, 4
Michieli, Venetian Ambassador, 113, 205
Middle-class, 236
Mirandola, Pico della, 53
Monluc, 186
Montaigne, 266
Montaigu, Madame de', letter from Diane de Poitiers to, 66
Montargis, Huguenot revolt at, 191
Montgoméry, 95, 210
Montmorency, Connétable de, 90, 91, 97, 112
— Catholic League and, 180
— death of, 222
Montmorency, Maréchal de, 176
Montmorency, Louise de, Madame de Châtillon, 122
Montpellier, fighting at, 191
Montpensier, Duchesse de, 115-16, 122
Montreuil, Dame de, 36
Morata, Olympia, 231
Murate, Convent, 31
Muret, 247

N

Nanteuil, Catherine de' Medici's visit to the Duc de Guise at, 164
Napoleon Bonaparte, 25
Nemours, Duc de, 164
Neo-Platonism, 231-2
Netherlands, 18, 20
Nevers, Duchesse de, 36

"New Learning," 137
"New Opinions," 105, 137, 164, 173
Nostradamus, 76
Notre Dame, 77, 96

O

Oléron, 154
Olivier, Chancellor, 110
Orléans, Duc d' (Henri II), 31, 33, 39
— Court of, 153
— ordinance of, 164
— Condé's advice concerning, 208
Orme, Philibert de l', 63, 249, 295, 299
— summary of career of, 300-1
Orsini, Alfonsina, grandmother of Catherine de' Medici, 29

P

Palais de Justice, meeting in Golden Chamber of, 166
Palissy, Bernard, birth and education of, 307
— character of, 305, 306
— artistic capabilities, 311
— attitude to religion, 310, 313-14
— journeys and profession, 307
— married life, 307, 309
— labours to discover white enamel, 307-10
— relations with Montmorency, 310-14
— arrest at Bordeaux and liberation, 314
— relations with Catherine de' Medici, 314, 319
— at Tuileries, 314
— lectures of, 315, 318
— publications of, 315
— style of, 317
— his imprisonment and death, 318
— quotations from his writings, 313, 316-17
Paré, Ambrose, 315
Paris, cold reception of Catherine de' Medici by, 35
— sixteenth century, 77-8
— consistory at, 106
— agitated condition of, 166, 194
— Montmorency appointed Governor of, 176
— excited by Catholic preacher, 200
Passerini, Cardinal, 30
Pasteur, Louis, 307
Peace of Amboise, 226, 237
— of Câteau-Cambrésis, 90
— negotiations for, 222
— of Vaucelles, 82, 84, 90

327

INDEX

Peele, George, quotations from poems of, 267
Périers, Bonaventure des, 54
Périgord, Huguenots in, 112
Perussel, Huguenot director of the Princesse de Condé, 124, 310
" Petite Bande," 36
Philibert de l'Orme, see Orme
Philip II of Spain, 20, 90, 104, 159, 165
Pickering, William, English Ambassador, 60
Piedmont, 162
Pilon, Germain, 297
Pisseleu, Anne de, see Chateaubriant, Madame de
Pius IV, Pope, 119
Place des Grèves, 105
Planche, Régnier de la, 61
Platonism, 53-5, 232
Pleïade, 247, 261
Poetry, French and English, comparison of, 241
— Elizabethan, 268
Poggio Caiano, Palace of, 30
Poissy, Council of, 21, 161, 195, 219
— arrival of de Bèze at, 168
— Coligny's proposal for equal terms at, 163
— confusion of de Bèze at, 172
— document signed by de Bèze at, 173
— first sitting of Council of, 171
— result of Council of, 182
— tactics of Cardinal de Lorraine at Council of, 175
— monastery of, 168
Poitien, Prince de, 184
— Princesse de, 122
Pole, Cardinal, 231
" Politiques," 105
Pontus de Thiard, 247
Postel, 77
Pourbus, 24
' Prêches,' 22, 126, 152, 167, 169, 178, 192-3, 196, 199, 208, 226
Prieur, Barthélmy, 315
Protestant cities, 210
— nobles, 171
— De Raymond's description of, 168
— important posts given to, 176
Protestantism, a political danger, 23
— a Court fashion, 20, 171-3
— failure of in France, 25, 234
— Henri II's attitude towards, 89
— Henri of Anjou's leanings towards, 173
— increase of, 105, 174, 199
— Palissy and, 310

Protestantism, science and, 300
— women politicians and, 137
Provins, 173

R

Rabelais, 266
Ramus, 55
Raphael, bold answer of to Antoine de Navarre, 217
Reconcilers, school of the, 231
Reformation, 159, 193, 231-2
— aristocratic leaders of the, 236
— literary movement of the time unaffected by the, 241
Reformed Churches, propositions for discussion advanced by the, 169
Reformers, freedom of, in theological discussion, 197
Regency, Catherine de' Medici's accession to the, 4, 101, 116, 159, 160-1
— difficulties of the, 162-3
Renaissance, women of the, 67, 140
— Neo-Platonism of the, 193
— and Reformation, the, 231
Renée, Duchess of Ferrara, Jeanne de Navarre compared with, 137-39
— letters from, 114, 139-40
— policy of, 122, 137
— religious views of, 152
— guardian of Prince Henri of Navarre, 216
Republic, desired by Calvinists, 105
Rheims, 106
Rochefoucauld, Duc de la, 184, 210
— Duchesse de la, 122
Roche-sur-Yon, Prince de, 217
Rome, 32, 253
Romorantin, Edict of, 111
Ronsard, Pierre de, parentage and boyhood of, 243
— reads Virgil, 244
— journeys in Germany, etc., 244
— deafness, 244
— at Collège de Coqueret, 245
— meets Du Bellay, and they form the Pleïade, 245
— his aims, 242, 246, 261
— his poetic work, 220, 241, 258-9, 268, 270-3, 276-84, 288
— success and honours, 248-9, 257, 259
— his love-affairs, 251
— attitude to religion, 259, 275
— — to Rabelais, 275
Rouen, 15, 216, 200

328

INDEX

Roye, Eléonore de, *see* Princesse de Condé
Rue de Grenelle, Hôtel de, 181
Rue St. Jacques, Bible-burning in the, 208
—— house in, meeting-place of Huguenots, 192

S

Saint-André, Maréchale de, 29, 124
—— Maréchal de, 103, 184, 222
St. Bartholomew's Eve, 9, 225, 234
Sainte-Beuve, 51
— criticism of Ronsard by, 247, 261
Sainte-Chapelle, 77
St. Denis, 96
Saint-Germain, 96, 103
— arrival of Papal Legate at, 176
— assembly at, 182
— Court assembled for Conference at, 168
— Protestant books sent to, 173
— preacher brought to, 200
Ste. Geneviève, Church of, 181
St. John's Eve (1561), 166
"Sainte Ligue," 62
St. Ladre, 96
Santa Lucia, Florence, convent of, 30
St. Marcoul, touching of the sick at, 78
Saint-Maur, 217
Saint-Quentin, siege of, 91–2
Saint-Vallier, Seigneur de, 51–2
Saintes, 307, 314
Saintonge, 307
Salviati, Maria, 32
Sardinia, 180
Sarto, Andrea del, 29
Savoie, Louise de, 58, 91
Scévole de Saint-Marthe, 247
Scotch Covenanters, 106
Sforza, Francesco, Duke of Milan, 33
— Catherine, 31
Silly, Sieur de, 164
Sir Walter Raleigh, poem of, 272
Socialism, Christian, 199
'Songe de Polyphile,' 312

Sorbonnists, petition of, 170-1
Spain, 90, 163, 165, 183
Spanish Navarre, 147, 179, 180, 215
Speyer, Diet of, 244
States-General, 107, 163, 166
Strasburg, Huguenots of, 107
Strozzi, Clarissa, 29
— Philip, 29
— Maréchal, 295
Suriano, 22

T

Tavannes, 18, 22, 57, 59, 82, 90, 195, 199, 227, 296
Tester, Guillaume de, 76
Tournon, Cardinal de, 172, 295
Treaty of Câteau-Cambrésis, 62
Triumvirate, Catholic, 181
Tuileries, 251, 301, 314

U

Urbino, Lorenzo of, father of Catherine de' Medici, 29

V

Valléry, Château de, 129
Vassy, massacre of Huguenots at, 189–91
— Bishop of Châlons sent to, 197–8
Vaucelles, Peace of, 82, 84, 90
Vendôme, Duc de, *see* Antoine de Navarre
— raid on, 185
Vielleville, Maréchal de, 80–1, 145

W

Wars of Henri II, 90
Watteau, Antoine, 256
Wolsey, Cardinal, 66, 88
Women, position of, 292

Y

Yuste, monastery of, 90

Z

Zwinglius, 236

Lightning Source UK Ltd.
Milton Keynes UK
UKHW011841241120
374029UK00001B/56